C000129841

*This book is sponsored by the Theological
Commission of the World Evangelical Fellowship*

RIGHT WITH GOD:

Justification in the Bible and the World

RIGHT WITH GOD:

Justification in the Bible and the World

edited by

D. A. CARSON

Published on behalf of the
World Evangelical Fellowship by
The Paternoster Press
and Baker Book House

British Library Cataloguing in Publication Data
Right with God: Justification in the Bible
and the World
I. Carson, D. A.
231.7

ISBN 0-85364-516-7

Library of Congress Cataloging-in-Publication data
Right with God / edited by D.A. Carson.
    p.   cm.
"Published on behalf of the World Evangelical Fellowship."
Includes bibliographical references and indexes.
ISBN 0-8010-2561-3
    1. Justification—Bible teaching.   2. Bible.   N.T.—Criticism,
interpretation, etc.   3. Justification—Comparative studies.
I. Carson, D. A.
BS2545.J82R54   1992
234'.7—dc20   92-15720
                                                        CIP

Typeset by Photoprint, Torquay, Devon,
and printed in the UK by
The Guernsey Press Co. Ltd., Guernsey, Channel Islands
for the publishers.

Table of Contents

Preface

This is the fourth volume to be produced by the Faith and Church Study Unit of the Theological Commission of the World Evangelical Fellowship. Like this one, the first three (*viz. Biblical Interpretation and the Church: Text and Context; The Church in the Bible and the World: An International Study; Teach Us to Pray: Prayer in the Bible and the World* — all published by Paternoster and Baker) were the products of consultations that brought together evangelical leaders from various parts of the world.

In each case, our method has been the same. Papers were assigned, prepared and circulated in advance. The consultation was spent not in delivering papers but in going over them paragraph by paragraph, sometimes line by line. Detailed notes were taken of the discussions, and each contributor was asked to revise his or her work in the light of the criticisms and suggestions raised. The revised papers eventually came to me, and I edited them and prepared them for the press.

The strengths and weaknesses of such an approach become more and more obvious each time we address a topic this way. To bring together people from such diverse backgrounds, facing challenges and experiencing God's blessing in ways far removed from the challenges and experiences of Christians in other parts of the world, goes some way to ensuring that our labour transcends merely parochial interests. The sense of personal enrichment and corporate oneness in Christ Jesus is considerable, something to be savoured and treasured. The procedure also makes it more likely that hermeneutical parochialism will be transcended.

On the other hand, the resulting papers are not uniformly 'technical' in the Western sense. That is both an advantage and disadvantage. Some Western readers will think (too quickly, in my view) that some of these papers are insufficiently rigorous; some readers in other parts of the world, little accustomed to the esoterica of Western academic debates, may be impatient (again, too quickly, in my view) with some technical discussions that have little immediate bearing on their own settings. Far better to learn from each other, so that by mutual forbearance we learn to correct our own (mis)understandings of the Word of God.

But perhaps the greatest difficulty with this sort of consultation came in the amount of disagreement that was aired at several points. I mentioned in the Preface of the second book of this series how gratifying it was to discover the degree of unanimity amongst people from so wide a diversity of denominations and cultures. Although considerable unanimity was achieved through this consultation as well, we were simply unable at several points to agree on a number of important matters. Doubtless this is not surprising when strong-minded individuals from Lutheran, Reformed, Baptist, Anglican, Charismatic and other backgrounds get together to talk about justification — the more so if they come from widely divergent languages and cultures as well. Nevertheless, I would like to think that if we had had more time we might have achieved more unanimity; but perhaps that is wishful thinking.

Still, there was no doubt in the mind of anyone at the consultation as to the importance of justification, and of its vital bearing on any evangelical understanding of the gospel. Division arose as to how best to articulate it, or to understand the contribution made to it by this or that biblical corpus. Some of these matters are briefly aired in the introductory chapter.

As is inevitable in this sort of international study, the division of labour was partly dictated by the contributors themselves, and partly by considerations of space. We have not attempted to treat the theme of justification in every part of the Bible, but to tackle enough of the crucial corpora to indicate where we would go. Discussion of Paul was divided into two papers, partly because the greatest debate has occurred over him, partly because it was judged wise to attempt to divide a survey of Pauline thought on the matter from consideration of the enormous body of secondary literature that has sprung up on the subject during the last couple of decades.

Especially strong, in my view, were the contributions of those who sought to show what bearing the doctrine of justification has on the proclamation of the gospel in their own cultures. Collectively, these essays remind us that our work on such matters must never descend to the *merely* academic. Responsible it must be, but to be ultimately responsible it must be put to the service of the church and the glory of the Head of the church. If reflection on justification does not drive us to our knees in gratitude and to the world in evangelism, we have denied in practice what we confess on paper.

The consultation was held in November 1988 in the excellent facilities of Tyndale House, Cambridge. We are grateful to the Warden, Dr. Bruce Winter, and his staff for the many kindnesses shown us. Most of us were billeted in homes connected with Eden Baptist Church, Cambridge. To the many people who helped us for the sake of Christ, and especially to Mr. Stan Blake, who looked after the local logistics, we again extend our deepest thanks. Perhaps I should add that the production of the volume has been delayed by unforeseen and unavoidable difficulties. For most of these essays, the delay makes little difference; in the case of the contribution of Peter T. O'Brian, I must extend my apologies: his failure to interact with N. T. Wright and a little more with J. D. G. Dunn is the fault of production delay – not oversight. My heartfelt thanks to Mr. Mark Krause for compiling the indexes.

As usual, any profits from the sale of this volume will go to helping responsible bodies in the so-called 'Third World' prepare any part of this book for translation and publication in other languages. Application should be made in the first instance to the Publications Working Group of the World Evangelical Fellowship.

Soli Deo gloria.

D. A. CARSON

Acknowledgement

Abbreviations

(Names of certain journals are shown in full in the text and notes, and are therefore not listed below.)

AB	Anchor Bible
ASV	American Standard Version
AV	Authorised Version
BAGD	Bauer–Arndt–Gingrich–Danker, *A Greek–English Lexicon to the New Testament*
BDF	Blass–Debrünner–Funk, *A Greek Grammar of the New Testament*
Bib	*Biblica*
BJRL	*Bulletin of the John Rylands Library*
Bl.–D.	Blass–Debrunner, *Grammatik des neutestamentlichen Griechisch*
BolT	*Boletin Teológico*
BS	*Bibliotheca Sacra*
BTB	*Biblical Theology Bulletin*
CBQ	*Catholic Biblical Quarterly*
CBSC	Cambridge Bible for Schools and Colleges
CD	Karl Barth, *Church Dogmatics*
CT	*Christianity Today*
EGT	*Expositor's Greek Testament*
EQ	*Evangelical Quarterly*
ERT	*Evangelical Review of Theology*
ET	English Translation
EvT	*Evangelische Theologie*
ExpT	*The Expository Times*
Fs.	Festschrift
GNB	Good News Bible
GTT	*Gereformeerd Theologisch Tijdschrift*
HBT	*Horizons of Biblical Theology*
HTR	*Harvard Theological Review*
IBD	*Illustrated Bible Dictionary*
IBS	*Irish Biblical Studies*
ICC	International Critical Commentaries

IDB	*Interpreter's Dictionary of the Bible*
IDBS	*Interpreter's Dictionary of the Bible Supplement*
Int	*Interpretation*
Inst.	John Calvin, *Institutes of the Christian Religion*
IRM	*International Review of Mission*
ISBE	*International Standard Bible Encyclopedia*
ISBER	*International Standard Bible Encyclopedia Revised*
JBL	*Journal of Biblical Literature*
JETS	*Journal of the Evangelical Theological Society*
JR	*Journal of Religion*
JRS	Journal of Religious Studies
KJV	King James Version
KB	Koehler-Baumgartner, *Lexicon in Veteris Testamenti Libros*
LCWE	Lausanne Committee on World Evangelization
LTJ	*Lutheran Theological Journal*
LW	*Lutheran World*
MHT	Moulton–Howard–Turner, *Grammar of New Testament Greek*
NASB	New American Standard Bible
NBCR	*New Bible Commentary Revised*
NBD	*New Bible Dictionary*
NCB	New Century Bible
NDT	*New Dictionary of Theology*
NEB	*New English Bible*
Neot	*Neotestamentica*
NICNT	*New International Commentary on the New Testament*
NIDNTT	*New International Dictionary of New Testament Theology*
NIV	New International Version
NKJV	New King James Version
NTS	*New Testament Studies*
RevThRev	*Reformed Theological Review*
RSV	Revised Standard Version
RV	Revised Version
SJT	*Scottish Journal of Theology*
SLJT	*Saint Luke's Journal of Theology*
SNTSMS	Society of New Testament Studies Monograph Series
SNTU	*Studien zum Neuen Testament und seiner Umwelt*
ST	*Studia Theologica*
Str-B	Strack-Billerbeck, *Komentar zum Neuen Testament*
SWJT	*Southwestern Journal of Theology*
TB	*Babylonian Talmud*
TDNT	*Theological Dictionary of the New Testament*
TDNTA	*Theological Dictionary of the New Testament Abridged*
TDOT	*Theological Dictionary of the Old Testament*
TEV	Today's English Version
THNT	Theologischer Handkommentar zum Neuen Testament
ThR	*Theologische Rundschau*
TNTC	Tyndale New Testament Commentary
TrinJ	*Trinity Journal*
TynB	*Tyndale Bulletin*
TZ	*Theologische Zeitschrift*

Up.	*Upanishads*
WEF	World Evangelical Fellowship
WTJ	*Westminster Theological Journal*
VE	*Vox Evangelica*
Zerwick	*Biblical Greek Illustrated by Examples*
ZNW	*Zeitschrift für die neutestamentliche Wissenschaft*
ZTK	*Zeitschrift für Theologie und Kirche*

1

Introduction

D. A. CARSON

It is possible to approach the question of justification from many angles. But much can be said for an approach that begins with the widest possible angle, the most fundamental question: How shall anyone be right with God?

Of course, to put the question that way already presupposes that God is of such a nature, and we are of such a nature, that we are *not* naturally right with God. It also presupposes that it is desirable and possible to be right with this God.

Biblical Christianity leaves no doubt on either point. The God 'who is there' (as Francis Schaeffer used to say) is both personal and transcendent, and utterly holy. He is the Creator and the Sovereign; the basis of our responsibility lies in creation (he made us for himself), and the wretchedness of our defection must be gauged by his greatness, holiness and love. But if we were made for him, we shall be restless until we find rest in him, as Augustine rightly observed. If instead we pursue self-interest and cater to self-will, the heart of all sin, we shall find that this is God's universe still, and that we must give an account to him. On the last day, we shall confess him with joy at being forgiven, or with terror at being condemned. But confess him we shall.

Both for his glory and for our good, the most important thing we can pursue is being rightly related to God. The Bible insists that he alone lays down the ground-rules for such a relationship; it also insists that, because he is a God of grace and mercy, he provides the means of access to his presence that we could not gain ourselves.

That, in short, is what the Bible is all about: God pursuing sinful human beings to bring them into a right relationship with himself, both for their good and for his own glory. That is why we have placed the essay by Edmund Clowney at the head of the collection. Unless we see the plot-line of the Bible on a large canvas now and then, we are tempted to get lost in myopic discussions, or to conclude, quite falsely, that 'justification' is largely restricted to the Epistles to the Galatians and the Romans, simply because certain technical vocabulary congregates there. One does not have to agree with every detail of the exegesis in this sweeping essay to admire its breadth and power, and to appreciate its call to think about justification in a broader biblical context than is often done today.

The two essays that follow both focus on Paul, because that is the primary storm centre of the contemporary debate. The first, by Brian C. Wintle, the

Principal of Union Biblical Seminary in Poona, India, approaches Paul's thought primarily by the careful exegis of several passages in Romans and Galatians, largely against the background of Judaism. Purposely, Wintle restricts the amount of interaction with secondary literature, partly so as to devote as much attention as possible to listening to the text, and partly because the next essay in the collection is entirely given over to an evaluation of current trends in such literature.

The second essay on Paul, then, by Peter O'Brien, the Vice-Principal of Moore College, addresses the contemporary debates directly. Amongst its more important findings are these: (1) S. K. Williams is right to argue that the meaning of the expression 'the righteousness of God' should not be established as a subset of the meaning of 'righteousness' (*dikaiosynē*): there are linguistic and contextual reasons for thinking that the former denotes God's righteous faithfulness to his covenant promises to Abraham, while the latter points to the resulting gift, a righteous status before God. The concerns of the magisterial Reformation are safeguarded in the latter; they should not be imported into the former. This analysis has substantial bearing on the debate over justification largely initiated by Ernst Käsemann. (2) O'Brien offers some thoughtful analysis of the slipperiness of much debate over the 'centrality' of justification in Paul, and, while interacting with some of the more important literature on the 'centre' of Pauline theology, argues that justification is central for Paul in the matter of becoming a Christian. Justification is thus foundational in that it marks the entry into Christian life, so that it is the fundamental blessing from which other blessings flow. (3) O'Brien also weighs the contribution of E. P. Sanders, and wrestles with current essays that argue for justification by faith but judgment according to works.

Norvald Yri examines 'justification' (*dikaiosynē*) in Matthew, and adopts a classic Lutheran resolution: here too, he argues, the 'righteousness' that outstrips that of the scribes and Pharisees can only be that which God himself provides. He candidly acknowledges that other Christians within the broadly 'evangelical' tradition might take a somewhat different approach to Matthew, but he reminds us of one broad stream in the church's approach to this question that is tightly self-consistent and exceedingly important in its own right.

The essay by Richard Gaffin, tracing the place of justification in Luke–Acts, begins by adopting a methodological posture rather different from that of Yri: it begins with some of the dominant themes in Luke–Acts and examines their bearing on the subject of justification, leaving aside word-studies and the exegesis of passages where certain relevant terms appear, until the broad strokes have been painted in. In particular, Gaffin studies, first, the relationship between the Holy Spirit and the judgment theme in Luke–Acts, i.e. the relationship between Pentecost and justification; and second, the forgiveness of sins and its relation to saving faith. Only then are the disputed texts, Luke 18:14 and Acts 13:39, carefully probed. The result is a picture of justification in Luke–Acts that may not be articulated in the categories of Paul, but which is nonetheless bound up with God's saving activity at the end of time to bring men and women into a right relationship with him, a salvation that is apprehended by faith.

Andrew H. Trotter, Jr., reverts to the study of the δικ- (*dik-*) word-group in his study of the Fourth Gospel. He is aware, of course, that Barrett thinks the *thought* of Jn. 5:24 is 'closely akin to the Pauline doctrine of justification',[1] that 1 Jn. 2:2 can be tied to the crucial Pauline passage Rom. 3:20–26 through the ἱλασμός (*hilasmos*, 'atonement', 'propitiation') word-group, that at least in 1 John δικαιοσύνη (*dikaiosynē*, 'righteousness/justification') is something that one *does* (1 Jn. 2:29ff.), but he prefers to examine the vocabulary in the Fourth Gospel itself, and concludes that even here the δικ- (*dik-*) root is primarily forensic.

In a lengthy essay, Ronald Y. K. Fung of the China Graduate School of Theology subjects 'justification' in the Epistle of James to fresh analysis. He competently surveys the complex options, and concludes that the different usages to which the same vocabulary in Paul and James is put stem in the first instance from the quite different crises confronting them.

The concern of Russell Shedd is to demonstrate that a forensic understanding of justification must never be allowed to stand so entirely alone in one's system of theology that one fosters (wittingly or unwittingly) some weary and inexcusable form of antinomianism. Rightly understood, justification is never merely a 'legal fiction'. It is the entry-point to a life committed to holiness. Guillermo Mendez is concerned to tie justification to the still broader demands of social justice, without losing the forensic and individual focus of the concept in the New Testament. Along the way he takes us through a thoughtful survey of some of the debates that currently rage in Latin America, trying to tie down the concept of 'justice' to biblical categories, trying, too, to relate it to the fall, to eschatology, and to the nature of the church.

Of course, the debate over justification first arose to sharp prominence during the Reformation. It would be inexcusable, therefore, not to analyse current treatments of justification among some representative Roman Catholic scholars, and especially to evaluate the bilaterally-produced documents of Lutheran/Catholic and Anglican/Catholic discussions. Klaas Runia of the Reformed Theological Seminary in Kampen isolates many positive advances represented by careful and sympathetic attempts to understand one another's position, but concludes that the differences that remain are more substantial than ARCIC II allows, much more in line with the candid expressions of unresolved differences in the Lutheran/Catholic discussions. Runia's essay brings a great deal of order and careful evaluation to a debate made complex by the peculiar mix of biblical, historical and systematic theologies that lie behind it.

For many readers of this volume, the last three essays will prove the most innovative and informative: the relevance of justification by faith in Hindu, Muslim and Buddhist contexts is surveyed by three Christian leaders who have discharged their ministry in those three contexts respectively. Sunand Sumithra argues that a biblical grasp of justification cannot be appreciated in Hindu culture until the Bible's presentation of God is understood, and monism is rejected. Out of one's understanding of God emerges one's understanding of sin, and therefore of how to be reconciled to God. Chris Marantika, who has enjoyed years of fruitful ministry in Indonesia, which comprises the largest Muslim group in the world, emphasises those elements in justification (such as the sovereign initiative of God) that find a hearing amongst many Muslims. At the same time, he carefully lays out the

Christological connections that must also be unpacked in any honest proclamation of the gospel, and outlines from his own experience the ways these can best be presented so as to cause least unnecessary umbrage while making Christian distinctives clear and persuasive. And finally, Masao Uenuma relates justification to the Buddhism found in Japan, especially the Jodoshin Shu sect, which is often said to embrace a notion of grace very similar to that in Christianity. Uenuma allows the similarities, but carefully insists on the differences — differences which, once again, finally turn on the very nature of God.

Other topics cry out for treatment. A colleague who was scheduled to write a paper on the relevance of justification in an animist culture in Africa found himself overstretched and unable to meet the deadlines. Equally, a paper might have been commissioned to deal with the relevance of justification to the materialistic and increasingly secularised North Atlantic countries. But if these essays have not said all that needs to be said, perhaps they will have served an adequate purpose if they stimulate reflection and discussion amongst Christians in many parts of the world, as to the nature of the good news to which we bear witness, and how best to present it in the diverse contexts in which we live.

2

The Biblical Doctrine of Justification by Faith

EDMUND P. CLOWNEY

For Martin Luther the doctrine of justification was 'the main doctrine of Christianity', the scriptural teaching that opened the gate of heaven to his anguished soul.[1] But the world has changed since Luther sat by his great tile stove in the mediaeval monastery of Wittenberg. Biblical studies have changed, too. Luther's understanding of the apostle Paul is challenged today, and the concerns of the apostle are thought to belong only to the distant past.[2] Indeed, it is urged that even Paul did not always put justification at the heart of his gospel. Rather, it is said, he made 'righteousness' a central gospel theme only when he had to refute those Jewish Christians who were demanding that Gentile believers be circumcised.[3]

Archbishop Cranmer in his *Homily on Salvation* wrote that no man can, by his own deeds, 'be justified and made righteous before God: but every man, of necessity, is constrained to seek for another righteousness or justification, to be received at God's own hands'.[4] Did Cranmer make justification too pivotal in the definition of salvation? Had the controversy with Rome given the Reformed church too narrow a view of the gospel? The Anglican divine, Richard Hooker, wrote: 'The grand question, which hangeth yet in controversy between us and the Church of Rome, is about the matter of justifying righteousness.'[5]

A recent statement by an Anglican–Roman Catholic commission on 'Salvation and the Church' affirms: 'We are agreed that this is not an area where any remaining differences of theological interpretation or ecclesiological emphasis, either within or between our Communions, can justify our continuing separation.'[6] An author in a reference dictionary admonishes: 'It is erroneously held by many that Roman Catholics and Protestants differ widely on justification.'[7]

Such statements raise our hopes. Moved by zeal for the unity of Christ's church, we do desire to leave behind the bitterness and misrepresentations of past polemics. We recognise, too, that both during and after the Reformation there has been a history of the elaboration of the doctrine.[8] We do well, therefore, to consider again what the Bible teaches about this aspect of God's great work of salvation. Did the reformation major in a minor? How central to the theology of the Bible is the doctrine of justification? Does the teaching of the apostle Paul represent a specialty, almost a quirk, in the theology of one converted rabbi who was never with Jesus? Is it an optional emphasis, one perspective from which salvation may be described for the benefit of people with a legalistic mind-set? Does it function only to undergird the assurance of the faint-hearted? Or is it indispensable for a clear understanding of the gospel, and therefore at the heart of the Christian message?

Two initial questions may be asked. What is the place of Paul's theology in the history of revelation? And what is the place of justification in Paul's theology? To the first question, Paul gives no uncertain answer. He confidently claims to have understanding in the mystery of Christ that was hidden from past generations (Eph. 3:4). That understanding is his by revelation, revelation that he shares with the other apostles and prophets as foundation-layers to the church (Eph. 2:20; 3:5). Moreover, the revelation that he has received goes beyond that of the other apostles. He is the last of the apostles, the apostle to the Gentiles; for this calling he has been given the gospel for the Gentiles. He speaks of it as 'my gospel', the distinctive revelation that undergirds the outreach of his ministry with a profound understanding of the fulfilment of all things in Jesus Christ.[9]

The breadth of Paul's missionary calling cannot be separated from the depth of his understanding of salvation through Jesus Christ. He carried to the nations the good news that they could receive God's finished salvation by faith. Paul rejoiced in the God of his fathers, and saw himself as God's servant, bearing the witness of the true Israel to the nations. But he did not summon the Gentiles to become Jews by submitting to circumcision and the law of Moses. As Saul of Tarsus, a Jew of the dispersion, he knew that the scattering of Jews throughout the Roman empire had drawn many Gentiles to the testimony of the synagogue. Jewish resistance to the worship of the Gentile pantheon had won Imperial recognition of Jewish monotheism. In spite of outbreaks of anti-Semitism, Judaism was successful in attracting a considerable number of proselytes.[10]

The Jewish attitude toward Gentile inquirers was decidedly mixed. There were rabbis and Pharisees who would 'travel over land and sea to make a single convert' (Matt. 23:15). That very expression, however, as used by Jesus, suggests the difficulty with which they saw the task, since their goal was to 'tie up heavy loads and put them on men's shoulders' (Matt. 23:4). Indeed, the outcome of Pharisaical legalism was to 'shut the kingdom of heaven in men's faces' (Matt. 23:13).

Paul, the separatist Pharisee, had kept that door shut and the wall high. He had been separated from less exacting Jews, and from all Gentiles, by his punctilious observance of the law. Now, however, he was separated to the gospel of God (Rom. 1:1). His new separation bound him to the whole Gentile world (Rom. 1:14). He owed it to the Gentiles to tell them of the open door that admitted them to the kingdom of God. Salvation is by grace through faith in Jesus Christ: Paul's message became his mission.

But Paul's message was not just for others. No one needed it more than he. He was a Jew by birth, and not a Gentile sinner (Gal. 2:15). He had struggled to merit God's favour by his keeping of the law. Yet his zeal for the law had yielded only a self-righteousness that could never be acceptable to God. Worse than that, his very zeal had led him to persecute God's saints. He blasphemed the name of the Son of God; he pursued Christians to the death, determined to force them to join his blasphemy (Acts 26:11). Paul never makes his doctrine of justification more explicit than when he is describing his own experience (Phil. 3:1–11). When the Lord shattered his pride on the road to Damascus, Paul discovered the folly of his own righteousness. All that he had counted to be gain was loss; his labour had fabricated a blindfold that veiled from his eyes the righteousness of Jesus Christ. Paul's doctrine of justification had opened the gate of heaven to him — or, rather, the opened gate of heaven brought his understanding of justification!

J. I. Packer has succinctly summarised the central place of justification in Paul's theology.[11] For Paul, it is God's fundamental act of blessing, providing pardon for the past and sure hope for the future (Rom. 5:1–11; 8:28–39). It is the key to God's history of redemption; God's promise of salvation in the Old Testament is fulfilled in the work of Jesus Christ, in the saving significance of his obedience and his death (Rom. 3:24–26; 5:16–19). Paul's quotations from the Old Testament in Romans and Galatians show how completely he sees the Scriptures as preaching the gospel, whether to Abraham (Gal. 3:8; Gen. 12:3) or to us. The old covenant points to the new covenant in the blood of Jesus Christ, in whom we have redemption and reconciliation, that we might be justified by God's grace (Gal. 3:10–16; 2 Cor. 5:18,19).

Justification lies at the heart of Paul's gospel. We may, indeed, reflect on its relation to other aspects of his teaching. It may well be urged, for example, that Paul's understanding of our union with Christ is the assumption from which his doctrine of justification flows. Yet apostolic revelation is of a piece; union with Christ and justification must be understood in relation to each other. God's work—for us and in us—is all centred in Jesus Christ.

I.   THE OLD TESTAMENT REVELATION OF GOD'S SAVING GRACE

What are the roots of Paul's doctrine of justification in the Old Testament? Do those Scriptures on which Paul was brought up teach a religion of works in contrast to Paul's message of grace? If the contrast is not complete, does not the Old Testament theology of the covenant at least require faithfulness as well as faith for justification?

A.   God's Initiative in Redemption and Revelation

The story of the Old Testament is the story of God's work in creating, ruling, and saving. It does not glorify the exploits of human beings; it glorifies the work of God. His sovereign rule over nature and history is always assumed and often celebrated (e.g. Psalms 33, 147, 148), but the great message of the Scriptures is God's lordship in *salvation*. Paul traces the mystery of God's plan of salvation, then sums up the testimony of Scripture: 'For from him and through him and to him are all things. To him be the glory forever!' (Rom. 11:36).

God's power to deliver and care for his people is pictured in many Old Testament figures: he is a warrior, the captain of the hosts of heaven, who comes to save his people in battle (Josh. 5:13–15; Isa. 59:16–19); he is a shepherd, leading his sheep to green pastures, and guarding them with his rod and staff (Ps. 23; Isa. 40; Ezek. 34:11–16); he is a farmer, harvesting the grapes of his vineyard (Isa. 5:1–7; Ps. 80:8–19); he is a husband, buying back his wayward wife from slavery (Hos. 3:1–5); he is a divine kinsman, redeeming his inheritance (Isa. 44:6,24); he is a father, who gives life to his people and nurtures them (Deut. 32:6,18; Exod. 4:22; Hos. 11:1,3). Even simpler images are used: God is a rock, a fortress, the refuge of his fugitive servants (Exod. 17:6; Deut. 32:3,4; Ps. 18:2; 31:3; 91:2; 95:1). He is also a fire: his transcendent holiness burns in wrath against sin (Deut. 4:24; Isa. 9:19; Dan. 7:9,10). Yet the fire of God's glory may become a flame to purify God's people (Isa. 4:4; 33:14; Mal. 3:2,3); a curtain and a covering to protect them (Exod. 14:20; Isa. 4:5; *cf.* 1 Kings 6:17), a judgment to consume their enemies and renovate their inheritance (Deut. 9:3; Isa. 10:17; 66:15–24). These many figures are taken up in a common pattern. One presupposes another: the gentle care of the shepherd carrying the lambs in his bosom gains dramatic force from the fact that he is the royal shepherd before whose coming every mountain is levelled, who holds the seas in his hand and has measured out the span of heaven (Isa. 40:4,11,12).

Quite clearly God's revelation used a wealth of metaphors to instruct us about our relation to him. The metaphors of the temple reflect the holiness of God. They speak of our approach into his presence, and of the purification we need to stand before him (Isa. 6:1–17). The metaphors of the market-place use the economic sphere to describe our redemption from slavery to be made God's possession. We claim the inheritance that we have in God, as he claims his inheritance in us (Isa. 43:3,4; Exod. 34:9; Deut. 4:20; Num. 18:20). The metaphors of warfare present the Lord as our champion, delivering us from all that would oppress and enslave us (Isa. 59:15–21). The metaphors of family life present the Lord, as we have noted, in the role of father and husband.

Some metaphors are used more intensively than others; some are so deeply grounded that they surpass the merely figurative. Some are complex, linking with others: the concept of a covenant, for example, may be structured in the form of a political covenant: the treaty established by a sovereign with a vassal king.[12] It may also take the form of a marriage covenant (Ezek. 16:8). Both forms are used to describe the bond between God and Israel. When theologians seek to summarise and apply the teaching of Scripture, they may fasten on one figure and seek to use it as a master metaphor. The Roman Catholic Church, for example, used the figure of the body of Christ as a master metaphor in ecclesiology. At Vatican II there was vigorous debate about replacing or supplementing this figure with the concept of the 'people of God'.[13]

Two evident dangers appear in our use of scriptural figures. One is to fill the horizon with a single figure to the neglect or prejudice of others. The other is to ignore the teaching of a figure, or to minimise its significance. This may be done by dismissing a figure as an optional perspective rather than a unique and essential contribution to our understanding.

It is the context of a court of justice that defines the concept of justification. The question of our relation to God is viewed from the standpoint of God's just judgment. The courtroom scene includes, to be sure, a metaphor. The process of reaching a verdict in the gate of an ancient Near Eastern city differed from the procedures used today in the Old Bailey or the Supreme Court of the United States. To interpret the biblical figure we must take account of the judicial customs that the text assumes. At the same time, interpretation seeks to appropriate the substance of what the courtroom language expresses. When the apostle tells us that we must all appear before the judgment-seat of God, his language may recall the *bēma* before which Paul himself was arraigned at Corinth; yet Paul is describing a real event — unimaginable to us, no doubt — but an actual encounter with God as the final judge.

As we turn to the judicial language that holds such a conspicuous place in scriptural revelation, we must therefore respect the substance of what is revealed. We dismiss it only at our own peril (Rom. 2:3–6).

Among the figures used to describe the glory of the Lord, that of the king has preeminence. So basic is it that we may need to be reminded that it is a figure, and that it cannot contain all that we need to know about God. It is used only rarely in the Pentateuch.[14] The link of kingship with many of the other figures is evident. For instance, 'shepherd' was a title borne by kings in the ancient Near East.[15] Kings like David were warriors, leading their armies into battle.

Above all, kings were judges with power to enforce their decrees (1 Sam. 8:5,6). The peace of their realm depended upon their enforcement of justice. Their defence against attack from without also had a judicial aspect. They were to defend the right of their kingdom against violation by an invader. As the divine king, the Lord is the just judge, able to enforce his judgments by his omnipotence. The Song of Moses in Deuteronomy proclaims the name and greatness of God the Rock of Israel:

> He is the Rock, his works are perfect,
>   and all his ways are just.
> A faithful God who does no wrong,
>   upright and just is he. (*Deut. 32:4*)

Abraham pleads God's justice as he intercedes for Sodom, where his nephew Lot lives:

> What if there are fifty righteous people in the city? Will you really sweep it away and not spare the place for the sake of the fifty righteous people in it? Far be it from you to do such a thing — to kill the righteous with the wicked, treating the righteous and the wicked alike. Far be it from you! Will not the Judge of all the earth do right? (*Gen. 18:24f.*)

Abraham's appeal would bind God to absolute standards of justice, yet these are God's own standards: he is the supreme and universal judge. Further, God is the judge, not as the sovereign of a world empire might be, but as the Creator and Sustainer of heaven and earth. In contrast to the treachery, injustice, and oppression brought on Jerusalem by her human rulers, there stands the perfect justice of God:

> The LORD within her is righteous;
>   he does no wrong.
> Morning by morning he dispenses his justice,
>   and every new day he does not fail. . . (*Zeph. 3:5*).

The first line of that passage could be interpreted as starting with a divine name: '*Yahweh Saddiq* is in the midst of her'. God is named 'Yahweh the

Just' or 'Yahweh the Righteous'. (As has often been pointed out, a single set of words in Hebrew may be translated by two sets in English: just/justice/ justify and righteous/righteousness.[16]The same is true of the set of Greek terms corresponding to the Hebrew.)

As judge and king, God's seat of justice is located, not in the gate of the city, but in his holy temple. The symbol of the holy of holies as God's throne-room links the thought of the *holiness* of God (and the fear with which he must be approached) to the *justice* that is the foundation of God's throne. The temple in Jerusalem symbolises God's heavenly temple and his throne of glory. David sings of the heavenly sanctuary:

> The LORD is in the temple, his holy place;
> The LORD is in the heavens, his throne
> His eyes behold, his eyelids try, the children of men. (*Ps. 11:4*ASV)

The holy Lord is the just Judge; he is no respecter of persons, and cannot be bribed (Deut. 10:17). His justice must be the norm for judicial practice of Israel. Judges must be impartial and incorruptible (Lev. 19:15; Deut. 1:17). In particular, God's justice cannot be perverted to favour the powerful and influential against the poor and friendless (Deut. 10:18). Human justice must also be impartial and open to the cause of the helpless (Deut. 24:17).[17]

God's justice is applied to individuals: he renders to every man according to that man's righteousness and faithfulness (1 Sam. 26:23). The distributive justice of the Lord, in its basic form, determines with respect to both cases and individuals who is in the right and who in the wrong (*cf.* Exod. 9:27; 1 Sam. 24:17).

Justice is shaped by the concept of a *verdict*, declaring one to be in the right or in the wrong. When Saul declares to David, 'You are more righteous than I' (1 Sam. 24:17), he is not saying that David has compiled more merit than he, or that he scores higher on a general scale of virtue. Rather, he is confessing that David has done him good, while he has done David evil (v. 7). David had appealed to the Lord's judgment ('May the Lord judge between you and me') and Saul acknowledges what the just verdict must be.

The question of comparative righteousness does come more clearly into view when Solomon condemns Joab to death for having killed two men 'more righteous and good than he' (1 Kings 2:32; *cf.* Gen. 38:26). Yet, in the context, the blood of the two victims is said to be 'innocent blood' (v. 31). Even when a comparison is made, the judgment is in terms of innocence or guilt rather than weighted merit.[18]

Alister McGrath has called attention to the differences in the associations ('semantic fields') of the terms for righteousness in the Hebrew Old Testament, in Greek, and in Latin. In Latin, righteousness is *iustitia*, understood as merit, that which deserves recognition or recompense. For the Latin church father Tertullian, therefore, the man who does good works can be said to make God his debtor.[19] In Hebrew, however, a man's 'righteousness' is seen in the context of the verdict that could be pronounced upon him: his being 'in the right' as over against an accusation. (The Greek terms were used of civic virtue in classical literature, but were drawn into the orbit of Hebrew use by the Greek translation of the Old Testament.)

A further difference in the connotation of the Hebrew terms appears in the use of the verb *haṣdîq*, 'to justify'.[20] This term always means 'to declare to be in the right', and therefore to acquit or vindicate. It never means to punish or condemn. The opposite is true of the corresponding term in classical Greek. *Dikaioun* means 'to do justice to', but almost invariably with a negative verdict in view. To do justice to someone is to punish him. In the Greek translation of the Old Testament, however, the use of the verb *dikaioun* to translate *haṣdîq* has forced a change in its implied meaning. *Dikaioun* takes on the meaning of 'to justify' as over against 'to condemn'.

The judges of Israel are commanded to 'justify the righteous and condemn the wicked' (Deut. 25:1). In Hebrew the expression repeats each of two roots: an English approximation might be 'to justify the justifiable and condemn the condemnable'. It is clear that 'condemn' must mean 'to *declare to be* wicked', not 'to *make* wicked', and that 'justify' must mean 'to declare to be righteous', and not 'to make righteous'. This meaning is consistent in the Old Testament. It is clear in the Book of Job where 'justify' is used with God as the object. Job is accused of justifying himself rather than God (Job 32:2). The just God declares that he will not justify the wicked (Exod. 23:7; 20:11). The synonymous verb *nāqāh* 'to clear' also has in view the pronouncement of status: God will not clear, or acquit, the guilty (Exod. 34:7).[21]

God's own standard of justice is perfect and has been revealed in his law, his ordinances. Given God's perfect standard and his perfect justice in applying it, what hope can there be for mankind? 'How can man be just before God?' (Job 9:2). When Isaiah sees God enthroned in the temple, he can only cry, 'Woe is me!' (Isa. 6:5). If there is none that does good, not even one (Ps. 14:3), if no man living can be justified in God's sight (Ps. 143:2), how can there be any escape from the universal verdict: the soul that sins must die (Ezek. 18:20)?

The biblical prophets and poets struggle with this issue. Indeed, it is the great question for the whole Old Testament. Sin has entered the world, and the death-knell sounds through the genealogies of Genesis. The doom that a holy God pronounces on sinful mankind is everywhere at hand: the expulsion from the garden, the universal flood, the curse on Babel, the annihilation of Sodom and Gomorrah, the death of the first-born in Egypt. Yet God's judgments are not total. He spares a remnant and proclaims his promise. Adam and Eve must leave the garden, but they are spared. Noah's family survives the flood to repopulate the world. The nations are scattered from Babel, but God gives them their boundaries on the earth (Gen. 10; Deut. 32:8; Acts 17:26).

The apostle Paul believed that there must be an explanation for the fact that a righteous and holy God could spare a world of sinners through the ages. He found that explanation in the atonement to be brought by Jesus Christ:

> God presented him as a sacrifice of atonement, through faith in his blood. He did this to demonstrate his justice, because in his forbearance he had left the sins committed beforehand unpunished — he did it to demonstrate his justice at the present time, so as to be just and the one who justifies the man who has faith in Jesus. (*Rom. 3:25f.*)

Paul's understanding has deep grounding in the Old Testament. There is no scaling down of the infinite height of the divine holiness, and no puffing up of human pretence in the sight of the Holy One. Israel is given the account of Adam and Eve in the garden to teach them that all hope begins with God's initiative in grace. Adam and Eve deserved the verdict of death for their rebellion against the word of the Lord. Yet they did not fall dead at the foot of the tree; God withheld his judgment in order to proclaim his promise (Gen. 3:15). The measured judgment that God did pronounce gave order to human life in the midst of death. Adam must labour in a world under Gods curse, but his labour could be fruitful. Eve must know the anguish of childbearing, but through a child to be born would come the destruction of the evil one. The word of the Lord that had declared 'Let there be light' also declared to the serpent,

> And I will put enmity
> Between you and the woman,
> And between your seed and her Seed. (*Gen. 3:15* NKJV)

God's word of promise is not less sovereign than his word of creation.

Human history is set under a suspended sentence, but a sentence that awaits a time of judgment and of final restoration. In the course of history the promise of God is repeated and expanded. The God who intervenes with his word of promise also bridges the gulf by mighty acts of deliverance. No Babel tower of man's building can avail to join earth to heaven and to determine where God should descend. God comes down his own stairway at his own time to make Bethel the house of God, the gate of heaven (Gen. 11:4; 28:12–17).

Just as God is the judge whose verdict is final and just, so God is the Saviour, the only one who can provide deliverance from the penalty of his own judgment. The great theme of the Old Testament is that 'salvation is of the Lord' (Jon. 2:9).

Perhaps our familiarity with the separate narratives of the Old Testament has blunted our grasp of the history as a whole. It unfolds under the shadow of God's judgment: on all mankind in the generation of Noah, on Sodom and Gomorrah, on Egypt, on the Canaanites, on Israel, on Judah, on the world empires employed by the Lord to bring judgment on his people.

Yet God's promises are never forgotten. It is God who calls Abram out of Ur, and who promises to bless him and to make him a blessing to all the families of the earth. God insists on promising Abraham and Sarah a son; after both Abraham and Sarah have laughed at the absurdity of such a promise (at *their* age!), God makes good on it. Is any promise too wonderful for God? (Gen. 18:14). It is God who swears to Abraham, by the dread symbol of a divine dismemberment, that he will not forget his promise to him and to his seed (Gen. 15; Jer. 34:18–20).

How can a man be just with God? The whole history of the Old Testament hinges on God's answer to that question. The black clouds of divine wrath are edged with the rim-light of his promises, the signs of his saving deeds. God chooses the descendant of Abraham, the son of David. God demonstrates the freedom of his choosing: the claims of human custom and tradition are overturned. The right of primogeniture is repeatedly set aside: God chooses not Cain, but Abel, then Seth; not Ishmael but Isaac; not Esau, but Jacob; not Reuben, but Judah; not Eliab, but David; not Amnon, but Solomon.

God purposes to show that his deliverance does not depend on the wisdom or strength of men. Moses was first preserved as an infant, then called as a senior citizen when his self-confidence was long gone. The story of the judges is the record of unlikely leaders whom God raised up and used as his instruments. Israel had to be shown that deliverance could come from Deborah, a woman; from Gideon, a younger son with a limited band of warriors; from Samson, a solitary hero whose power was of the Spirit, and who worked his greatest victory as a blind captive.

The author of Hebrews is exactly right in seeing the history of God's people as a chronicle of faith.[22] Not the war-chariot or gold brought Israel's salvation, but the power of God.

B. Covenantal Religion

God's covenant with his people expresses this principle: salvation is indeed of the Lord. The bond of the covenant is the bond of God's grace. The delay of judgment is due to the forbearance, the patience of God (Neh. 9:30; Rom. 2:4). It awaits the fulfilment of the promise. But why should God make such promises? What purpose lies behind the suspended sentence? The prophet gives the Lord's answer:

> 'For I know the thoughts that I think toward you,' declares the Lord, 'plans to prosper you and not to harm you, plans to give you hope and a future.' (*Jer. 29:11*)

God's ordering of history, his calling, his intervention to deliver his chosen, all this expresses the purpose of grace that moves him. God's covenant with his people is not a contract worked out at a bargaining table. It is a bond that God himself sets in place as he calls his people to himself. God's calling and choosing establishes his covenant with Israel in fulfilment of the promises that he made to the fathers. It is as the God of Abraham, Isaac, and Jacob that God calls Moses to deliver his people from Egypt (Exod. 3:6). God did not set his love upon Israel because they were more in number than any other people, for he chose them as the fewest of all peoples (Deut. 7:7). Neither was it for their righteousness that they were given the land of Canaan (although it was for the wickedness of the Canaanites that they were judged and destroyed — Deut. 9:4–6). The basis for God's calling of Israel was not to be found in them, but in him. Because the Lord loved them he delivered them and carried them on eagles' wings to himself (Exod. 19:4; Deut. 7:8).

The covenant that God made with Israel at Sinai bound him to the nation as he had already bound himself to the fathers. God threatened judgment on Pharaoh's son unless Pharaoh released Israel, God's son. God first claimed Israel as his own, then brought them out of Egypt that he might bring them to himself. They had been Pharaoh's servants; God would make them his servants. They would serve him in the sense that they would be his people, and he their God. Their service would be worship[23], but also subjection to his lordship. It was to a delivered people that God addressed the words of his covenant at Sinai. God presented his covenant in the form of a treaty, the treaty of a victorious sovereign; he required of them that they bind themselves to its stipulations. The introduction to the Ten Commandments is revealing. God identified himself as the Saviour God, the Lord who had redeemed them from bondage in Egypt, and who required of them that they worship him alone.

The question as to how human beings can be acceptable to God is given new form in God's covenant. God's declaration defines the covenantal relation: 'I will . . . be your God, and you will be my people' (Lev. 26:12). That relation exists as God's claim. For example, the law of God's covenant forbids Israelites to keep other Israelites in permanent servitude. God gives a simple reason: 'The Israelites belong to me as servants. They are my servants, whom I brought out of Egypt. I am the LORD your God' (Lev. 25:25).

There can be no doubt as to the closeness of relation that the covenant establishes. A full range of figures is used to describe the intimacy of God's care for his people. They are the apple of his eye; they are graven on his hands (Deut. 32:10; Isa. 49:16). His devotion toward them is crystallised in the term *hesed*. This term described a gracious love, and not a mere covenantal obligation.[24] Yet it is a love of devotion, a love in which God binds himself to those who cannot demand or deserve such commitment. The *hesed* of God's covenant reflects the amazing grace of the Lord's goodness toward his people.

How can there be such intimacy? How can the Lord claim Israel as his own? How can he walk and live among them without destroying them by the flame of his holiness?

This question is dramatically put and answered in the book of Exodus. At Mount Sinai the Lord met with Israel and established his covenant with them by his word spoken from heaven. The people could not bear that dread voice; they asked Moses to serve as the medium of God's communication. Moses ascended the mountain into the cloud of the divine presence. There he received the Ten Commandments, inscribed by God himself on tablets of stone. There he also received God's instructions for the building of the tabernacle, the tent of God's own dwelling to be set in the midst of the encampment of Israel.

Moses was up on the mountain for more than a month. In his absence, the people grew restive; they pressured Aaron to make them a golden calf for a religious celebration. When Moses at last descended from Sinai, he heard the noise of a heathen orgy in the camp of Israel. A full civil war ensued before Moses could put down the rebellion and restore order. If such blatant idolatry was possible at the very foot of the mountain from which the voice of the Lord had forbidden it, what hope could there be for Israel?

In that situation the Lord proposed another plan. Since the people were so wilfully disobedient, so 'stiffnecked', it was too dangerous for the holy Lord to be in their midst. Instead, he would go before them in the presence of his angel, drive out the inhabitants of Canaan and give them the promised land. Plans for the tabernacle would be cancelled. Rather than dwelling in the midst of the people, the Lord would meet with Moses outside the camp. A temporary arrangement would be made permanent. Joshua would live in a tent outside the camp, and that tent would serve as a tent of meeting. Moses would go out of the camp to the tent, and God would meet with him at the tent door. Contact with God would not be lost, but the intimate fellowship pictured by God's tent of residence would not take place. It was simply too dangerous. God would go before his people, lead them into the land of the promise, but he would not, could not go among them (Exod. 33:3).

We might have supposed that Moses would welcome God's alternate plan with enthusiasm. Surely it offered what the people most wanted without the danger of too intimate contact with God. Moses, however, reacted with total dismay. If God were not to go up in the midst of his people, there was no point in their going to the promised land: 'If your Presence does not go with us, do not send us up from here' (Exod. 33:15). The journey from Egypt to Canaan was not for a change in diet: to substitute milk and honey for fish and onions. Nor was it just to exchange slavery for freedom. At the goal of the journey and along the way, the meaning of the exodus was that Israel should be the people of God: to know him, to have fellowship with him. Moses therefore prayed that the Lord would show him his glory. He asked for what the tabernacle symbolised: the revelation of the presence of the Lord in the midst of his people.

God granted the prayer of Moses: he revealed his glory, hiding Moses in the cleft of the rock. He proclaimed his name to Moses. He is Yahweh, the God of *ḥesed* and *'emeth*: covenant grace and faithfulness. Moses was right in appealing to the revelation of the Lord himself. What else could he plead? That Israel was not so stiffnecked, after all? That, given another chance, they would become good enough so that the presence of the Holy God would cease to be a threat? God's presence in the midst could be established only in the depth of the Lord's mercy and the commitment of his grace. After God had revealed himself, Moses prayed:

> If now I have found favour in thy sight, O Lord, let the Lord, I pray thee, go in the midst of us; for it is a stiffnecked people; and pardon our iniquity and our sin, and take us for thine inheritance. (*Exod. 34:9* ASV)

Is the prayer contradictory? Because Israel was a stiff-necked people, God had said he could not dwell in the midst (Exod. 33:5). Yet, for that very reason, Moses now asks God to dwell in the midst. The only basis for that reversal is God's revelation of his covenant mercy. Confident of God's *ḥesed*, Moses can pray: 'Pardon our iniquity and our sin'. If God were to dwell among a sinful people, there must be abundant pardon for sin. Only then could God make them *his* inheritance (much more than giving them *their* inheritance!).

It is precisely this pardon for sin, flowing from the *ḥesed* and *'emeth* of the Lord that is symbolised by the tabernacle. The tabernacle would be built; God, in symbol, would dwell in the midst of his people. The veils of the tabernacle would insulate, as it were, against the fire of God's presence. But at the same time, the tabernacle imaged a way of approach into God's presence. At the entrance to the court stood the great bronze altar of sacrifice. Only through shed blood could the stiffnecked people come into the presence of God. The blood marked the death of the sacrificial animal in the place of the sinner. The blood of the altar, the water of the laver: cleansing was necessary to come before the Lord — a cleansing that his ordinances provided.

This incident set in the heart of the book of Exodus shows us how central the tabernacle must be for the worship of Israel. It shows again that God's covenant must be established in blood: the blood that was sprinkled on the

altar and the people when they stood before the Lord to enter his covenant
(Exod. 24:6–8).

How can a sinful people be acceptable to God? By the blood of the
covenant, the provision of his grace. By the revelation of his mercy in the way
of approach that he provided. The ceremonial system is governed by the
concept of cleanness. That concept describes a status, a status that is
symbolised by the right of the clean Israelite to enter the courts of the Lord
and to stand before the Holy One. Gerhard von Rad has pointed out that the
formula 'He is righteous' as used in Ezekiel 18:9 is of the same sort as the
formulae pronounced by the priest who had to declare what the status of an
individual was: clean or unclean, blood-guilty or innocent (Lev. 13; 7:18;
17:4).[25] Von Rad thinks of this cultic declaration as offering one model of
viewing a man as acceptable to God. The keeping of God's commandments
would represent another way (Deut. 6:25).

It may seem attractive to regard the cultic and the moral as two paths
leading to divine acceptance. But the prophets from Samuel onward
distinguish ceremonial performance from true righteousness:

> Does the LORD delight in burnt offerings and sacrifices
>   as much as in obeying the voice of the LORD?
> To obey is better than sacrifice,
>   and to heed is better than the fat of rams. (*1 Sam. 15:22*)

Yet the prophetic condemnation of empty and hypocritical formalism does
not reject the symbolism of cleansing and atonement. Jesus quoted the
prophets to condemn the formalism of his day, but he also cleansed the
temple. His word and his deed were consistent with the message of the
prophets. Ezekiel preaches God's demand of righteousness but also sees
God's future blessing in the vision of a glorious temple. The word of the Lord
to Zechariah condemns the fruitless fasting of the disobedient exiles (Zech.
7:5,6), but Zechariah hails the cultic cleansing of Joshua, the royal priest, and
sees all Jerusalem made as holy as the temple (Zech. 3:4,5; 14:16–21). Isaiah
brings the most eloquent description of divine displeasure against hypocrites
trampling his courts (Isa. 1:11–17), but Isaiah's call comes from a vision of the
Lord's glory in the temple, where he must be cleansed by a coal from the altar
(Isa. 6:6). In Isaiah's song of the suffering servant the righteous sin-bearer is
led as a lamb to the slaughter that his soul might be made an offering for sin
(Isa. 53:7,10).

In God's covenant, his people are accepted because he freely chose and
called them in his grace. The issue of their disqualification and sinfulness is
always met with the symbolism of sacrifice. God delights in the sacrifice of a
broken heart, but bullocks continue to be offered on his altar. The last two
verses of Psalm 51 are not a rebuttal to the two that precede (Ps. 51:17,19). In
the ceremonies of worship, the status of the people before God is declared by
the priest in God's name; the ritual of the Day of Atonement provides that
declaration for Israel as a whole.

There are not two alternate ways of being accepted by God, but there are
two figures by which acceptance is expressed: the verdict of the judge and the
blessing of the priest. Both are found in the New Testament. In Romans, the
language of the law-court is used to describe our justification; in Hebrews the

language of the sanctuary includes the same truth. Christ's once-for-all sacrifice makes forever perfect those who are thereby sanctified (Heb. 10:14). Hebrews 'clearly locates this perfecting *in the past with respect to its accomplishment and in the present with respect to its enjoyment*'.[26]

It is true that the language of sanctification in the New Testament speaks of the work of God in us rather than the declaration of God for us, particularly when progress in sanctification is spoken of (2 Cor. 7:1). Yet the language of the cultus can be used to describe the status of those who are acceptable to God through the atonement of his altar.[27]

The bond of the covenant and the status of Israel as the people of God lead to two consequences in the Old Testament. First, God's people are distinguished from the world by their position. They are a righteous nation, given righteous laws and ordinances to serve the Lord. Second, they are called and commanded to live in obedience to their God, and to suffer the greater judgment if they prove unfaithful to their calling.

The first consequence of the covenant, Israel's righteousness, leads to a rather startling use of the term. When Israel prays for the display of God's righteousness, it is with a view to the vindication of Israel's position as righteous over against the threats and oppression of the wicked. The people of God are presented as the congregation or the generation of the righteous (Ps. 1:5; 14:5). They are constantly distinguished from 'the workers of iniquity' (Ps. 14:4–NIV 'evildoers'). The Psalmist pleads his righteousness as he calls upon the Lord to vindicate his cause against his enemies (Ps. 7:8,10). Such pleas are standard in the Psalms of refuge, for the psalmist is appealing his case to the Lord as judge (Ps. 11:5–7). He has fled, figuratively, to lay hold on the horns of God's altar; he would carry to the highest court of appeal the charges that have been laid against him. His protestations of righteousness are made as a 'not guilty' plea to the accusations of his enemies. He calls upon God for justice; he asks the Lord to judge his case in righteousness and to grant deliverance (Ps. 31:1), a full deliverance that will include retribution as well as vindication (Ps. 58:10,11).

'The righteous LORD loves righteousness' (Ps. 11:7 ASV). The noun in the plural suggests the righteous deeds of the Lord (see Judg. 5:11). David, the psalmist, is affirming that the Lord delights to exhibit his justice in actions. When Samuel reminds Israel of (lit.) all the 'righteousnesses of the Lord which he did to you and to your fathers' (1 Sam. 12:7), he is not speaking of acts of judgment *upon* Israel, but *on behalf of* Israel: that is, acts of justice against their enemies.

Because the showing of God's righteousness/justice brings deliverance to God's people, it is celebrated in the Psalms as a saving righteousness (Ps. 40:10; 88:10,11). Put in parallel with God's faithfulness (*'emûnah*), covenant devotion (*ḥeseḏ*), and even his deliberate favour (*raṣôn*) the righteousness of God comes to express the triumph of his holy purpose for his people (Ps. 88:11,12,16,17). In the sight of the nations God is revealed as righteous in that he remembers his mercy and truth toward Israel (Ps. 98:2,3). The covenant devotion of the Lord is forever fixed on those that fear him, and his righteousness to their grandchildren (Ps. 103:17). God's righteousness is therefore most closely connected with his faithfulness (*'emûnah*). He will hear the prayer of his servant, for he is faithful to his covenantal promise, and will show his righteousness by answering (Ps. 143:1). To appeal to God's righteousness is like appealing to his name, and therefore also to his sure mercy (Ps. 143:11,12). The psalmist may actually appeal to God's righteousness/ justice with a prayer that the Lord not enter into judgment with him, since in God's sight no one living may be justified (Ps. 143:1,2). We may sense a tension, or even find a contradiction here. How can one seek relief from the Lord's justice by appealing to his justice? The resolution is to be found in God's promise of saving mercy. The basic expression of this Psalm corresponds to the New Testament affirmation that God is 'faithful and just [*dikaios*, 'righteous'] and will forgive us our sins and purify us from all unrighteousness' (1 John 1:9).

The psalmist's plea for the revelation of God's righteousness even while confessing his own unrighteousness comes from a penitent and dependent heart. To claim God's saving righteousness is to claim his gracious promise. The prayer may be urgent and even bold in its desperation, but it is a prayer of faith, not an accusatory claim against God. In Job, in the Psalms, in the history of Israel, it is clear that the proud cannot command or manipulate the righteous judgments of God. Not pride, but repentance marks the man who has been restored to the Lord's favour. Elihu takes pains to remind Job of this truth, although he fails to consider Job's true situation (Job 33:26–28). It is the penitent sinner, not the self-righteous Pharisee, who leaves the temple justified in the sight of God (Lk. 18:9–14). The sinner who turns to God cannot offer his sorrow for sin as atonement for his transgression. To the contrary, he sees his sin as justifying God's judgment (Ps. 51:4). The penitent can only confess his iniquity and seek the Lord's mercy (Ps. 32:5). Yet David pledges to sing of God's righteousness as the Lord delivers him from bloodguilt (Ps. 51:14). David will praise God's righteousness as the God of his salvation. David's sin showed God to be righteous in condemning him, but David's deliverance from condemnation will show God's righteousness in saving him. There is no mystery in the righteous wrath of God against David's adultery and murder. There is great mystery in the righteousness of God's deliverance. David is indeed blessed to have his sin covered, to be a man to whom the Lord does not reckon iniquity (Ps. 32:1,2). But how can God's righteousness not only allow, but provide such a reckoning?

Certainly the answer must lie with God. The psalmist who seeks God's covenant love and righteousness looks to the divine faithfulness in redeeming his people, not only from their enemies, but from their sins. God's *righteousness* accomplishes that, the righteousness of his saving purpose and promise. As the centuries trace the sin of Israel, the need for God's saving righteousness becomes ever plainer. The prophets make explicit what has always been implied. God's forgiveness of sin, his acceptance of his people as a holy nation, a kingdom of priests, must require that his righteousness not only provide for them, but be their provision. The righteousness of God's judgment must become the righteousness of God's gift.

C. God's Righteousness as Promise

The apostle Paul well shows that the gift of righteousness is required by the reality of grace and promise inherent in God's salvation (Rom. 4:16). The Old Testament is structured by the unfolding of God's promise. Abraham believes the promise of grace, and is accounted righteous in God's sight (Gen.

15:6; Rom. 4:3). The righteousness of his position before God is but the application to him of the promise he believes. Paul has been accused of spiritualising God's covenant promises to Abraham. Does not the promise of many nations descending from Abraham refer to the Ishmaelites, and to the Semitic peoples descended from the sons of Keturah (Gen. 25:1–4)? How, then, can the apostle speak of Abraham as the father of many nations of the *Gentiles* in fulfilment of the promise (Rom. 4:16,17)? Does not the inheritance given to Abraham refer to Canaan, the land of the promise (Gen. 15:7; 17:8)? How, then, can Paul speak of Abraham being made heir of the *world* according to the promise (Rom. 4:13; *cf.* Eph. 6:3)?

Paul does not remove elements of the promise and substitute others more congenial to his gospel. Rather he argues from the unity and therefore the depth of the Old Testament promises.[28] Through the seed of Abraham all the nations of the earth would be blessed, and the blessing they are to receive is that given to Abraham. The heart of the blessing is that God himself is Abraham's shield and reward (Gen. 15:1). The covenant that God made with Abraham promised the fundamental blessing of a restored relationship between God and sinful mankind. Abraham was separated from the nations that he might be a blessing to the nations through the seed of the promise. For that reason, Paul can speak of the gift of the Spirit as the fulfilment of the promise to Abraham (Gal. 3:14). Abraham looked beyond earthly real estate to desire a 'heavenly country', a restored relation with the living God (Heb. 11:16). The God of Abraham, who could revivify Abraham's aging body and Sarah's dead womb to keep his promise, is the God of the impossible, who brings life from the dead and calls into being things that are not (Rom. 4:17). 'Is any word too wonderful for the Lord?' (Gen. 18:14; Luke 1:37). Paul does not misread the promises of God to Abraham when he finds in them the kernel of God's whole plan of redemption. Rather, Paul recognises the continuity of the promises of God. The glorious visions of the prophets are not alien to the promises to Abraham, but show more fully what those promises imply.

The righteousness of the promise given to Abraham and received by faith is the gift-righteousness of which the prophets speak. God is the source of all righteousness: 'There is no God apart from me, a righteous God and a Saviour' (Isa. 45:21). For that reason, 'They will say of me, "In the LORD alone are righteousness and strength" . . . But in the LORD all the descendants of Israel will be found righteous and will exult' (Isa. 45:24,25). 'This is the heritage of the servants of the LORD, and their righteousness is from Me, saith the LORD' (Isa. 54:17 NKJV).[29]

The focus of the Old Testament on the gift of God's righteousness appears as God promises to come himself to save his people. The account of Israel's apostasy and exile shows that the righteousness of the God of the covenant is directed against his rebellious people. Israel presumed on the covenant promises, thinking that the presence of the Lord made the temple indestructible and their own deliverance inevitable (Jer. 7:1–15). The word of the Lord to Jeremiah reminds the people of Judah of the fate of the sanctuary in Shiloh because of the apostasy of Israel in the north (Jer. 7:12). In proud self-confidence Israel supposed that they could 'steal and murder, commit adultery, and perjury, burn incense to Baal and follow other gods', but still call on the name of the Lord for deliverance (Jer. 7:9). To such rebels God's covenant righteousness brought not comfort but a dread threat. Their special relation with the Lord would assure special judgment. 'You only have I known of all the families of the earth; therefore I will punish you for all your iniquities' (Amos 3:2 NKJV).

In view of that principle it might seem that all of God's promises would prove empty: golden, perhaps, but inaccessible, shut off by human sin. 'For what profit is it to us if the eternal age is promised to us, but we have done works which bring death?' (4 Ezra 7:119).

The message of the prophets, however, proclaims hope. The sin of Israel does, indeed, bring destruction and exile. Their situation is hopeless: they are scattered in captivity like the bones of men long dead strewn on the valley floor (Ezek. 37). Can these bones live? Not by human power, but by the Spirit of the Lord. The situation of the people is too hopeless, and God's promises too great for any human programme or leadership. God himself must bring salvation to his people. Here is the hope of the prophets. God's judgment will not be total: he will spare a remnant, small and insignificant before men, but a remnant that carries the seed of the promise. From that remnant will come renewal. Israel will be cut down like a cedar of Lebanon, but from the stump will grow up a shoot that will be an ensign to the nations (Isa. 10:33–11:5). The branch from the stump of Jesse is a royal figure who will judge the poor with righteousness, for righteousness will be the belt of his waist (Isa. 11:3,5). The daughter of Jerusalem can rejoice at the coming of the king who is righteous, and having salvation (Zech. 9:9).

Most pointedly, the coming branch is to be identified with the servant of the Lord, a suffering servant who by the knowledge of himself will justify many; 'and he will bear their iniquities' (Isa. 53:11). Like Moses, the servant of the Lord will be a prophet who endures hostility to represent the cause of the Lord. But while Moses could only desire to be blotted from God's book along with a sinful people, the servant to come will not only make intercession for transgressors, he will be 'cut off out of the land of the living, stricken to death for the transgression of my people' (Isa. 53:8).[30] His soul will be a sin-offering. Henri Blocher states clearly the significance of this passage:

> The Book of Leviticus rules that if sinful man, under the holy wrath of a holy God, would approach the Lord, he must sacrifice a spotless victim in his place (see Lev. 4 and 5). This is how atonement is made. This is the core of the institution of sacrifice. The Servant 'makes *himself* an offering for sin'; he offers not another life, but his own, as a sin-offering. Since he offers the sacrifice, he is the priest; since he offers himself, he is the sacrifice. He himself is the Lamb of God.[31]

Sinful Israel cannot make atonement for their own sins. God must provide: the arm of the Lord must be revealed. The righteousness of God must be his provision through his own servant and Son. Only so can God's righteousness be his gift to sinners. The name of the righteous branch who will be raised up in the line of David will be 'The LORD our righteousness' (Jer. 23:5,6). He will bear the name of the Lord, not just as his people may do through him (Jer. 33:14–16), but in a unique sense, for he will be identified with the Lord himself, the Angel of the Lord in the midst of his people (Zech. 12:8; Mal. 3:1,2).

Only by the coming of God himself can his righteousness deliver his people. He will be the divine warrior, wearing the helmet of salvation and the breastplate of righteousness to come as their redeemer (Isa. 59:16,17). As he once led Israel through the wilderness, so he must come again, marching through the desert to bring salvation to his people (Isa. 40:3–5).

God's people have despised the oath that bound them to his covenant; they have broken his covenant and brought its curse upon them (Ezek. 16:59; Jer. 11:10). But God's promised grace will yet triumph. He will remember his covenant in mercy (Ezek. 16:60f.); indeed, he will renew it as a new covenant, written on their hearts (Jer. 31:31–34). The Lord will indeed be their God, and they his people, for they will all know him, from the least to the greatest (Jer. 31:34). As God came down at Sinai to make his covenant with those he had delivered, so he must come again, in a yet greater revelation of his presence. The new covenant comes with the Lord.

When John the Baptist uses Isaiah's gospel of divine epiphany to announce the coming of Jesus, he is true to the Old Testament message. The coming of the Lord is joined with the coming of the Messiah, who bears the divine name (Isa. 9:6,7).

D. The Response of Covenant Devotion

God's gracious initiative in establishing his covenant with his people calls for their response. Because salvation is of the Lord, that response looks to God, receives his word of promise, trusts in his provision. Human response recognises and acknowledges the relation into which God enters with humankind.[32] The worshipper approaches the courts of the Lord in the time and place of his appointment. 'Man is never the one who initially establishes this relation. Even in passages where there is no express mention of this the presupposition of faith is always the fact that God is the true author of the relation between God and man.'[33]

At the same time, God's initiative in salvation does seek a response from the creatures made in his image. After the sin of Adam and Eve in the garden God came calling them. Jesus described the heavenly Father as seeking worshippers (John 4:23). The heart of the covenant is a relation in which the objects of God's redeeming love respond to his grace with hearts that are circumcised. Nothing less than complete and whole-souled devotion is called for. The one true God commands the unity of a total response:

> Hear, O Israel: the LORD our God, the LORD is one. Love the LORD your God with all your heart and with all your soul and with all your strength. (*Deut. 6:4,5*)

How does this full response of devoted love relate to the saving faith taught in Paul's epistles? Does the Old Testament make loving obedience the requirement of the covenant while the New Testament asks faith alone? The question is wrongly put, of course. Faith in the New Testament does not remain alone; it works through love (Gal. 5:6). On the other hand, the whole Old Testament presents salvation as God's plan and work from start to finish; it is received, not merited. The Deuteronomy passage just quoted (the *shema*) proclaims the name of the Lord who has claimed Israel as his own. The response of love is grounded in the hearing of faith. God's proclamation must be credited as true; more than that, it must be acknowledged and embraced in covenant commitment.

The place of faith in the Old Testament is illumined by the study of the term *'āman* and its cognates.[34] The use of the verb in the *hip'îl* form gives strong witness to the importance of believing. Nevertheless, the number of occurrences where the term is used in a positive sense for faith in God is limited.[35] There is no noun meaning 'faith' in this group (unless Habakkuk 2:4 be taken as an exception). It would be a mistake to conclude from this that the Old Testament has little to say about faith, or to limit our understanding of the Old Testament doctrine to these words. At the least, we must take account of the synonyms most closely related to the *'āman* group.[36] These include the terms for 'trust' (*bātaḥ*), for 'seek refuge' (*ḥāsāh*), and for 'hope in' and 'wait for' (*yiḥāltî, ḥikāh*). The common term to 'fear' the Lord (*yārē*) is also used in a positive sense to express trust in him. When these terms are taken together, it is clear that there is no lack of emphasis on the importance of faith as trust in the Lord and commitment to him.

As might be expected, terms for trust are common in the Psalms, particularly in psalms of lament and of refuge. It is notable that the psalmist confesses his trust in the mercy and grace of the Lord.[37] As may be seen in Psalm 22, the psalms of lament regularly include confessions of trust (Ps. 22:3–5, 9–10), and entire Psalms are extended celebrations of trust (Psalm 23). The very heartbeat of the Psalms is the cry of total dependence on the Lord. David's trust in God was learned at his mother's breast.

> As the eyes of slaves look to the hand of their master,
>   as the eyes of a maid look to the hand of her mistress,
> so our eyes look to the LORD our God,
>   till he shows us his mercy. (*Ps. 123:2*)

Trust in God reviews the past to remember God's mighty acts of deliverance, the tokens of his lovingkindness. His present help is sought so that others might see his salvation and learn to trust in him (Ps. 40:1–4). The Psalms breathe the confidence that the Lord will hear and will deliver. The psalmist concludes his lament by offering his vow of praise. He anticipates deliverance that it is assured although it has not yet been realised (Ps. 22:22–25).

Trust always looks to the future. In part, this is forced upon the Lord's anointed by the intolerable anguish and oppression of his situation. His trust is in the Lord as his refuge, a hiding place where he can find shelter until the storm of calamities has passed. Secure in the Lord's protection he can wait in hope. Deliverance, however, means more than protection. It also means vindication and victory. The psalmist trusts the word and promise of God. He recalls that when God delivered Israel from Egypt, the people believed his words (Ps. 106:12; Exod. 14:31). He appeals to God's righteousness to express his confidence that God will be true to his covenant promises.

Trust in God is often contrasted with trust in idols (Isa. 42:17; 59:4; Ps. 115:8; 135:18; Hab. 2:18). The same contrast is made with a whole-earth catalogue of the things in which men put their trust: horses (Ps. 20:7), chariots (Isa. 31:1), the bow (Ps. 44:6), riches (Ps. 49:6), oppression (Isa. 30:2), power (Ps. 49:6; Prov. 28:26), military allies (Isa. 36:9), cultural accomplishments (Jer. 48:7), or their own understanding (Prov. 3:5). The wisdom literature contrasts those who are wise in their own eyes with those who fear the Lord and depart from evil: in their hearts they trust the Lord, in their lives they keep his commandments (Prov. 3:7).

For Rudolf Bultmann Old Testament faith is not properly existential, because 'the question of death is not set under the concept of faith'.[38] Faith is directed to this-worldly deliverances; the psalmist may apeal to his own piety. 'Piety, then, is not radically understood as faith.'[39] It is true that David and the other psalmists seek deliverance and blessing in this life. It is untrue that 'death is not set under the concept of faith'. David, who meditated while the fire burned, prayed for the Lord to show him his mortality, his life as a mere breath, and concluded: 'And now, Lord, what wait I for? My hope is in thee' (Ps. 39:7 ASV). While it is true that only the resurrection of Christ put the hope of resurrection from the dead in the full light of glory, Jesus himself showed how the Old Testament taught it: in the unbreakable communion that exists between the living God and those whose name he bears (Matt. 22:32). Psalms 23,73 and 90 eloquently testify to the radical trust in God that rises from a pilgrimage under the shadow of death. Old Testament piety looks to the Lord as the only Saviour and hope, to the exclusion of anything in man. As Moses desired to know the Lord and to see his glory, so David prays, 'Unite my heart to fear Your name' (Ps. 86:11 NKJV). His piety holds fast to God, and is upheld by God's right hand; it is the piety of faith (Ps. 63:8).

The New Testament beautifully presents the depth and power of Old Testament faith, even while acknowledging its incompleteness. The epistle to the Hebrews does not mistake the dynamic of Old Testament piety when it traces Old Testament history by the category of faith (Heb. 11). The author concludes:

> These were all commended for their faith, yet none of them received what had been promised. God had planned something better for us so that only together with us would they be made perfect (Heb. 11:39,40).

As the apostle Paul teaches, grace and faith go together (Rom. 4:16). If God's mercies can be earned, so that God owes wages to the saints, then they are no longer mercies, grace is no longer grace, and faith is no longer pivotal. The overwhelming witness of the Old Testament to the saving grace of God carries along a parallel witness to the faith of those who receive it.

These passages in Hebrews and Romans both join faith not only to God, but to his promise. Old Testament faith is forward-looking, for it accompanies the unfolding of the history of redemption. In every period of that history believers are pointed toward better things to come. Childless Abraham, a pilgrim in the land of promise; exiled Moses sent to free a nation of slaves; David, an anointed outlaw, hiding in the desert; these all wait for God to keep his word.

The great test of faith was the doom of exile. Did not that destruction put an end to the promises of God? We have seen that it did not. Rather, those promises came with greater lustre, and with global outreach. Isaiah tells of the faith that rests in the final great salvation of God. The prophet warns King Ahaz that if he does not believe, he will not be established (Isa. 7:9).[40] His lack of faith is challenged by the marvellous sign the Lord will give (Isa.

7:14). In judgment God has hidden his face from the house of Jacob, yet the prophet is summoned not to share their fears, but to hallow the Lord of hosts himself: 'he is the one you are to fear, he is the one you are to dread' (Isa. 8:13). The prophet will wait for the Lord, and hope in him (8:17). The apostle Peter, in his epistle, repeats the exhortation not to share the fears of others, but to sanctify the Lord. But where the Greek version of Isaiah reads, 'the Lord himself', Peter writes, 'the Lord, the Christ' (1 Pet. 3:15).

The movement of the history of redemption leads to the coming of the Lord himself to fulfil his promises, and to the coming of the servant of the Lord, the greater son of David. Isaiah, the 'evangelical prophet', announces the coming of the Lord (chap. 40), and of the servant (chap. 49), who bears the name of the Lord (Isa. 9:6). With the soaring of the promise, the call to faith also rises. When the overflowing flood passes through, those who have sought refuge in lies will have no place to stand, but those who are grounded on the foundation that God lays will not be moved. 'The one who trusts will never be dismayed' (Isa. 28:16).

> You will keep in perfect peace him whose mind is steadfast,
>   because he trusts in you.
> Trust in the LORD forever,
>   for the LORD, the LORD, is the Rock eternal. (*Isa. 26:3,4*)

The futile panic of the unbelieving is contrasted with the quiet confidence of those whose trust is in the Lord (Isa. 30:15–17). Trust in the Lord is also confident submission to the servant of the Lord (Isa. 50:10). The prophetic theme of quiet confidence appears in Habakkuk as well. He can quietly await the coming devastation of the invader because he knows the vindicating judgment of God is sure. God will come in cosmic power for the salvation of his people with his anointed (Hab. 3:13). The haughty man will fall by his iniquity, but the righteous will live by his *'emûnāh*. The term is usually translated 'faithfulness', describing the righteous as one to be relied on, rather than one relying. In the broader context, however, the faithfulness of the truly devout is the faithfulness that patiently awaits the coming of God's salvation in spite of the dark horizon of judgment. It is conceivable that *'emûnāh* here could bear the active sense. In view of the use of the verb in the *hip̄'îl*, the noun could possibly mean 'firmness' as relying, rather than 'firmness' as reliability. The Greek word *pistis* that translates *'emûnāh* here in the Septuagint may mean either 'faithfulness' or 'faith'. In any case, Paul does not betray the thrust of the prophecy by emphasising *pistos* in the Greek translation (Rom. 1:17; Gal. 3:11; *cf.* Heb. 10:38).[41]

The deepening emphasis of the prophets on faith flows from the promise that they bear. Because the Lord will both preserve and renew a remnant, their trust in him must be intensified. Again, the glory of the promises heightens the anticipation with which the disciples of the prophet await their coming (Isa. 8:16–18). Further, the election of the remnant, a choosing within the choosing of Israel, is at the same time the flinging open of the doors of promise to others who will trust in the Lord to come. The promise of blessing to the nations through the seed of Abraham will reach out to the enemy nations, who may be named by the tenderest expressions of covenant privilege (Isa. 19:19–25).

All the intensifying comes to a burning focus as faith is pointed to the coming Lord: 'But for you who revere my name, the sun of righteousness will rise with healing in its wings. . . . See, I will send my messenger, who will prepare the way before me. Then suddenly the Lord you are seeking will come to his temple; the messenger of the covenant, whom you desire, will come . . .' (Mal. 4:2; 3:1).

II.   THE REVELATION OF GOD'S SAVING GRACE IN CHRIST

A.   The Coming of Salvation in Jesus Christ

How can a man approach the presence of God? The Old Testament answers: 'Jehovah Jireh', the Lord, will see to it. The fulfilment of the New Testament answers to the promise of the Old. The Lord himself must come. Angels in the fields of Bethlehem announce that he has come: 'Today in the town of David a Saviour has been born to you; he is Christ the Lord' (Luke 2:11).

Agur, the wise man of old, professed great ignorance as he put the questions:

> Who has gone up to heaven and come down . . .
> Who has established all the ends of earth?
> What is his name, and the name of his son?
> Tell me if you know! (*Prov. 30:4*)

Agur's ignorance is widely shared, as he no doubt implies. But his questions have an answer. When the Pharisee Nicodemus came to Jesus by night, Jesus gave that answer. 'No one has ever gone into heaven except the one who came from heaven — the Son of Man, who is in heaven' (John 3:13).[42] Jesus then used an amazing figure to tell how he would be lifted heavenward. 'Just as Moses lifted up the snake in the desert, so the Son of Man must be lifted up, that everyone who believes in him may have eternal life' (John 3:14).

Who shall ascend into the hill of the Lord? It must be the King of Glory, the one who has come from heaven, and who can tell Nicodemus about heavenly things. But he will ascend by first being 'lifted up' a few feet from the ground on a cross (John 12:32,33). Like the serpent in the wilderness, he will be lifted up as the accursed, the sin-bearer, who gives his life a ransom for many (Mark 10:45). The faith of Israel was directed to a symbol of the curse that had punished their unbelief. The venom of the poisonous serpents would cease its deadly work when they looked to the bronze symbol on the pole. Now they must look to the Son of Man, the mysterious figure whom Daniel had seen coming on the clouds of heaven to receive an eternal kingdom from the Ancient of Days (Dan. 7:13,14). His origin was, and is, heavenly, but his mission is redemptive.

The coming of Jesus was announced by John the Baptist, his forerunner, who served as Elijah to proclaim the coming of the Lord (Mal. 4:5,6). The proclamation of John and of Jesus was that the kingdom of God was at hand. That kingdom was promised in the Psalms and the prophets as the establishment of God's righteous rule. It brought into view the judgment of God in which his purposes and justice would be fully vindicated. N. T. Wright has well stated, 'Although, therefore, the *doctrine* of justification is discussed quite rarely in the NT, the *fact* of it is everywhere apparent.'[43] In the Old Testament, God's coming judgment is seen as the vindication of his oppressed people, but, as we have seen, the Scriptures are also concerned with the issue of the sin of Israel: who indeed can abide the coming of the Lord?

John the Baptist preached the message of Isaiah 40, presenting himself as the voice, crying in the wilderness, 'Prepare the way of the Lord!' The one that was to come, whose sandals he was not worthy to tie, would bring in the righteousness of God's kingdom. The axe was lying at the root of the tree of wickedness, and the Coming One would wield it. John preached repentance; his hearers were to flee the wrath to come by seeking God's forgiveness and cleansing, symbolised in the water of baptism. John preached both judgment and renewal, the judgment as promise (vindication), and the promise as judgment (baptism in the fire of the Spirit). The issue was squarely raised: John did not simply proclaim deliverance to the poor and oppressed through the vindication of God's justice; rather, his message called on all to repent. God's judgment must be encountered by those who sought his deliverance. The message of God's kingdom must be received and believed.

John's preaching brought division in Israel, division that was deepened by the ministry of Jesus. Jesus continued the proclamation of the coming of the kingdom; he taught the demand of God's righteousness. But where was the vindicating righteousness John expected Jesus to bring? Jesus did not take up the axe to begin the work of judgment. It was not from any lack of power. The miracles of Jesus included even the raising of the dead. John, however, because of his boldness in condemning sin in high places, found himself a prisoner of Herod, at the mercy of that arbitrary ruler. From his cell John sent two of his disciples to Jesus: 'Are you the one who was to come, or should we expect someone else?' (Luke 7:18).

If Jesus was the righteous judge, where was the judgment? If he had been anointed of the Spirit to release the oppressed (Luke 3:21,22; 4:18), why did he not release his forerunner? Jesus kept John's disciples with him while he performed more of his signs, showing them how directly he was fulfilling the promises of the prophets (Luke 4:22; Isa. 35:5,6). At the same time, Jesus sent word to John calling him to faith: 'Blessed is the man who does not fall away on account of me' (Luke 7:23).

This encounter between Jesus and John dramatises the unexpected way in which Jesus was bringing in the kingdom. He came with kingdom power, but he did not yet bring kingdom judgment. The explanation lay in the profound meaning of a message John himself had brought. Jesus was the Lamb of God who would take away the sin of the world (John 1:29). The Son of Man had come to give his life a ransom for many (Mark 10:45). Jesus came, not to bring the judgment, but to bear it. He was the suffering servant of Isaiah 53 (Matt. 8:17). Jesus knew that it was written of him 'that he should suffer much, and be rejected' (Mark 8:31; 9:12; Isa. 53:3).

Jesus also spoke of a time when he would come again in glory, with the angels of his Father, and when he would indeed bring the judgment (Matt. 24:27; 25:31–46). There was, therefore, an interim between the coming of Jesus to bring in the saving righteousness of the kingdom, and his coming again to bring in the final judgment of the kingdom.

The whole ministry of Jesus and the whole message of the kingdom has salvation as its key. The promised kingdom of God is not his sovereign rule over all things; that does not come, it always exists. God's kingdom that comes is the sphere of his saving power. It describes his triumph over all the power of sin and Satan. When Jesus by the finger of God casts out demons, it becomes evident that the kingdom of God is present. Where the king is, there the kingdom is: where his saving power operates, the kingdom is revealed.

Matthew emphasises the teaching of Jesus about the righteousness of the kingdom.[44] The good news is that the kingdom has come; Jesus announces the righteousness of the kingdom as a blessing: 'Blessed are those who hunger and thirst for righteousness, for they shall be filled' (Matt. 5:6).

The heirs of the kingdom, those who will be filled with righteousness, are not those who are confident of their own righteousness. To the contrary, Jesus says that 'unless your righteousness surpasses that of the Pharisees and the teachers of the law, you will certainly not enter the kingdom of heaven' (Matt. 5:20).

But if the righteousness of the scribes and Pharisees is not adequate for the standards of the kingdom, what hope can there be for harlots, tax-swindlers, and open sinners? Every hope, it appears, for Jesus not only fraternised with such people, he welcomed them as his disciples. The righteousness of the kingdom cannot be the achievement of proud human beings. It is the fruit of grace for those who know themselves to be sinners. The Pharisee in the temple, thanking God that he is so much better than others, cannot be pronounced just in God's sight. The defrauding tax-collector prays in deep contrition, 'God, be merciful to me, a sinner', and goes home justified through divine forgiveness and acceptance (Luke 18:9–14).

Jesus himself is the key to the question, 'How shall a man be right with God?' Jesus teaches with authority, exposing the legalism of the traditions of the elders. They have burdened people with heavy loads of observances, fencing God's law with their own teachings. But they have shown no understanding of what the law means or how it may be kept. Their misconstruction has shut the door against those who would enter; their hypocrisy has kept them from entering themselves.

In contrast to the wisdom of the scribes, Jesus presents himself as the Son of God. He alone knows the Father, even as only the Father knows him. He alone, therefore, can reveal the Father. He summons those labouring under the bondage of legalism to come to him, and promises rest, the easy yoke of the disciple who learns of him (Matt. 11:25–30).

In no way does Jesus destroy or set aside the law of God.[45] His teaching of the righteousness of the kingdom takes the law with seriousness for what it really is: the revealed will of the Father in heaven. The examples that Jesus gives of what it means to keep the law show the radical authority that the law has in view of the righteousness of God (Matt. 5:21–48).

Jesus has come, not to destroy the law and the prophets, but to fulfil them (Matt. 5:17). He does so by his own coming, for in him the kingdom comes, God's righteousness comes. He does so in his obedience, an obedience to the will of the Father that goes far beyond what any legalist could imagine. Jesus knows the meaning of the love that fulfils the law. It is the love of the Father's heart, the love of his saving righteousness, the love that sent his beloved Son into the world. This is clear when the legal scholar asks Jesus what he must do to inherit eternal life (Luke 10:25–37). Jesus asks him how the law reads. The

lawyer gives the summary of the law that Jesus himself gave on another
occasion: ' "Love the Lord your God with all your heart . . .'' and, "love
your neighbour as yourself." ' 'Do this', says Jesus, 'and you will live.'

But having given the right answer, the lawyer proceeds to ask the wrong
question: 'Who is my neighbour?' The motive of the question is plain. The
lawyer wants to minimise the number of people he must love. He thinks in
terms of loving for merit: earning heaven on points. Jesus' parable of the
'Good Samaritan' reverses the lawyer's question. It is not a matter of asking,
'How many people must I love?' but to whom may I show the love of
compassion — the love with which God has loved me? The law of God's
kingdom is the law of his saving love revealed in Jesus Christ.

The same lesson is to be drawn from the parable of the 'Prodigal Son'.
Jesus pictures his Pharisaical critics in the figure of the elder brother who
refuses to join his father's feast of welcome for the returning prodigal. Like
the elder brother, the self-righteous Pharisees would never eat with sinners,
and they criticise Jesus for doing so (Luke 15:1). But Jesus does more than eat
with sinners. As their true elder brother, he brings them home to heaven's
feast. He does so because he understands his Father's heart of love, the
Father's joy in heaven over one sinner who repents. Jesus, the true elder
brother, is also the good shepherd who seeks out the sheep that is lost and
brings it home rejoicing.

He it is who forgives sins, as only God can. The one who is forgiven much
loves much: the sinful woman lavishes her devotion at the feet of Jesus, for he
is her Saviour (Luke 7:36–50). Jesus declares that her faith has saved her and
sends her away with his blessing of peace.

Because Christ brings salvation as a gift, faith is the key. Belief in the
power of Jesus to heal and to forgive sins comes down at last to the same
thing: to acknowledge his claim as the only Saviour, the one sent by the
Father (Mark 2:9–11).

In the words, the work, the person of Jesus Christ we find the resolution of
tensions that might seem contradictory. How can Jesus, on the one hand,
trace the demands of the law back to the profound depths of the Father's
compassion, and on the other hand welcome tax-collectors who have
exploited others for money? How can Jesus make a righteousness surpassing
that of the Pharisees a condition for entering the kingdom, and on the other
hand welcome a dying thief to paradise? Can we read the Sermon on the
Mount and say that his yoke is easy and his burden light?

In the teaching of Jesus we do not find an uneasy truce between law and
grace. Rather we find a harmony that illumines for us the same themes in the
Old Testament. 'For, indeed, the principal part of the law consists of justice,
mercy, and faith (Matt. 23:23), i.e., in the certainty of God's help and
salvation.'[46] The prophet Jeremiah had brought the promise of God's grace
to Jerusalem under siege, on the brink of exile: 'Call to Me, and I will answer
you, and show you great and mighty things, which you do not know' (Jer. 33:3
NKJV).

The unimaginable blessings of God's promise go far beyond return from
exile after seventy years. They include the new covenant when God's law will
be written on their hearts, and when, in the branch, God himself will be their
righteousness (Jer. 31:33; 33:15,16). Jesus repeats, in the fulfilment of the
kingdom, 'Ask and it will be given to you; seek and you will find; knock and

the door will be opened to you' (Matt. 7:7). The Father will give good gifts to his children, indeed, the greatest gift: the gift of his Holy Spirit (Luke 11:13).

It is the high, holy righteousness of the Father in heaven that Jesus must both require and fulfil, because it is the righteousness of God. Jesus teaches his disciples to pray to the Father, 'Your will be done.' God's righteousness will prevail in grace and judgment. In the suffering of his ministry, in the agony of Gethsemane, in the sacrifice of Calvary, Jesus establishes the righteous will of God. He whom the Father has appointed judge bears the penalty of sin, and therefore he can forgive sinners. On the cross he triumphs over the power of the devil, and establishes the new covenant in his blood. The triumph of his resurrection and ascension brings the baptism of the Holy Spirit who writes the law of God on the hearts of his people (Jer. 31:33).

In the day of judgment, he will know his own sheep, and they will know him (Matt. 7:23; John 10:14, 27–29). Their lives will show in their care for their brothers how they cared for him (Matt. 25:31–46). In their lives they have found his yoke easy, because he who bore the cross for them gives them to drink of his Spirit.

In all the Gospels, and in John with special emphasis, Jesus presents himself so that men and women might believe in him. Even those of 'little faith' may become his disciples; a Gentile centurion with 'great faith' represents a great multitude of believers who will come from the east and west to sit down with Abraham, Isaac and Jacob in the kingdom of heaven (Matt. 8:11).

In Jesus, God's answer is given as to how a man may be just before God. In his beloved Son, God is well pleased. David's greater Son is, indeed, a man after God's own heart. He is the glorious Son of Man who receives the kingdom that cannot be shaken. As the Holy One of God, he welcomes sinners, speaking words of grace given him by the Father; he came to seek and to save that which was lost. But in order to heal the wounds of the curse, he must himself endure the very afflictions that he removes (Matt. 8:17). In order to bear away sin and bring in righteousness, he must give his life a ransom for many. The Gospels tell the story of what the suffering servant did for his people in his life and his death; they show us that he is the triumphant Son, one with the Father. He fulfils the promise that God himself must be the Saviour of his people.

The Gospels focus their witness on the work of Christ before his ascension. In the rest of the New Testament the revelation of the ascended Christ is given to his church.

B. The Gospel of Salvation in Christ

The church as the new covenant form of the people of God is built upon the foundation of the apostles and prophets, Christ Jesus himself being the chief cornerstone (Eph. 2:20). The gospel message answers to the Old Testament promises, and is the mystery of Christ, revealed to the holy apostles and prophets in the Spirit (Eph. 3:5). The fullest exposition of justification is found, of course, in Paul's letters to the Galatians and the Romans. From the perspective of God's ongoing revelation, these do not represent just one literary episode in the course of early church history. They are to be seen, rather, as the inspired understanding given to the last of the apostles as he defends and summarises the full revelation of Christ granted to him. While they are not the last texts of the New Testament to be written, they do present the theology of revelation as it reaches its decisive climax. Paul's words must be understood in the context in which they were written, yet they present apostolic truth that is foundational for the church of all ages. They teach us that the gospel of Christ is the gospel of God's righteousness, that righteousness to which all the Scriptures testify. They summon us to faith in Jesus Christ in whom that righteousness is made ours.

The apostolic gospel centres in Jesus Christ, the risen Lord. We see this in Luke's summary of Peter's preaching in the house of Cornelius, the Gentile centurion. The witness of the apostles begins with two givens: the astonishing life and ministry of Jesus that led to his crucifixion (Acts 10:37,38), and the promise of the prophets (Acts 10:43). It was the apostolic task to show the meaning of both and to demonstrate their deep unity. As to the first, the witness of the apostles completed the account of the ministry of Jesus by proclaiming his resurrection and ascension. Jesus is 'Lord of all' (Acts 10:36). As to the second, the apostolic teaching explained the gospel of Jesus Christ from the Old Testament Scriptures. Both the sufferings of Christ and his resurrection glory had been predicted as the necessary climax of God's great work of salvation. From the outset, then, the apostolic message set out to show the *meaning* of the work of Jesus. Only in the light of God's purpose could either the crucifixion or the resurrection be understood.

To understand that purpose was not a matter of satisfying curiosity. It was a matter of life and death: indeed, eternal life or eternal death. That Jesus was alive from the dead and the judge and Lord of all had a terrifying consequence for those who had cried out 'Crucify him!' Gripped by the power of the Spirit as Peter preached on Pentecost, they now cried out, 'What must we do to be saved?' They were not confronted with a curious report of the revivification of one who was clinically dead. They were confronted with the proclamation of Jesus as the Lord of glory. In Peter's message, as in all apostolic preaching, the glory of Jesus implied his coming judgment: the gospel called to repentance.

Yet what hope could repentance bring to those who had denied, betrayed, crucified the prince of life? Luke reports the astonishing answer in Peter's preaching. The death of Jesus, the crime of all crimes, was nevertheless determined by the divine plan (Acts 2:23). It fulfilled what God had promised through the prophets, that his Messiah should suffer (Acts 3:18). The crucifixion did not mean that Jesus was not the Messiah; to the contrary, it showed that he was. The question must be answered: Why did the Messiah have to die? The death of Jesus implied his atonement for sin: because of the cross, the gospel promised forgiveness. The central fact of the gospel could be expressed in a cry of praise reminiscent of the Psalms, 'Jesus is Lord of all.' But the gospel necessarily included more: 'Christ died for our sins according to the Scriptures, . . . he was buried, . . . he was raised on the third day according to the Scriptures' (1 Cor. 15:3,4).

New Testament scholars have called attention to citations in the epistles from earlier Christian creeds or hymns.[47] Debate continues about the number of such citations, but in any case there is ample evidence from these and other passages that the apostolic church regularly used the Old Testament to interpret the meaning of the person and work of Christ.

One such passage is 1 Peter 3:18. Peter's succinct statement may cite an early confession; it may simply repeat a formula from his own teaching. It expressly connects the righteousness of Christ with his death for the unrighteous:

> For Christ died for sins once for all, the righteous for the unrighteous, to bring you to God. He was put to death in the body, but made alive by the Spirit. (*1 Pet. 3:18*)[48]

The background of the connection 's Isaiah's prophecy of the suffering servant, directly alluded to in 1 Peter 2:22–24. Jesus was silent before his accusers in his suffering; by his welts we are healed, for he bore our sins in his own body up to the cross (Isa. 53). In particular, Peter's words reflect the language of the prophets: (lit.) 'the righteous one, my Servant, shall make many to be accounted righteous' (Isa. 53:11). The figure of the suffering righteous servant of the Lord from the Psalms and the prophets is actualised in Jesus Christ.[49] Jesus is the righteous one who is the 'end of the law' — the one who is the goal of the law, and in whom the law is fulfilled (Rom. 10:4,5; Acts 22:14; Lev. 18:5).[50]

From the outset, apostolic witness was grounded in the teaching of Jesus in the period between his resurrection and the ascension. Luke summarises that teaching at the conclusion of his Gospel, and assumes it in Acts. The confused disciples on the way to Emmaus that day of resurrection were rebuked by Jesus for their lack of understanding. They were foolish, slow of heart to believe all that the prophets had spoken (Luke 24:25).

Before leaving his disciples, Jesus did more than show them the reality of his resurrection life. He taught them from the Old Testament Scriptures the meaning of his sufferings and his resurrection glory. Their witness was to the fulfilment of the Scriptures, and their mission itself fulfilled the promises (Luke 24:45–47).

Paul, like the other apostles, preached the sufferings and glory of Christ 'according to the Scriptures' (1 Cor. 15:1–4; Acts 17:2,3). His distinctive emphasis on justification by faith is his defence of the gospel of salvation against misunderstanding and contradiction. His letters to the Galatians and the Romans are structured as responses to the attacks of his enemies and to the misunderstanding — actual or possible — of the churches. That Galatians is an anguished response is stamped on every paragraph of the letter. Romans is a longer treatment of the objections that have been raised to Paul's teaching. His use of questions in the epistle is more than an effective teaching device; it plainly distils real dialogues that the apostle has carried on.

Nothing could be plainer from both epistles than that Paul knew the very heart of the gospel to be at risk. The Judaising teachers in Galatia who would require the Gentile believes to be circumcised were presenting another gospel. Their teaching could not be regarded as a modification, even a major modification of the apostolic gospel. It was something else entirely, a 'gospel' that was not a gospel, for there was only one gospel of the one Lord Jesus Christ. The radical antithesis that Paul saw between the gospel and a religion of works warns us against supposing that the contents of these two epistles were only an episode in Paul's teaching ministry. If we do not see the need for his response to the Galatians, or for its passion, we do not understand the gospel that he preached. Neither Galatians nor Romans was written as a comprehensive 'systematic theology'. The challenge of a fatal corruption of the gospel led the inspired apostle to the Gentiles to proclaim the salvation of Christ that goes forth to the nations.

Paul proclaims that salvation in terms of the 'righteousness of God' (Rom. 1:17; 3:21,22). He uses Old Testament terminology, not simply because the false teachers sought to use the Old Testament against him, but because the Old Testament provides the revelation from which the salvation in Christ must be understood.

What is the antithesis that Paul must make clear? He states it repeatedly; for example, in Romans 4:16:

> Therefore, the promise comes by faith, so that it may be by grace and may be guaranteed to all Abraham's offspring — not only to those who are of the law but also to those who are of the faith of Abraham. He is the father of us all.

Grace, faith, the promise, for the nations: these resonate in harmony, for one implies the other. To them we may add hope and the gift of the Spirit (Gal. 5:5). Each of these is contrasted with an opposite: grace, not merit; faith, not works; the promise, not the law; for the nations, not exclusively for Israel; hope, not bondage; the Spirit, not the flesh. Paul makes the division with one question: (lit.) 'Where then is the glorying?' (Rom. 3:27). On the one side the glorying is in human achievement. On the other side, the glorying is in God (Rom. 4:20; 1 Cor. 1:26–31; Gal. 6:14; Phil. 3:2,3). No question could better indicate the burden of the Scriptures: 'Salvation is of the Lord!' (Jon. 2:9).

Glorying in God is also glorying in Christ. Paul defines the gospel to which he has been separated as an apostle:

> . . . the gospel of God which He promised before through His prophets in the Holy Scriptures, concerning His Son Jesus Christ our Lord, who was born of the seed of David according to the flesh, and declared to be the Son of God with power, according to the Spirit of holiness, by the resurrection from the dead . . . (*Rom. 1:2–4*NKJV)

The gospel is God's because it is the good news of his righteousness, not only the righteousness that judges and vindicates, but the righteousness that is the gift of his salvation. The gospel concerns God's Son, for it is he who is the righteous Saviour, through whom we receive the righteousness of God. The gospel concerns the Holy Spirit, in whose power Christ rose from the dead, and who is both gift and giver; he is the reality of the blessing promised to Abraham (Gal. 3:14), and the Author of the new life that we have in Christ (Gal. 4:29). In the work of salvation, all is of God, through God, and to God's glory (Rom. 11:12).

Paul is not ashamed of the gospel, for in it God's power operates (Rom. 1:16f). It is saving power, but it appears against the dark background of the righteous wrath of God that is also revealed by the gospel's demand (Rom. 1:18; 2:4; 3:19; 5:9). Paul constantly affirms that he is preaching what the Scriptures promised: the revealing of the righteousness of God in salvation. As we have seen, the prophets foretold the coming of God's righteousness in judgment. In righteousness God would vindicate (Ps. 98:2,9), purify (Isa.

46:12,13), and renew (Isa 51:4–6). But God would also hear the prayer of his prophet to plead his case, execute judgment, and bring him forth to the light, to behold God's righteousness (Mic. 7:9). He would tread the iniquity of his people under foot, and give the covenant mercy he had promised to Abraham (Mic. 7:19,20). God's righteousness must come in redemption (Isa. 45:21–25; 54:17; Jer. 33:16); it would come through the righteous branch, the Messiah (Jer. 23:6; Isa. 53:11; 61:1–3,10,11).

Debates about the meaning of Paul's use of the term 'righteousness of God' reveal the richness rather than the confusion of his thought. Paul readily assumes the understanding of God's righteousness as his attribute, an attribute that is shown by the way in which he justifies the ungodly. What might seem to be a paradox is resolved: God may be righteous, and yet declare sinners to be righteous in his sight (Rom. 3:25,26). This is possible because of the gift of God's righteousness attributed to them, and received by faith. In Christ, believers receive 'the abundant provision of grace and of the gift of righteousness' (Rom. 5:17). Paul speaks of righteousness as God's gift when he says,

> But now apart from the law a righteousness of God hath been manifested, being witnessed by the law and the prophets; even the righteousness of God through faith in Jesus Christ unto all them that believe. . . (*Rom. 3:21,22* ASV)

Believers are 'justified freely by his grace through the redemption that is in Christ Jesus' (Rom. 3:24 ASV). In sharp distinction from one's own righteousness, which is of the law, this revealed righteousness is through faith in Christ, 'the righteousness that comes from God and is by faith' (Phil. 3:9).

The revelation of God's righteousness as gift requires us to think in Old Testament categories. As we have seen, righteousness in the Old Testament has to do with the standing of a man in the sight of God, the supreme and just judge. It is paralleled by the figure of cleanness, the ceremonial purity required to enter into God's courts. The language is forensic in the sense that it speaks of God's seat of judgment. God pronounces condemnation upon the condemnable, and justification upon the justifiable (1 Kings 8:32). Human judges should seek to do the same, and not accept a bribe to justify the wicked (Deut. 25:1; Isa. 5:23). To 'justify' is not to make righteous, but to pronounce righteous, to acquit one of the charge of guilt. God, the righteous judge, will not justify the wicked (Exod. 23:7).

How then shall any sinner escape condemnation before the judgment seat of God? This, we have seen, is a problem the Old Testament addresses. God's righteous refusal to clear the guilty is joined to the revelation of his covenantal faithfulness and grace (Exod. 34:7). The prophets spoke of the coming of God in grace, when God's people would receive his righteousness. Paul announces the fulfilment of the promise. God's righteousness has come through Jesus Christ. For the verdict 'Not guilty' to be pronounced upon sinners, their sin must be atoned for. For them to be reckoned righteous, there must be another righteousness than their own put to their account. This has happened through Christ: 'For He made Him who knew no sin to be sin for us, that we might become the righteousness of God in Him' (2 Cor. 5:21 NKJV). 'It is because of him that you are in Christ Jesus, who has become for us wisdom from God — that is, our righteousness, holiness and redemption' (1 Cor. 1:30).

The gift of righteousness from God is the righteousness of Jesus Christ; the atonement God provides is the sacrificial death of Jesus Christ. Free justification comes 'through the redemption that is in Christ Jesus, whom God set forth to be a propitiation, by His blood, through faith . . .' (Rom. 3:25 NKJV). 'It is this decisive, central act of propitiation, executed before the eyes of heaven and earth, in which God himself, passing over all the sacrifices that had formerly been offered, provides the means of propitiation and places it in the midst of all.'[51]

We must recognise the twin pillars of Paul's understanding in order to perceive how he accounts for justification. One is his doctrine of our union with Christ; the other is his grasp of the history of redemption. We see how he joins the two when he presents Christ as the second Adam (Rom. 5:12–21; 1 Cor. 15:20–23). When Christ died for us, so that we might be justified by his blood (Rom. 5:9), he died in our place, as our representative. His representation is not accidental or artificial. Paul sees an analogy between Adam as the representative of the old humanity descended from him, and Christ as the representative of a new humanity joined to him. Adam represented us when he sinned; through his sin death passed on all humanity. Christ is the representative head of a new humanity, those who have been chosen in him from before the foundation of the world (Eph. 1:4). Our union with Adam is vital as well as representative: we are physically descended from him. Our union with Christ is also vital, for we are joined to him by the presence of his Spirit. Yet Paul's comparison of Christ with Adam and his use of the 'in Christ' forumula shows that our union with Christ is not simply mystical, but representative.[52] 'In Christ' we secure the blessings that are *through* Christ (*cf.* Eph. 1:3–5). They who are blessed in the heavenly places *in* Christ are those who were raised together *with* him (Eph. 1:3, *cf.* 2:6,7; Col. 3:1,2).

Paul presents union with Christ in terms of the history of redemption. 'In the fulness of time' God sent forth his Son, born of a woman (Gal. 4:4). Sin and death entered through Adam, but Jesus Christ is the promised son of the woman (Gen. 3:15). God's covenant with Abraham promised that in his seed all the nations of the earth would be blessed. Christ is that promised Seed (Gal. 3:16). As 'minister of the circumcision' he is the servant of the Lord who fulfils the role of Israel to confirm the promises given to the fathers (Rom. 15:8). Paul sees the unfolding of God's plan through the ages. He marks out the giving of the law at Sinai in relation to the periods beginning with Adam and with Abraham; he notes the priority of God's covenant promise to Abraham which could not be voided by the covenant at Sinai (Rom. 5:12f; Gal. 3:15–17; 4:1–5). Indeed, the apostle sets his own calling in the context of the history of redemption, for he is called to carry the gospel to the nations and to minister in the offering up of the Gentiles to the praise of God (Rom. 15:15,16).

The goal of all the history of God's covenants is found in the new covenant in Jesus Christ (1 Cor. 11:25). He is the creator and sustainer of all things, the image of the invisible God, and in him we have redemption, the forgiveness of sins (Col. 1:13–23).

Only Jesus Christ, the Lord of glory, could offer full satisfaction for all our sins and propitiate the wrath of God, wrath that Paul so powerfully describes. The Lord became a curse for us (Gal. 3:13). As Saul the Pharisee, Paul had been assured that Jesus could not be the Messiah. Jesus had been crucified, and the law pronounced accursed everyone who hung on a tree (Deut. 21:23; Gal. 3:13). But after he had encountered the risen Lord, Paul found that he had erred completely. The cross, so far from proving that Jesus was not the Messiah, proved that he was. Only by becoming accursed for us could Jesus save us.

Just as only Christ's sacrifice could make satisfaction for our sins, so, too, only Christ's obedience can merit eternal life. The inheritance that we receive in Christ is the free gift of God, eternal life (Rom. 6:23). The righteousness of God, so long sought and promised, is given in a way beyond all imagining: it is the righteousness of the Son of God himself.

Because God's justifying verdict pronounces us righteous in his sight, it takes account of that which is attributable to us. If we had earned the inheritance by our own efforts, it would be credited to us as a debt, as wages due for work performed (Rom. 4:4). But since we are justified by what Christ has done for us, the reckoning is of grace. God reckons our sin to Christ's account (makes him to be 'sin' — not a sinner — for us), and reckons Christ's righteousness to our account (2 Cor. 5:21). To those who have not grasped the wonder of our union with Christ, such reckoning may seem artificial. Not to Paul. Paul knew the Christ who had loved him, and given himself for him (Gal. 2:20). He knew the love of God for his enemies (sons of disobedience, children of wrath) proven in the giving of his Son (Rom. 5:8,10). Abraham was spared offering his son Isaac; that sacrifice was offered by the heavenly Father, who 'did not spare his own Son, but gave him up for us all' (Rom. 8:32).

Since Christ's life, death, and resurrection accomplished our salvation, our part is not to achieve it, but to receive it. Our justification does not await the last day when all shall appear before God's judgment. Since we are united to Christ, what is true of him is true of us. When he died to sin, so did we; when he rose to eternal life, we rose with him. When he ascended to heaven, we entered the heavenly places with him. For that reason, our justification is not simply a future hope but a present reality, made ours through faith. We now have access to God, standing in his grace; we now have peace with God, the blessing of sins forgiven. 'Who will bring any change against those whom God has chosen?' cries Paul. Referring to the words of Isaiah in a passage that expresses the sure hope of God's suffering servant, he says,

> It is God who justifies. Who is he that condemns? Christ Jesus, who died — more than that, who was raised to life — is at the right hand of God and is also interceding for us. (*Rom. 8:33; Isa. 50:8,9*)

There is a past, present, and future aspect to our justification. The past stretches back to God's electing purpose when he chose us in Christ (Gal. 3:8; 1 Pet. 1:1,2; Eph. 1:5). The plan of God for the salvation of sinners includes his purpose to call, justify, and glorify (Rom. 8:30). Christ was chosen before the creation of the world as the Lamb of God, whose precious blood would atone for sin (1 Pet. 1:19,20). God could withhold punishment for sin in the ages before Christ's coming because of his justifying purpose in Christ (Rom. 3:25).

God's purpose was accomplished when Jesus Christ finished his work of obedience and atonement on the cross (Gal. 4:4,5; 1 Tim. 2:6; Rom. 4:25; 5:9; 6:6,7; 2 Cor. 5:19; Isa. 53:11).

The present is the moment when the Holy Spirit applies to us the benefits of Christ's redemption (Col. 1:21,22; Gal. 2:16; Tit. 3:4–7). The future, for which we are guarded by faith, is the salvation ready to be revealed at the last time (1 Pet. 1:5). At the last judgment God's justifying verdict will be publicly declared; God's saints will be vindicated, and God's judgment will bring them joy and salvation (1 Thess. 5:9; 2 Thess. 1:6–10; Rev. 6:10,16).

Justification is by faith. Faith is the appropriate response to grace, for it acknowledges complete dependence on God as Saviour. It does not earn a reward, but receives a gift. By its very act of looking to the Lord and not to oneself, it is abandonment; it includes commitment, but commitment in the sense of fleeing for refuge. We have seen how God's grace called for faith in Old Testament times. Paul underscores this when he cites Genesis 15:6 to show that Abraham was justified by faith. Abraham believed the word of God, the promise of God, hoping against hope because he trusted God to do the impossible (Rom. 4:17,18). The gospel that Paul preached was a word of faith, that is, a word to be believed as it announced the meaning of Christ's death and resurrection (Rom. 10:8–10,14,15). Paul reports the unbelief of Israel, citing Isaiah: 'Lord, who has believed our message?' They would not hear, that is, heed and trust the word of the Lord (Rom. 10:16–21).[53] In contrast, believing Jews and Gentiles are children of the promise, who like Abraham trust in God and receive his righteousness.

Faith is the sole instrument of justification because it has the unique function of receiving and resting upon Christ in whom alone believers are justified.[54] Paul distinguishes faith in this respect from all the graces that are also the gift of the Spirit. Faith is distinctive, not because it is a gift of grace, but because it receives Christ, the gift of grace. In a context where Paul is maintaining that neither circumcision nor uncircumcision avails, but only faith, Paul does not hesitate to add 'faith working through love' (Gal. 5:6). Paul is certainly a theologian of love, and of the loving obedience that we offer to the Lord. But even that love cannot serve as the ground for our justification. That ground is found only in Jesus Christ. It is not the presence of love or any other accompanying grace that makes faith the appropriate receptor of justification. Faith justifies not because it produces the fruit of love for Christ, but because it receives the fruit of Christ's sacrificial love.

The clarity of Paul's teaching appears in the objections that he has anticipated (and, no doubt, had often heard). If salvation is God's free gift, through grace alone, to be received by faith, and not earned, why should anyone bother about obeying God's commandments? Since God overrules our sin to his own glory, why not sin all the more to give him more opportunity to display his free grace (Rom. 6:1)?

Paul's reply shows how completely such an objection lies outside the range of his own thought. To be united to Jesus Christ is not only to be justified in his righteousness; it is also to gain in him the fountain of a life of new obedience and holiness. Our union with Christ in his death is not a fiction. It is a reality wrought by grace (Rom. 6:2). God's righteousness given for us must result in God's righteousness established in us.

Paul teaches with the other New Testament writers that there will be a day of judgment when complete and searching justice will be done (Rom. 2:5–16; 1 Cor. 4:5; 2 Cor. 5:10). He sees no contradiction to his doctrine of justification by faith when he tells us that God will render to every man according to his works, and welcome into eternal life those who by patience in well-doing seek for glory, honour, and incorruption (Rom. 2:6,7).[55] Those who are circumcised in heart keep the law in the Spirit (Rom. 2:27–29; 8:4). Faith does not make void God's law; it establishes it in obedience. James rightly observed that Abraham's faith was made evident in his deeds. He says, 'I will show you my faith by what I do' (James 2:18). When James demands works, and not only faith, for justifiction, he does not set works without faith over against true faith. Rather, he contrasts the empty shell of faith, such as demons may possess, with the commitment of true faith made evident in Abraham's deed of obedience. A dead and empty faith cannot justify, but this is not because it lacks works as a supplement. It is because it lacks the living bond of trust from which works must flow.

The good works of believers, imperfect as they are, are accepted by God, because they are accepted in Christ. Their new obedience is a genuine fruit of Christ's saving work for them and in them; it will therefore be recognised as appropriate to justification and admittance to eternal life. The judgment will disclose that they know Christ and are known by Christ (Matt. 7:23; 25:40), who delivers them from the wrath to come (1 Thess. 1:10). For the believer, the judgment brings vindication after a life of suffering shame for the name of Christ (2 Thess. 1:6–10). Like the Old Testament saints, God's new covenant servants pray for the deliverance and vindication of the final judge (Rev. 6:10). They do not avenge themselves, but trust God's justice (Rom. 12:19–21). At the same time, they pray for their enemies, seeking their conversion and eternal good (Matt. 5:44).

God's judgment will search the thoughts and deeds of believers as well as those who persecute them. Paul can appeal to that judgment against the judgment of others, or, indeed, his own (1 Cor. 4:3–5). It is for God to determine his faithfulness as a steward of the gospel. Paul seeks not the praise of men, but of God (1 Cor. 4:5). By the same token, Paul does not boast of having achieved, but presses on to the goal of his calling: to share resurrection glory with Christ (Phil. 3:12–16; 1 Cor. 9:25ff).

We misunderstand Paul if we separate in principle between the justification that is ours when we believe in Christ and the justification to be pronounced in the day of judgment.[56] In its most extreme form, this separation makes *faith* the way of justification now, and *works* the way of justification then.[57] It teaches that believers are washed of sin in baptism, and have the resources of institutionalised grace to live a godly life. In the day of judgment, however, they will be judged according to their works. This is not Paul's teaching. He makes no stronger statement of justification through the righteousness of Christ than in Philippians 3:9 (righteousness not my own, from God, through faith). Yet he there speaks of how he continues to count all his self-righteousness to be garbage in order that he may 'gain Christ' and 'be found in him' when he reaches the goal — in the day of judgment. Then, too, he will be justified, not by his own righteousness, but by Christ's.[58] This is again clear when Paul speaks of the unworthy works of some Christian teachers being consumed in the fire of judgment, although they themselves will be saved as believers (1 Cor. 3:15).

The point of the assurance of present justification is that the believer is already in Christ, and that the verdict of the day of judgment is already rendered (Rom. 5:1). The reality of the day of judgment remains, however, and must be taken with full seriousness. It brings God's evaluation of the quality of our stewardship; it is also the goal that will bring to light the evidence of our continuing faith. Peter assures Christians as persecution looms that their inheritance is kept for them. Unlike the earthly inheritance of Israel, it cannot be laid waste by invasion, polluted by idolatry, or withered by drought (1 Pet. 1:4; Isa. 24:3–5; 40:7). Believers are also kept under guard for their inheritance (1 Pet. 1:5). But they are kept through faith; God keeps them by keeping them believing. To do so, he purges their faith in suffering, like gold in a furnace. True faith is incombustible, and will result in 'praise, glory and honour when Jesus Christ is revealed' (1 Pet. 1:7).

The Lord will graciously reward all that has been done for his name's sake, yet his blessing does not mean that such obedience has earned heaven, but that it marks those who have found in him their salvation. The secrets of men will be judged, Paul says, by Jesus Christ, 'according to my gospel' (Rom. 2:16). The Lord of the *gospel* is the judge.

Paul's doctrine of justification is grounded in the Old Testament promises. Paul finds them all fulfilled in Jesus Christ, and rejoices in the world-wide scope of the blessings promised to Abraham. His own ministry as apostle to the Gentiles carries those blessings to the nations. Looking back over the history of redemption, he can see how the demands of God's covenant law served as what we might call a school-bus driver to bring us to Christ. The law detected, and even provoked transgression because of our sin (Gal. 3:24; Rom. 3:20; 5:20; 7:5,7–13). Israel's experience under the law fueled the message of the prophets, who pointed to the righteousness that must be given by God, and be found in him. That righteousness, Paul said, is now revealed in Jesus Christ. Those who receive it by faith learn to reckon for themselves what God has reckoned for them. They did die with Christ; they did rise with him, and by the power of the Spirit they are called to live that way. For Paul faith in Christ always lies between two loves: the love of God that did not spare his Son, but gave him up for us all, and our love for the Lord that is the fulfilling of the law (Rom. 5:8; 13:10). Paul's fervour for justification through Christ's righteousness and not our own is fervour for grace: jealousy for the love of God for the ungodly.

3

Justification in Pauline Thought[a]

BRIAN. C. WINTLE

I.   JEWISH PREMISES REGARDING THE LAW AND JUSTIFICATION

Although the churches addressed in Paul's letters were predominantly Gentile, his teaching on justification can be appreciated fully only in the light of its Jewish[1] background. Luke tells us in his account of the ministry of Paul in the Book of Acts that he was most successful among the Gentile God-fearers — people who were familiar with the Jewish faith but were held back from becoming full proselytes by an aversion to the rite of circumcision. During his ministry, the apostle was persistently dogged by Judaisers[1a], who attempted to impose the Jewish law and its observances on the Gentile converts in the churches he founded. In his letters, much of his teaching on justification and the law is given to counter these attempts and to expose the basic misunderstanding of the OT faith on the one hand, and of the gospel on the other, underlying these attempts.

A.   Righteousness and the Law

The 'giving of the Law' was the high point of the Exodus tradition. It was an intrinsic part of the renewing of the covenant with the generation that had been redeemed out of Egypt. As a Jew, Paul had seen no eschatological aspect to the significance of the law. To the Jews, the OT was a closed book, a compendium of theology and morals, by which God himself was bound. All that remained to be done was the codifying of their teaching and careful and detailed obedience to its demands and precepts. Therefore they concentrated on pursuing the righteousness of the law.

In Phil. 3 Paul is concerned to warn the Philippian church of his Judaising opponents, whose visit to Philippi seems imminent. They will encourage the Philippians to put their confidence in the flesh and will themselves boast in such matters. Paul warns these Christians by undermining beforehand the attraction of the claims and arguments of his opponents. His strongest point is that he himself once boasted in the very things these men boast in, but for the sake of Christ, he regarded these things as loss, indeed, as refuse[2] — so glorious was the privilege of knowing Christ and belonging to him.

Among these grounds for confidence in the flesh Paul names four to establish that his Jewish descent was impeccable. He then goes on to speak of his religious achievement as a Jew. As regard the law, he had belonged to the Pharisees, the party whose very *raison d'être* was the complete and exact fulfilment of the law's demands. He had been an extremely zealous Pharisee and his violent persecution of the church was clearest testimony to this fact. Paul insists that as a member of the people of the law, he had not, so far as his conscience could tell, failed to observe the law in its every detail: 'as for legalistic righteousness, faultless'. This verse concurs with Paul's self-assessment in Gal. 1:14 and is a significant testimony to Pharisaic self-understanding. The Pharisaic ideal was righteousness consisting in blameless observance of all the commands and prohibitions of the law. In v. 9 this righteousness is described as 'a righteousness of my own, that comes from the Law', and contrasted with 'the righteousness that comes from God and is by faith'.

This relationship between righteousness and repentance in Jewish thinking is better understood when seen against the background of the rabbinic view that the law was given to deliver people from the tyranny of the evil impulse.[3] The evil impulse was represented in Jewish literature primarily as the subjective origin of temptation or more correctly as the tempter within. It was used to explain the human inherent tendency to sin and was understood as implanted in human beings at birth. God had also created in man the good impulse so that he did not complacently acquiesce in the courses in which the evil impulse impelled him. In this conflict of impulses, however, on even terms it was recognised that the evil is stronger. Indeed, this was precisely why the Torah was given — it was a patent means to succeed in overcoming the evil impulse.

> Paul's definition of righteousness as perfect conformity to the law of God would never have been conceded by a Jewish opponent, to whom it would have been equivalent to admitting that God had mocked man by offering to him salvation on terms they both knew to be impossible — God, because he had made man a creature of the dust with all his human frailties (Psalm 103:4) and implanted in him the 'evil' impulse; man, above all the conscientious man, through his daily experience. God was too good, too reasonable, to demand a perfection of which he had created man incapable.[4]
>
> The righteous man is one . . . who strives to regulate his whole life by the rules God has given in his twofold law. The sincerity and supremacy of this purpose and the strenuous endeavour to accomplish it are the marks of the righteous man. Such a man shares in the universality of sin (Eccles. 7:20); but he is not for that denied the character and name of a righteous man, much less must he be called a sinner. For righteousness, in the conception in which Judaism got it from the Scriptures, had no suggestion of sinless perfection. What distinguishes the righteous man who has fallen into sin is his repentance.[5]

It is clear from these quotations that it is because righteousness to the Jews is primarily an attitude to God's law, that repentance plays an important part in his thinking.

B. Righteousness and the Gentiles

This legalistic understanding of righteousness was closely related to the Jewish sense of superiority over the Gentiles. In Gal. 2:11ff. Paul recounts the incident at Antioch, when Peter under pressure from the circumcision party had withdrawn from table fellowship with Gentile Christians. Paul perceived that such an action could lead to a serious division of the church into Jewish and Gentile factions, and took steps to prevent such a split from occurring. In vv. 14ff. he points out that such behaviour was not consistent with the truth of the Christian gospel. Paul's argument in these verses indicates that he believed that a basic weakness in the Judaistic position was the inadequate conception of sin. In v. 15 he refers to the Gentiles as 'Gentile sinners' and contrasts them with those who were 'Jews by birth'. He is probably using a catch-phrase of the circumsion party (v. 12) because in v. 16 he implies that neither he nor Peter and his fellow Jewish Christians any longer restricted sin to Gentiles only. Indeed, such a conception of sin made nonsense of their faith in Christ. The Jew believed that evil was not a necessary circumstance of life but only a deficiency which man had the power to remedy. Sin was only a latent disposition or an acquirement easily corrected. Therefore, Judaism laid its emphasis on moral conduct — on the observance of the law. This is reflected also in Jewish thinking on Abraham. He was seen as an outstanding example of perfect[6] obedience to the commands of God.[7] It was believed that he kept the whole Torah, as yet unwritten[8] (*cf.* Kiddushin 4:14: 'We find that Abraham our father had performed the whole law before it was given, for it is written, because Abraham obeyed my voice and kept my charge, my commandments, my statutes, and my laws [Gen. 26:5]'). The Gentile, therefore, was a sinner because he did not have the law and hence did not conform to it. In other words, since righteousness was based on obedience to the Jewish law, Gentiles by definition were excluded from the very possibility of being justified. This thinking led, inevitably, to a spirit of boasting in one's religious achievements, and in the absence of such religious achievements to a presumptuous confidence in their very possession of the law.

It is for these reasons that the Jews valued very highly their status as God's chosen and elect people. The mark of this election was circumcision and the Jews accordingly placed much emphasis on the rite. 'The significance of the initiatory rite was not entrance into a religious community, it was naturalisation in the Jewish nation, that is, adoption into the Jewish race, the convert entering into all the rights and privileges of the born Jew and assuming all the corresponding obligations.'[9] They looked on the rite as that which distinguished them from all the nations around them.

This is brought out very clearly in Eph. 2:12ff. where Paul reminds his Gentile readers that in Christ there is no Jew or Gentile. In him, this distinction has been transcended — he died to create in himself one new humanity. Paul speaks here in the light of the Christ-event, but behind his words it is possible to detect Jewish thinking that he had once shared.

He reminds them that to the Jews, their outstanding characteristic as Gentiles had been their uncircumcision. This is brought out by his description of them as '(those who) are called uncircumcised' (v. 11). Since the rite was intended to point beyond itself to an attitude of heart, Paul refers to the Jews as 'those who call themselves "the circumcision"' and emphasises the outwardness of the rite by the words 'one in the body by the hands of men'. He implies that to the Jews the physical rite was most significant in that it distinguished them from the uncircumcised Gentiles.

II.   JEWISH OPPOSITION TO THE CHRISTIAN GOSPEL

It is against this backcloth of Jewish particularism that the Pauline gospel of justification through faith in Christ to all who believe — Jews and Gentiles — must be understood. The New Testament evidence appears to support the conclusion that the Jews regarded the message of the apostolic church as a threat essentially because according to it salvation was not restricted to the Jews. The Christians proclaimed that God had acted in Christ to effect the salvation of mankind. From the Gospels we know that the attitude and teaching of Jesus himself was often contrary to Pharisaic opinion. Besides, the opposition of the Jews to the apostolic witness as recorded by Luke in the early chapters of Acts was similarly based on its implications for the traditional Jewish position on the law and their worship. 'Jesus had not been condemned by irreligious, immoral men but by conscientious, devout Jews who believed they were defending God's law. It was Judaism at its best that put Jesus on the cross.'[10]

In an autobiographical passage Paul gives us an important insight into his motives as a Jew in opposing the Christian message. In Gal. 1:11–16, the apostle is defending his apostleship and the gospel message that he was called upon to preach among the Gentiles. He tells the Galatians that in his pre-conversion days, he regarded the message of the primitive church a threat to the 'traditions of (his) fathers' (v. 14). It was his zeal for these traditions that had led him to persecute the Church so violently. *Paradosis* ('tradition') is used in the NT to refer to teaching or instruction that has been transmitted from one person (or generation) to another. The qualifying phrase 'of (the) fathers' indicates that Paul is referring to the oral traditions observed by the Pharisees as having come down from the fathers of the nation and considered by them as no less binding than the written law. It has been objected that Paul is not used to making a distinction between the written and oral traditions, and that the reference here must be to the whole law.[11] However, Paul consistently presents Christ and faith in him as the fulfilment of Old Testament faith, and it would be very strange if he was saying here that the Christian gospel was contrary to that faith. Moreover, it is significant that Paul refers here to his life as a Pharisee as his life in 'Judaism'. Paul does not use the term elsewhere in his letters and it is quite likely that he uses it here to distinguish the Pharisaic religion from Old Testament faith, properly understood — that is, as that which looked forward to Christ as its fulfilment.

In v. 12 Paul declares that the gospel he preached had not been received by him from man and he had not been taught it. It had come 'by revelation from Jesus Christ'. Although the content of the 'revelation' he received on the road to Damascus was that the crucified Jesus of Nazareth had been raised from the dead and was alive, it was the implication of this resurrection that is reflected in his gospel. 'It was an intuition of the truth of the resurrection, which involved an acknowledgement of Jesus as Son of God and also compelled a reinterpretation of the crucifixion.'[12]

In Gal. 1:4 Paul states three facts that are basic to his new perspective: the Lord Jesus Christ had given himself up for sin, to deliver his people from the 'present evil age', this being in accordance with God's will and purpose. In other words, in the light of his experience on the road to Damascus, Paul viewed the facts of the ministry, death and resurrection of Jesus — the Christ-event — from an eschatological perspective. In the Christ-event the transition from the present age to the age to come had already taken place. God had acted in human history to effect the deliverance of his people from the powers that characterise the present evil age, and to bring them into the liberty and new life that characterise the age to come. In Judaism, however, the eschatological aspect received less attention than the historical, temporal advantages of the Jews as God's elect people. This explains to some extent why the Christian message was unwelcome to the traditionalists. The kind of Messiah they proclaimed posed a threat to Jewish particularism.

In his letters, Paul refers to the message of the cross as a stumbling block to the Jews (e.g. 1 Cor. 1:23). Now it can hardly be disputed that the very concept of a crucified Messiah was nonsense to the Jews. There is no reason to believe, however, that it is not only the concept of a suffering and crucified Messiah but, more importantly, the significance of the cross particularly in relation to the traditional Jewish teaching, that caused offence.

In Gal. 5:11, Paul appeals to the fact that he is being persecuted to establish that he cannot be advocating circumcision. He argues that if he were still preaching circumcision the 'offence of the cross' would be removed. In Gal. 6:12, there is further reference to persecution, this time of those who were endeavouring to persuade the Galatians to submit to circumcision. Once more, circumcision appears in contrast to 'the message of "the cross" '. If circumcision was primarily valued by the Jews because it set them apart as those who belonged to the 'commonwealth of Israel' from the uncircumcised aliens to this commonwealth, their persecution of those who preached the message of the cross might well have been motivated by fear that this message undermined this distinction between Jews and Gentiles and implied that circumcision was no longer relevant.

In what sense did the message of the cross of Christ threaten Jewish distinctiveness? To answer this question one must consider the significance of the message of the cross for the Jewish understanding of the law and of righteousness.

The clear implication of the early Christian preaching was that the Jewish understanding of sin and of righteousness was inadequate, and, indeed, misleading. If what the Christian church claimed was true, that is, that the Jewish Messiah had come in fulfilment of Scripture to die for the sins of his people, then the traditional understanding of righteousness as consisting in legal observances could not be right. The very necessity of the cross indicated that righteousness could not be by works of the law (*cf.* Gal. 2:21). The corollary to this was that true righteousness was not a Jewish prerogative. It was a gift of God's grace. It was precisely this emphasis on the grace of God as manifested in the cross that caused offence to the Jews. If the call is to submit to God's righteousness, the Gentiles could not *a priori* be excluded from this call.[13]

II. THE PAULINE CRITIQUE OF JEWISH THINKING

In his letters Paul argues long and hard against this legalistic and exclusivistic understanding of righteousness. One of his major foci is the law and its role in salvation history.

A. The Purpose of the Law in Salvation History[14]

1. *Legal Righteousness — an impossibility*

Paul establishes in Gal. 3:10–12, on the basis of Scripture and of the very nature of law, that the law does not make righteousness possible, but rather brings a curse. He declares in v. 10 that 'all who rely on observing the law' are under the curse that it pronounces on transgressors. 'All who rely on observing the law' stands in direct contrast to 'those who have faith' in v. 9 and the 'for' indicates that v. 10 substantiates the point made in the preceding verses. The general sense is, 'It is people of faith who are blessed with believing Abraham, for all who are of law-works are (not blessed but rather) under a curse'. He then proceeds to cite Deut. 27:26, 'Cursed is everyone who does not continue to do everything written in the Book of the Law.'[15] All that the Deuteronomy text states is that all who seek righteousness by works of law are under the threat of a curse. But Paul assumes that 'all who are of law-works' will come under the category of those 'who do not continue to do everything written in the Book of the Law'. The emphasis in Deut. 27:26 is on the 'doing' of the law, but since no one has fulfilled all the law the threatened curse has become a reality.[16] In vv. 11–12 Paul argues that Scripture and the very nature of the law confirm that this conclusion is right. On the basis of Lev. 18:5 ('The man who does these things will live by them'), he points out that the law depends on works for its basis; but Hab. 2:4 makes it clear that it is the righteous by faith who shall live. Faith for Paul involves the renunciation of works and therefore the combined testimony of these two passages is that 'no one is justified before God by the Law'.

There has been much discussion amongst scholars as to whether Paul cites Hab. 2:4 here in the sense, 'He who is righteous-through-faith shall live', or in the sense, 'He who is righteous shall live through faith'. In other words, it is debated whether Paul intends to contrast faith-righteousness with law-righteousness at all or whether he is using 'righteous' in the Jewish sense of the word — that is, to refer to the person who by his conduct shows that he is right with God. The context favours understanding *dikaios* ('righteous') in a forensic sense rather than a moral sense since Paul is dealing with justification before God. *Pistis* in that case bears its active sense of 'belief' or 'faith' rather than 'faithfulness'.

In its context in Hab. 2, the Hebrew text means that the righteous man shall survive the impending political catastrophe — that is, the Babylonian invasion (*c.* 587 BC) by his faithfulness and loyalty to Yahweh. The LXX reads, *ho de dikaios ek pisteōs mou zēsetai*. *'Emûnah* means 'faithfulness', 'steadfastness' or 'integrity'; but understanding *pistis* in its active sense involves no perversion of the original passage because the two senses overlap and vary only in stressing different aspects on the total range of meaning of the word-group. Moreover, 'the particular sense which the words bore for Paul and which he intended to convey to his readers is (undoubtedly) to be determined by Pauline usage in general and by the part which the sentence plays in the Apostle's argument rather than by the meaning which the original Hebrew had for the prophet'.[17]

However, commentators who interpret this passage as a contrast between law- or works-righteousness and faith-righteousness are in danger of misinterpreting Paul. For him, there is no law-righteousness. The fact that no one has ever fulfilled the whole law precludes such a possibility. Paul is arguing rather on the basis of the nature of the law. The law depends on works for its basis (Lev. 18:5), whereas according to Hab. 2:4, it is he who is righteous-by-faith who shall live. Therefore, it is clear (so his argument goes) that no man is justified before God by law.[18] This is confirmed by his statement in v. 21 which makes it clear that the law does not 'impart life' and therefore, there can be no such thing as law-righteousness — that is, legal observance that justifies man before God. Therefore, 'all who rely on law-works' not only do not attain life, but find themselves subject to the curse of the Law — the penalty of death.

Although Paul's view of legal righteousness, as outlined above, is contrary to mainstream Jewish thinking, there is evidence that he was not alone in recognising the impotency of the law and the resulting sense of failure and frustration. The Jewish apocalyptists often came close to his evaluation of life under the law (e.g. 2 Esdras 3:19–22; 8:31–36; 9:31–37). The Qumran literature likewise confirms that there was such a stream of thought in Jewish circles, different from the official view but nonetheless detectable (1 QH 1:21–23; 3:24–26; 4:5–40; 1 QS 11:9–10). However, Paul recognises that his refutation of the Jewish assumption that the law was given to make righteousness possible will not carry full conviction unless he can posit an alternative purpose for the law in salvation history.

2. *The Preparatory Function of the Law*

In seeking to establish what was the actual role of the law in salvation history, Paul argues *a minori ad maius* from the basic principle that once a covenant or contract has been formally ratified, no one but the parties involved can alter its conditions or annul it by adding to it.[19] Since the covenant with Abraham was established 430 years before the law was given through Moses, the latter could not be regarded as a codicil to the covenant-promise made to Abraham. It must have other significance and be related to the promise differently. In v. 18, Paul argues from the essential difference between law and promise. 'Law means demand, conditions; the promise, on the contrary, means free grant, guarantee, unconditionality.'[20] The inheritance offered was God's free gift, but this gift would be robbed of its initial fulness and freeness if it were subsequently made dependent on obedience to the law.

In the parallel passage, Rom. 4:16, the apostle argues similarly. The promise was given in a context of faith rather than obedience to the law (v. 13). The essence of the divine promise is that it is kept and faith is the confidence that God will keep it. Therefore the basis must be faith on man's part and sheer generosity on God's. What God provides by his free grace can be appropriated by man only through faith.

However, it ought to be noted that although Paul keeps the promise and the law strictly separate, he takes pains to make it clear that the law is not against the promise. His contention is simply that there is no conflict between them because they have extremely different functions and different spheres of operation. The reason for the superiority of promise over law is not due to any failure on the part of the law to achieve what it was designed to do. It had brought no life because it had never been intended for that purpose. The unfulfilled condition construction is often used to prove the falsity of the hypothesis from the unreality of the apodosis.[21] 'To impart life the law would need to pardon the condemned, that is, justify him or give him a righteous standing, but this is beyond the province of-the law. Both the law and the promise had their respective sphere which neither overlapped nor conflicted. God could pardon those whom his own law condemned, but this was an act of grace as the promise was also an act of grace.'[22] So once more, the underlying assumption of the apostle's argument is that the Jewish position is based on an inadequate understanding of sin.

But if the law was not intended to bring life, what was its purpose? It was added, says Paul in Gal. 3:19, because of transgressions. The apostle consistently distinguishes sin from transgression. Man may sin in ignorance but he transgresses only when he has a recognised standard of what is right. It was to provide such a standard that the law 'was added'. The NEB renders: 'It was added to make wrong doing a legal offence'.

This recognition of sin as concrete transgression of the law was a necessary preliminary to understanding the significance of the coming of the Seed — the Messiah. 'So that' (*hina*) (v. 22) implies that the reign of the law was a strictly limited one and would be terminated with the fulfilment of the promise. (*Cf.* further 'until faith should be revealed' [v. 23] and 'until Christ came' [v. 25 mg].)

Paul develops this point further in Romans 3:20. In summing up his argument in the section 1:18–3:20, the apostle says, 'Therefore no one will be declared righteous in his sight by observing the law; rather, through the law we become conscious of sin'. The damning conclusion in the first part of the verse undermines the very basis of the Jewish hope and security in the law. The 'for' (RSV) at the beginning of the second part of the verse indicates that it substantiates this conclusion — justification could not be attained by works of the law because the law was not given to make justification possible. It was given rather to bring to human beings an awareness of sin in the form of concrete transgression. That this is a necessary preparation for true justification, that is, that which is by grace through faith, is implicit in Paul's insistence in vv. 21,31 that his message of righteousness is not contrary to the law.

In Rom. 4:14–15, Paul develops this thought further. The promise 'is by grace' (*kata charin*) (v. 16) and comes through the righteousness of faith, whereas 'the law brings wrath'. The next statement, 'where there is no law, there is no transgression', makes it clear that Paul is thinking of God's wrath in terms of appropriate penalties fixed to specific transgressions and associated guilt. In the absence of any specific law, man's proneness to sin can remain undetected. It takes a legal or statutory prohibition to crystallise a sinful tendency into positive transgression, and positive transgression brings a sense of liability to God's wrath—that is, guilt.

Similarly in Rom. 5:20, Paul speaks of the law 'coming in' (RSV) so that the trespass might increase. The dispensation of the law is merely an interlude in salvation history.[23] When it was given through Moses there was thereafter a multiplication of the sin exemplified in Adam's trespass — disobedience to a clearly revealed commandment. However, Paul is careful not to abstract this purpose served by the law from the more abundant provisions of grace. The ultimate purpose was that 'grace might reign through righteousness to bring eternal life through Jesus Christ our Lord'.

A second focus in Paul's argument against a legalistic understanding of righteousness is the implication some held to the effect that righteousness is reserved exclusively for the Jews.

B. Righteousness not a Jewish Privilege

One of the basic tenets of the Jewish faith was that God is impartial. He is no respector of persons. But many Jews apparently believed that, even if their lives were no different from that of the Gentiles, they would not be subject to divine wrath.[24]

In Rom. 2, Paul argues that this is a wrong, indeed a dangerous, assumption. In the preceding section of the letter (1:18–32), Paul begins with a general statement concerning all mankind — 'the wrath of God is being revealed against all . . . men' — and then proceeds to show how this is true in the case of the Gentile world of his day. However, Paul then proceeds to dismiss any attempt made by the Jew to assume the role of accuser and thereby exclude himself from the indictment. 'You do the same things' repeated thrice over in vv. 1–3 is so categorical precisely because he assumes that no one can deny that it was true.

Paul's emphasis on works in vv. 6–16 is directed against another related — and false — premise: that the criterion of God's final judgement will be the possession or lack of the law. To put it otherwise, it was the Gentiles who would be judged, because they did not have the law and hence did not conform to the righteousness it prescribed. Against this, Paul argues from the fact that God as the righteous Judge of all mankind will show no partiality in his judgement. There will be a distinction made in the criterion of judgement and it will be the Jew and not the Gentile who will be judged on the basis of the Jewish law. Moreover, the criterion of judgement will be man's obedience (or his lack of obedience) to the law and not his possession of it.[25] There is evidence that some rabbis taught that it was to Israel's credit that she accepted the law, because the Gentiles too had been offered the law but had rejected it.[26] Therefore, the latter would be judged. Paul gives no credence to this tradition at all. He assumes that it was to Israel alone that the law was given, and therefore, Israel would be judged by the law.

In vv. 17ff., Paul refers to this privileged possession of the law and its accompanying prerogatives. The three members of v. 17 are closely related to each other and reflect the Jewish historical self-consciousness. Israel regarded her possession of the law as the token of her special relationship to God. She confidently believed that, as the people of the law, she was called to teach it to the less-privileged nations around her. Paul's language in these verses reflects Jewish missionary preaching in Hellenistic circles. The concluding clause, 'having in the law the embodiment of knowledge and truth' (v. 20b), is the climax of this description of all that was involved in the Jewish view of Israel's possession of the law.

Paul does not deny any of this, but in vv. 22–22 he declares that their possession of the law notwithstanding, the Jews stand condemned because they do not keep the law themselves. The four rhetorical questions are in effect accusations. Their privileges and prerogatives carried responsibilities that the Jews had failed to bear. They boasted in the law and yet transgressed it. As he did in vv. 1–3, Paul assumes that the Jew cannot deny his charge.

The Jews recognised their failure to keep the law perfectly but were able to compare themselves favourably with the nations around them.[27]

Finally, in vv. 25–29 Paul turns his attention to Jewish thinking on circumcision. In Judaism, law and circumcision belonged together, but the unbalanced emphasis on the privileges of election — that is, to the neglect of the accompanying responsibilities — was reflected in their misunderstanding of the nature of true righteousness and hence the function of the law, and the true significance of the rite of circumcision. To the Jew, circumcision constituted the perfect commandment. To elude it was almost an unforgiveable sin; to receive it gave protection against Gehenna. Paul argues that the religious significance of the rite was that it was the mark of the covenant people — the people of the law. Therefore, unless the law was kept, and the covenant honoured, circumcision was of no value. To treat it as a protective rite divorced from its covenantal context and obligations was empty superstition.

Paul's argument in this chapter is based on the assumption that man is incapable of fulfilling the Law. From elsewhere in his letters we learn that this is not because of any inherent defect in the law which, as God's revealed will, is 'holy, righteous and good' (Rom. 7:12) but rather because people are fleshly and sold under sin (Rom. 7:14). As long as a person is weakened by the flesh, he or she is incapable of fulfilling the law. This assumption in itself is not inconsistent with contemporary Judaism. Schoeps[28] cites the opinion of Rabbi Alexandrai given in *Ber.* 17*a*: 'Lord of the worlds, it is open and known to Thee that it is our will to do Thy will and that we are prevented from doing so by nothing other than the leaven in the dough'. The reference to leaven in the dough is presumably to the evil impulse in one's body.

Paul's argument, however, is based on the further assumption that unless the law is observed perfectly, a person will not be justified or attain righteousness. Now this assumption would have been rejected outright by his Jewish contemporaries. Schoeps continues the quote from Rabbi Alexandrai given above as typical of Jewish piety: 'May it be Thy pleasure that we return to fulfil the commands of Thy will with all our hearts'. In other words, the Jews believed that as long as a Jew desired to keep the law, even if he fell into sin, he would be 'righteous', provided he repented. Schoeps' comment is very revealing: 'It is because Paul does not know the Jewish belief in the power of turning again to God, he does not understand the question of the fulfilment of the law is in the last resort unimportant. For whether the law is fulfilled by man or not, the mere intention to fulfil it brings man close to God'.[29] Nevertheless, it is interesting that there was an inherent danger of presumption in their conception of righteousness and repentance. The Mishnah *Yoma* 8:9 warns against this: 'If anyone says to himself, "I will sin, and repent, (and again) I will sin and repent (and thus escape the consequences), no opportunity is given to him to repent" '. Therefore, it is not without significance that apart from Rom. 2:4, Paul never refers to repentance in connection with failure to attain law-righteousness, and in that verse he accuses the Jew of presumption!

The apostle picks up this argument again in Rom. 3:27ff. Having established in 1:18–3:20 that all are under sin (3:9) and that 'no one will be declared righteous in his sight by observing the law' (3:20), Paul introduces into his argument the fact that God has brought about a change in the situation. In the death of Christ, his righteousness has been revealed — 'the righteousness from God [that] comes through faith in Christ Jesus to all who believe' (3:22). Justification is a gift of God's grace through the redemption which is in Christ Jesus (3:24). In v. 25 Paul says God presented him as a *sacrifice of atonement* through faith in his blood. There has been much debate over the meaning of the Greek word *hilastērion*. It is generally argued that although in extra-biblical Greek the predominant meaning of the word is 'propitiation', in the LXX the thought expressed by the word is the expiation of sin, or of God being gracious, merciful and forgiving. However, in answer to this, it has been shown that in most, if not in all the passages where *hilaskesthai* and its cognates are used, the idea of God's wrath is present.

In Rom. 3:25 God is the subject. It is he who purposes or presents Christ as *hilastērion*. It is very likely, therefore, that the intended object is sin, or the sinner, rather than God. In other words, the primary reference here must be to the cancelling or removal of sin. However, the very context of this passage in Rom. 1–8 demands a reference also to the setting aside of God's wrath. This section closely follows Paul's exposition of God's wrath that is revealed against 'all the godlessness and wickedness of men' (Rom. 1:18). What Paul is saying is that the consequence of man's sin being removed by the sacrificial death of Christ is that he no longer experiences the wrath of God which his sin provoked. He has been forgiven. He has been reconciled.

In vv. 27–31, Paul states two corollaries to his assertion that it is in Christ that the righteousness of God has been revealed. In the first place, justified man has no grounds for boasting because his righteousness comes apart from works based on the law. Inasmuch as the law serves to nourish man's pride and encourage him to establish his own righteousness before God, it gives rise to 'boasting' — a characteristic of the piety that emphasises merit and obedience to the law.[30] We have already observed that Paul as a Pharisee had taken great pride in his religious achievements (Gal. 1:4; Phil. 3:6). He knew from past experience that an understanding of righteousness as consisting in keeping the precepts of the law was closely related to the conception of this obedience as meritorious and led to boasting and pride. But since a man is justified through faith, apart from observing the law, there is no room for 'boasting' and taking pride in one's own personal righteousness. For Paul, boasting denotes the basic attitude of the Jew as one of self-confidence which seeks glory before God and relies upon itself. It is the very antithesis of faith which receives righteousness as a free gift of God's grace.

Paul's second corollary is that both circumcised Jews and uncircumcised Gentiles can be justified through faith — that is, circumcision is not a pre-condition for justification. Rom. 3:28 is the counterpart to 3:20. Faith consists in accepting this conclusion and renouncing all attempts to justify oneself before God.

Paul's questions in v. 29 ('Is God the God of Jews only? Is he not the God of Gentiles too? Yes, of Gentiles too') in effect point out that the Jewish understanding of righteousness as consisting in keeping the Law is contrary to a basic tenet of the Jewish faith — monotheism.[31] Paul has already argued in 2:6ff that God is the Judge of all humankind. There he was refuting the Jewish assumption that the uncircumcised Gentile cannot be justified before God.

This emphasis on the implications of monotheism occurs repeatedly in

Paul's letters. His argument exposes a constitutive element in the Jewish misunderstanding of their election. For monotheism necessarily implies universalism. In the Old Testament, Jewish monotheism is perhaps most clearly presented in Isa. 40–55. But in this same section a universal emphasis is very noticeable too. Similarly, we have an emphasis on both Israel's election and her world mission (e.g. 42:6–8; 41:8–9; 44:1; 43:10). Similarly, Isa. 2:2–4 implies that the religion of Israel was not for her alone but for all people. Israel, however, had lost sight of this universal aspect of her election. She had become inward-looking, at least inasmuch as she came to believe that salvation was the prerogative of Jewry alone.

Both these foci (3:1 and 3:2) appear in Romans 9:30–10:31. In this section of the letter Paul's primary concern is to substantiate the argument in the preceding section (9:14–29) that God is sovereign in his choice of people as instruments to carry out his purposes. That his election purposes for Israel will be carried out through a mere remnant of the nation was the consequence of the unbelief of the rest, and this was in turn the outcome of their misunderstanding of the nature of true righteousness.

'What then shall we say?' (9:30) introduces the implication of the argument in the preceding section. 'That the Gentiles, who did not pursue righteousness, have obtained it, a righteousness that is by faith; but that Israel who pursued a law of righteousness, has not attained it.' This contrast between the Gentiles and their success, and the failure of Israel, is explained on the basis of the different means used: Israel had pursued righteousness as if it were based on works of the law. They had zealously observed the law which prescribed this righteousness but had failed to fulfil it.[32] Moreover, their misunderstanding of the nature of righteousness had resulted in their failing to recognise true righteousness, the righteousness that comes from God (10:3). That it was a misunderstanding is underlined by the words 'as if it were by works' in 9:32. Their zeal was an unenlightened zeal and the result was that when the righteousness of God was revealed in Christ, the Gentiles received it gladly in faith, but the Jews stumbled in unbelief. They stumbled over the stumbling-stone — God's Messiah. The revelation that true righteousness is attained by faith in Christ proved a stumbling-stone to the Jews because it put them on a par with the Gentiles. To a people who revelled in their privileges as God's peculiar people, this was indeed a hard lesson to learn.

The Jewish emphasis on righteousness based on works of the law was the consequence of their having lost the eschatological perspective in their understanding of their election and the law. Paul, on the other hand, sees in Christ alone the full significance of Israel's election. For him, the law, rightly understood, was a temporary and limited measure meant to point beyond itself to Christ. Therefore, the zeal for God of the Jews in their striving after righteousness based on works of the law was 'not based on knowledge' (10:2). They were ignorant of the righteousness that comes from God and zealously sought to establish their own righteousness instead of submitting to God's righteousness.[33]

It must be emphasised that Paul is not contrasting two types of righteousness but two methods of attaining righteousness before God — represented tersely by the antithesis 'works — faith' (9:32).

'For Christ is the end of the law, so that there may be righteousness for everyone who believes' (10:4 RSV). The 'for' (*cf.* RSV) indicates that this statement is meant to explain or substantiate v. 3, which in turn explains Paul's statement in v. 2 that the Jewish religious zeal is 'not based on knowledge'. They sought to establish their own righteousness based on works of the law because they did not realise that true righteousness was from God and received by faith. In other words, Paul is saying that the Jews had misunderstood the nature of true righteousness and the true purpose of the law. If they had understood God's purpose aright, they would have seen that Christ is the end (*telos*) of the law and that righteousness from God was received by faith.

Lexically, the word *telos* can mean 'termination' or 'end'[34] or 'goal' or 'aim'.[35] In the context here where Paul is explaining that the Jews had failed to see that the law looked beyond itself to Christ, the word primarily means 'goal' or 'aim'. However, if it looked forward to Christ, its function came to an end with his coming.[36] By failing to see this, the Jews had come to believe that righteousness was their prerogative because they were people of the law, but God had never intended to confine the possibility of righteousness to the Jews alone. That the distinction between Jews and Gentiles that the law had come to represent was intended to be temporary was proved by the fact that the law looked beyond itself to Christ. In him, true righteousness that comes from God could be received by 'every one who believes'.[37]

In 10:5–13 Paul elaborates on what he has already said. The 'for' (*cf*. RSV) in v. 5 indicates that he is explaining further or substantiating v. 4b. The possibility of righteousness based on works was necessarily confined to those who possessed the law — the Jews. The righteousness that comes from God, however, was accessible to all. This is Paul's main point in these verses.[38]

Paul's central thesis that in Christ righteousness and salvation are accessible to Jew and Gentile alike is grounded strikingly on the fundamental tenet of the Jewish faith: monotheism. For him the truth that God is one and, therefore, is the God of Jews and Gentiles alike made it imperative that the election of Israel be understood as primarily having eschatological-universal significance. His conviction that in the Christ-event the 'age to come' had arrived led to his understanding and interpretation of the Old Testament faith and hope solely in Christological terms.

C. Abraham the Father of the Justified

In introducing himself to the church in Rome Paul describes the gospel that he preaches as 'the gospel [of God] he promised beforehand through his prophets in the Holy Scriptures' (Rom. 1:2). This emphasis on the gospel of justification through faith in Christ being witnessed to by the law and the prophets is a further focal point in Paul's thinking.

The Jewish understanding of the election of Israel was, of course, intrinsically connected with the covenant made with Abraham. Paul insists that Abraham is not to be interpreted through Moses or determined by him. This is consistent with his emphasis that the law of Moses came later and could not alter the fundamental basis of God's relation to his elect — namely, faith. So Paul appeals to the faith of Abraham as a pre-figurement of the faith in Christ that justifies.

In Romans 4, Paul first establishes that 'boasting' did not characterise Abraham's piety as it did those of his posterity who relied on their observance of the law. If Abraham had been justified by works, he would indeed have had something to boast about before God, but Scripture (Gen. 15:6) clearly indicated that Abraham was justified through his faith.[39] Abraham's faith was demonstrated in obedience, but Paul's point is that the Scripture emphasises his faith, not his works. The frame of mind that boasted in one's obedience was the very antithesis of faith — the faith that Abraham displayed.

He elaborates this in vv. 4–5. The antithesis in these verses is between those who work to earn their wages — in this case, acceptance before God being regarded as the just reward of punctilious observance of the law — and those who rather rely on the grace of God, the God who receives even the ungodly if they trust in him. Since the contrast 'the man who works — the man who does not work' is used to explain how Abraham was not justified 'by works', the terms have reference to the ground of a person's relationship to God. 'The man who works' denotes one who sees this relationship as determined by his works. On the other hand, one who declines such a view — 'the man who does not work' — is alternatively described as a believer (v. 5). The eye of faith sees God as 'he who justifies the wicked'. Faith accepts God's judgment that all men are ungodly and that the basis of justification is not to be found in man and his works. 'Credited' (vv. 4,5) connects the Old Testament quotation in v. 3 to its interpretation in these verses. It explains on the one hand the reward as 'an obligation'; on the other, the free act of justification is 'as a gift'. Paul clearly understands Scripture to support his contention that Abraham falls into the latter category.

In vv. 6–8, Paul appeals to a passage from the Psalms to support his exegesis of Gen. 15:6. He introduces the quotation from Psa. 32:1–2 by summarising it in the concept of 'blessedness'. The relative clause 'to whom God credits righteousness apart from works' connects the quotation to the preceding train of thought. The Psalm itself does not speak of the righteousness of God or of the crediting of righteousness. However, the parallelism makes it clear that the expressions 'whose transgressions are forgiven' and 'whose sins are covered' explain 'whose sin the Lord will never count against him'. For Paul, this non-reckoning of sin is the same as the reckoning of righteousness. Justification includes the verdict of acquittal at the divine judgment bar.

Paul's emphasis on God justifying the ungodly and on justification involving a verdict of acquittal is crucial to his argument in this passage. The Jewish emphasis on works reflected their neglect of the seriousness of sin, but the apostle insists that sinful man could not be justified before he submitted himself to the divine judgment that he was in need of forgiveness. Implicit in this forgiveness was the gift of God's grace — righteousness. 'God shows his divinity in that he acts forgivingly — that is, turns towards the ungodly. The centre of our passage is to be found in Paul's separation between faith and what is generally called goodness; and he can only bring this out when he gives a challengingly new definition, contrary to the prevailing view of what the nature and work of the true God really is.'[40]

In vv. 9–12, Paul deals with Abraham's circumcision and its relationship to his righteousness. The apostle appeals to the order of events in the patriarchal narrative. Abraham responded in faith to God's word of promise and God established a covenant with him (Gen. 15:18). In Gen. 17:10–11, God tells Abraham that as a sign of the covenant he must be circumcised. Paul concludes from this that Abraham's faith that was reckoned as righteousness was independent of his circumcision. The rite was a subsequent and external seal of the righteous status that the Abraham of Gen. 17:10–11 already enjoyed as God's gracious gift. It was a ratification of his faith and justification and not a precondition.

The purpose clauses in v. 11 indicate that Paul is emphasising the divine purpose in the call of Abraham, and in him, his descendants. He infers from the sequence of events that, since it was only a subsequent ratification of Abraham's righteous status, circumcision, the strongest mark of Jewish separation, was intended to point beyond its immediate exclusiveness to an ultimate inclusion of Gentiles as well. Abraham's circumcision ratified a spiritual reality — an attitude of faith — and he was the father, not of those who imitated his circumcision (that is, Jews whether believing or not), but those who shared his faith (that is, believing Jews and Gentiles). God was the God of Jews and Gentiles and his purpose in calling Abraham was that both the Jews and Gentiles might be blessed.

This overruling purpose of God in the call of Abraham forms part of Paul's argument in the letter to the Galatians too. In 3:6–9, Paul appeals to the same text, Gen. 15:6, to establish that it was his faith that was reckoned to Abraham as righteousness and that he is the father of all who believe. However, there is a significant difference in his argument. When God called Abraham, he indicated his purpose in doing so when he gave him a promise: 'All nations will be blessed through you' (v. 8). The point that Paul makes in Rom. 4 on the basis of the sequence of events in the Genesis narrative, that is, that the call of Abraham had significance for Gentiles as well as Jews, he deduces here from the promise recorded in Gen. 12:3 and frequently repeated in the subsequent narrative. Paul sees the promise as fulfilled in the Gentiles being justified by faith in Christ (v. 8). Since 'all nations' were included in the promise, physical descent or the rite of circumcision could not be the criterion. It was faith. The verb 'foresaw' implies a continuity of the new order ushered in by Christ with the old. Similarly, 'announced the gospel in advance' shows Paul's conviction that the promise made to Abraham foreshadowed the gospel and, indeed, was fulfilled only in the gospel. Paul views Israel's history as salvation history and hence the significance of Abraham lies in his particular role in the divine plan of redemption.[41]

The parallel that Paul draws between Abraham's faith and the faith that justifies is important. Just as Abraham was prepared to take God at his word, regardless of how incredible the promise seemed at the time, the faith that justifies is essentially trust in God's activity without consideration of what is attainable or possible by human effort. Vincent Taylor thinks the parallel between Abraham's faith and the faith by which men are justified is far from satisfactory. 'The OT quotation [Gen. 15:6 quoted by Paul in Gal. 3:6 and Rom. 4:3]', he says, 'encourages the thought: A man is justified because he believes something'.[42] However, the actual content of Abraham's faith, intellectually speaking, is of so little consequence that no reference is made to it by Paul in Gal. 3:6f. It is his assent of mind and will that Paul refers to. Openness of mind to the divine revelation whatever its content, and response of will—this is the faith by which a person is justified.

In Rom. 4:16–25 Paul describes the characteristic of Abraham's faith that makes him the father of all believers, and it is quite clear that it was his faith in God, rather than in the promise, that God honoured. He clung to the God who promised rather than to what had been promised. When God's promise to Abraham, 'I have made you a father of many nations' (Rom. 4:17; *cf.* Gen. 17:5), was made, neither Abraham nor Sarah was in a position to give birth to descendants. He was a hundred years old and his body was as good as dead. Sarah's womb was dead too, but faced with these facts his faith did not weaken. 'The believing man hopes at the very point where there is, in the earthly sense, nothing more to hope for.'[43] He rather rested confidently upon the character of God who had made the promise as having the power to do what he had promised. He is the God who gives life to the dead and calls into existence the things that do not exist (v. 17). He could give life to Abraham's dead body and to Sarah's dead womb and bring into existence the many nations in whom the promise would be fulfilled.

Therefore, Abraham was strengthened in his faith and gave glory to God. 'To give glory to God is to reckon God to be what he is and rely upon his power and righteousness'.[44] This was the faith that was credited to Abraham as righteousness (v. 22). In v. 23 Paul continues: 'The words, "it was credited to him", were written not for him alone, but also for us.' Faith in the God and Father of the Lord Jesus Christ is essentially the same as the faith in God that Abraham displayed — an obedient trust in God, the Source and Giver of life, and it is this faith alone that justifies. Paul's portrayal of Abraham's faith illustrates the fundamental motif of the Pauline conception of faith: openness to and, finally, participation in the redemptive power of God operative in Christ's death and resurrection.

At this point we would do well to clarify the relationship between faith and righteousness.[45] The righteousness that accrues to the believer in the form of redemptive benefits of the work of Christ is both objective — justification — and subjective — new life in the Spirit. Both are eschatological realities, belonging to the 'age to come', yet both have nevertheless become objects of present experience in 'this age'. Justification is both forensic and eschatological. As forensic it has to do not with a sinner's personal condition but with his relation to the Ruler and Judge of the universe. It is the pronouncement of the righteous Judge that the believer is acquitted from all guilt of sin. As such it is essentially eschatological, that is, it belongs to the eschatological day of judgment (*cf.* Gal. 5:5; Rom. 8:33); but Paul asserts that by virtue of the death of Christ, the eschatological judgment which belongs to the age to come has reached back to the cross of Christ, and the man of faith is living in the new age as far as his relationship is concerned.

However, while it is important to understand justification in relational terms, we ought not to confound justification with faith by suggesting, for example, that righteousness must be understood in a qualitative sense — as a comprehensive attitude of mind and will.[46] According to this view, a believer is pronounced righteous because his faith shows that he really is righteous in mind and purpose although not yet in achievement. But this is to emphasise the relational aspect to the neglect of the forensic. Rather it is faith that is an attitude of trusting surrender to God.

IV. JUSTIFICATION AND LIFE IN THE SPIRIT

We turn, finally to a consideration of Paul's presentation of the life in Christ as a fulfilment of the promise made to Abraham and his descendants.

In Gal. 3:11,21 Paul practically equates this new life and faith-righteousness. Since righteousness includes the forensic aspect of acquittal, the believer 'lives' because he has been acquitted at the divine judgment-bar. The apostle makes essentially the same point in Rom. 5:12–21, where he contrasts the disobedience of Adam and its disastrous effects on mankind with the obedience of Christ, the last Adam, and ts consequences for all men. In the case of Adam, through his trespass sin came into the world and death through sin. Death reigned (v. 17) because sin did (v. 21). In Adam, all human beings sinned and all died (v. 12, *cf.* v. 15) — that is, all came under the sentence of death. (Condemnation, like righteousness, is an eschatological concept.) In Christ, however, God offers the gift of righteousness and life. Paul lays particular emphasis on two facts: (1) life is the gift of God's grace; and (2) it is offered to all human beings. In v. 18 justification is contrasted with condemnation — the sentence of death pronounced on all sinners. In Christ, we receive the verdict of acquittal and enter into life. It is clear from this passage that eternal life is also an eschatological concept (vv. 18–21).

In Gal. 3:27–4:7 Paul describes the believer's new standing in terms of filial favour with God. God acknowledges the believer in Christ as a son. 'In Christ Jesus' (v. 26) must be taken with 'you are all sons of God' rather than with 'through faith'. The phrase 'sons of God' or 'children of God' in Paul mostly conveys the idea of liberty, and this is certainly the emphasis here in this passage.[47]

In 4:6 the apostle makes the further point that 'adoption' and the gift of the Spirit are concomitant events. The causal *hoti* at the beginning of 4:6 indicates that the 'sonship' is the basis of the receiving of the Spirit. The believer's present possession of the Holy Spirit is an important aspect of Paul's soteriology. In Gal. 3:14 he describes the results of Christ's atoning death as twofold: (1) Abraham's blessing (that is, righteousness through faith) had become universally available; and (2) all human beings, Jews and Gentiles alike, could receive the Spirit through faith. The second purpose clause, 'so that by faith we might receive the promise of the Spirit', is an expansion of the first. Paul conceives the universal activity of the Spirit in people of faith as the fulfilment of the promise made to Abraham, that in him all nations would be blessed.

It is likely that the concept of sonship here in Gal. 4:1–7 also implies the conferring of the right to inherit. An heir is, by definition, one who is 'in the line to receive' and waits for the receipt of something which is not yet given. The inheritance is still to come, but the one who is designated as an 'heir' thereby has a new status already.

In the parallel passage in Rom. 8:18ff. the apostle makes it clear that 'sonship' too is an eschatological concept. In v. 19 he describes the climax and consummation of God's work of salvation as the revealing of the sons of God. Believers are already sons but their sonship is not as yet manifest. Their adoption is still to be publicly proclaimed. However, although they await their full adoption as sons of God, when they will be like Christ, God's Son, they already possess the Spirit as the firstfruits of their redemption (v. 23). Firstfruits, the first portion of the harvest, is both the first instalment and the pledge of the full harvest yet to come. Just as they have already been justified, although justification is strictly an eschatological event, they already live in newness of life by the Spirit who gives life.

The believer's life in Christ is therefore regarded by Paul as the fulfilment of the promise of life made by the law. The law 'promised life' (Rom. 7:10 RSV) but was never intended 'to impart life' (Gal. 3:21). Rather God shut up human beings under sin and the law so that 'what was promised, being given through faith in Jesus Christ, might be given to those who believe' (Gal. 3:22).

In 2 Cor. 3:3–6 Paul contrasts the Spirit of the living God with the written letter of the law. In contrast to the letter of the law which kills, the Spirit gives life. In vv. 7–9 the new dispensation, 'the dispensation of the Spirit' (RSV), is also described as 'the dispensation of righteousness' and is contrasted with the Mosaic dispensation, 'the dispensation of condemnation' (v. 9) and 'of death' (v. 7). This contrast between condemnation and death on the one hand, and righteousness on the other, occurs once more in Rom. 8:1–11, where again it is the Spirit who brings deliverance and life. In v. 4 Paul declares that the deliverance that has been made possible by Christ's atoning death was 'in order that the righteous requirements [*dikaiōma*] of the law might be fully met in us, who do not live according to the sinful nature but according to the Spirit'.

What does the apostle really mean when he says that the 'righteous requirement of the law' is fulfilled in believers? In Rom. 9:30–32 Paul says that the Gentiles 'obtained . . . righteousness' whereas Israel 'did not attain it'. The context makes it clear that it is the righteousness that the law promised; but it was to be attained 'by faith' and not 'by works'. Therefore, the 'righteous requirement of the law' that is fully met in believers must refer, at least in some measure, to their justification.[48] Barrett observes: 'Here the thought is not so much that what the Law requires is righteous as that what the Law requires is righteousness. The Law tells us that God has the right to summon us to his court and that he requires that we be found righteous.'[49]

However, since 'condemnation' in Rom. 8:1 probably refers to the penal servitude that follows the verdict of condemnation rather than to the verdict itself, Paul may well mean that the 'righteous requirement of the law' is fully met in believers in the sense that they have been freed from bondage to sin and death. The believer's life 'in Christ', as one justified and freed, is a fulfilment of the righteous requirement of the law. However, Paul's further description of believers in v. 4b as those 'who do not live according to the sinful nature but according to the Spirit' indicates that this fulfilment is realised only as believers conduct themselves under the direction of the Spirit.[50]

4

Justification in Paul and Some Crucial Issues of the Last Two Decades

P. T. O'BRIEN

Paul's understanding of God's righteousness and justification by faith have been, in recent times, at the heart of a lively, diverse and even heated theological debate.[1] The questions raised have not been on the periphery of Paul's teaching, and it has been claimed that 'all the major issues in Pauline interpretation are contained (at least by implication) in this debate'.[2] Recent histories of interpretation indicate that no scholarly agreement has yet been reached as to what the apostle meant by *dikaiosyne theou* and how his teaching on this motif is to be related to the rest of his theology. One wonders whether anything approaching a consensus can ever be reached! However, new insights have opened up fresh interpretative possibilities and some genuine advances have been made in the understanding of this theme.

The issues raised in this paper are not simply of academic interest, but have important pastoral, evangelistic and theological ramifications as well. This study will reaffirm the importance of justification by faith alone. If in Paul's teaching it is foundational, as we shall argue, then it deals with the basic issue of a man or woman's entering into and being in a right relationship with God. There are important implications for contemporary teaching and preaching where the term 'gospel' has become either so vague or broad in its meaning as to include almost anything. A proper grasp of the theme of righteousness and justification should result in a preaching of the gospel which focuses on Christ's saving work in relation to God's justifying the ungodly. Further, it is only through a proper understanding of justification by faith alone that we are able to have a true estimate of sin and a proper grasp of the significance of the cross. With the loss of clear teaching on God's justifying work there has been a loss of Christian assurance on the part of many church members. Good works, even miraculous good works, have intruded as Christians have looked to these to provide the grounds for their day-to-day confidence and assurance.

A historical survey such as this, even if limited in its scope and in the period assessed, has the advantage of drawing our attention to the strengths of earlier formulations as well as alerting us to some of their pitfalls or dangers. So, for example, Bultmann's stress on the gift aspect of righteousness can lead to a false individualism and to a theology which is in reality centred on anthropology, while Käsemann's brilliant and influential contribution to the debate is in danger of ending in universalism. If salvation is for everybody, then the urgency of preaching the gospel has diminished, everyday actions do not have to be read in the light of a final judgment and the Christian is robbed of that assurance which is based on God's justifying activity.

At the same time the debates of the last two decades have shown that yesterday's answers do not solve today's questions. Our study of this period, and particularly since 1977, demonstrates that, although there is a fundamental theological core that is constant, many of the issues raised in the recent debates are considerably more nuanced than previously. Further information has come to light and fresh insights have been provided as scholars have wrestled fresh with the Pauline texts. These need to be evaluated so that the wealth of the apostle's teaching can be appreciated.

In approaching this vast subject of justification and righteousness in Paul over the last two decades it is intended to limit the areas of inquiry to the following:

(a) What is the meaning of the expression 'the righteousness of God'? In endeavouring to come to answers to this critical question, Ernst Käsemann's magisterial contribution will be taken into account, together with representative positive and negative reactions to it. The nature of the genitive [δικαιοσύνη] θεοῦ, ([*dikaiosyne*] *theou*) needs to be examined: does the expression denote: (i) human righteousness which counts in God's eyes (a so-called objective genitive); (ii) God's own saving power or activity (a subjective genitive); (iii) God's gift of righteousness (a genitive of origin), or (iv) some combination or variation of these?

(b) What role does the doctrine of justification play in Paul's thought? Is it correct to speak of the centrality of justification? Or, indeed, to 'search for a centre' in Paul's teaching at all?

(c) The meaning, place and significance of the Pauline teaching on righteousness and justificiation have been questioned afresh with the publication of several significant works by E. P. Sanders and the debate that follows. The basis of justification or a righteous standing before God in Paul is at the heart of these discussions and needs to be addressed[2a].

(d) Finally, the apparent contradiction between Paul's teaching on justification by faith and his affirmation of a future judgment according to works, while not a new issue, has been addressed in fresh ways during the past two decades, and some attention will be given to this.

I. THE MEANING OF 'THE RIGHTEOUSNESS OF GOD'

A. Käsemann's Contribution

One cannot account satisfactorily for the last two decades of research into the Pauline doctrine of justification without first examining the highly influential contribution of Ernst Käsemann which has been described as 'a turning-point in the history of interpretation'.[3] Käsemann introduced new terminology into the debate (e.g. the 'power character of the gift', 'change of lordship', and 'transformation of existence') as he sought to provide new perspectives on the relationship between God's action in Christ and man's existence under faith.

At the time of the Reformation Luther had claimed that the important

Pauline expression, 'the righteousness of God', referred to that righteousness which counts before him and which humanity possesses as a gift from him.[4] Emphasising the gift-character of God's righteousness Luther described it as 'his gracious and creative and redemptive activity on behalf of man'.[5]

Luther's legacy was developed and expounded by later writers, notably by Rudolf Bultmann, who interpreted 'the righteousness of God' from his anthropological starting-point and within the framework of existential philosophy. In dependence on Pauline texts such as Rom. 10:3 and Phil. 3:9 Bultmann understood *dikaiosyne* as a forensic eschatological term (formally Paul had it in common with his Jewish heritage) which referred not to the ethical quality of a person but to a relationship. 'Righteousness' was the 'favourable standing' a person had in the eyes of others (*theou* is a genitive of origin or authorship). Judaism viewed this in terms of a future hope which was directly related to keeping the works of the law. Paul, however, understood this forensic-eschatological righteousness as being imputed to a person in the present on the presupposition of faith.

'Therefore, the righteousness which God adjudicates to man (the man of faith) is not "sinlessness" in the sense of ethical perfection, but is "sinlessness" in the sense that God does not "count" man's sins against him (2 Cor. 5:19)'.[6] The individual is righteous, not in the sense that he or she may *be* righteous but in the sense of being acknowledged as innocent by God. Taking the genitive '[the righteousness] *of God*' as one of authorship Bultmann thus claimed the expression referred to that righteousness from God which is conferred upon humanity as a gift by his free grace alone.[7]

Käsemann recognised that *dikaiosyne theou* ('the righteousness of God') — perhaps the most significant expression in the writings of Paul — was not the apostle's creation but was taken over by him from apocalyptic Judaism. As an independent technical term it can be traced back to the OT (Dt. 33:21) and from this into late Judaism (Dn. 6:10; 1 QS 11:12). This ready-made formulation is not to be subsumed under the general concept of *dikaiosyne* and then interpreted as either a personal, ethical quality[8] or in terms of a juridical-forensic concept which focuses on the gift character of righteousness. Käsemann had forcefully criticised Bultmann's interpretation of *dikaiosyne theou* (with its genitive of origin or authorship) for focusing on this gift character and for isolating the gift from the Giver. He considered that Bultmann had provided an anthropocentric rather than a theological understanding of the gospel, and had understood righteousness in purely individualistic terms.[9] By contrast, Käsemann claimed that *dikaiosyne theou* — a subjective genitive — speaks of a divine activity: it is for Paul 'God's sovereignty over the world revealing itself eschatologically in Jesus'.[10] 'The righteousness of God' is a salvation-creating activity and has been defined as '*God's victorious, creation-covenant-faithful power-action*'.[11]

God's righteousness was manifested in an apocalyptic event that caused the change of aeons. It is cosmic in scope, for Paul saw in the revelation of God's righteousness in the Christ-event God's faithfulness towards the entire creation: his righteousness 'reaches out for the world, and the world's salvation lies in its being recaptured for the sovereignty of God'.[12] Over against Bultmann Käsemann argued that *dikaiosyne theou* 'does not refer primarily to the individual and is not to be understood exclusively in the context of the doctrine of man'. 'The Gift can never be separated from the

Giver; it participates in the power of God, since God steps on to the scene in the gift'. As a more balanced presentation Käsemann sought to replace the alternatives with a dialectic along the following lines: 'The justification of the ungodly certainly in the first place affects, in concrete terms, myself. But the phrase is robbed of its full significance if it does not mean salvation for everyone and for the whole world'.[13] For Käsemann this double aspect of righteousness as both 'gift' and 'power' in the context of God's redemptive action is the only satisfactory solution to the subject-object orientation of the genitive 'the righteousness *of God*'.[14] In bringing a new perspective to the discussion he believes that he has avoided the one-sidedness of an anthropocentric presentation which treats *dikaiosyne* as a pure gift or the sinner's deliverance, as well as a one-sided theocentric approach in which the revelation of God's righteousness appears to be external to man. The 'power-character of the gift' requires that an encounter takes place within man while at the same time a response is demanded from man.[15] Käsemann has thus suggested a new meaning for *dikaiosyne* and a new understanding of *theou* based on an apocalyptic phrase now reinterpreted by Paul in the light of Christology. In the cross of Jesus Christ God has triumphed over the world: on that basis the ungodly can be justified and set free to hear God's word in a new way and to serve him with a new sort of obedience.

B.   Käsemann's Influence on Recent Scholarship

Käsemann's dynamic interpretation of 'the righteousness of God' in Pauline thought has had a profound influence on subsequent NT scholarship. Both Protestant and Roman Catholic writers up to the present have interacted with his explanation and utilised elements within it for expounding their own interpretations. The following are some of the more important constructions:

(1) *C. Müller*

Christian Müller,[16] who sought to interpret the 'Israel problem' within Paul's understanding of God's righteousness and the sinner's justification, explained *dikaiosyne theou* in terms of God's victory. Believing that the apostle was working within OT and Jewish apocalyptic traditions, Müller claimed that this key expression had to do with God's sovereignty and rights as Creator. He has an unconditional claim over against his creation and calls the whole world to account in a cosmic trial. God emerges victorious from this eschatological judgment trial by establishing the guilt of the world and by calling for all to submit to his 'forensic' judgment. Justification occurs when 'the believer acknowledges God's free and sovereign action in Christ, and in this acknowledgement [which is by faith] becomes a new creation'.[17]

(2) *P. Stuhlmacher*

Peter Stuhlmacher, a student of Käsemann who was dependent on his interpretation of *dikaiosyne theou* as 'salvation-creating power', emphasised the soteriological aspect of the righteousness of God in terms of God's faithfulness as Creator towards his creation. He understands this expression in the context of Jewish apocalyptic where it had become a technical term signifying 'the power of the creating Word of God' against the backdrop of God's right as Creator, his covenant faithfulness, his forgiving mercy, and his demand for obedience.[18] Stuhlmacher supports his interpretation by an extensive examination of the Pauline texts. He regards Rom. 10:3 as particularly significant, for here various aspects of his understanding of *dikaiosyne theou* come together: 'God's righteousness is exclusively a redemptive event'. It is the creative activity of God as Creator, is personified in Christ and realised as 'word' in the kerygma.[19] This interpretation of 'the righteousness of God' lay at the heart of Paul's doctrine of justification.

Stuhlmacher raises the question as to how the concrete action of God as Creator (i.e. *dikaiosyne theou*) is related to his forensic and justifying activity (*dikaioun/dikaiousthai*). In answer he asserts that God's justification is a divine-creative activity, in which his righteousness (*dikaiosyne theou*) is actualised in terms of a word-event such that a new being is created. This creative work is not something mechanical for it calls for man's response as he is addressed in the kerygma, and it reaches its fulfilment when man acknowledges God as Judge and Creator.[20] There is a tension between present justification and the final judgment. But God's faithfulness towards his new creation outlasts the judgment. The apostle Paul looks forward to the final coming of God. It will be 'the final vindication of God's right, because only then will God give to his own the new being in its fullness'.[21]

In his later essay, 'The Apostle Paul's View of Righteousness',[22] Stuhlmacher makes the following points: first, Paul played a key role in the history of NT thinking about righteousness 'because he made God's righteousness in Christ the basic content of the missionary gospel'. In fact, from the time of Paul's ministry, '*the righteousness of God in Christ and the justification of all believers through Christ alone are the inalienable foundations and norms of Christian belief*'.[23] Paul's proclamation about justification was the direct consequence of his encounter with the risen Christ on the Damascus road. The righteousness of God is the 'embodiment of the saving action of God in Christ, which creates new life for believers as they face the judgment'.[24] After an examination of the phrase in Romans, 2 Cor. 5:21 and Phil. 3:21, Stuhlmacher concludes that one cannot reduce the formula *dikaiosyne theou* to 'the righteousness of faith that is accepted by God' or to 'God's own righteousness in Christ'. 'Both aspects belong indissolubly together' and the expression must be understood in the 'synthetic' sense in which Paul used it.[25]

(3) *K. Kertelge*

Käsemann's profound influence on recent NT scholarship has been felt by Roman Catholic writers as well as Protestant ones, and perhaps this is no more evident than in the case of Karl Kertelge's work, '*Rechtfertigung' bei Paulus*.[26] In agreement with Stuhlmacher he locates the expression *dikaiosyne theou* in the context of the OT and apocalyptic Judaism, though he recognises Paul has given new content to the formula. Like Käsemann, Kertelge agrees that the phrase describes neither the character of God nor the situation of man before God. Instead, it designates God's action in and on behalf of man.[27] But whereas Müller developed Käsemann's interpretation of God's creative, cosmic, redemptive activity in terms of his *victory* as Creator over against the creation, and Stuhlmacher gave emphatic expression to it with reference to God's *faithfulness* as Creator towards his creation, Kertelge explains 'the righteousness of God' as his redemptive activity that creates a new relationship between himself and mankind. In passages such as Rom. 1:17 and 3:21–26 *diokaiosyne theou* is clearly related to the eschatological revelation of God's redemption in Christ. Although the expression has to do with God's activity and not his gift of righteousness to man, it must not be overlooked that mankind is the object of this divine work. God's *dikaiosyne* implies a relationship between himself and man, and is directed towards man's salvation. The sinner is transferred into the sphere of God's righteousness and experiences justification as a result of God's gracious action.

Kertelge confronts the question: what happens to the sinner when he is 'declared righteous' or is 'justified'? Analysing the forensic and eschatological notions of the terms *dikaiosyne* and *dikaioun/dikaiousthai*[28] Kertelge states that in justifiction God declares the sinner righteous and on the basis of Christ's death freely absolves him from his 'being-in-sin'. The forensic declaration creates the sinner anew in the sense of a newly formed relationship to God. In seeking to avoid the problem of a legal fiction Kertelge argues that 'God's action is not exhausted in simply an external decree (a purely forensic declaration), but signifies the effective creation of a new reality through God. This new reality of the justified one, created by God, is not to be understood in terms of a static ontology, but rather as a "relational reality" . . . i.e., a reality which consists of nothing except that new relationship between God and man created by God, the content of which is, from the side of God, Lordship, and from the side of man, obedience'.[29]

Justification has an eschatological character to it, but in the Christ-event the final and decisive revelation of 'God's righteousness' is present; the eschaton has broken into this age so that justification is experienced here and now. God's eschatological redemption has come though its ultimate fulfilment is still outstanding.[30] In the meantime the justified person is called into service; such a person not only receives, but is also obligated.

C. Critiques of Käsemann's Interpretation

As indicated above there has been widespread support for Käsemann's explanation of the key Pauline expression, 'the righteousness of God'. Nevertheless the correctness of his interpretation has been challenged by some significant New Testament scholars.

Bultmann in a brief response to Käsemann is 'unrepentant',[31] judging the latter's criticisms of his own work to be wide of the mark, while C. E. B. Cranfield, who acknowledges that Käsemann's theological objections to Bultmann's individualistic, anthropocentric and disjunctive interpretation of righteousness (in which the gift was isolated from the Giver) has real point to them, continues to maintain that it is 'perfectly possible to hold that Paul meant by δικαιοσύνη Θεοῦ in some of the places where he uses the expression the status of righteousness which may be had as a gift from God'.[32]

H. Conzelmann[33] reaffirmed Bultmann's thesis, arguing that Pauline theology must be interpreted anthropologically. He dismissed the subjective meaning of the genitive construction, *dikaiosyne theou*, as a reference to God's character, but failed to consider the subjective genitive as a designation of God's action (as Käsemann had understood it). Conzelmann's return to the

Bultmann line, according to Brauch, has been a failure for it has given us neither a clearer understanding of Paul's teaching on justification nor of his theology as a whole.[34] G. Klein[35] denied the validity of Käsemann's thesis and presented a view of 'the righteousness of God' which distinguished 'the fact of justification and the possibility of moral renewal'. He argued that the unity of justification and sanctification which Käsemann claimed to have established by interpreting the righteousness of God as both gift and demand had been shattered by his criticisms.

Several other challenges to Käsemann's reconstruction have appeared in the last decade.[36] Of particular significance are those of K. Stendahl and S. K. Williams. We shall examine these before making some comments on the Käsemann-oriented line of interpretation as reflected in Müller, Stuhlmacher and Kertelge. The debate between Stendahl and Käsemann touches on the search for the centre of Paul's theology, and as such would normally be considered later (see below). However, since Stendahl's critique brings salvation-history to the fore, and this has been perceived by some to be a significant lack in Käsemann's interpretation, it is convenient to treat the matter here. Williams' contribution naturally follows on from this, though it deals particularly with the meaning of the expression *dikaiosyne theou* by examining it linguistically and exegetically.

(1) *K. Stendahl*

Twenty-five years ago Krister Stendahl, in a now famous article 'The Apostle Paul and the Introspective Conscience of the West',[37] warned of the danger of modernising Paul. He especially challenged the current picture of Paul, inherited from Augustine and Luther, in which the apostle was thought to have suffered from a bad conscience with soul-searchings and agonies prior to his 'conversion'. For Stendahl chapters 9–11 were the real centre of Romans and salvation-history was the basic content of Paul's theology. Justification by faith was part of Paul's apologetic in connection with the place of Gentiles within the church. Käsemann responded that salvation-history was opposed to the true Protestant teaching of justification by faith with its basis in the cross. Stendahl asserted in his rejoinder that it begs the question to begin with the traditional doctrine of justification. After all 'the justification of the ungodly' is mentioned rarely by Paul and one might wonder whether it lies at the centre of his thought in the way Käsemann claimed. In fact, 'the very argument about justification by faith functions within [Paul's] reflection on God's plan for the world'.[38]

Stendahl has made some telling points about Paul's robust conscience. More significant for our purposes is his recognition of the links between justification and salvation-history (note the important connections in Rom. 1–4, 9–11; Gal. 2–4 and Phil. 3), whether he is right or not about the centrality of justification (see below). Käsemann has rightly been criticised for failing to interpret justification in a salvation-historical framework, and thus for allowing justification to become anthropology or unhistorical mysticism (both of which he rejects).[39]

(2) *S. K. Williams*[40]

Recognising that the 'righteousness of God' is a key motif in the letter to the Romans (a thoroughly theocentric epistle), Williams argues that the genitive 'of God' is parallelled in two other genitive phrases in the letter, *viz.* 'the faithfulness of God' and 'the truth of God'. *Dikaiosyne theou* brings to mind that aspect of God's nature which describes his steadfast adherence to what is right and fitting, his constancy and trustworthiness. Williams concludes on the basis of his study of Romans and related passages (e.g. Gal. 3) that this expression denotes God's faithfulness to his covenant promises to Abraham. The gospel that Paul preaches is the power of God that leads to final salvation for both Jew and Gentile. In the proclamation of this law-free gospel God's righteousness is being revealed and this is bound up with the consummation of his purposes in history (Rom. 1:17). According to Williams, Paul's use here of Hab. 2:4, which is nothing less than 'the prophetic summary of the gospel' and affirms that 'he who is righteous by faith shall live [that is, in God's presence, at the end]', is consistent with this interpretation of *dikaiosyne theou*.

Against Käsemann's view Williams contends that any attempt to define 'the righteousness of God' as God's power does not take seriously enough the precision of Paul's statement in 1:17. It is not the righteousness of God which he describes as God's power; rather, the gospel is God's power for salvation because God's righteousness is being revealed in it. Otherwise Paul is making the absurd statement that 'the activity of God' (*dikaiosyne theou*) is being revealed in the power of God, *viz.* the gospel. Further, the object of the verb *apokalyptein* in other Pauline texts is never an activity (Rom. 1:18; 1 Cor. 2:10; 3:13; 14:30; Gal. 1:16; 3:23). The activity to which the apostle refers in Rom. 1:17 is the *revealing* of God's righteousness, not the righteousness itself. When he wishes to speak of bestowing righteousness he typically uses *dikaioun*.

Likewise, Williams rejects the view that 'the righteousness of God' refers to a gift from God (i.e. a righteous status). This, he argues, is to confuse the apostle's language and make no distinction between *dikaiosyne* and *dikaiosyne theou*. The former can be used to describe the resulting gift, but not the latter. Paul speaks about the free gift of righteousness (Rom. 5:17) or the Gentiles having attained righteousness but he does not describe *dikaiosyne theou* as a gift or of its having been received or attained (*cf.* ch. 4; 5:17,21; 8:10; 9:30; 10:4,10; 14:17). Instead, Paul speaks of the righteousness of God being revealed, shown up, manifested, demonstrated or known (1:17; 3:5,21,25; 10:3).

On Williams' view Bultmann and others appear to go astray when they begin with the general category of 'righteousness' and consider 'the righteousness of God' as a subheading under the larger, general heading. The latter is not to be subsumed in this way for it deprives the particular expression 'the righteousness of God' of its special nuances.

In relation to Rom. 3:21–26, a passage that may be used as a test-case for Williams' interpretation, we note that God's righteousness has been manifested apart from or independently of the law, although the OT bears witness to it. At v. 22 Paul provides a more explicit statement of the key phrase *dikaiosyne theou* with special reference to Christ's involvement. Williams renders the expression as 'the righteousness of God which *is* [lit.] through the faith of Jesus Christ'. This amounts to a repetition of the verb 'manifested' from v. 21.

Pistis Iesou Christou (lit. 'the faith of Jesus Christ') has been taken to refer to 'the faith[fulness] of Jesus Christ', in which case the thought is almost synonymous with v. 24, and is a reference to Christ's faithful obedience to death on the cross. Christ proved his trustworthiness by relying on God in complete obedience to the divine will (*cf.* Rom. 5:18–19). If Paul does mean 'the faith of Christ' it becomes clear as to why he uses the perfect tense in 3:21 (*pephanerōtai*) rather than the present tense as in 1:17: the righteousness of God has been manifested in the past, in the faith/obedience of the crucified one.

The contrast between Rom. 3:20 and 3:21f. is not between two types of human initiative, two categories of human endeavour, *viz.* obey law or have faith. It is a contrast between a human endeavour and a possibility that comes from beyond, a new possibility that 'comes' with Christ. When Paul employs the terms *dikaiosyne theou* in 3:21–26 he is thinking about how God is righteous, how he has shown his righteousness in these last days. So he understands v. 26b to indicate that God *is* righteous in that he sets man right with himself, *i.e.* he justifies. Rom. 3:24–26 ties the righteousness of God directly to God's 'setting forth' the crucified Jesus as a means of propitiation. This means God has now made available to both Jews and Gentiles whose sins he had previously 'passed over' and allowed to accumulate. Paul saw in the formula *dikaiosyne theou* an allusion to God's fidelity to his covenant promise to Abraham, a promise that centres on the blessing granted to all nations, Jews and Gentiles, through the death of Christ.

Whether one agrees or not with his interpretation of *pistis Iesou Christou* as a reference to 'the faith[fulness] of Jesus Christ', in our judgment Williams' linguistic and exegetical criticisms of the above-mentioned alternatives are valid. He has made a good case for understanding *dikaiosyne theou* as 'God's faithfulness to his covenant promises to Abraham' (with *theou* being a subjective genitive).[41] His observation that many have confused the apostle's language and not picked Paul's distinction between *dikaiosyne theou* and *dikaiosyne* is most pertinent and has important theological ramifications. The latter term describes the resulting free gift of righteousness which comes to the believer who trusts in the God who is faithful to his covenant promises. Accordingly, the gift aspect of righteousness, about which the Reformers were so concerned, is accounted for by Williams under the term *dikaiosyne*, while he has given to *dikaiosyne theou* connotations that make considerable sense in their Pauline contexts and an overall salvation-historical framework.[42]

The Käsemann-oriented line of interpretation[43] into Paul's teaching on the righteousness of God helpfully brings certain emphases to the fore. We note some of these and make a number of critical observations:

First, the OT context of God acting righteously on behalf of his people is the theological presupposition of Paul's statements on God's righteousness and the justification of man. However, in equating God's righteousness with his power, and only referring to the *context* of God's covenant faithfulness, we judge that important nuances from the OT have been missed (note Williams' criticisms above).

Secondly, we agree that *dikaiosyne theou* describes neither God's essence nor man's essence before God. However, this newer interpretation has not distinguished clearly between *dikaiosyne* and *dikaiosyne theou*. The latter has been interpreted under the broader umbrella of *dikaiosyne*, and this method is faulty. With Williams *dikaiosyne theou* denotes God's faithfulness to his covenant promises to Abraham, while *dikaiosyne* (as well as the passive of *dikaioō*), points to the resulting gift, a righteous status before God. The Reformers' concerns are accounted for, on William's view, in relation to *dikaiosyne* rather than *dikaiosyne theou*.

Thirdly, while recognising that Paul's justification terminology arises out of the law court, it is helpfully interpreted within the context of personal categories and presupposing personal relationships. The notion that justification in Paul is purely a 'legal fiction' does not come to grips with either this context of personal relationships or the close conjunction of justification and sanctification in the apostle's letters.

Fourthly, there is considerable emphasis in Käsemann and others (though they vary at significant points) on God as Creator, and his righteousness as his powerful intervention in his creation. Stuhlmacher, for example, speaks of 'the faithfulness of the Creator towards his creation'. Paul, however, emphasises 'the new creation', and Brauch rightly asks whether it is appropriate to speak of a 'Pauline transfer of God's faithfulness from the covenant-people to the entire creation?' Kertelge is closer to the apostle with his emphasis on the new creation. Further, whenever the expression *dikaiosyne theou* occurs in Paul, God's action as Creator appears to be in the background, not to the fore. In a desire to avoid Bultmann's individualistic and anthropological approach, Käsemann makes mention of God's acting redemptively on behalf of all men and of the old covenant being universalised to include the whole creation. But here the danger of universalism raises its ugly head as the quote from Käsemann (cited above) shows: 'the phrase [*i.e.* the justification of the ungodly] is robbed of its full significance if it does not mean salvation for everyone and for the whole world'.[44] On this view the urgency of preaching the gospel is removed, everyday actions now have no significance in the light of a final judgment and Christian assurance which is based on God's justifying activity has evaporated.

Finally, as noted above in relation to the Stendahl-Käsemann debate, Käsemann himself did not set Paul's teaching on the righteousness of God firmly enough within the framework of salvation-history. Stendahl's criticisms at this point were telling, and subsequent writers seem to have made a number of necessary corrections.

II.   THE CENTRALITY OF JUSTIFICATION IN PAUL

A.   Introduction: A Recent Survey of the Debate

The second area in which Paul's concept of God's righteousness and his teaching on justification have been at the heart of lively, sometimes heated, theological debate over the last twenty years concerns the status of this doctrine and the search for the centre of Paul's theology. Martin Luther considered justification by faith to be the article of a standing or falling church. From the Reformation to the mid-nineteenth century this doctrine was generally held to represent the content or at least the centre of Paul's theology. But for the past 150 years many have challenged this estimate of the doctrine and given it a different status in Paul's thought. During the last two decades the debate has not only continued but become more nuanced as scholars have sought to locate precisely the central theme or the underlying principle of coherence in his theology.

Ronald Fung[45] has recently provided a helpful survey of the course of scholarly research into the place and status of justification during the modern period. We shall highlight a number of his salient points and use his survey as the point of departure for raising several further significant issues. In the nature of the case these have to be selective.

Fung claims in his review of the status of justification that four broad positions may be distinguished. They are as follows:

(1) The doctrine of justification by faith is *of merely subsidiary significance* to Paul, for the centre of his theological thought lies elsewhere. Fung lists many scholars of an earlier generation[46] who for a variety of reasons denied that justification lay at the heart of the apostle's teaching. W. Wrede claimed it was a 'polemical doctrine of Paul' that arose in his controversy with Judaism and Jewish Christianity while the true essential Pauline doctrine was redemption. Albert Schweitzer, whose celebrated comment that justification by faith was 'a subsidiary crater' in Paul's teaching, stated that the *mystical* doctrine of dying and rising again with Christ lay at the heart of Paul's thought. In more recent times W. D. Davies and E. P. Sanders have heartily endorsed Schweitzer's evaluation of the subsidiary nature of justification, while the following, to name only a few, have been chosen as the central and integrating themes in Paul's teaching: 'the necessity of faith' (R. Bultmann), 'salvation' (C. S. Anderson Scott, A. M. Hunter), 'salvation history' (K. Stendahl), 'an apocalyptic vision' (J. C. Beker), 'reconciliation' (P. Stuhlmacher, R. P. Martin), 'Jesus' death and resurrection' (C. E. B. Cranfield), 'the turning point of the ages' (C. J. A. Hickling), 'participation in Christ' (E. P. Sanders) and 'the unity of God' (E. F. Osborn).

(2) Justification by faith is of *fundamental significance and central* to Paul's theology. Wrede, Schweitzer and others were not without their critics who, for a variety of reasons, argued that Paul's doctrine of justification by faith lay at the heart of his gospel and was not simply used in polemical situations. G. Bornkamm, for example, asserted that Paul 'expounds and develops the *Christian gospel as the gospel of justification by faith alone*'. Bornkamm added that 'his whole preaching, even when it says nothing expressly about justification, can be properly understood only when taken in closest connection with that doctrine and related to it'.[47] Others, such as J. G. Machen, G. Schrenk, H. D. Wendland, H. Conzelmann, E. Käsemann and J. I. Packer on the Protestant side, as well as O. Kuss and K. Kertelge on the Roman Catholic side, endorsed justification as the theological centre of gravity in Paul's main epistles and regarded it as of more than passing or polemical value since it dealt with the real need of man in his relation to God.[48]

(3) Justification by faith is *one of a number of formulations and metaphors* used by Paul to describe the new relationship of man to God in Christ. This third view took a mediating position, dissenting from those who regarded justification as of merely subsidiary significance in Paul and

from the opposite position which accorded to the doctrine the central place. J. Jeremias, for example, regarded justification as one of 'a multitude of illustrations', originally taken from the judicial sphere, which describes God's grace in baptism in terms of unreserved pardon.

(4) The fourth position reviewed by Fung is one which he describes as 'a modification of the Reformation view of Paul's doctrine of justification as the centre and content of Paul's gospel'.[49] Advocates regard *justification by faith as central* to Paul's gospel, but *as set within a salvation-historical framework of the redemptive work of Christ.* In other words, several writers who stand within the Reformed tradition agree that the central place in Pauline theology belongs to the doctrine of justification since it deals with the fundamental issues of God's relationship with man. However, they are concerned lest justification be unhinged from its historical moorings so that it becomes inconsistent with both Paul's teaching specifically and that of the Bible as a whole. As a result, F. F. Bruce, G. E. Ladd, R. B. Gaffin and R. Fung himself stress that this doctrine must be interpreted within a *heilsgeschichtlich* framework that focuses on God's work of new creation in Christ.

B. Some Further Questions and Responses

At the conclusion of his survey Fung observes that the primary issue in the modern debate on the status of justification in Paul's thought is, to use K. Kertelge's words, 'whether the doctrine of justification plays only a subordinate role in the totality of a doctrine of redemption which proceeds on a multiple track, or whether, from its basic intention, the central place in Pauline theology belongs to it'.[50] But this raises a series of more fundamental questions: In what sense is it correct to speak of a theme in the apostle's teaching as being central? Indeed, what is meant by the term 'centre'? Is it an underlying principle of coherence in his theology? A convenient label by which one might describe or even summarise the apostle's teaching? A yardstick, a canon by which one might determine whether other material or documents are genuinely Pauline? In fact, is it appropriate to speak of a 'centre' in Pauline theology at all? And if so, then what are the criteria for determining such a centre?[51]

J. Reumann has rightly pointed out that there are difficulties in speaking of 'the centre' (however this is defined) of someone's theology unless it is expressly described as such (and followed) by the writer himself, while to refer to 'a centre' is illogical and introduces the notion of a cluster of themes in which some may be more significant than others.[52] Further, the noun 'centre' and its cognate 'central' have been used in various ways in this debate: they can describe, for instance, what is basic to a writer's thinking, however infrequently mentioned by him. An example of this is C. H. Dodd's reference to the OT as the 'substructure' of Paul's theology. Reumann has suggested that a theme may be 'the centre' because it has been inherited by the apostle, e.g. his teaching on the cross of Christ; or because it has been uniquely developed or sharpened by him as, for instance, the notion that justification is 'by faith, not by works'. A motif may be central inasmuch as it is the basis on which other teaching stands or because it is the final goal to which events move.

In a methodological investigation, H. W. Boers addresses 'the Problem of the Coherent Centre of Paul's Thought'.[53] Starting from the premise that Paul's thinking was not systematic (an incorrect premise, in our judgment, for the issue is whether his letters contain a *systematic exposition* of his theology), but was directly related to the pastoral needs of his congregations, Boers takes up the question of contemporary scholarship: what is the 'Pauline centre'? After surveying a number of recent scholarly options as to what was 'the underlying principle of coherence' in Paul's theology, Boers concludes that it is whatever 'links all the themes structurally. What holds everything together, syntactically and paradigmatically, is the grammar of his thought, constituted. . . . by its syntactic and semantic components'.[54] But Boers' own tentative conclusion is unsatisfactory: the 'coherent centre' is 'contradiction at its most fundamental level'.[55] Perhaps, he argues, this is what underlies or forms the sub-structure of Paul's thought!

Ernst Käsemann had earlier expounded the centrality of Paul's *dikaiosyne theou* and the justifying of the ungodly in a comprehensive way. This teaching is the 'theme which dominates the whole of his theology'. While recognising that for Paul justification by faith is 'a fighting doctrine, directed against Judaism', Käsemann argues that 'the struggle which it represents is not a merely anti-Jewish affair and is not superseded even today'.[56] For Käsemann, however, the centrality of justification has other connotations. It is not only the centre of Scripture (*als Mitte der Schrift*), but also the single formula which maintains both the historical-apocalyptic and existential-eschatological dimensions of history, as well as being the legitimating principle of the apostle's theology.[57] By means of *Sachkritik* ('content criticism')[58] Käsemann concludes that the doctrine of the justification of the ungodly must function as the 'deciding criterion', the *norma normans*. According to R. P. Martin, it 'informed and controlled his [Käsemann's] pre-understanding, his selection of the material, his exegesis, his assignment of suitable life-settings and his conclusions throughout'.[59]

Underlying the Pauline teaching on justification by faith, according to Käsemann, is Christology. This does not primarily refer to Jesus' divinity and/ or humanity but is rather a shorthand term for the 'theology of the cross', i.e. the revelation of God's righteousness in the cross, by which the world is defeated and on account of which the believer is challenged and enabled to live by faith.

Not only does justification serve as the criterion by which other doctrines are judged by Käsemann to be important, it also functions as a 'canon within the canon' so that documents within the Pauline corpus, not to say the rest of the NT, are judged according to their proximity to this cardinal teaching of the apostle.

Many of Käsemann's conclusions have rightly been rejected. While it is one thing to say that justification is central to Paul's theology, it is another matter to suggest that it dominates the whole of his theology or is the deciding criterion by which documents are judged to be post-Pauline or down-graded in the canon below others. Käsemann's methods and conclusions have been subjected to strong criticism by both Protestant[60] and Roman Catholic[61] scholars alike. He has not only banished 'important lines and basic thoughts of Scripture into powerless darkness', to use Maier's phrase, but has understood the notion of 'the centre' of Paul's teaching in too comprehensive a manner. In our judgment there is a better approach which recognises the fundamental nature of justification (appropriately defined and understood) and at the same time retains the whole canon of Scripture (see below).

C. 'Reconciliation' as the Centre?

(1) *A Case Study*

Within the broad stream of evangelicalism, Ralph P. Martin, in his search for the centre of Paul's theology, expresses dissatisfaction not only with the conclusions of many previous writers (including Käsemann), but also, and more significantly, with their failure to provide adequate criteria for determining what is central. He claims that there was no way of escape from the dilemma, and that Paul's theology was to be treated as fragmentary responses to pastoral situations delivered *ad hoc*, unless adequate criteria (which could be carefully tested) were found and judiciously applied to the material. Martin discerns five basic patterns in Paul's theological teaching. Any theme which is central to his thinking has to take these five factors into account:

(i)   There is an insistence upon the primacy of God's grace, which initiates and effects man's salvation;

(ii)   God has acted in human history in the person of his Son, Jesus Christ, and his work has had repercussions that affect both the cosmic scene and mysterious spiritual intelligences, as well as man;

(iii)   The cross is crucial to Paul's salvation teaching, and equally crucial as the instrument in the sinner's self-denial (*cf*. Gal. 2:20);

(iv)   The gap between the historical 'is' and the ethical 'ought' needs to be bridged; and

(v)   Finally, Paul's theology has to be set 'in the context of his own self-description . . . both [as] a Christian and a missionary-apostle'.[62] For Paul, word and life go together.

Martin follows and develops the lead of T. W. Manson and P. Stuhlmacher, and believes it is the overall theme of 'reconciliation' which takes each of these factors into account. Reconciliation 'can be presented as an interpretative key to Paul's theology; and if we are pressed to suggest a simple term that summarises his message, the word reconciliation will be the "chief theme" or "centre" of his missionary and pastoral thought and practice'.[63] In a later article Martin set forth his basic thesis, the first section of which is as follows:

> Paul's soteriology and eschatology — the twin distinctives of Paul's theology are linked by their common anchorage. They are both fideistic and christological through and through. His ground of salvation and confidence for the future are centred in the person of Jesus Christ, the reconciler of the Gentile world and the hope of Israel.[64]

Forty years earlier Vincent Taylor had called reconciliation 'the best New Testament word to describe the purpose of the Atonement'. Peter Stuhlmacher,[65] whose contribution to *dikaiosyne theou* (as we have seen) was significant, came to see that the basis for Paul's teaching on justification lay in Jesus' atoning death. Paul's gospel of justification expressed who Jesus was and where the crown of his messianic work of reconciliation was focused, *viz.* in his substitutionary sacrifice on the cross. Stuhlmacher views *dikaiosyne theou* in its continuity with the OT and the Jewish backgrounds and with reconciliation as the overarching theme. He states: 'the gospel of reconciliation in Christ' or 'the Versöhnung of God with his creation through the sending of Messiah Jesus Christ' is 'the centrepiece of the New Testament'.[66]

Reconciliation has deep meaning in our age of estrangement and over the last several decades has had a wide and growing use. It is a metaphor drawn from human relations rather than the lawcourt (*cf.* forensic justification) and is used in the Pauline letters to speak of reconciliation between humanity and God and of persons with each other.[67]

Martin recognised that the reconciliation (*katallag–*) word-group is not prominent in Paul's writings (it turns up in only four major passages) and that it is not used with the same nuance wherever it appears. However, he contends that it provides a suitable umbrella — it is a broader category than justification — under which Paul's *kerygma* and its practical outworking may be set. Further, reconciliation is closely tied in with the historical events of Jesus' passion and with moral transformation in human lives.[68] After an exegetical examination of Rom. 5:1–11; 2 Cor. 5:18–21; Col. 1:18–23 and Eph. 2:12–19 Martin concludes that the far-ranging and distinctive ideas of these passages 'covering cosmic, personal, societal and ethnic areas of our human story, are . . . part of a pattern . . . There is an emerging design and a coherent picture . . . the most adequate and meaningful title for the resulting product is "reconciliation" '.[69] 'Reconciliation is indeed a central, organising theme in Paul's theology'.[70]

(2) *An Evaluation*

The arguments in favour of 'reconciliation' as the centre of Paul's have convinced a number of contemporary scholars. At the same time this proposal has not gone unchallenged. By way of response the following points ought to be noted:

First, the term 'reconciliation' is clearly related to the saving work of Christ in Paul and can be understood on a broad canvas (e.g. reconciliation of the world) as well as in personal terms. However, the paucity of references to the word-group in the Pauline corpus (*katalassō*, 'reconcile': six times; *katallagē*, 'reconciliation': four times; *apokatallassō*, 'reconcile': three times) raises doubts about its possible centrality in the apostle's teaching and suggests that reconciliation is but one element, albeit an important one, in the NT lexicon to describe the work of Christ in relation to the world and in harmony with the divine purpose. Martin claims in his monograph as well as in his more recent article on Rom. 5:1–11 that the notion of 'reconciliation' is on view when atonement vocabulary (e.g. *hilaskomai*) as well as the language of peace (Rom. 5:1) are used. But this raises the question as to whether Martin has varied or broadened his definition of 'reconciliation' in order to meet his earlier critieria.[71]

Secondly, it may be helpful to speak of reconciliation as an overarching or 'umbrella' term. However, it is inappropriate to regard it as the 'interpretative key' or the underlying principle of coherence which links together the major themes of Paul's theology. Indeed, it is questionable whether any motif fulfils this role in Paul's teaching.

Thirdly, while the two concepts of justification and reconciliation contain elements which are common, it is incorrect to speak of them as being the same (*cf.* Reumann) or describing the same act (C. K. Barrett). On the other hand, in the light of our earlier discussion about the meaning of 'the righteousness of God', it is tendentious to refer to justification in essentially negative and non-personal categories, and to reconciliation in essentially positive ones (*cf.* Martin).

There are positive and negative elements relating to both. Perhaps it is best to regard the two notions as functioning at different levels, with justification providing the *basis of the relationship with God*, a point which Martin himself seems to concede when he acknowledges that God vindicates himself and offers "justification" . . . as a ground on which he extends the grace of reconciliation'.[72]

D.   Justification as Fundamental or Foundational⁻

We are led to conclude that justification is not the 'centre' of Paul's theology in the sense that it is dominant, all-embracing or the underlying principle of coherence by which the other major themes are interlocked. In our view, no Pauline motif fills this role in spite of the many scholarly claimants for such a position. (This assertion needs to be tested further, including an evaluation as to whether the 'in Christ' motif meets the necessary criteria.)[73] Rather, justification is foundational to Paul's gospel (*cf.* Rom. 1:16–17) in that it deals with the basic issue of a person's entering into a right relationship with God. (This is not to deny that justification has ramifications regarding the continuance in that relationship.) It is for Paul God's 'fundamental act of blessing, for it both saves from the past and secures for the future'.[74] However, justification must be understood within the redemptive-historical framework of Paul's thought (note the discussion above about the righteousness of God referring to God's faithfulness to his covenant promises to Abraham); if it is unhinged from this context serious misunderstandings arise.

As God's foundational blessing which is linked to entry into the Christian life, other blessings flow from it. Accordingly, one may acknowledge the interconnections between justification and other Pauline motifs noted by J. I. Packer: (a) The doctrine of justification lies at the heart of Paul's gospel as expounded in Romans (*cf.* esp. 1:16–17; 3:21–26); (b) Paul writes personally about his conversion in the language of justification (Gal. 2:15–21; 2 Cor. 5:16–21; Phil. 3:4–14), while his need in relation to the law's condemnation is expressed in terms of God's justifying sentence in Christ (Rom. 8:1f; Gal. 3:19–4:7); (c) Justification has an eschatological significance because the judgment of the last day is brought into the present with its final verdict. Justification is linked with both adoption and heirship (Gal. 4:4ff.; Rom. 8:14ff.), while according to Rom. 5:1–2 justification brings peace with God (because sins are forgiven) and the hope of God's glory (because the sinner is accepted as righteous); (d) It is the basic reference-point of the apostle's doctrine of salvation[75] and (e) It is the key to his philosophy of history, for the language of justification appears to be central to God's dealing with mankind through Adam and Christ (*cf.* Rom. 5:16ff.), and with Jews and Gentiles (Rom. 9–11).

If justification is foundationally tied to entry into the Christian life (without minimising its eschatological element; see below), so that it is the fundamental blessing of God from which other blessings flow, then several consequences follow. First, in contemporary teaching and preaching the term 'gospel' has become either so vague or broad in its meaning that it includes almost anything (it is sometimes used synonymously with 'Christianity' as understood sociologically). Justification lay at the heart of Paul's gospel, since it focused on God's saving work in Christ with reference to man's basic need of being out of a right relationship with his Creator (Rom. 1:16–18); in the contemporary context there ought to be a return to that preaching of the gospel which focuses on Christ's saving work in relation to God's justifying the ungodly. Secondly, it is only through a proper understanding of justification by faith alone that we are able to have a true estimate of sin and a proper grasp of the significance of the cross. Thirdly, with the loss of clear teaching on God's justifying work there has been a loss of Christian assurance on the part of many church members. Good works, even miraculous good works, have intruded as Christians have looked to these to provide the grounds for their day-to-day confidence and assurance.

III. THE SANDERS DEBATE

A. The Substance

The meaning, place and significance of the Pauline teaching on righteousness and justification have been questioned afresh with the recent publication of several significant theological works by E. P. Sanders. The first of these, *Paul and Palestinian Judaism*, appeared in 1977 and was described as the most important work on its subject to appear in a generation. This volume gave much more space to Palestinian Judaism than to Paul, but six years later with the publication of *Paul, the Law and the Jewish People* the imbalance was redressed. Sanders has provided, it has been argued, a new perspective on Paul. His basic claim is that the picture of first-century Judaism from the apostle's writing is 'historically false, not simply inaccurate in part but fundamentally mistaken'.[76] For more than a hundred years the majority of NT scholars have maintained a fundamental antithesis between Paul and Judaism, especially rabbinic Judaism. Two such influential scholars, Rudolf Bultmann and Ernst Käsemann, have read Paul through Lutheran eyes, regarded justification by faith as the central and organising theological principle and viewed Paul as rejecting a perverted attempt on the part of the Jews of his day to use the law as the means of earning righteousness by good works. Although Jewish scholars and experts in early Judaism had protested against such interpretations, regarding them as a parody of first century Judaism, their protests had been rejected. They had argued that the emphasis in rabbinic Judaism was on God's goodness and generosity, his invitation to repentance with its offer of forgiveness. Paul was interpreted by the majority as presenting Judaism as 'coldly and calculatingly legalistic, a system of "works" righteousnness, where salvation is *earned* by the *merit* of good works'.[77]

Against the scholarly tendency to seize on certain statements that appeal to Christian prejudice and neglect others that put Palestinian Judaism in a better light, Sanders attempts to compare whole patterns of religion, not particular themes. As a result he builds up a different picture of Palestinian Judaism at the time of Paul, under the broad category of soteriology, which he calls 'covenantal nomism'. To the first century Jew Israel's covenant relation with God was basic to his sense of national identity and his understanding of religion. The one God had chosen Israel to be his particular people and to enjoy a special relationship with him. The law was given as an expression of this covenant and was intended to maintain and regulate the relationship. Righteousness referred to conduct appropriate to the relationship and in accord with the law. Sanders makes the point again and again that obedience to the law in Judaism was not thought of as the means of *entering* the convenant or of establishing the relationship with God, but the means of *maintaining* the covenant relationship — not for 'getting in' but for 'staying in'.

Furthermore, Paul and Judaism do not stand in contrast as so many contemporary interpreters claim. Sanders makes the following critical statement: 'on the point at which many have found the decisive contrast between Paul and Judaism — grace and works — Paul is in agreement with Palestinian Judaism . . . salvation is by grace but judgment is according to works; works are the condition of remaining "in", but they do not earn salvation'.[78]

Where then do the differences lie between Paul and Palestinian Judaism and why is the apostle critical of Judaism? Put simply, Sanders says the difference is a salvation-historical one. It is not because 'Jews seek to save themselves and become self-righteous about it'.[79] Rather, it is because they are dependent upon 'their status as God's covenant people who possess the law and as a result miss out on the better righteousness based solely on believing participation in Christ'.[80] The difference between Jewish righteousness and God's righteousness in Christ 'is not the distinction between merit and grace but between two dispensations. There is a righteousness which comes by law, but it is now worth nothing because of a different dispensation . . . It is this concrete fact of *Heilsgeschichte* which makes the other righteousness wrong'.[81]

In relation to Paul's testimony regarding his former life in Judaism (Phil. 3:2–11) Sanders rejects the suggestion that 'the righteousness which comes from the law' (v. 9) is a 'meritorious achievement which allows one to demand reward from God and is thus a denial of grace'. He claims that the apostle was critical of his former life, not because he was guilty of 'the attitudinal sin of self-righteousness' but because he 'put his confidence in something other than faith [*sic*!] in Jesus Christ'.[82] The expression in Phil. 3:9, 'my own righteousness' does not designate what we call today 'self-righteousness'. Rather, it is that righteousness which comes by law and is 'the peculiar result of being an observant Jew, which is *in and of itself a good thing*'.[83] 'The only thing that is wrong with the old righteousness seems to be that it is not the new one; it has no fault which is described in other terms'.[84] So, according to Sanders, Paul's attacks on the Judaizers' teaching are to be explained simply as a dogmatic denial: Judaism is wrong because it is not Christianity.

D. An Evaluation

Sanders has been commended for questioning contemporary reconstructions of first-century Palestinian Judaism and for his insistence that whole patterns of religion (e.g. in Judaism and Paul) should be compared, and not simply particular themes. Often in the past statements within Judaism that appealed to Christian prejudice had been seized upon, to the neglect of others that put Palestinian Judaism in a better light. Sanders' handling of both primary Jewish materials and secondary literature has been impressive, while his focus on soteriology in Judaism has been regarded as broad enough to cover all the essential points in this religion thus enabling one to understand its overall thrust.

Further, it is true that many contemporary students of Paul have interpreted the apostle through Lutheran and existential eyes with the result that Palestinian Judaism has been seen in a wholly negative light within a law-grace dichotomy.[85] Some, though not all, of those conclusions are incorrect. Sanders' views on the centrality of the 'in Christ' motif in Paul and its relation to justification by faith are to be seriously questioned. Nevertheless, his criticisms of some presentations of the centrality of justification by faith are pertinent. And further, he is quite right in pointing out that Paul (like Palestinian Judaism) was particularly concerned about the issue of remaining in the covenant.

But Sanders' assertion that Paul and Palestinian Judaism do not stand in contrast, as so many contemporary interpreters claim, has to be rejected.[86] For, first, if we weigh the emphases of the two systems — and this is a difficult task since one has to work on impressions — Palestinian Judaism appears to be centred on 'works-righteousness', while Paul's focus is on grace. R. H. Gundry admits that this is an historical judgment, not necessarily a theological one. But in Palestinian Judaism the law is stretched, applied and pulled, as rabbis build a fence around it to prevent pious Jews from inadvertently breaking it. Paul, by contrast, moves in the direction of freedom of conscience, not legal definition.[87] Secondly, against Sanders, Paul is not in agreement with Palestinian Judaism, for it is not the case that for both 'salvation is by grace but judgment is according to works; works are the condition of remaining "in", but they do not earn salvation'.[88] There are significant differences. Paul, who in Galatians and Romans, [89] at least, is dealing with the issue of staying in the covenant, 'repeatedly identifies faith and rejects works as the principle of continuance in salvation'.[90] It is the activity of God, not human effort, which is the ground of one's perseverance. Human effort is the effect, not the cause (2 Cor. 1:24; 3:5; Phil. 1:6; 2:12f.). Sanders claims that Paul's demand for good works from Christians is evidence that: (1) salvation is by grace, and (2) judgment is according to works which are the condition of remaining in the covenant. However, for the apostle good works are *evidence* of having received God's grace through faith. They are not *instrumental* for maintaining grace. 'For Paul, then, getting in and staying in are covered by the seamless robe of faith as opposed to works, with the result that works come in as evidential rather than instrumental'.[91]

For Sanders the differences between Paul and Palestinian Judaism are to be explained in terms of a salvation-historical perspective: the reason the apostle is critical of Jewish righteousness is not because it has to do with merit rather

than grace. Instead, the righteousness which comes by law is now worth
nothing because of a different dispensation. 'It is this concrete fact of
Heilsgeschichte which makes the other righteousness wrong'.[92] Paul's attacks
on the Judaizers' teaching are to be explained simply as a dogmatic denial:
Judaism is wrong because it is not Christianity.[93] But Sanders is only partly
right in interpreting the distinction as a dispensational shift. Two Pauline
passages which focus on righteousness bear out this point:

(1) The first is *Phil. 3:2–11*. The key expression in this paragraph is found in
v. 9, 'a righteousness of my own that comes from the law' (*emēn
dikaiosynēn tēn ek nomou*). Sanders rejects the view that this expression
designates what we call today 'self-righteousness'. Instead, it describes
that righteousness which comes by law and is 'the peculiar result of being
an observant Jew, which is *in and of itself a good thing*'.[94] But against
Sanders the expression is about 'attitudinal self-righteousness'. It
describes Paul's own previous moral achievement — not simply the
righteousness which he possesses but that which he has acquired —
gained by obeying the law, which was intended to establish a claim upon
God, particularly in view of the final judgment. In Phil. 3:2–11, although
Paul begins by recounting the privileges of his Jewish heritage (v. 5), he
quickly moves on to describe his personal achievements (vv. 5,6) in which
he had previously placed his confidence (v. 4). Sanders' belief that Phil.
3:6,9 indicate righteousness by the law is attainable rests on his failure to
recognise that Paul speaks from the standpoint of a *false human estimate*:
'If anyone *thinks* . . ., I more'.[95]

There is a shift in dispensations in Phil. 3, and clearly salvation-history
does play a part, as Sanders recognises. But, as R. H. Gundry rightly
argues, 'Salvation-history does not account for all that Paul says, much
less for the passion with which he says it; we are dealing with an
autobiographical as well as a dispensational shift'.[96] The three *kata*-
expressions ('according to . . .') of v. 6 point to individual performance
alongside Jewish status. A zeal for the law was good, but not the self-
righteousness that resulted. Gundry lists eight items in vv. 2–11 (including
'boasting', 'thinking to have confidence', his 'considering' past achievements as gain) which are clearly attitudinal elements and which show that
'self-righteousness' is an accurate description of a significant element in
Paul's previous attitudes.

(2) Commenting on *Rom. 9:30–10:13*, Sanders acknowledges that Israel
failed to fulfil the law, not because they tried to fulfil it (*i.e.* by works
rather than faith), but because they lacked faith in Christ — again an
appeal to a dispensational shift. Accordingly, 'their own righteousness'
(10:3) means 'that righteousness which the Jews are alone privileged to
obtain' rather than 'self-righteousness which consists in individuals'
presenting their merits as a claim upon God'.[97] But 'Paul is not criticizing
the Jews' unbelief in Christ *instead of* their attempt to perform the law,
but he is criticizing their unbelief *as caused by* an attempt to perform the
law'.[98] It is this latter which leads to self-righteousness, boasting and an
obedience that ends in or arises out of a man-made religion.

Sanders' interpretation of other Pauline righteousness and justification
passages in relation to Palestinian Judaism have been subjected to similar
critique.[99] The conclusion reached is that Paul rejected Judaism and Judaistic

Christianity not simply because he was convinced God had revealed his Son Jesus in him (Gal. 1:15–16), but also 'because of a conviction that works-righteousness lay at the heart of Judaism and Judaistic Christianity and that it would corrupt what he had come to believe concerning God's grace in Jesus Christ'.[100] Thus, although E. P. Sanders has placed the NT scholarly world in his debt by challenging many presuppositions about interpreting Paul and Palestinian Judaism and their respective teaching on salvation, arguing that whole patterns of religion are to be compared, not particular themes, I conclude that his new perspective on Paul is flawed and that his major conclusions regarding Paul's teaching on righteousness and justification are incorrect.

IV. JUSTIFICATION BY FAITH, JUDGMENT ACCORDING TO WORKS

The fourth issue of the last two decades in which there has been lively if not heated theological debate arising out of Paul's teaching on justification is the apparent contradiction between his doctrine of justification by faith and his affirmation of a future judgment according to works. The apostle uses justification language to affirm in the strongest way possible that God is for us, that he takes our side contrary to all our deserts or expectations (Rom. 4:5; 5:6–11; 8:31–34). Yet in the final judgment God will judge us according to our works (Rom. 2:12; 14:10; 1 Cor. 3:15; 4:5; 2 Cor. 5:10; *cf.* 1 Cor. 1:8; Col. 1:22; Phil. 1:10). The controversy is not a new one, for it arose in the early church, and a succession of scholars from the time of Origen and Augustine onward grappled with the issue. But it has continued to vex interpreters, as a survey of recent approaches to the problem will reveal.[101] For the sake of convenience we shall present and attempt to evaluate the most significant of these approaches before suggesting ways forward to a possible solution.

A. K. P. Donfried[102]

Donfried's lecture in 1974 on justification and the last judgment in Paul, which anticipated some of E. P. Sanders' conclusions published three years later, developes Käsemann's thesis that the righteousness of God represents both gift and demand. As such this righteousness partakes of both the present and the future with obedience the link between the two. Within Paul's writings there is the tension between the 'already' and the 'not yet'. 'For the justified man salvation is not yet completed in the present; it has still to be consummated and fulfilled on the last day.'[103] After an examination of the relevant terminology Donfried discerns the following 'Pauline pattern':

(1) *justification* — a past event, which has present implications through sanctification;

(2) *sanctification* — a present event, dependent upon a past event, justification, which has future implications, *viz.* salvation;

(3) *salvation* — a future event, already anticipated and partially experienced in justification and sanctification and clearly dependent upon them.[104]

Donfried's thesis regarding the relationship of justification to last judgment is as follows: for Paul the person who receives the gospel of God's grace is justified and will receive the gift of final salvation at the last judgment. But if that person 'makes a mockery of God's gift by his gross abuse and disobedience, such a one will not receive the gift of salvation at the last judgment and he will suffer the wrath of God . . . the final criterion at the last judgment is, for Paul, not how many good works man has performed . . . but whether . . . [he] has held fast and remained obedient to his new life in Christ'.[105]

While we must recognise that Donfried has provided some fresh insights, his solution with its three-fold Pauline pattern has been criticised at a number of significant points. First, it is argued that the justification, sanctification and salvation terminology does not fall into a neat past-present-future schema. Sanctification can refer to a past event (1 Cor. 6:11; *cf.* 1:2) as well as the future (1 Thes. 5:23), while some salvation texts are taken as pointing to the past (*cf.* Rom. 8:24; 1 Cor. 15:2) or present (1 Cor. 1:18).[106] Most importantly, Donfried's presentation fails to account for the apostle's future justification statements (Rom. 2:13; 8:33; Gal. 5:4–5; 1 Cor. 4:4–5 by implication). Justification language appears in Paul in relation to the beginning of the Christian life *and* to its final consummation.

B. E. P. Sanders

As already indicated, Sanders has contended that the apostle is in agreement with Palestinian Judaism in that 'salvation is by grace but judgment is according to works; works are the condition of remaining "in", but they do not earn salvation'. But it was argued above that for Paul good works are *evidence* of having received God's grace through faith. They are not *instrumental* for maintaining grace. The material Sanders cites from the literature of Palestinian Judaism shows overwhelmingly that good works are *a condition as well as a sign* of remaining in the covenant. For Paul good works are only (albeit significantly) a sign of staying in; faith is the necessary and sufficient condition of remaining in, as well as of getting into, the covenant.[107]

Sanders' interpretation of Paul, however, does not solve our present question regarding the apparent contradiction between justification by faith and judgment according to works. Like Donfried he regards justification as an initiatory event which does not contradict the idea of a future judgment according to works in either its negative or positive aspects. But he too has failed to account for Paul's future justification statements (Rom. 2:13; 8:33, etc.; see above).[108] Justification carries with it the assurance of deliverance from the wrath to come (Rom. 5:9f.; *cf.* 1 Thes. 1:10; 5:9). For the believer the last judgment has been anticipated and the verdict of acquittal already pronounced (Rom. 8:30–34). This message of eschatological finality cannot be reconciled with the warnings of a coming judgment in the way Sanders suggests.

C. N. M. Watson[109]

The important article of N. M. Watson, in which he seeks to resolve the tension in Paul between justification by faith and judgment according to works, builds on and refines the studies of E. Synofzik and W. Joest.[110] The former had collected all the references to *judgment* and *recompense* in Paul's letters, and arranged them in accordance with the different types of passages in which they occurred, eight in all. Synofzik concluded that Paul had integrated this judgment-recompense motif into his own theology and used it for his own purposes (see for example Rom. 2). However, in answer to the question, 'What is the place of this motif of judgment in Paul's theology?' Synofzik claimed that the apostle used it exclusively as a tool in his argument (*'Argumentationsmittel'*), directing his readers to the consequences for their present conduct which flow from it. He was not interested in a detailed description of the more precise circumstances of the judgment or its content or mode. But this exclusively 'functional' interpretation leaves too many unanswered questions. For example: did Paul believe in a future judgment? If not, then this motif is a poor tool in his argument (*'Argumentationsmittel'*), since he has urged Christians to godly behaviour on the basis of a future reality which he believes will not occur. If, on the other hand, he did believe in this future judgment, would Christians be judged on the basis of works when they had already been justified by faith? How is the original dilemma resolved? Further, as Watson has rightly pointed out, the presence of a practical (paraenetic or polemical) aim does not invalidate in any way the doctrinal statement. Synofzik, with his purely 'functional' interpretation, has failed to show how justification by faith and judgment according to works represent a unified concept in Paul.

Watson himself, noting Synofzik's insight that the judgment-recompense motif appears in different types of Pauline passages, and refining W. Joest's dialectical solution, argues that the apostle directed his message of justification and the warning of judgment to different addressees. Paul's warnings of judgment to come were consistently addressed to those who were puffed up, guilty of presumption and living in a state of illusion (e.g. the Corinthians), and were intended 'to demolish assurance'. Again and again there are indications in these passages that 'Paul does not intend the message of judgment to be his last word to his readers but rather as the word they need to hear so long as they remain in a state of illusion'.[111] On the other hand, there is at the same time the assurance 'that for those who are living in penitent faith the judgment will hold no terrors'.[112] According to this view, justification by faith is the apostle's 'ultimate and unshakable word of divine address', while judgment according to works is a penultimate word, contextually determined and addressed to those who presume upon God's grace.[113]

Watson is clearly right in speaking about the different epistolary situations to which Paul's letters were directed. It is all too easy to regard them as addressed to the same readers in the same context. However, when the apostle writes about the future judgment according to works his word is addressed to *all* in the congregation. It is not as though this future judgment will apply only to some in the church. 2 Cor. 5:10 makes this clear. The apostle, addressing the Corinthians, asserts: 'We must *all* appear before the judgment seat of Christ, that *each one* may receive what is due him for the things done while in the body, whether good or bad.' The words 'we all' and 'each one' include not only Paul, his colleagues and the Corinthians, but also all other Christians. The word of judgment and recompense applies to all, for Paul speaks of that future day not only negatively by way of warning, but also positively, as a hope of reward or commendation for obedience (*cf.* Rom.

2:6–7; 1 Cor. 4:5). It is not simply the case that 'for those who are living in penitent faith the judgment will hold no terrors'; for such Christians there will be a reward or commendation on the basis of their godly deeds. The word of judgment according to works cannot therefore be simply a penultimate word as Watson would have us believe. At the future judgment every believer will be judged according to his or her works. As a penultimate word for Watson it seems only to function as a device. Certainly, as he claims, the message of judgment is intended as a warning for those who are 'puffed up', guilty of presumption and living in a state of illusion. The word for them is to turn back to the living God in repentance and faith. That faith ought then to be evidenced in godly actions. But the message of judgment and recompense is also directed to the humble and contrite Christian as a word of warning, that he or she may truly fear God and live in a way that pleases him; it is also a word of encouragement with its hope of reward and commendation for obedience. The message of judgment- recompense is not to 'demolish all assurance' but only that assurance which is improperly based.

Further, as already noted in relation to Donfried and Sanders, it is not only the judgment passages that seem to clash with Paul's teaching about justification by faith, but also certain justification statements themselves. The dialectical solution does not resolve this issue. Even less does it deal with the dilemma of 1 Cor. 4:3–5, where justification and vindicating future judgment are equated.

We conclude, then, that the apparent contradiction between Paul's teaching on justification by faith and judgment according to works is not resolved by Watson's dialectical solution. The word of recompense-judgment is not tied in theologically with the message of justification by faith, for in Watson's schema the former ends up being only functional. At this point it is subject to the same criticisms as Synofzik's proposal.

D. K. R. Snodgrass[114]

A solution of a different kind has been proposed by K. R. Snodgrass who claims: 'Judgment according to works is not the contradiction of justification by faith, but its presupposition'.[115] Building on the work of K. P. Donfried, Snodgrass argues that the obedient Christian who remains in Christ will be saved on the last day. Paul frequently mentions the theme of judgment according to works without it apparently causing any difficulty. He expects a final judgment for Christians which can result in salvation or wrath. Focusing on Rom. 2, which he seeks to fit into the framework of Paul's theology, Snodgrass thinks that God grants eternal life or salvation to those who live obediently in accordance with the revelation they have received. This is not a doctrine of works righteousness, but a description of those who, by doing the good, show that their obedience is the direct result of the activity of God.

The purpose of Romans has to do with the vindication of God. Chap. 2 with its focus on the end-time reward and punishment from God fits this theme of vindication well. The passage is not about justification but judgment according to works. Because Paul really did believe in this, then 2:7,10,13,14–15,26 all point to the granting of eternal life or salvation to those who live obediently in accordance with the revelation they have received.[116]

Snodgrass acknowledges that several difficulties in his interpretation have to be resolved. First, perfection is not required of the 'doer' of Rom. 2 to whom God gives life. Such a requirement has validity only when the issue of 'works righteousness' is in view, i.e. when people attempt to present themselves as righteous in order to be accepted by God. Godly obedience is the issue, not perfection. 'There is nothing in Romans 2 to suggest that perfection is required for salvation.'[117] But has Snodgrass really solved this difficulty, or left us with a double standard, viz. perfection when it is works-righteousness that is in view, 'non-perfection' when it is only obedience?

Secondly, do not statements such as Rom. 3:20 ('From works of the law no flesh will be justified before him') contradict Snodgrass' handling of Rom. 2? In response to this criticism it is suggested that *erga nomou* ('works of the law') is a negative expression for Paul which falls within the sphere of 'works righteousness', whereas the terms used in Rom. 2 (including *ergon*) all refer to godly obedience. However, there is considerable scholarly dispute about this, not least of which is the function of Rom. 2 in the context of 1:18–3:20.

Finally, Paul believed that 'salvation is to the doers' and it is appropriate to understand him as referring to this issue in Rom. 2 which is concerned about judgment according to works, not justification by faith. Snodgrass ties faith and obedience together and claims, quite correctly, that a new creation for Paul meant a life of faith working through love (Gal. 5:6; *cf.* 6:15; 1 Cor. 7:19). But is Rom. 2 dealing with the eschatological judgment according to works? If so, who are those being judged? Further, is it appropriate to understand the chapter within the suggested purpose of Romans regarding the vindication of God?

E. A Linguistic Solution?

Having acknowledged what he judges to be the basic insights of K. P. Donfried and E. P. Sanders into the relationship of justification and judgment in Paul, C. H. Cosgrove tackles the problem left unresolved by them, *viz.* how the language of justification can be applied to 'both the moment of reconciliation through Christ's death and the ultimate vindication of the believer's works in the final judgment'.[118] He acknowledges, on the basis of Gal. 2:16 and Rom. 3:20, that Paul's exclusion of justification by works of the law must refer to both the present and the future.

After a wide-ranging examination, in hellenistic literature generally and then in Paul, of the verb *dikaioun* ('to justify') and its prepositional phrases, Cosgrove concludes that the apostle 'expresses the relationship of justification and works or faith always in terms of means or instrumentality, never in terms of juridical or evidential basis'. He employs the verb *dikaioun* with *ek-* or *dia-* constructions, for example, to express instrumentality and not the evidential basis. (The latter was designated in the hellenistic world by *dikaioun* with *epi* plus the dative case or *kata* with the accusative.) Thus, the sentence 'no one shall be justified by (*ek*) works of the law' (Gal. 2:16; Rom. 3:20), states that 'works of the law' are not an *instrument* by which the sinner is acquitted. However, once a person is justified 'through the faith[fulness] of Christ' (*dia* and *ek* in Gal. 2:16), enlivened by the Spirit and liberated from sin's power, he or she then does what is pleasing in God's eyes, i.e. 'the good', and will be judged on the occasion of the great assize in accordance with (*kata*) those works. The doing of good works is the *evidence* of salvation, not its *instrument.* In the judgment 'the empirical reality of one's life before God as "works" will be revealed and evaluated'.[119] According to Cosgrove, this is the understanding of judgment that we meet in 1 Cor. 4:3–5; Rom. 2:10, 13; 2 Cor. 5:10 and Rom. 8:33. And the expectation of the believer is that this judgment on the final day will be according to works and will result in acquittal; in other words, justification.

Cosgrove completes his presentation with a discussion of Rom. 8:33 in its context and concludes that this future judgment scene understands 'justification' in terms of the 'Vindication of Cruciform Existence'. In effect, he has overcome the problem of the future reference of the 'justification' terminology by treating it as 'vindication'. He concludes: 'The two moments of justification cohere in the apostle's understanding of God. In justifying the ungodly and vindicating those conformed to the image of his crucified Son, God's own righteousness is displayed . . . justification remains at every point God's prerogative . . . That is clear in reconciliation, where God justifies the ungodly. But it is no less evident in future justification, where God vindicates his elect.'[120]

F. Concluding Remarks

The dichotomy between 'faith' and 'works' has been presented in some traditions of Pauline interpretation as absolute, instead of being viewed as a contrast between the grace of God on the one hand, and human achievement as the ground or instrument of justification on the other. *Faith* and *works* are in this sense mutually exclusive. But the apostle expects that faith will work through love (Gal. 5:6), while he conjoins 'faith' with 'work' in one of his first references to 'faith' (*pistis*) *viz.* 1 Thes. 1:3 (in fact, the very first instance if 1 Thessalonians is Paul's first letter). Speaking of the Thessalonians' 'work of faith' he refers to that activity which arises from faith (a genitive of origin) and which can be mentioned in the same breath with their labour of love and steadfastness of hope. If the two notions, 'work' and 'faith', were to be understood as always dichotomous, it is hard to see how the apostle could have risked such a misinterpretation (!) by placing them together in the same phrase.

Herman Ridderbos points out that justification by faith and judgment according to works are two poles of the same matter:

> [The] first expresses as pregnantly as possible that the ground or cause of divine justification does not lie in human work as merit, but only in the grace of God. And in the second all the emphasis is placed on the work of faith, in the sense of its indispensable fruit.[121]

But this does not signify that justification by faith is the initial judicial act of God in the present which is later followed by a further justification on the ground of works at the judgment. The ground of justification lies not in works, nor in faith, but 'in the revelation of God's grace in Christ embraced by faith'.[122] Works are indispensable for they demonstrate the presence of true faith and are evidence of one's being united with Christ in his death and resurrection. Yet even these works are acceptable to God only as they are wrought in Christ and on account of his death and resurrection.

Eph. 2:8–10 makes the point well: 'For by grace you have been saved *through faith . . . not of works*, lest any man should boast. For we are his creation, *created* in Christ Jesus *for good works*, which God prepared beforehand that we should walk in them'.

5

Seek God's Righteousness: Righteousness in the Gospel of Matthew

NORVALD YRI

I. INTRODUCTION

A survey of the literature dealing with the Gospel of Matthew, not to mention that which discusses in particular the theme *dikaiosynē* ('righteousness') in Matthew, reveals that there is little consensus as to the meaning of righteousness in this book.[1] Moreover, the various positions taken do not seem to be tied to traditional theological or ideological categories. Thus it is very difficult to assign a particular view of righteousness in Matthew to a typically 'liberal' or 'evangelical' position, a typically 'Lutheran' or 'Reformed' position, or the like. But some classification of the discussion is possible. Przybylski has shown that at root there are two diametrically opposed views regarding righteousness in Matthew: some hold that *dikaiosynē* refers to God's gift to humankind, and others that it is God's demand upon humankind. Despite this polarity, however, he also shows that there are several mediating positions which hold to the *priority* of righteousness as the gift of God, or to the *priority* of righteousness as God's demand.[2]

The question is more than a theoretical one to be reserved for the study of the theologian. The Christian church always needs guidance in the fundamental issues relating to righteousness. The most that this article can claim to do is to set forth the understanding of the present writer on the subject, in the hope of stirring up renewed interest.

Evangelicals emerge from the framework of classical, Protestant hermeneutics, which presupposes a unity in the testimony of the biblical revelation as to how human beings enter a right relationship with God. Of course, this does not mean that 'righteousness' must have the same meaning in Matthew as it does in every other part of Scripture. But the larger question must be asked: is it reasonable to assume that Matthew has adopted a meaning for the word or the concept seriously at odds with an understanding of righteousness that lies at the very heart of both the Old and New Testament revelation? In this article we shall proceed in three steps. First, we shall consider what Matthew says about the need human beings have for righteousness. Second, by examining the theme of the promised kingdom and the nature of the king, we shall probe Matthew's portrayal of Jesus Christ as the righteous one, and in particular the nature of his relationship to righteousness. Finally, we shall discuss what it means to seek righteousness. In this context most of the *dikaiosynē* texts in Matthew will be scanned, along with some other Matthean material that throws light upon the principal theme.

II. THE NEED FOR RIGHTEOUSNESS

One of Matthew's principal themes concerns the kingdom, the king, the importance of entering the kingdom (especially chapters 2,13,22,24–25; *cf.* also 4:17). Linked to this theme of the kingdom is a continuous line of references insisting that what is taking place in the life and ministry of Jesus is the fulfilment of what God had promised in what we call the Old Testament. But these promises were not given in a vacuum: the historical and existential background is the lost condition of the human race. Jesus the Messiah came to save people from *sin* (Matthew 1:21; 20:28).

The question as to what the people of Jesus' day needed was crucial not only for public sinners and tax collectors, but also for the Pharisees and the teachers of the law. Jesus himself describes the former as 'sick' (9:9–13). Clearly he is not referring to physical illness, but to those who suffer and have pain — indeed, as is clear from 9:13, those who are called sinners (*hamartolos*, cognate with *hamartia*, 'sin', envisages the sinner as one who misses the mark). But when Jesus refers to the Pharisees as those who are 'healthy' (9:12), and explains what he means by designating these people 'righteous' (9:13), he cannot possibly mean that they are entirely spiritually well, that they are entirely righteous in meeting God's demand in his law. Otherwise Matthew's Gospel would be at odds with itself, for in this Gospel Jesus has already demanded a righteousness that surpasses that of the Pharisees and teachers of the law (5:20).[3] In referring to the Pharisees as 'righteous' in 9:13, therefore, Jesus must be characterising them according to their own interpretation of the Mosaic code and the body of oral tradition that had grown up around it.

Clearly then, as Przybylski also notes, the scribes and the Pharisees had some form of righteousness. But we find it difficult to agree with Przybylski's inference when he argues from this observation that righteousness in Matthew must not be construed as a gift from God: 'If *dikaiosynē* [righteousness] is to refer to the gift of God, then this meaning must apply both to the righteous-ness of the disciples and to that of the scribes and Pharisees. Since the whole point of 5:20 is that the righteousness of the scribe and Pharisees is not sufficient to enter the kingdom of heaven, it is quite unlikely that their righteousness is based upon the gift of God.'[4]

But Przybylski assumes that the word 'righteousness' must always have the same meaning. We heartily agree that the righteousness of the Pharisees was not God's gift, but it does not follow that the same should be said of the righteousness of Jesus' genuine disciples. The thrust of the argument in Matthew's Gospel is adequate demonstration that the righteousness of the Pharisees is presented as *not* being from God: it is self-righteousness, it is based on a man's ability to obey what he himself has understood to be God's will in the written law. But a failure to recognise the distinction between this kind of righteousness and that which Jesus demands makes it impossible to grasp the profound hiatus between human ability and God's demand for righteousness (e.g. Matthew 9:9–13; frequently in Matthew 5;7–23; compare also Luke 18:9–14, and especially Philippians 3:1–11, where Paul contrasts his own righteousness gained from the law and the righteousness that comes from God — and we must remember that Paul is speaking of himself as a Pharisee, 3:6).

From the time of Martin Luther, it has been repeatedly shown that no class was as highly honoured in the Jewish nation as that of the Pharisees and the scribes. For many people the embodiment of what it meant to be holy was the Pharisee. Yet here Jesus condemns their righteousness as inadequate (5:20).[5] Calvin goes so far as to say that the Pharisees fabricated a righteousness which effectively closed the door of heaven to those who pursued it, for by attaching God's law to outward duties they trained their disciples in hypocrisy like monkeys.[6]

Although the expression for 'surpasses' in Matthew 5:20 (*perisseuē pleion*) is formally quantitative, in Semitic thought such quantitative expressions are frequently used to refer to qualitative distinctions. Granted that the Pharisees represented the very apex of Jewish piety, it is unlikely that Jesus is merely demanding *more* righteousness of the same kind, more righteousness fundamentally construed as human activity.[7] Rather, the righteousness of the disciples must be of an entirely different kind if they expect to enter the kingdom.

Many scholars agree that Jesus here insists upon *perfection* — perfection according to the law of God. What is needed from a disciple is righteousness that will meet all of God's demands, righteousness that is measured by the perfect doing of God's will. It has been pointed out that in Isaiah 26:2 righteousness is the presupposition for entering the kingdom of God.[8] Psalm 118:20 may also stand behind the theology of Matthew 5:20. A righteousness is needed that will open up the gate of heaven.

The Pharisees were not slack; they were indeed seeking perfection. They were strict in their interpretation of the law. But according to Jesus their attainment does not give them access to God's kingdom. Thus the best Jews are not able to enter in: what then shall we say for all the others? It is clear that another perfection is needed. The Sermon on the Mount as a whole is a protest and a rejection of any view of righteousness that is based upon achievement and merit. By showing the law's demands to be so rigorous, Jesus makes it clear that meeting God's demands cannot be achieved within the framework of the approach of the Pharisees.[9]

Any interpretation of the righteousness that Jesus demands in 5:20 that is understood to be nothing more than more demands, greater requirements for a perfect life and greater obedience or the like, will not satisfy the fundamental challenge of the text. What Jesus is requiring is a righteousness that goes beyond what human beings are able to achieve. Not even the life of righteousness expected of a disciple is of such a nature that it can open up the gate of the kingdom. Of course, this does not mean that a life of righteousness is unimportant to the disciple, as a consequence of the righteousness that God gives. It would be wrong to deny that good works, profound obedience and upright conduct of the disciple are fruit of his or her new relationship to God. Nevertheless, it is crucial to argue that, without a righteousness that is fundamentally 'greater' — that is, of a different kind — than that of the Pharisees, it is impossible to enter the kingdom.[10]

God's demand for righteousness is so high and so fundamental that it requires that the disciple be *perfect* (Matthew 5:48). Is this 'perfection' merely relative, that which a human being is able to achieve? Is it nothing more than the obedient, righteous life of a disciple? Or is it better to interpret 'perfect' (*teleios*) in the absolute sense — to be perfect as God is perfect? Does not the text insist, 'Be perfect, therefore, as your heavenly Father is perfect' (5:48)?

Przybylski takes 5:48 as both a qualitative and a quantitative summary of righteousness, but he argues that *teleios* ('perfect') is redactional. This he argues on the basis of Luke 6:36: 'Be *merciful*, even as your Father is merciful.' This redactional change was made, according to Przybylski, because Matthew wanted a concluding statement for 5:21–47, and only the use of the adjective *teleios* ('perfect'), rather than *oiktirmon* ('merciful') would contribute to this purpose.[11] Przybylski also refers to the *Didachē* (an early second-century Christian document) and the Dead Sea Scrolls to support his claim that 'perfect' has to be understood as an attainment of the highest rank according to specific standards. The perfection sought is thus fundamentally quantitative, even though some qualitative meaning is presupposed. The attainment of qualitative perfection is also to be seen in passages such as 3:15; 5:18; and 28:20. The demands for *all* righteousness and for *everything* to be accomplished are summarised in the insistence that Jesus' disciples observe *everything* that he commanded (28:20). Przybylski argues that the 'all' or 'everything' (*pas*) in all three places is redactional, and that we are here faced in each case with a demand for an activity that is to be measured in a quantitative way.[12]

We remain unpersuaded by the redaction-critical arguments. But even if they could be established, it would not necessarily follow that 'perfect' in 5:48 is to be taken primarily in a quantitative sense. Surely the flow of the argument from 5:20 to 5:48 demands a righteousness and a perfection that outstrips anything a human being can perform or achieve. Certainly it is possible to understand the perfection in 5:48 as an eschatological goal which the disciple of Jesus only imperfectly achieves. In this view a complete perfection is possible only at the end. In this life, then, a relative perfection is gained when a disciple of Jesus does his or her best in holy living, seeking to be obedient, wholeheartedly committing himself or herself to the will of God. Certainly we agree that the disciple is expected to live in accordance with God's will.[13]

Nevertheless, we argue that in this context an absolute meaning of 'perfect' is called for. Maier holds that the background of 5:48 is Leviticus 19:2 and Deuteronomy 18:13. The standard of measurement in such passages is taken away from the human being: it is God himself who is the measure of perfection. He requires that we be like him. This demand is so high that no person, no disciple, is able to achieve it. If the form of Matthew 5:48 is thus tied to Leviticus 19:2 and Deuteronomy 18:13, this absolute demand constitutes a natural link with our interpretation of 5:20. In that case, 'perfect' must here be taken in the absolute sense: Jesus points to a requirement that is impossible for us to achieve.[14] Impossible though it may be for us to achieve it, it is nevertheless demanded.[15]

Similarly, Grundmann points to the law's requirement that we be holy as God is holy, and this he binds together with the fundamental demands summarised in the demand for love in Matthew 5:43–48. But this love (*agapē*) resides in God alone. In Jesus' teaching, this love of the Father is directed toward human beings: he wants to give his love. The disciple must give himself over to this love: the disciple is characterised as being 'poor in spirit' (5:3), and must follow Jesus, not least in his explanation of the law (5:7–47) where he finds he is asked to be complete, perfect just like the Father (5:48). Here Grundmann compares Matthew 5 with Romans 1:16–8:28 with reference to the study of what it means to regain the *imago Dei* ('the image of God'). Perfection and wholeness, the image of God, are in Jesus Christ.[16]

Ladd takes a similar position: the righteousness explained in 5:20–48 includes freedom from anger, from lust, from retaliation. If the attainment of such a perfect righteousness is left to human effort, no one can acquire it.[17]

We are driven to the conclusion that unless Jesus does infinitely more for the world than give it a code of ethics, he has but mocked our impotence, and revealed our weakness.[18]

The word *teleios* ('perfect') is also used in an illuminating way in 19:21. There a rich young ruler wants to know what good he should perform in order to gain eternal life. Jesus responds to his concern by telling him he must keep the commandments. Although the young man claims that he has kept these, he nevertheless has the grace to display some doubt: 'What do I still lack?' (Matthew 19:20). Now Jesus replies, 'If you want to be *perfect* . . .' (19:21). Gundry suggests that the meaning here should be 'mature'. The young man was lacking in 'maturity' — taking this lack of 'maturity' or 'perfection' to be equivalent to a failure in discipleship.[19] Others claim that the meaning is 'complete' in the sense of having reached the goal (*telos*).[20] A possible interpretation is to take 'perfect' to refer to full-hearted obedience, to self-surrender and unqualified discipleship. The young man needs to surrender himself; he needs this display of the triumph of grace.[21]

But surely it is also wise to emphasise the absoluteness of the perfection required (as in 5:48). The rich young man, Rienecker says, did not understand that God asks for more than good deeds: he asks for the whole person — thoughts, words, deeds, love. Jesus is asking him to love God above all things. Both this rich young ruler and the disciples are facing the question of how to obey the first commandment.[22] Other interpreters have taken a similar line.[23]

No one, then, is able to perform the will of God in this absolute sense. All break the law; all are unclean. Who then shall be saved? Surely Jesus is painting a picture of human beings that is far more radical than all the pictures they draw of themselves. No one is able to save himself.[24]

We human beings break God's holy law from our very heart. We forfeit fellowship with God. Our relationship to him is characterised by sin: we face him in the perfection demanded by the Decalogue and the Sermon on the Mount.[25]

It appears, then, that there is justification for our interpretation of *teleios* as referring to absolute perfection. In this view, the rich young ruler must be absolutely perfect to gain eternal life. He has to be without sin for this is the requirement of the law. In the ensuing dialogue with the disciples, Jesus makes it clear that this is impossible for all, not least for them (19:23–26).

But if human beings need such absolute righteousness, it is utterly clear that we are not able to produce this ourselves, for we are evil. As Carson has pointed out, Jesus in Matthew's Gospel presupposes the sinfulness of human nature (7:11) while at the same time he does not include himself.[26] The human heart (*kardia*) is hard. Although this was not the situation from the beginning, it is now the source of evil thoughts, murder, adultery, sexual immorality, theft, false testimony, slander, and the other things that make one unclean (Matthew 19:1ff.; *cf.* 15:19–20).

Even so, God's demand that human beings be perfect is unfaltering: 'Love the Lord your God with all your heart, and with all your soul, and with all your mind. This is the first and greatest commandment. And the second is like it: love your neighbour as yourself. All the Law and the Prophets hang on these two commandments' (Matthew 22:35–40).

Thus the sinner with an evil heart is asked to be perfect, to love God and his neighbour with a pure heart. Is this possible? Jesus himself says no (Matthew 19:23–26). It is impossible for a human being to gain eternal life by doing his or her best to keep the law; but God has found another way (Matthew 19:26).[27]

III. FULFILLING ALL RIGHTEOUSNESS

The Gospel of Matthew presents Jesus as the Messiah, the king promised in the Old Testament. John the Baptist's announcement was 'Repent, for the kingdom of heaven is near' (3:2). The kingdom of heaven was coming with Jesus. Jesus is also presented as God's Son, the holy one who is fit for the ministry God expects him to fulfil (especially chapters 3,17). He is the righteous one who would fulfil all righteousness, the servant of the Lord.

When people came to John the Baptist confessing their sins and seeking baptism from him in the Jordan River (3:2–6), Jesus also approached the Baptist demanding to be baptised by him. John tried to deter Jesus: 'I need to be baptised by you, and do you come to me?' (3:14). Jesus replied, 'Let it be so now; it is proper for us *to fulfil all righteousness*' (3:15). Both John the Baptist and Jesus were under obligation to do what God had arranged for them. Understanding himself to be the servant of the Lord of Isaiah 53 (and other passages), Jesus knows he has come to take the sin of the world. He, the holy one, places himself under the burden of sin in front of God. Jesus does not himself need the baptism of sinners. Nevertheless, in this way he shows he is taking the sin of the world upon himself, in order to fulfil all righteousness. Isaiah 53 had to be fulfilled, and all Jesus' efforts are directed to the fulfilment of the Father's will. By his obedience in this instance he simultaneously reveals his commitment to pursuing God's will without any attempt to change it, and shows himself to be the righteous one who self-consciously stands before the holy will of his Father.[28]

Jesus acts as the substitute for sinners.[29] The concept 'all righteousness' is to be compared with the righteousness that must surpass the scribes and the Pharisees.[30] Jesus is the servant who obeys God: he fulfils all righteousness since ultimately he suffers and dies to accomplish redemption in obedience to the will of God, thereby demonstrating his willingness to take on the servant's role.[31]

This is the 'righteousness' (*dikaiosyne* — surely the gift!) — that will satisfy God's will. As Grundmann argues, to obey God's demands and commandments, Jesus shows that he himself is the gift satisfying God's will

(1:21) — the *dikaiosynē* is full and whole. Jesus fulfils all righteousness, establishing himself as the righteous one of God, by giving himself without reserve to the obedience of the Father's will (11:29).[32] To use the language of John's Gospel, Jesus knows himself to be the Lamb of God who takes away the sin of the world; he knows he is going toward the cross.[33]

Jesus did not come in order to abolish the Law and the Prophets (5:17); he came to *fulfil* them. Jesus fulfils the Law and the Prophets inasmuch as they point to him.[34] They demand righteousness; he himself is the righteous one. To this point the law of God had only been broken, but now one has come who always does what God requires. Thus the eschatological fulfilment of the Law and the Prophets is itself realised in the *obedience of Jesus*, the obedience that leads him to the cross. Thus he not only teaches the righteousness of the requirement of the law 5:21–48; 7:12); he himself is willing to satisfy all of God's demands on him in the most absolute sense.[35]

The Scriptures had already established that human beings lost fellowship with God because of their sin and disobedience (Genesis 3). By graciously giving the law with its rules and regulations, God revealed the need for sacrifice, for atonement for sin. In the course of time God also revealed that a righteous sufferer was needed in order to fulfil God's demands — one who would give his life a ransom for many (Isaiah 53). In Matthew's Gospel Jesus says he has come to give his life as ransom (20:28). He himself serves as the vicarious atonement.[36] The Son of Man is none the less God's Son (16:13–16), who came in order to give himself for humankind. He came to take the place of others: the 'ransom' (*lytron*, 20:28) is the purchase-price, the deliverance price. With Isaiah 53 in the background, Jesus' death is simultaneously guilt-offering[37] and the price paid to free a prisoner or a slave.[38] We have seen that Jesus was recognised by God as his Son: 'And a voice from heaven said, "This is my Son, whom I love; with him I am well pleased" ' (3:17). Jesus was accepted by God without reservation; he was fit for the ministry of fulfilling all righteousness (3:15; compare 17:5). Through his ministry, suffering, death and resurrection, Jesus completed everything required to fulfil all righteousness. His entire life was lived within this framework (compare 22:5). His obedience was climaxed when his blood was 'poured out for many for the forgiveness of sins' (26:28).

IV.   SEEKING GOD'S RIGHTEOUSNESS

The meaning of another key text is disputed, namely Matthew 6:33: 'But seek first his kingdom and his righteousness . . .' Przybylski takes the meaning of righteousness here to be 'the norm governing man's conduct'.[39] It refers not to God's righteousness through which man is justified, but to a righteous life in agreement with the will of God. In this view, it is God's righteousness as the norm of human behaviour; but it remains God's demand upon man, rather than God's gift to man.[40] In this framework, the injunction is not to seek justification, but to pursue righteousness of life in full submission to the will of God.[41]

Yet in this verse too we can identify two principal lines of interpretation. The one emphasises the obedient and holy life a disciple must lead as he seeks to follow God's commandments in his life; the other stresses the importance of receiving the righteousness that comes with the kingdom. As Przybylski has noted, once again there are mediating positions.

Odland interprets the righteousness here to be the righteousness of a life lived according to God's will and demand. By prayer and work one seeks to do God's will, to partake in the kingdom of utter righteousness.[42] Frvig takes the same position.[43] Gundry is not dissimilar: ultimately the promise of receiving this righteousness is fulfilled not in the present life of the disciples, but in the coming age.[44]

Calvin relates the word 'righteousness' to God and to his kingdom, for the kingdom of God consists in righteousness, which leads to spiritual newness of life.[45] Luther has a similar view: the kingdom embraces a righteousness of its own, different from that of the world, a righteousness that comes from a faith that is busy and active in good works. Although Luther speaks about the forgiveness of sins, at the same time he here pictures good works as the fruit that grows from a good tree.[46] Guthrie insists that this righteousness cannot be obtained through man's efforts. He emphasises that humble repentance is at the root of this pursuit. Although justification in a purely forensic sense does not occur in the teaching of Jesus, he says, nevertheless the widespread requirement of both faith and righteousness in Jesus' followers prepares the way for the classic exposition found in the doctrine of Paul.[47]

We would not deny that the Christian disciple needs to live a righteous life, indeed that there is a demand laid on all disciples to follow God's will. In this context, however, it is better to follow the line of interpretation that more closely links righteousness with the kingdom. The kingdom of God brings in God's gift. We are asked to seek the kingdom; at the same time we are asked to seek this righteousness.

Grundmann points out the connection between what is said here about God's kingdom and righteousness and what is said in the Lord's prayer about the will of God and the coming of the kingdom (6:10). The realisation of God's will among men and women is the same as the coming of the kingdom. Similarly, the righteousness of God is given to a human being as he is forgiven his sins, and simultaneously he is given the impetus to new conduct. It is impossible for anyone to enter the kingdom on any other path than that of *dikaiosynē*.[48] Ladd takes a similar view: what is at stake is not primarily ethical quality, but the forgiveness of sins, divine acquittal of guilt. That is what we are to pursue; that is what it means to seek God's kingdom and God's righteousness. To receive the kingdom is to receive the accompanying righteousness.[49]

Aalen discusses four interpretations of righteousness in this text:

(a) Ethical righteousness. This he dismisses on the ground that it is *God's* righteousness that is in view.
(b) The righteous situation in God's kingdom. This, Aalen insists, does not suit the context.
(c) God's act of salvation.
(d) God's final judgment and the consequent acquittal.

Aalen finds points (c) and (d) to be natural in this context. The background from 'righteousness' in Isaiah shows that 'righteousness' is very close to meaning to 'salvation'. What human beings are to pursue is God's righteousness, that is, salvation from God.[50]

Maier takes much the same line: the text presses human beings to pursue a part in the eternal kingdom of God. He compares this passage with Romans 3:21–26: to gain righteousness (Matthew 6:33) is the same thing as to be set free from sin. This is possible only as a person enters into fellowship with Jesus.[51] By pronouncing us righteous and thereby making us partakers of his kingdom, God is justified both in his royal rule and in his own perfect righteousness.[52]

What, then, of the interpretation of Matthew 5:6? Is it possible that this passage pronounces a blessing on those who hunger and thirst for the righteousness that is God's gift? Martyn Lloyd-Jones understands this verse to exhort us to seek holiness, the life of righteousness. The righteousness in view is Christ-likeness, becoming more and more holy.[53] Similarly, Przybylski understands the righteousness in this passage, as in other places in the Sermon on the Mount, to refer to human conduct.[54] Carson surveys a variety of interpretations, and discusses the views of scholars who argue that the references are to the imputed righteousness of God, the eschatological salvation, or, more narrowly, justification: 'This is certainly plausible, since the immediate context does arouse hopes for God's eschatological action, and hungering suggests that the righteousness that satisfies will be given as a gift.'[55] Carson himself, however, interprets the meaning to be simultaneously a reference to personal righteousness and to justice in the broader sense (with reference to the views of Ridderbos). There is a longing for the advent of the kingdom, as the outgrowth of the disciples' personal and social righteousness.

By contrast, Maier follows the interpretation that Carson judges 'plausible'. He refers to Psalm 119:123 and argues that salvation and righteousness once again are one and the same. The person who has righteousness is the one who stands before God without guilt (Maier compares Romans 1:17; 3:28). Thus Matthew 5:6, Maier insists, refers to people who stand before God without guilt. They cannot now claim for themselves deeds that are good enough to stand before him. Nevertheless, the righteousness is provided to them as a gift, and their full satisfaction will be enjoyed at the end of time when they will personally realise complete righteousness.[56]

We interpret the reference to righteousness in 5:10–11 along much the same line. The persecution that is applied 'because of righteousness' cannot be differentiated from the persecution mentioned in the next verse, applied to believers *because of Jesus*. Here, too, of course, there are different interpretations, and many follow the view that the righteousness at stake in this passage is the life of obedience before God.[57]

It has been argued, rightly, that Jesus does not teach about things that are separated from his own person. Thus the fundamental cause for persecution against his followers lies in their obedience to Jesus and his teaching. But his teaching is more than mere instruction; it affects their entire lives. Insofar as his own death and resurrection have been the cause of their becoming disciples, so far is he also the genuine divine cause of their persecution as disciples. Thus to say that disciples are persecuted because of righteousness, or because of Jesus, is to say the same thing: Jesus Christ is himself both truth and righteousness. It is in this sense that the persecution is because of Jesus.[58]

To summarise: the righteousness that is greater than that of the scribes and the Pharisees is that brought about by Jesus. Only this righteousness is able to open the door of the kingdom (5:20). Disciples need a righteousness built upon a complete and perfect fulfilment of the law: God's will as revealed in the Old Testament had to be fulfilled. This is what Jesus came to do (5:17–19). Only on the basis of his fulfilment of the law is it possible to receive a righteousness that is of a different nature from that of humankind — a righteousness that gives entrance to God's kingdom. No fulfilment of the law which even the best of Christ's disciples were able to achieve can admit them to the kingdom. The kingdom is not gained by good works. But Christ's fulfilment, the righteousness from his redemptive work, provides the foundation for a different *dikaiosynē* ('righteousness') that opens up the gate of the kingdom (5:17–20). The perfection asked for (5:48) cannot be found in human efforts to meet God's demand. An extremely meticulous observation of the law will still not provide the answer sought for in this context. Gaining this highest righteousness is possible only as a person gains a righteousness other than that which is achieved by human efforts. Attainment of the *perfect* is impossible, unless that righteousness is understood to be God's gift.[59]

What of the wedding clothes in Matthew 22:1–14? The symbolic force of these clothes is explained in a variety of ways. Aalen says it is impossible to know whether they refer to faith or good deeds, or to something else.[60] Other suggestions include works of righteousness, righteousness of life, righteousness to remain in the kingdom, faithfulness and obedience that can be expected of those who are members of the kingdom or church, and obedient discipleship — to mention only a few interpretations that are close to one another.[61]

But it makes sense to regard the symbolic force of the wedding clothes as referring to the righteousness given by God himself. Says Guthrie: If the garment is symbolic of God's own provision of salvation, the message is clear: those who stand in their own strength have no part in salvation.[62]

Several scholars (including Grundmann, Maier and Lenski) see in Isaiah 61:10 a natural biblical background for the interpretation of the symbolic force of the wedding garment (see also Genesis 45:22; Judges 14:12; 2 Kings 5:22; 10:22; Esther 6:8; 8:15; compare Revelation 19:8–9). 'Garment', insists Grundmann, in the categories of apocalyptic, is a picture for having part in the eschatological fulfilment of God's redemptive purposes. One gains such a part by conversion, entering into the new existence of salvation (Isaiah 61:10).[63]

It is worth noting that the perfect passive form (*endedymenon*) is passive: literally 'having been garmented', something that takes place at another's initiative. The person who is cast out of the wedding feast 'had not been garmented'.

The analogy of the faith likewise excludes works and moral fitness. Works do not admit anyone into the kingdom; only the righteousness of Christ can do that. If faith is the garment, it is the faith that like a cup holds this free gift of righteousness; no other saving faith exists. All the bridal linen is provided for the bride by the bridegroom, and this is the righteousness of the saints (Revelation 19:8).[64]

In brief: human beings need righteousness. We are not able to fulfil God's demand, for we are not perfect, but are in fact evil. God's demands reveal the need we have to receive another righteousness: we are asked to seek the righteousness that comes with the kingdom and the king.

6

Justification in Luke–Acts

RICHARD B. GAFFIN, JR.

I. PRELIMINARY OBSERVATIONS

1. The question of justification in the various non-Pauline writings of the New Testament brings into view the much debated issue of unity and diversity in the New Testament.[1] This is especially the case since justification by faith, whether or not it be *the* centre, is surely an integral element in Paul's teaching. To pose the question of justification elsewhere in the New Testament is, in effect, to raise the issue of its unity, and to do so in a fundamental way. To explore the theme of this chapter, then, is, — at least implicitly — to measure Luke–Acts by Paul.

Luke–Acts makes up approximately one-fourth of the volume of the New Testament; Luke–Acts and the letters of Paul, taken together, constitute about one-half. When that fact is joined with the Christologically-based harmony of New Testament teaching and the importance of justification in Paul, then we are warranted in expecting to discover at least positive, even substantial lines of connection between Paul's teaching on justification and the concerns of Luke.

At the same time, however, that anticipation ought not to lead us to mistake the unity of the New Testament for didactic uniformity. The unity of New Testament teaching is a unity in diversity — a diversity readily apparent, for instance, from the indelible imprint left in the various documents by the personalities of the respective authors, as well as from the assorted, markedly different literary genres contained within the New Testament. In exploring justification in Luke-Acts we must be on guard against reading Paul into Luke. On balance, two extremes are to be avoided: setting Paul in opposition to Luke, on the one hand, and 'Paulinising' Luke, on the other.

2. To our advantage Luke[2] indicates clearly at the beginning of his Gospel something of his procedure and objectives in writing (1:1–4). That his reader may have 'certainty' about what he has been taught (v. 4), Luke's concern is to provide a 'carefully investigated', 'orderly account' (v. 3), based on the accounts of authorised, most probably apostolic 'eyewitnesses' of 'the things fulfilled among us' (v. 1). In view of the virtually universal consensus that the two volumes to Theophilus are a literary unit, the prologue almost certainly covers Acts as well.[3] Even if that were not Luke's intention, or even if it

refers primarily to the Gospel, Acts could hardly be excluded from the same general arena of endeavour.

The subsequent narrative makes clear that the focus of 'the things that have been fulfilled' is primarily Christological, or, more concretely, a focus on messianic suffering and glory: 'the sufferings of Christ and the glories that would follow', to borrow from the language of 1 Peter 1:11. Globally considered, the Gospel (chapters 1–23) documents the humiliation of Christ (with its concomitants), while Acts (along with Luke 24) focuses on his exaltation (with its immediate consequences).

This brief overview prompts a further observation. Surely the Gospel, as well as Acts, is written from a postexaltation perspective. No doubt the Gospel reflects the circumstances in which Luke wrote, and his selection and presentation of material is shaped by that situation. But Acts 1:1 distinguishes, implicitly but plainly, between 'all that Jesus began to do and to teach' previously on earth and what he has done subsequently, as the exalted Lord. It misrepresents Luke badly to suppose that he is not really much concerned to distinguish the pre- and post-Easter situations. In fact, that distinction — together with a concern for the actual historical profile involved — remains fundamental for him.

Over the past two hundred years many scholars have rejected Luke's claim, or at least have failed to take that claim seriously.[4] Suffice it here to say that such scepticism is unwarranted. Careful investigation confirms that Luke is the creditable historian he claims to be.[5] In keeping with what we have already noted about his prologue, his accounts of the activities and teaching of Jesus, Peter, Paul, and others may not be precise, verbatim records (nor were they intended to be), but they are accurate and reliable as general, summary descriptions.

3. A permanent result of redaction criticism has been to heighten our awareness that the Gospels and Acts are not neutral, disinterested chronicles: they were written with a definite bias, 'from faith to faith'. Their design, as narrative focused on Christ's person and work, is not only to inform but to convince, to convict and convert (e.g., so much is stated in John 20:31). To achieve this and other related, contributory goals, the Evangelists select from the larger volume of their own eyewitness impressions and the (oral and written) traditions at their disposal; and they arrange and edit these materials (Luke 1:1–3; John 21:25). In a word, these documents are *kerygmatic* and *theological.*

The theological and (in a positive sense) biased, tendentious character of the Gospels and Acts is undeniable; and sensitivity to that dimension is important for sound exegesis. It is another question, however, whether Luke–Acts and the other Gospels each provide us with their own complete theology. The Pauline corpus comes closest to providing a comprehensive theology; but it goes too far, certainly beyond what the texts warrant, to try to discover represented in each New Testament document, or group of documents, an independent, more or less complete theology-type. 'Lucan theology', therefore, is a problematic expression — helpful in one sense, misleading in another. At any rate, our concern in this chapter is not only Luke's view of justification but Luke's witness to the proclamation of Jesus, Peter, and Paul on justification. Attention must be paid to his presentation of the teaching of others — both their actual teaching, as he reports it, and his own distinctive, carefully crafted presentation of that teaching. But in the light of his prologue, surely the former is primary for him.

4. Initially Luke–Acts may not appear to have much material pertinent to justification. A quick glance at a concordance seems to confirm an unpromising situation.[6] The adjective 'righteous'/'just' does occur slightly more frequently in Luke–Acts than in Paul, but the nouns for 'righteousness' and 'justification' and the verb 'to justify' are found only a handful of times compared to the dominant place they have in Paul, especially in Romans and Galatians. The key Pauline expression, '(the) righteousness of God' (e.g. Rom. 1:17; 2 Cor. 5:20; Phil. 3:9) is missing in Luke–Acts. Furthermore, even at the most direct points of contact Luke appears to have with Paul (Luke 18:14 and Acts 13:38–39), interpreters remain sharply divided as to whether the justification spoken of is the same eschatological-forensic reality that it is in Paul's letters.

It could appear, then, that, unlike Paul, Luke just does not see justification as basic to understanding the gospel — or better, to understanding the gospel as presented by Jesus, Peter, Paul, and others — so that whatever attention is given to the handful of references to justification in Luke-Acts, a prime requirement is to guard against reading them through the eyes of Paul. In fact, even with the advent of redaction criticism, monographs and articles on the theme of justification in Luke–Acts are few indeed.[7]

There are two basic approaches to our topic. We may begin with an exegetical survey of the relatively few passages where justification/righteousness terminology occurs, move on to consider others with alternative language or closely related ideas, and then see what general conclusions may be drawn. Alternatively, we may take a more holistic approach, by identifying central, controlling themes in Luke–Acts, considering whether these themes involve elements that bear on the idea of justification, and then examining the justification/righteousness references and related passages in the light of this perspective. I will follow the latter approach as the more fruitful.

II. THE HOLY SPIRIT AND JUDGMENT IN LUKE–ACTS (PENTECOST AND JUSTIFICATION)

1. For Luke, no less than for the other Synoptics, the central, controlling theme in the proclamation of Jesus is the kingdom or rule of God (or heaven). The gospel, in its totality, is the gospel of the kingdom (4:43; 8:1; 9:2; 16:16) — the kingdom not simply as a timeless, ideal moral order, more or less equivalent to divine sovereignty; but as an eschatological reality, as the fulfilment of the Old Testament promises, the reign that has finally begun with the ministry of Jesus (see e.g. Luke 3:4–6; 4:17–21; 11:20). This well-established conclusion[8] is a presupposition for further study of Luke–Acts.

Also, few (if any) will care to dispute that a major theme in Luke-Acts is the coming of the Holy Spirit. Pentecost is not only the high point, or at least the decisive turning point, of the narrative in Acts, but has a central place in the entire history Luke relates to Theophilus. Lampe's thesis that 'Pentecost [is] the great-turning point, the hinge, as it were, of the two-volume narrative'[9] is only slightly overstated. Indeed, if we connect Pentecost with the death but especially the resurrection and ascension of Christ as an inseparable complex of events (as Peter does, Acts 2:32–33), then that thesis is not an overstatement at all.

These observations suggest a tie between the Spirit and the kingdom integral to the message of Luke-Acts.[10] Such a tie is in fact apparent at a number of places throughout the Gospel — in key events such as the birth of Jesus (1:31–35), his baptism (3:21–22), and his temptation–conflict with Satan (*cf.* 4:1 with vv. 5–6), as well as in his preaching activity as a whole (*cf.* 4:14–15,18 with v. 43). The casting out of demons by 'the finger [= Spirit] of God' is a manifestation of the kingdom of God (11:20). A certain equation exists between the Spirit and the kingdom: the incomparably highest gift that the Father will give to the disciples is the Holy Spirit (11:13), while the greatest blessing that the disciples are to seek and the Father is pleased to give them is the kingdom (12:31–32).

The importance of this tie comes out in the overlap between the end of Luke 24 and the beginning of Acts 1. On the one side, the summary of Jesus' teaching activity over the entire 40 days between his resurrection and ascension is, in a single phrase, that he 'spoke about the kingdom of God' (Acts 1:3). Related to that, verses 4–5 recall Jesus' command to wait in Jerusalem for baptism with the Holy Spirit. Luke 24:44–49, on the other side, is best read as providing a brief description of what typified the instruction of Jesus during this interim. These verses are 'an extremely succinct account of what happened further'.[11] Verses 44b-47 show this period to have been a kind of 'crash course' in Old Testament hermeneutics for the disciples: Jesus teaches that the (necessary) fulfilment of the Old Testament, in all its parts and as a whole, is centered in his suffering and death, his resurrection, and world-wide gospel proclamation. But all 'this', he begins by saying, 'is what I told you while I was still with you' (v. 44a), referring to the entire period prior to the resurrection. So in effect, the focus of Jesus' entire post-resurrection teaching is the kingdom. And to facilitate their own impending kingdom role as gospel witnesses (vv. 48–49), the disciples are to stay in Jerusalem (v. 47), until they receive 'what my Father has promised' and are 'clothed with power from on high' — obvious references to the imminent coming of the Spirit at Pentecost.

Furthermore (without here settling the exegesis of Acts 1:6) the point of the well-known eighth verse, together with verse 7, is that the apostles'[12] concern about the kingdom ought not to be about its *future* but about the *present, impending* kingdom-task of world-wide witness — for which task the Holy Spirit will come upon them at Pentecost. Confirmation for this point is found in the fact that subsequent references to the kingdom in Acts are all within summary descriptions of the content of gospel preaching and teaching (8:12; 19:8; 20:25; 28:23,31 — the note on which Acts ends).

A controlling perspective of Luke-Acts, then, is that Pentecost is a decisive juncture in the manifestation of the kingdom of God. The events narrated in Acts generally, and the coming of the Spirit at Pentecost in particular, are kingdom phenomena; they take place within the context of the coming of the kingdom — the eschatological rule of God inaugurated by Christ. The Spirit that comes at Pentecost is the Spirit of eschatology; the pentecostal Spirit is the eschatological Spirit.

2. In Acts 1:5 the resurrected Jesus points forward to Pentecost ('in a few days') and backward to the ministry of John the Baptist. Furthermore, he

does so by echoing John's prophecy in Luke 3:16 — 'I baptise you with water. But . . . he will baptise you with the Holy Spirit and with fire.' The context in Luke 3 shows that the tie between these baptisms is that between forerunner (v. 4) and messianic (v. 15) fulfiller, between Spirit and fire baptism as reality and John's water baptism as the sign/symbol pointing to that reality.[13] The point is not so much John the Baptist as Jesus the Baptiser.

This messianic baptism, it is important to grasp, is essentially the reality of *judgment*, not only in a negative sense but as a judicial event with two, mutually exclusive outcomes. For some it will result, positively, in acquittal and blessing; for others, negatively, in condemnation and destruction. The surrounding context makes this forensic point clear. First, John's water baptism is essentially related to judgment. It points to repentance in the context of impending (eschatological) wrath (v. 7) and the threat of imminent, justly deserved destruction (v. 9); it signifies repentance as the means of escape from God's punitive, judicial anger toward sinners.

More importantly, verse 17 amplifies Spirit and fire baptism; syntactically, the subject of the relative clause in v. 17a is the messianic baptiser in v. 16. His activity is pictured by the metaphor of the threshing floor — of a piece with the harvest metaphor, a favourite biblical picture for (eschatological) judgment (e.g. Isa. 17:5; 21:10; 41:15–16; Jer. 51:33; Joel 3:12–13; Matt. 13:30, 39; Rev. 14:14–20): it will issue in salvation (the grain), on the one hand, and destruction (the chaff), on the other; the Spirit and fire baptiser is a harvester-judge. Finally, 'fire' is a key word, with distinct connotations of judgment; in its other occurrences in the surrounding context (vv. 9,17) it refers to the inextinguishable fire of punitive destruction.

'With/in the Holy Spirit and fire' almost certainly describes one baptism, not two[14] — especially if one considers the background of the Old Testament prophetic tradition (in which John stands, *cf.* 7:26–27; 16:16), where both Spirit and fire refer to judgment that either purifies the righteous (Isa. 4:4; 32:15–17; 44:3; Mal. 3:1–3) or destroys tr wicked (Isa. 11:2–4,15; Mal. 4:1; *cf.* Acts 5:3–5,8–10; 2 Thess 2:8). In view is a composite medium, 'the fiery *pneuma* in which all must be immersed'.[15] The messianic baptism-judgment contemplated is one act with two facets: it will be experienced by the repentant as blessing, by the unrepentant as destruction.

Whatever may be its full significance and outworkings, then, a proper understanding of Pentecost begins by seeing it in the context of eschatological judgment. The immediate fulfilment of John's prophecy at Pentecost is a part of the final, end-time judicial action of God.

3. The prophesied Spirit and fire baptism do not take place immediately — a fact, apparently, that confused even John (7:18–23). Why? What explains the delay between Luke 3 and Acts 2? The answer, the *gospel* answer, is that for that baptism to be blessing, not destruction, for those who repent, it must be preceded and mediated by a period based on the messianic baptiser's own submission to baptism, a baptism for which, too, a forensic dimension is basic.

For Luke, Jesus' baptism by John (3:21–22) is plainly not personal but messianic.[16] It marks, not the occasion when Jesus first becomes the Messiah, but, in effect, his 'coronation' as Messiah, publicly inaugurating his kingdom ministry. In particular, by submitting to John's baptism Jesus shows his solidarity with his people. Pointedly, though himself 'holy' (1:35;[17] Acts 3:14) and 'righteous' (23:47; Acts 3:14; 7:52; 22:14), he identifies with them in their sins — the sin presupposed by the repentance symbolised by John's baptism. By being baptised Jesus reveals that dealing with sin is at the heart of his messianic task. Accordingly, the Father confirms his messianic identity and, in so doing, endows him with the Holy Spirit for carrying out his messianic role; the Jordan is Jesus' own baptism with, and reception of, the Spirit.

The necessity of this messianic solidarity in sin (that takes Jesus from the Jordan into the desert on the way, eventually, to the cross) ultimately lies in the eschatological-forensic reality of God's wrath, highlighted by John's baptism/ministry (3:7; *cf*. v. 9). Not the 'horizontal' consequences of sin, but God's judicial anger on sin (reflected, to be sure, in resultant human misery and suffering) — that is the ultimate exigency sin creates. To save his people Christ must propitiate that justly deserved divine wrath, by identifying with them in their guilt and enduring judgment for them; the Messiah is judicial sin-bearer.

Subsequently, in 12:49–50, a passage found only in Luke, Jesus declares that he has 'come to bring fire on the earth' and, correlatively, has 'a baptism to undergo'. The overtones of John's prophecy are unmistakable: both 'fire' and 'baptism' (noun and verb), and clearly with connotations of discriminating judgment (*cf*. Jesus as the bringer of 'division', v. 51). This impending situation (note the air of tension, even 'distress' in the subordinate clauses, vv. 49 and 50) has two components: Jesus' bringing ('casting' = baptising with) fire on earth and, correlatively, a baptism with which he has to be baptised; the messianic baptiser must himself be baptised.

In view in that baptism, without question, is the cross as the climax of Jesus' suffering. In Mark 10:38–39, the near parrallel to verse 50a, 'the baptism I am baptised with' is, alternatively, 'the cup I drink', and that 'cup', according to Luke 22:42 par., is plainly the imminent ordeal of the cross (from which Jesus recoils in agony, v. 44).[18] This passage reinforces the forensic nature of baptism in Luke 3. It also warrants viewing the entirety of Jesus' ministry, from the Jordan to the cross, as a kind of baptism, as one large submission to the baptism-ordeal of God's judicial wrath.

4. At Pentecost Jesus' disciples are not consumed like chaff by the 'fiery *pneuma*' because he, the baptiser, has already been baptised for them. On their behalf he has passed through final judgment — enduring the condemnation and destruction their sins deserve and emerging from that baptism–ordeal triumphant and vindicated in his death and resurrection. In their case God's wrath has been quenched, the fire of destruction exhausted; only the blessings of messianic baptism remain. As resurrected and exalted Lord, and so now in reception of the Spirit as gift (Acts 2:32–33; *cf*. 1:4; Luke 24:49), his baptising is totally saving; the presence of the Spirit at Pentecost is manifestly gracious.

Fire is in fact present at Pentecost, in the form of 'what seemed to be tongues of fire' resting on each of the disciples (Acts 2:3) — present, in other words, not as a substantive reality but as a sign, a fire-like phenomenon. In view of the extensive forensic background Luke has already developed, it seems difficult to deny that this theophanic presence (*cf*., e.g., Exod. 3:2; 13:21–22; Psa. 78:14), whatever else may be involved, demonstrates that in their (the church's) case the fire of destructive judgment has been dissipated, the guilty verdict has been annulled. The gently-positioned, non-consuming fire-tongues reveal that the conflagration of God's eschatological wrath and judgment on sin, which Christ himself will kindle at the end of history (*cf.* Luke 12:49; Acts 2:19–20; *cf.* 2 Thess. 1:7–8; 2:8), and which will consume the unrepentant like chaff, will not consume those who repent, because, in their stead, he has already endured that holocaust in history. As the Joel passage cited by Peter intimates (just beyond the portion cited in vv. 17–21), through him all who call on the name of the Lord for salvation are 'survivors' of eschatological judgment (2:32; MT 3:5).

(There is no need to force a choice between this and the view that the tongues of fire symbolise purification,[19] although, against the Old Testament background, judgment appears to be the more basic, controlling idea. In Isaiah 4:4, notably, the Spirit is closely associated with fire in the context of [messianic, v. 2] judgment: Zion/Jerusalem will be cleansed 'by the Spirit of judgment and the Spirit of fire'; which can be compared to the fire of purifying eschatological judgment in Malachi 3:2–3. The cleansing work of the Spirit is a function of judgment.)

Pentecost, then, is the *de facto* justification of the church. Along with Christ's resurrection and ascension (with which it forms a complex of inseparable, once-for-all events; *cf.* 2:32–33) it is a declaration, in effect, of the church's righteous standing before God. Pentecost is not only the efficacious empowering of the church for kingdom-service (it is that, to be sure), but is also the effective demonstration that the church is no longer subject to God's wrath. The eschatological life of the Spirit poured out on the church at Pentecost seals its acquittal and the definitive removal of its guilt. The baptism with the Holy Spirit openly attests that 'there is now no condemnation for those who are in Christ Jesus' (Rom. 8:1). The Spirit of Pentecost is the Spirit of justification.

The reality of justification is as central to the message of Luke-Acts as is Pentecost, no more no less. Where that is not appreciated it will be difficult to see that justification has any substantive importance for Luke, and treatment of materials (by themselves relatively sparse) that deal more or less explicitly with justifiction will remain limited to a largely inconclusive exegesis in their immediate contexts. Such materials are seen in a true light only when they are assessed, as Luke intends, from that basic and comprehensive point of reference provided by the forensic significance of Pentecost.

III.   THE FORGIVENESS OF SINS IN LUKE-ACTS

1. 'Forgiveness of sins' is an expression that does not appear in the New Testament with great frequency. But of the 11 occurrences 8 are found in Luke–Acts.[20] In the Gospel, explicit references to the remission of sins, though few, are pivotally placed. The first occurs in Zechariah's song (the 'Benedictus'): John, the final prophet-forerunner (*cf.* 16:16), will give the Lord's people 'the knowledge of salvation through the forgiveness of their sins' (1:77). Not to be missed here is the association of remission with salvation. The latter is a major theme in Luke–Acts.[21] In this instance, at the outset (note the earlier references to salvation in vv. 47,69,71), the promised messianic salvation is defined more exactly as salvation from sin, by means of forgiveness.

Consequently, in the summary account of John's ministry the essence of his preaching and baptism is 'repentance for the forgiveness of sins' (3:3), forgiveness in view of what the Messiah, the one through whom 'all mankind will see God's salvation' (v. 6), the Spirit and fire baptiser (vv. 15–16), is to accomplish. Accordingly, in Jesus' synagogue teaching at Nazareth (4:16ff.), introduced by Luke to epitomise the Galilean ministry from its outset,[22] Jesus identifies himself, in the words of Isaiah, as the Lord's Spirit-anointed (v. 16), whose mission, among other things, is 'to proclaim freedom for the prisoners' and 'to release the oppressed' (v. 18). 'Freedom' and 'release' translate the word (*aphesis*) usually rendered 'forgiveness', and that latter sense is likely included here.[23] What it treats is the entire range of indebtedness and bondage created by sin.

One of the petitions found in Luke's shorter version of the Lord's prayer is for the forgiveness of sins (11:4; *cf.* 17:3–4). And at the close, the gist of the gospel to be preached worldwide in the name of the now crucified and resurrected Christ is 'repentance and/for forgiveness of sins' (24:47). Thus while explicit mention of forgiveness may be relatively sparse, the reality of remission is integral to the message of this Gospel.[24]

2. There are just two places in the Synoptic tradition where Jesus explicitly declares someone's sins to be forgiven. One is found in all three Gospels (Luke 5:17–26, par.), the other is unique to Luke (7:36–50). Because of this and other common features, for our purposes we may consider the two passages together.

In 5:17ff., where Jesus heals the paralytic, the issue relates to what has attracted increasing attention in the course of his Galilean ministry — the authority of his teaching (4:32), the efficacy of his word, whose performative power is evidenced, for instance, in exorcisms (4:36). Here, however, the specific issue is his authority to forgive sins (5:24). The crux of this incident in all three Synoptic accounts is not the healing but Jesus' declaration (to the paralytic) 'your sins are forgiven' (v. 20). The healing, strictly speaking, is in reaction to the sceptical questioning of 'the Pharisees and the teachers of the law' (v. 21; this is not to suggest that he would not have otherwise healed the paralytic).

The unheard-of radicality of Jesus' declaration must not be muted. At issue is not merely the possibility or promise of forgiveness, or his teaching that God forgives and will forgive; — that was Old Testament teaching (e.g. Ex. 34:6–7; Ps. 86:5; 103:3; Is. 43:25) familiar to the Pharisees. If this were all Jesus meant, then they would not have made their charge of blasphemy (v. 21). More is at stake in this gospel pronouncement of Jesus, and the Pharisees sense that and respond accordingly.

That 'more' involves at least two facets: the remission of sins itself, i.e. (complete) forgiveness as a present reality; and the capacity and authority of Jesus to grant that reality. The present actuality is accented by Luke's use of the verb for forgiveness in the (Greek) perfect tense (v. 20), which 'expresses the abiding force of the forgiveness',[25] and the indication that forgiveness has taken place 'on earth' (v. 24).

The authority claimed by Jesus is authority as 'the Son of Man' (v. 24). This is the initial occurrence in Luke of what is 'a favourite self-designation of Jesus'[26] to affirm his messianic identity. Specifically, against the background of the royal figure foreseen in Daniel 7:13–14, it brings into view his heavenly

origin and, with increasing clarity as the Gospel unfolds, his prerogatives —
as the eschatological baptiser 'more powerful' than John (3:16) — for final
rule and judgment (9:26; 12:8,40; 17:22,24,26,30; 18:8; 21:27,36; 22:69).[27]
Used here in response to the Pharisees it involves an implicit divine claim,
which they sense and cannot tolerate. He has the authority to do what God
alone can do.

A primary thrust of this passage is that true healing — salvation — concerns
the whole person, not just physical affliction such as that of the paralytic or,
in general, conditions of human misery resulting from sin. Rather, it heals
the entire person as sinner; most specifically, the person as *guilty* sinner.[28]
Where that guilt is pardoned, the eventual, eschatological restoration of the
whole person is bound to follow (as the physical healing of the paralytic is
intended, in part, to signify). The coming of the Son of Man means that the
sentence of justification will not only take place before the future, heavenly
tribunal, but is also pronounced now, on earth; or, better: the irreversible,
eschatological verdict of absolute, unqualified acquittal is already rendered
in history. This is the prerogative of the Son of Man, the eschatological king
and messianic baptiser–judge; this, too, is perhaps the most awe-inspiring of
the 'paradoxes' witnessed by the crowd that day (v. 26).

In 7:36ff. Jesus' announcement of sins forgiven is two-fold: first to Simon
the Pharisee concerning the woman, in view of her lavish act of devotion to
Jesus (v. 47; *cf.* 37–38); and then, in words virtually identical to those to the
paralytic (5:21), to the forgiven woman herself (v. 48). What heightens the
impact of these declarations is the context: Jesus is dining, by invitation, in
the home of a Pharisee (v. 36) and the (uninvited and no doubt unwanted)
woman is a notorious 'sinner' (v. 37, probably a prostitute[29]), a fact that is
accented by Simon's unvoiced indignation and scepticism about Jesus (v. 39).
Particularly startling, climaxing Jesus' response to Simon (whose silent doubts
about him as a prophet he prophetically intuits), is the comprehensive scope
of the pardon affirmed: not just one particular sin but the 'many sins', no
matter how heinous, of this infamous sinner are forgiven (v. 47).

This pronouncement leaves the other guests astounded and asking: 'Who
is this who even forgives sins?' (v. 49). Luke gives no indication of Jesus'
response, if any, to this question. But for the attentive reader it is
undoubtedly a rhetorical question with a Christological answer to be supplied
by the eschatological claim of the Son of Man already heard in 5:24.

3. An important aspect of both these passages is the role of faith. In each
instance the remission is sovereign and gracious (it is not even sought, at least
not explicitly) but it is not indiscriminate or gratuitous in the sense of being
granted without faith. The declaration of forgiveness to the paralytic is tied
directly to the fact that 'Jesus saw their faith' (5:20a; that is, interestingly,
the faith of those who brought him, as well as his own).

Neither the content of their faith nor its precise function in relation to
forgiveness is spelled out. Exactly what they understood about Jesus' true
identity is not made clear, so that we must avoid undue speculation about
their state of mind. Still, in the context of Israel's history and its covenant
consciousness, it does seem in order here to see an instance of the faith of
Abraham, the trust that 'the Lord will provide' (Gen. 22:8,14). However
unclear and elemental their grasp of Jesus' significance may have been, they
recognise him to be the Lord's promised provision and seek him out, relying

on his power to meet their need; however seminally, they entrust themselves and their most basic concerns to Jesus.

Noteworthy also is the fact that Jesus *sees* their faith. In view of his ability to read the thoughts of the Pharisees (v. 22; *cf.* 7:40), it would be wrong to eliminate from this 'sight' insight into their attitude and the true disposition of their hearts. But it would also be wrong to restrict it to such insight. What Jesus saw is what all present saw: people so intent on getting to Jesus that they were ready to make every effort, no matter how extraordinary (v. 19), to do so. Their faith was visible, embodied in and inseparable from the actions they took.

These same considerations are present in 7:36ff., even more emphatically. The culmination of the entire narrative is Jesus' declaration to the woman: 'Your faith has saved you; go in peace' (v. 50). This amplifies his prior declarations, both *about* and *to* her (vv. 47–48), that her sins are forgiven: her salvation consists in remission of her sins, with the resultant state of peace with God, in view of her faith. As in 5:17ff., the content and function of her faith are not elaborated, but something of its nature comes to light as much of the narrative is taken up with contrasting her faith and Simon's unbelief, in order to unmask the latter.

The salient point can be appreciated by focusing on the much-debated statement in verse 47: 'her many sins have been forgiven — for she loved much'. Here the conjunction 'for'/'because' (*hoti*) introduces love as the result or evidence, not the basis or cause of forgiveness — contrary to the traditional Roman Catholic view and some Liberal Protestant commentators.[30] Only this sense fits the context where the whole point of the parable of the two forgiven debtors (vv. 41–43) is that being forgiven leads to loving, not the reverse. Furthermore, the reverse side of the woman's situation reads, 'But he who has been forgiven little loves little' (v. 47b), so that, by the parallelism involved, the woman, in contrast, illustrates the truth, 'the one who has been forgiven much loves much'. The statement in question can be paraphrased: 'Her many sins are forgiven, as her much love evidences' (*cf.* Zerwick §422).

What Jesus affirms climactically in her heartfelt ('weeping', v. 38) outpouring of love and devotion is her faith, again not only because of his unerring insight into the hidden recesses of the human heart (*cf.* v. 40) but also because of what is available for all to see. As in 5:17ff. so here too faith, focused profoundly and even more evidently on his person, is embodied in action. The (justifying) faith of the woman is certainly not faith formed by love or acts of contrition, but it is 'faith working through love' (Gal. 5:6).

Elsewhere, in instances of physical healing — either independently in Luke or in parallels — Jesus declares that faith has 'saved' someone (8:48; 17:19; 18:42; *cf.* Acts 14:9). An underlying connection between these incidents and those we have been considering is suggested by the bond (already seen in 5:17ff.) between *sin and sickness*, on the one hand, and *forgiveness and healing*, on the other.

In other passages in the Gospel forgiveness is tied not to faith but to repentance — in summary descriptions of the preaching of John the Baptist (3:3; *cf.* v. 8) and of the proclamation authorised by the resurrected Christ (24:47), and in 17:3–4. In the latter Jesus' insistence that repentance is the condition of forgiveness deals with human interpersonal relationships; but, in the light of the Lord's prayer (11:4 — 'forgive us . . ., for we also forgive'), he undoubtedly has in mind the pattern of God's dealing with sinners as well.

In the other two instances (3:2; 24:47) — because of their comprehensive, summary nature — faith is probably included in repentance or so closely associated with it that to speak of the one necessarily brings into view the other. That is borne out by 22:32, where Jesus' prayer that Peter's faith may not fail is to be answered by his 'turning (back)', an idea (conversion) closely related to that of repentance (17:4; *cf.* Acts 3:19; 26:20). The 'sinner who repents' (15:7,10) is the sinner who believes (7:50). Similarly, in Acts 11:18 the salvation granted to the Gentiles is, comprehensively, 'repentance unto life'.

All told, as more careful study could show, in Luke–Acts faith/repentance/ conversion all refer to the decisive movement away from sinning and self-reliance toward God, to relying on his power (especially his power to forgive sins) and doing his will. Faith, as we have already seen, often describes that movement as directed specifically to Jesus and his word (e.g. also, Acts 10:43; 16:31; 20:21 — 'repentance toward God and faith in our Lord Jesus Christ', NASB). Etymologically considered, the Greek term for repentance (*metanoia*) describes a change of mind. But that change is hardly a bare mental act. It engages the whole person and does not exist in isolation, apart from specific, concrete manifestations; like faith, it is embodied in 'fruit in keeping with repentance' (Luke 3:8; Acts 26:20).[31]

4. Luke, as noted, has only two places where Jesus pronounces sins forgiven. But both these incidents have to be seen within the broader context of Jesus' table fellowship and other ongoing associations with sinners. That such conduct was typical is suggested by the reproach of the Pharisees and law-experts that Jesus was 'a friend of tax collectors and sinners' (7:34; *cf.* v. 30). They said he 'welcomes sinners and eats with them' (15:2; *cf.* v. 1).

A clear instance of this fellowship is the calling of Levi, culminating in Jesus' announcement that 'it is not the healthy who need a doctor, but the sick', and that he did 'not come to call the righteous, but sinners to repentance' (5:31–32). Also, unique to Luke, Jesus lodges with Zacchaeus, 'a chief tax collector' (19:2), and declares, as the high point of the account, that 'the Son of Man came to seek and to save what was lost' (v. 10). The three parables in chapter 15, two of which are found only in Luke (the Lost Coin, vv. 8–10 and the Lost Son, vv. 11–32), illumine this salvation of the lost, of sinners in distinction from the righteous (vv. 7,10,32).

On Jesus' lips the sense of this distinction is deliberately elusive. On the one hand, he apparently took it over from his opponents (usually identified by Luke as 'the Pharisees and law-experts', e.g., 15:2), who, because of their knowledge of the law and their commitment to observing it faithfully, considered themselves to be the 'righteous' (before God and man), in distinction from 'sinners' — Gentiles and other Jews who did not keep the law and in some instances, like tax collectors and prostitutes, were notoriously dishonest and immoral.[32] In taking over this distinction Jesus is not simply being ironic. He recognises its relative validity; he does not facilely reduce the conduct of each group to the same level, and recognises, in some instances, the moral earnestness of the 'righteous' (*cf.* the rich ruler, 18:21–22).

At the same time, Jesus' friendship with 'sinners' and his assertion that he has come to save them and not the 'righteous' relativises that distinction. His ministry of salvation to 'sinners' kindles such intense conflict and animosity because it implicitly challenges the system of salvation of the 'righteous' at its core. Given the cultural-religious circumstances, Jesus' table fellowship with 'sinners' itself shows vividly that acceptance with God and acquittal in the forum of his judgment is not based on 'righteous' conduct, no matter how scrupulous, but on God's unmerited mercy, mediated through commitment to Jesus and his word. Jesus' calling of 'sinners' to repentance is as well an unmistakable sign and challenge to the 'righteous' that they, too, are sinners and in need of repentance. The parable of the lost son, for instance, is not only about that son — his sin, his repentance, and the gracious treatment he receives from the father; it is as much about the older ('righteous') brother and his anger.[33] Despite the evident contrast between his conduct and the profligate behaviour of the younger brother, that anger reveals just as evidently that he is lacking the love and compassion that are at the heart of what the law in fact requires (*cf.* 10:27–28). The closing words of the father (15:31–32) are an implicit invitation to the elder son.

Jesus' fellowship with 'sinners' should not be construed as indulgent or indifferent acceptance; he does not tolerate their sin. Among the synoptists, it is Luke who accents the call to repentance (5:32; *cf.* Matt. 9:13; Mark 2:17). Levi leaves everything to follow Jesus (5:28), and Zacchaeus, reminiscent of the woman who anointed Jesus' feet (7:36ff.), responds with a spontaneous display of generosity and restitution.

5. Two motifs in the Lucan account of Jesus' ministry of forgiveness, already noted, will bear emphasising: the *Christological* and *antithetical* nature of his conduct and proclamation.

Jesus' message is not the timeless truth that 'God forgives', without further qualification but an eschatological reality. It functions within the concrete historical context of the actual arrival of God's kingdom. It does not have a general validity, apart from him; its truth is staked on his unique person and activity. The Son of Man is the eschatological judge and has the authority already, on earth, to render a verdict of acquittal, because he is the Son of Man who must suffer and be rejected and killed and raised to life on the third day (9:22,44; 18:31; 22:22,48; 24:7). Strictly speaking, the perfect tense in 5:20 ('your sins are forgiven') depends on his future death and resurrection. The messianic baptiser can grant remission from guilt to the believing and repentant because by his own baptism on the cross he bears away God's just wrath and punishment on their sins.

Sometimes this Christological dimension is either denied outright or otherwise obscured or restricted. Such views are usually variations on the view that the content of Jesus' gospel is the Father and not the Son.[34] This tradition persists in the view, for instance, that the parable of the lost son is by itself a complete statement of the gospel (its portrayal of the father's unconditioned love is a self-contained paradigm of the gospel), or in the view that forgiveness is based solely on repentance.

But there is no place in Luke for a gospel of Jesus without Christ. Individual pericopae on forgiveness, faith, and repentance were never meant to be detached from the larger, controlling framework of Luke-Acts, focused on the event-complex of Jesus' death, resurrection, ascension, and outpouring of the Spirit — in its eschatological, forensic significance. The parable of the lost son is distorted as soon as it is read in isolation from the reality of messianic suffering and glory.

These observations apply as well to the view that Luke has no real interest in Jesus' death as an atonement or satisfaction for sin.[35] The case here rests on the facts that (1) in the accounts of apostolic preaching in Acts there is only minimal mention of Christ's death; (2) Luke's only references to the atoning significance of Christ's death are two traditional formulae (Luke 22:19–20; Acts 20:28); and (3) he omits the 'ransom'-word (Mark 10:45; *cf.* Matt. 20:28). Why Luke does *not* include the saying of Mark 10:45 is an interesting question to ponder, and we may wonder why there is not more in Acts about the significance of Christ's death. But to conclude that for Luke the atonement is at best peripheral is so to focus on details that the larger picture vanishes — that total picture whose centre includes messianic Spirit and fire baptism, conditioned on the sin-bearing, wrath-propitiating baptism experienced by the Messiah himself. Luke knows of no remission of sin apart from this reality. In fact, it does not go too far to say that he knows no remission that is not based on that messianic work.

The Christological, salvation-historical aspect of Jesus' ministry of forgiveness gives rise to its antithetical character. Because Jesus, especially in his messianic suffering and glory, is the focus of the entire Old Testament (Luke 24:25–27, 44–47), fundamental conflict between him (and later the church) and the main streams within contemporary Jewish soteriology was inevitable. These were all based on thoroughly misconstruing God's covenant with Israel, especially his righteousness and mercy, as well as the function of the law.[36]

Leaving aside the question as to how self-consciously merit-oriented these systems were, there is no question that a righteous, 'not guilty' standing before God was viewed not as his undeserved gift but as a human attainment. The Pharisees exemplify this. The law became effectively detached from God; it no longer functioned in an already existing, graciously established and maintained fellowship of righteousness with him, but to acquire and maintain a right standing before him. On the negative side the key issue was guilt — an issue which, with the final judgment in view, was always open and unresolved. Such confidence as was to be had in that respect was based on reward acquired through observance of the specific stipulations of the law; and in some cases, such as the Pharisees, oral tradition ostensibly built upon it.

Such a system is self-centred rather than God-centred. It presupposes a high, perfectionistic view of human beings and a correspondingly low view of sin that, at its worst, gives rise to self-righteousness and hypocrisy. There was room for the mercy of God and repentance; but the repentant sinner was always at a disadvantage in comparison with the righteous. A daily, 'self-sustaining system of penitential achievement and forgiveness'[37] was maintained; one that simply could not comprehend the radical, once-for-all repentance and the eschatological forgiveness foreseen by John the Baptist and actually granted by Jesus. Jesus' acceptance of 'sinners' rather than 'the righteous' created a break with this system that was total.

This antithesis explains why the fruitful, obedient nature of the repentance and faith elicited by Jesus in his disciples may not be confused with the conscientious scrupulosity of the Pharisees. The two are poles apart. Outside the kingdom of God every form of discipleship and spiritual regimen is self-serving in the deepest and most ultimate sense — efforts at establishing one's self before God and in the world, forms of self-aggrandisement and self-justification. But in the kingdom sinners have been set free from the impossible task of self-justification. They have been freed from serving themselves and so, unlike the elder son, they are free to love and serve God and others. Before God they are no longer servile but servant-sons.

6. In the light of our preceding discussion, references to the forgiveness of sins in Acts may be considered much more briefly. These all occur in sermons or other speech material of Peter or Paul. Luke certainly intends these sermons to be read against the background of his Gospel, and the proclamation of John the Baptist and of Jesus; a reading which discloses, among other things, the essential identity of their proclamation of the remission of sins with that of the apostles. Specifically, Acts provides examples of that preaching of forgiveness commissioned by the resurrected Jesus in Luke 24:47.

Without becoming embroiled here in the much-mooted question of the purpose of Acts, surely 1:8 functions as a programme statement: Luke intends to document, as the resurrected Christ had promised, the world-wide spread of apostolic gospel preaching, from Jerusalem to 'the ends of the earth' (Rome). To this end the sermons in Acts are not verbatim transcripts but summaries, carefully selected and shaped to illustrate what was typical of that preaching in its progress. They are to be read not as characterising the distinctives of the theology of Peter or Paul but as showing, in summary profile, what was common and prominent in earliest Christian witness and proclamation, primarily to those outside the church. Taken with these qualifications, they are faithful historical accounts, not free literary creations of Luke to advance his theology in the face of other competing, even conflicting alternatives current at the time of writing.[38]

The first mention of forgiveness in Acts is in the conclusion to Peter's Pentecost sermon: 'Repent and be baptised, every one of you, in the name of Jesus Christ for the forgiveness of your sins. And you will receive the gift of the Holy Spirit. The promise is for you and your children and for all who are afar off — for all whom the Lord our God will call' (2:38–39). This gospel declaration responds to the entreaty of those in the crowd who are deeply convicted by Peter's indictment of their complicity and guilt, along with wicked, 'lawless' men (v. 23), in crucifying Jesus (v. 37). Their plea, in effect, is that of the Philippian jailor: 'What must I do to be saved?' (16:30; *cf.* 2:40). (The summary nature of Peter's response is intimated by 'many other words', v. 40.)

Among the key elements in this declaration are those already present in the Gospel, beginning with John the Baptist's ministry (3:3): baptism associated with repentance and remission, and remission conditioned on repentance — as amplified above. Now, however, there are notable additions: baptism 'in the name of Jesus Christ' and reception of the gift of the Spirit, as well as an indication of the universality of the gospel-promise (not only for Israel but for 'all who are far off').

The explicit connection of (water) baptism with the name of Christ (*cf.* 8:16; 10:48; 19:5) points to the new situation of messianic glory introduced by his death and resurrection, and, probably, to confession of him, the crucified, as the now exalted Christ (*cf.* v. 36). This baptism is neither the same as, nor completely divorced from, John's baptism. As signs they both point to the same reality: the messianic Spirit and fire baptism with its benefits for the repentant. But they do so from decisively different salvation-historical vantage points — John's from the angle of promise, Christian baptism from that of fulfilment.

This suggests how the gift of the Spirit is to be understood — not as an independent, presumably even subsequent, addition to forgiveness but as integrally and inseparably connected. This ties in with the forensic significance of Pentecost, discussed earlier: those who are justified are those who are Spirit-baptised, not as a supplementary benefit but as the essential validation of their justification. What Peter holds out to the crowd is not an individual experience of power such as they have just been observing in Peter and others (although similar experiences of power may have followed for some of those who repented). Rather, he offers inclusion into the church as the Spirit-baptised people of God, so that they share individually in what is true of that community corporately: the indwelling presence and power of the Spirit himself as the integral seal that their sins, too, are forgiven.

These observations are borne out later when Peter explains to the Jerusalem church the expansion of the scope of Holy Spirit baptism to include the Gentiles (11:1ff.). The bottom line of his assessment is that God has granted the Gentiles 'repentance unto life' (v. 18); that is, eschatological life, conditioned on (and a function of) the forgiveness of sins. And in verse 39 'the promise' probably embraces *both* the forgiveness of sins *and* the gift of the Spirit in verse 38. Both benefits are seen as inseparable aspects of a single promise — a promise, moreover, which in view of the Old Testament allusions made (Isa. 57:19 and Joel 2:32), lies at the heart of the old-covenant expectations (*cf.* Gal. 3:1–14).

Subsequent references to forgiveness in Peter's sermons do not add substantively to what we have found in 2:38. To a similar audience and with a similar tone, the call to repentance in 3:19 is joined with the idea of 'turning' (*cf.* 26:20; Luke 17:3–4), and the vocabulary of forgiveness is replaced by sins being 'wiped/blotted out' or 'cancelled'. This language has a no less forensic force (*cf.* Paul's usage in Col. 2:14; *cf.* v. 13 and the LXX of Psa. 50:1; *cf.* v. 4; Isa. 43:35; 44:22).

In 5:31 the testimony of Peter and the other apostles before the Sanhedrin (v. 27) is that God has exalted Jesus, whom they are killed, so that he might give 'repentance and forgiveness of sins to Israel'. The looser connection here is to be understood in the light of the other passages where the function of repentance is made more precise.

In 8:22 Peter admonishes Simon: 'Repent of this wickedness and pray to God. Perhaps he will forgive you for having such a thought in your heart.' This tentative way of speaking about forgiveness is not intended to cast doubt on its possibility, should Simon repent, but to accent the grave presumption of his sin.

In 10:43, before the household of Cornelius, Peter affirms as the concerted testimony of all the prophets that 'everyone who believes in him receives forgiveness of sins through his name'. Here faith replaces repentance, showing the interchangeability of the two, or at least their inseparability for 'receiving' forgiveness; and both faith and forgiveness are tied to Jesus, particularly his death and resurrection (vv. 39–41).

The tie with verse 44 should not be missed: as Peter speaks the Holy Spirit comes on all who 'hear' (= 'believe') his message. The faith that receives forgiveness, receives the Holy Spirit — among other things, the Spirit as the inseparable, attesting seal of that forgiveness.

Of interest in the wider context of chapter 10 is the description of Cornelius prior to the events narrated: he is 'righteous' (v. 22), which illustrates the truth that 'God does not show favouritism but accepts men from every nation fear him and do what is right' (vv. 34–35), and is heard by God in view of his gifts to the poor (vv. 4,31). By themselves these descriptions can appear moralistic, or to approve a religion of works — in tension, for instance, with the *sola gratia* of Paul.[39]

But that would be a very distorted reading. The key here is the further description of Cornelius as 'God-fearing' (vv. 2,22,35), that is, as one who, though uncircumcised, is otherwise included in the circle of God's covenant with Israel and embraces the religion of the Old Testmant. He is a true worshipper of the true God. He is like the other centurion whose faith is mentioned by Luke (Luke 7:1–10), and comparable to old-covenant believers like Zechariah and Elizabeth (1:6 — 'righteous in the sight of God'), Simeon (2:25 — 'righteous and devout'), and Anna (2:38). Cornelius' prayers and righteous deeds are 'fruit in keeping with repentance' and presuppose God's unmerited covenantal mercy and grace.

The issue is the continuity of the religion of the old covenant and the gospel of the kingdom, a continuity Luke affirms in accenting the *Christological* meaning and focus of the entire Old Testament (e.g. Luke 24:27, 44–47). Old Testament religion is Christ-centred religion. The point of Acts 10 is not the conversion experience of Cornelius as an individual, but the inclusion of the Gentiles in the church as the eschatological, Spirit-baptised people of God (v. 45; 11:1, 18; 15:7).[40]

There are just two references to the forgiveness of sins in accounts of Paul's preaching: 13:38 and 26:18. The former will be considered below. In his defence before Agrippa (26:1ff.), Paul recounts his commission from the exalted Christ: he was sent to Jews and Gentiles 'to open their eyes and turn them from darkness to light, and from the power of Satan to God, so that they may receive forgiveness of sins and a place among those who are sanctified by faith in me' (v. 18). Such a commission also involves preaching 'that they should repent and turn to God and prove their repentance by their deeds' (v. 20). The continuity with Peter's proclamation is apparent (in terms reminiscent of Colossians 1:12–14[41]), with its emphasis on the repentance and conversion that are the condition of forgiveness, and forgiveness tied to Christ's suffering and resurrection (v. 23). The sense of the associated idea of being 'sanctified' by faith is difficult to determine precisely. Luke uses the verb in only one other place in an almost identical phrase, also in Paul's mouth (20:32). Perhaps the thought, with the Greek verb used in the perfect tense, is to accent the bond (established through repentance and faith and by receiving the Spirit) between being forgiven and being set apart to God from sin.

There is a parallel account of Paul's conversion and commission in 22:16 ('Get up, be baptised and wash your sins away, calling on his name').

'Washing away' sins is almost certainly to be understood forensically, as a metaphor for forgiveness, associated here with baptism and faith in Jesus (*cf.* v. 14). Incidentally, baptism is mentioned here and in 2:38, but not in the other passages considered, which is an indication of its distinctive function: it does not have some *ex opere operato* necessity in parallel with repentance and faith, but is rather the external sign pointing to the reality (forgiveness and the gift of the Spirit) received by faith and repentance.

To sum up: in Acts, forgiveness of sins is the same forensic reality, conditioned on repentance and faith, that it is in the Gospel; but now the claim is made explicit that it is based on Christ's death and resurrection and validated by the gift of the Spirit.

IV. 'JUSTIFICATION' IN LUKE-ACTS

Luke uses the actual language of justification — the verb repeatedly used by Paul, especially in Romans and Galatians, to mean 'justify' — just a few times, and only two uses are directly pertinent to our inquiry: Luke 18:14 and Acts 13:39. We will consider them briefly in reverse order.

1. Toward the close of his synagogue sermon in Pisidian Antioch Paul announces: 'Therefore, my brothers, I want you to know that through Jesus the forgiveness of sins is proclaimed to you. Through him everyone who believes is justified from everything you could not be justified from by the law of Moses' (Acts 13:38–39). Here again we find remission tied to Jesus (the crucified and resurrected Jesus, vv. 27–37); but then comes the amplification that faith in Jesus *justifies* — the only place in the New Testament outside of James and the letters of Paul where faith and justification are explicitly related.

These verses are among those at the 'storm centre' of scholarly controversy over Acts in recent decades. For many, they are part of Luke's 'picture' of Paul that allegedly does not harmonise with the reliable portrait we have from his own letters.[42] In particular, 13:38–39 — along with 15:10 (where Peter says: 'Now then, why do you try to test God by putting on the necks of the [Gentile] disciples a yoke that neither we nor our fathers have been able to bear?') — are read as advancing, in tension or even in conflict with Paul's radical, unrelieved polemic against the law, a justification for Jewish Christians based on law and works with the addition of faith, and a law-free justification by faith for Gentile converts.

I cannot debate this viewpoint in its various shadings here, except to express the judgment that it thoroughly misconstrues both Luke and Paul. Its distorted conception of Paul results, in part, from failing to recognise his positive use and application of the law in passages like Romans 13:8–10 (*cf.* 7:12), 1 Corinthians 7:19, and 1 Timothy 1:8; while in both Acts 13:39 and 15:10 Luke has in view a justification by faith (salvation by grace) which is plainly not *relative* but *absolute*. As Peter says (15:11), 'No! We believe it is through the grace of our Lord Jesus that we [Jews] are saved, just as they [Gentiles] are' — grace that involves a justification by faith where there is no place for works other than as 'fruit in keeping with repentance'.

In Acts 13:38–39 Paul is not the mouthpiece for Luke's own, creative theologising; nor is Luke attempting to give in detail Paul's teaching on justification and forgiveness. Measured by his intention to provide reliable sketches of apostolic preaching, these verses are entirely adequate as a concise summary, in Luke's own words, of Paul's teaching on justification. That holds true regardless of the question of how familiar he was with Paul's letters, or even of how well he himself understood Paul (issues like these, strictly, are beside the point).

The same observations apply to 24:25. There, in speaking to Felix and Drusilla about 'faith in Jesus Christ' (v. 24), Paul confronts them concerning 'righteousness, self-control and the judgment to come'. There is no problem here — especially in view of the summary nature of the description, as well as the mention of final judgment and Felix's fearful reaction — with concluding that 'righteousness' at least includes the forensic dimension developed by Paul in his letters.

2. In the Gospel the verb in question is used five times: three times by Jesus (7:35; 16:15; 18:14) and twice in Luke's narrative commentary (7:29; 10:29). All five have either a forensic or quasi-forensic meaning with either a declarative or closely related demonstrative sense.[43] In 7:29, 35 the thought is that of vindication before a forum: in the matter of Jesus' teaching on John the Baptist, the listening crowd as a whole 'vindicates' God ('acknowledged that God's way was right', NIV), and wisdom, in general, is 'vindicated' ('proved right', NIV) by her 'children'. In 10:29 the law-expert 'wanted to justify himself' in the debate he had instigated with Jesus; before the forum of those present he seeks to vindicate himself, to show that he is in the right. (Luke 16:15 is best looked at with 18:14.)

The parable of the Pharisee and the tax collector is found only in Luke.[44] Standing at the close of Luke's lengthy insertion (distinctive among the Synoptics) into his account of Jesus' journey to Jerusalem (9:51–18:14), it provides 'a fitting finale'[45] to that insertion. In the well-known conclusion to this parable — 'I tell you that this man, rather than the other, went home justified before God' (v. 14) — justification is plainly soteric as well as forensic, particularly when it is seen within the framework of Luke–Acts already discussed.

The parable stands on its own in the immediate context, and the occasion for it is clear from verse 9: Jesus directs it to 'some who were confident of their own righteousness and looked down on everybody else.' A more literal translation is: 'some who were confident in themselves that [or perhaps even, "because"[46]] they were righteous'. Their confidence of being righteous, not only in comparison to others but before God himself (as the prayer of vv. 11–12 subsequently discloses), resides not in God but in themselves.

In view are the 'righteous', in terms of contemporary Jewish socio-religious categories. That these are the Pharisees, at least characteristically, follows from the parable (v. 10) as well as 16:15, where, in Jesus' words to them, they are 'the ones who justify yourselves in the eyes of men, but God knows your hearts'. This does not mean that they do not try to justify themselves before God. To the contrary, their assumption is that to establish or demonstrate their own righteousness before men is to do so before God. But it is just this presumed self-justification that Jesus immediately denies to them in the severest terms: 'What is highly valued among men is detestable in God's sight'. At issue, then, is righteousness before God. The parable answers the question: who is righteous in God's eyes?

The story Jesus tells, contrasting the two prayers and God's assessment of each, illustrates vividly the truth that he has not come to call the 'righteous' but 'sinners' (5:32). As often noted, the shock-effect on the original hearers — for whom, in general, the Pharisee would have been an admired or at least respectable figure in contrast with the thoroughly despicable tax collector — tends to be lost on those who can understand the parable and its conclusion within the broader biblical context. In fact, there is nothing wrong with what the Pharisee prays. It is a prayer of thanksgiving to God for the thoroughly commendable deeds enumerated, some of which (the amount of fasting and tithing) went beyond the law's requirements; it can even be said to reflect a certain theology of grace.

What is wrong and deeply flawed is what is missing (and present in the tax collector's prayer): a heartfelt confession of his own sinfulness and guilt, an acknowledgment that ultimately, despite the undeniable difference in their behaviour, he is 'even like this tax collector' (v. 11). This lack leads to his proud, self-confident stance in prayer (v. 11a) — unlike the tax collector, who 'stood at a distance' (v. 13) — as well as his contempt for the tax collector (and others).

The contrasting prayer, then, is not that of just *any* tax collector, but of one who knows he is a guilty sinner and reflects his deep contrition in demeanour as well as words. He knows his basic need is God's forgiveness, and his stark plea is 'God, have mercy on me, a sinner'. This usual translation is acceptable, but it should not be overlooked that the verb, against the background of well-established usage in the Greek Old Testament (e.g. Lev. 4:35; 10:17; 16:30), carries the idea of propitiation, of mercy that puts away anger and removes wrath.[47] The tax collector knows the wrath his sins justly deserve, and so his prayer for forgiveness is for God to be propitious toward him; he pleads that God will 'in wrath remember mercy' (Hab. 3:2).

Verse 14 gives Jesus' verdict: it was not the self-confident, self-justifying Pharisee but the self-condemning, mercy-seeking tax collector who 'went home justified before God'. The forensically declarative force of this justification is clear; other than in a forensic sense, he was not 'made righteous', nor was he 'shown to be righteous' before God. Though a sinner, he is pronounced righteous by God. Here, if anywhere, God is, as Paul will later say (Rom. 4:5), the God 'who justifies the ungodly'.

The latter part of verse 14 is not secondary, as some argue; it is by no means extraneous to the original sense of the parable. The principle of eschatological judgment expressed there — God will humble the proud and exalt the humble — accents important ramifications of the justification in view:

(1) Justification is by faith; the tax collector, in abandoning himself to the forgiving mercy of God, exemplifies the humility of faith (*cf.* Matt. 18:3–4).

(2) But especially, justification is eschatological. The tax collector's prayer, and Luke's unfolding of the all-encompassing centrality of messianic Spirit and fire baptism with its eschatological and forensic dimensions, demonstrate the same point. Justification is present deliverance from the eschatological wrath of God, a verdict, already rendered, of acquittal and right standing at the final judgment.

We can hardly quarrel with the conclusion, then, 'that not only the content of the Pauline doctrine of justification but also the terminology of an antedonated eschatological pardon goes back to Jesus'.[48] And we may even wonder whether in verse 14 the translation 'declared to be righteous' fully captures what was done for the tax collector; whether, 'without leaving the realm of the judicial or forensic', there is not 'reflection here upon the status constituted as well as upon the status declared to be'; whether, that is, there is not involved here a constitutive sort of declaration that approaches Paul's notion of imputed righteousness.[49]

At any rate, this key pronouncement of Jesus, along with the other components we have examined within the Luke's framework, supports the observation that 'Paul does nothing but explain the eschatological reality which in Christ's teaching is called the Kingdom'.[50] Paul's teaching on the righteousness of God has its roots in Jesus' proclamation of the kingdom of God. The gospel of justification by faith advocated by Paul is the fruition, the doctrinally more explicit and developed delineation, of the good news of repentance for the forgiveness of sins which was announced by Jesus, and which, more importantly, was actualised in his death, resurrection, ascension, and baptism with the Holy Spirit.

7

Justification in the Gospel of John

ANDREW H. TROTTER, JR.

I. INTRODUCTION

A paper with the title 'Justification in the Gospel of John' may strike the reader who knows something about the subject as a curiosity. The knowledge-able reader will wonder how the author is going to face the great problem of reconciling the paucity of teaching on the subject in John with the importance of justification for the Christian faith. The less serious reader will rank the attempt to discuss the subject in any depth with attempts to discuss a topic like baseball in Britain: there may be pockets of interest in a few places, and there may be some other, more popular, games that have similarities, but no right thinking person could ever say baseball was central to a discussion of games in Britain. The object of this essay is to try to answer the questions: (1) What does John's Gospel teach about justification?[1] (2) Is this soteriological motif central to John's thinking in any way? (3) What are the implications of our findings for the Christian doctrine of salvation and for our understanding of the theology of the New Testament, especially concerning its unity?

These three questions are central to any discussion of justification in John. This is of course obvious in the case of the first, but there are special circumstances that require closer attention to the question than might normally be given. First, the word-group most associated with the concept of justification, the *dikaio-* word-group, occurs rarely in John.[2] Secondly, when words in the group do appear, their meaning is disputed, especially the occurrence of *dikaiosynē* ('righteousness') in Jn. 16:8,10.[3] Thirdly, because it is dangerous to limit the discussion of *any* concept to a discussion of one particular word-group, we will need to justify doing so in this paper.

The second and third questions are relevant largely because of the prominence given to the concept of justification in Protestant discussion of New Testament soteriology,[4] to say nothing of the discussion of its unity.[5] If the idea of justification is not important to John, one of the major authors of the New Testament, then surely the high place accorded justification in the theological debate about salvation is jeopardised — or else we must assume the New Testament is deeply divided. If, on the other hand, we find the theme to be prominent in his thinking, then there is substantial unity in at least two of the most important thinkers in the New Testament, Paul and John. Of course, there are alternatives other than the black and white options, of John either focusing or not focusing on justification, and thereby meshing strongly or being at odds with Paul. He may show evidence of an underlying *presupposition* of justification; and thus, while not displaying it prominently in his soteriology, have a strong compatibility with Paul that undermines talk of a disunity in New Testament theology at this point.

We will concentrate our attention on passages where *dikaiosynē* and its cognate words occur, even though the Gospel contains few references to them. This may seem a backward sort of methodology. Why concentrate on them in our exegesis if John does not concentrate on them in his explication of the themes of salvation? We do so for two reasons. First, space requirements necessitate that we limit our discussion, and to bring in all the Johannine themes that show a correspondence with justification would be to go far beyond the scope of this essay. Second, the very paucity of references to the *dikaio-* word-group makes it all the more important to examine them thoroughly, and the passages in which they occur, if we are to understand John's view of justification; especially since these references have not to my knowledge been examined as a group before. In this way, we should be able to make a small contribution toward understanding John's relationship to the doctrine of justification and draw some tentative conclusions about the importance (or otherwise) of the doctrine for John.

By following this procedure we hope to avoid at least two pitfalls. To 'go looking' for justification in related concepts or in central Johannine themes without the linguistic connection of the *dikaio-* word-group may risk the extreme of what may be called the 'Barr syndrome'.[6] The syndrome so avoids concrete linguistic evidence that it does theology in something of a linguistic 'hard evidence' vacuum. True, it is important to pay due attention to contextual data for meaning and not depend too heavily on some pre-defined understanding of a particular word. It is equally important to realise that authors choose words because they mean certain things and avoid others for the same reason. Sometimes those meanings carry a complex freight of nuance for the author that must be recognised in order to understand a given passage. If the exegete moves too far afield from the words most commonly tied to the concept that he is attempting to study, he risks the error of finding what he wants to find and justifying its presence on grounds that, without the necessary linguistic controls, are simply too subjective to provide material for useful discourse.[7] This is not to give up entirely the proper hermeneutical advances made by Barr's contributions; it is simply to warn of a danger that is not often recognised in today's theological climate.

The second danger is related to the first. It stems from the problem of defining the identifiable related concepts for which we are looking as we delve into the Gospel and its teaching about justification. What semantic components are there to Paul's view of justification that can be isolated and then discerned as 'parts' of (or whole) concepts in John? To do this would be difficult enough for a simple term about which there is little debate, but for something as complex and as debated as the concept of justification in the writings of Paul, it could be deemed foolish even to try. In order to gain some control, I shall attempt to find elements of the *dikaio-* word-group in Paul about which there is little debate and search the *dikaio-* material in John's Gospel for evidence of those. There does seem to be at least some agreed common ground upon which to stand.

For example, if we were to find Johannine evidence of a gift from God to man that is tied to the forensic sphere, we would surely have a concept somewhat similar to that of Paul, regardless of whether the emphasis in Paul is found to lie upon the gift or the Giver, upon God as Creator/Redeemer or upon the eschatological activity of God.[8] More than just one of these 'correspondences' would have to be found, of course, to establish any Johannine interest in justification at all parallel to that of Paul, but this is at least an example of the sort of thing for which we would need to look.

Before we 'break down' justification according to Paul into identifiable structural elements and look for these elements in the Gospel of John, it will be helpful for us to look at the passages in John containing the *dikaio-* word-group.

II.   THE *DIKAIO-* WORD-GROUP IN THE FOURTH GOSPEL

A.   John 16:8–11

Jn. 16:8–11 is the only passage in the Gospel to contain the word *dikaiosynē*[9] and is part of what has been called 'one of the most baffling passages in the fourth gospel'.[10] Many of the most difficult problems in the passage have been worked out by D. A. Carson.

(1) *Elengchein peri* does not mean 'to prove the world wrong about' in the sense of intellectually convicting the world of wrong ideas about the three objects of sin, righteousness and judgment. Neither does it mean 'to prove to the disciples that the world is wrong about' (at least without any reference to the conviction of the world itself). Other alternatives such as 'to convict' and 'to expose in regard to' are also to be discarded. *Elengchein peri* is best thought of as embracing both subjective 'conviction' of sin and intellectual convincing: for the Paraclete 'to bring the world to the place where it is convinced of its sin, for instance, is to bring it to self-conscious "conviction" of sin, to self-conscious recognition of guilt'.[11]

(2) The *hoti* ('because' or 'that' or 'in that') clauses in 16:9–11 are not to be taken as explicative or as some mixture of causal and explicative, but rather each is to be taken as a causal clause, modifying the verb *elengchein* and giving the reasons why the Paraclete convicts the world of sin, righteousness and judgment.[12] Carson's explanations are on target and cogent; I would only slightly modify them in ways that accord with my different views of the meanings of sin, righteousness and judgment in the passage.

(3) The change to the second person in the second clause in v. 10 ('and you will no longer see me') is explained by the fact that this teaching is being given to the disciples in order to explain the Paraclete's ministry more clearly. Part of that ministry is to 'lead them into all truth' (Jn. 16:13). But part of it, as our passage shows, is to convict the world of its sin, righteousness and judgment.

> What that last clause, *kai ouketi theōreite me* ['and you will no longer see me'], introduces is not some refinement of the main reason for the Paraclete's *elengxis* advanced by the first part of the *hoti* clause but something more subtle. Once Jesus has departed, the disciples have no model, no 'master', no one to follow in the same sense that they followed Jesus in the days of his flesh. How, then, will they contribute to convicting the world of its false righteousness? The

Paraclete takes over this role from Jesus, as we have seen; but he does not convict the world *only* on his own but *also* through the disciples . . . thus, within short compass, [the clause] not only provides the reason why the Paraclete will convict the world of its 'righteousness', but frames that reason in such a way as to provide encouragement for the disciples in their witness.[13]

(4) Carson's solution unifies the passage not only by making all three of the *hoti* clauses causal but also by taking the position that all three of the objects about which the world needs to be convinced/convicted are *their* 'possession'. The fact that it is their sin about which they will be convicted comes as no surprise; neither is it surprising that the judgment is theirs, too. The sticking point comes when the *dikaiosynē* ('righteousness') spoken of in 16:10 is said to be that of the world and not that of the disciples or of Jesus or of God (as demonstrated in the cross, resurrection, ascension or some combination of the three). But Carson stands his ground well, and, largely on the basis of John's well-known proclivity for irony, argues that what is referred to here is a 'bad righteousness' after that of Isa. 64:5 LXX; Dan. 9:18 Th, Rom. 10:3, Phil. 3:6–9; Tit. 3:5 and Mt. 5:20.[14]

The major exception I take to Carson's interpretation of the passage comes in his explanation, not of the 'owners' of the three elements but of their content. Without much comment, Carson simply states that it is the world's 'sin' of which the Paraclete convicts it and, rightly, points to the parallel expression in Jn. 8:46 where Jesus asks the question of the Jews, 'Which of you convicts me of sin?' (*tis ex hymōn elengxei me peri hamartias*)? But what does sin (*hamartia*) mean in this context? Is it unbelief? This is unlikely in my view because, if this were the case, the following *hoti* clause would be more easily read as explicative than as causal. Does it mean sin in a broad sense, as I assume Carson accepts? This is more likely than unbelief since *hamartia* in John certainly sometimes carries no further elaboration (e.g. Jn. 8:34). But there are reasons for thinking that John intends something more precise in his use of *hamartia* in this passage.

'Guilt' in a forensic sense is probably the best definition for *hamartia* here. This conclusion stems from two factors. First, the parallel passage in Jn. 8:46 (the only other one in John to use the phrase *elengchein peri*) is best read in a judicial way. Jesus does not seem to be talking about being convicted of sin in a general way but about being found guilty of the very thing of which he is accusing the Jews: being a liar or telling lies. So, as Lindars puts it, '8.46 . . . does not mean "Which of you convicts me of actual sin?" but rather "Which of you finds me guilty (of the implicit charge of speaking falsehood)?" '[15]

Secondly, 1 Jn. 5:17 links *hamartia* with *adikia* in a strong way, and (as Lindars points out) since John does not use the normal biblical words for 'guilty'[16], and since there is a strong case for a forensic background to the passage anyway,[17] there is a good reason for taking the word as John's way of speaking of judicial guilt. This interpretation fits a number of appearances of the word in the Gospel in addition to the important occurrence in Jn. 8:46. Jesus' references to the Jews 'dying in their sin/sins' in Jn. 8:21,24 and the link between the metaphorical blindness of the Pharisees and their sin remaining (Jn. 9:41), hard upon the more general conception of the sin of either the blind man or his parents causing his blindness (Jn. 9:1–2), both have overtones of God's judgment upon the actors and present a view of 'sin' that asks for more than simply the general view of moral wrong. Hence judicial 'guilt' is the best way to take the word in this passage: the Paraclete will convict the world of its guilt because it has not believed in Jesus.[18]

Similarly, Carson sees the world's judgment, mentioned in v. 11, as being 'all false judgment, of which the condemnation of Jesus was the supreme example . . . The world is wrong in its assessment of all things spiritual, i.e. all things surrounding Jesus and his teaching and work. In these realms, mistaken judgment stems not from mere cognitive ignorance but from moral perversity, and so the Paraclete convicts the world in this area as well'.[19] His model for John's use of *krisis* ('judgment') in this verse is Jn. 7:24: 'Stop judging by mere appearances, and make a right judgment' where the judgment is of a more all-encompassing type.

It is certainly not wrong to assert that the world's judgments about all things moral and spiritual are wrong (the world is in darkness rather than light), and it is right to see here a judgment that is actually the world's 'possession' rather than a generic, unowned judgment ('The Spirit will convince you of a right idea about judgment'). Nevertheless, there is evidence that indicates John is here referring to a judicial verdict that has been handed down against the world. Though God the righteous judge has delivered the verdict, and in that sense it is his judgment, the verdict nevertheless condemns the world and so belongs to it.

The Johannine model for this view of *krisis* in the passage is therefore not Jn. 7:24, but rather Jn. 12:31–32. While it is true that Jn. 7:24 links judgment to righteousness by speaking of a 'righteous judgment' (*dikaios krisis*), connecting it verbally to Jn. 16:8–11, this connection must be made on an ethical view of *dikaiosynē* in Jn. 16:8,10, a view that we shall argue is incorrect. Further, Jn. 12:31 seems a much richer parallel in that it not only mentions the judgment of the world and not just 'judgments', but also mentions the judgment of 'the prince of this world'.[20] The judgment of Jn. 12:31–32 is in the form of a verdict that rests upon the world rather than a criterion for sentencing (*cf.* 3:19), an act of judging (*cf.* 5:24), or the condemnation stated in the verdict (*cf.* 5:29 and indicated in Jn. 16:8–11 by the *hamartia* of v. 9).[21] Thus the judgment of which the world will be convinced by the Spirit is the judgment of the cross, a judgment that will convict the world because it has judged the world's prince.

Lastly, and for our purposes most importantly, the *dikaiosynē* mentioned in Jn. 16:8,10 belongs not to Christ or to the neutral realm of ideas, but rather to the world just as the sin and judgment do.[22] Though Carson does not make a major point of defining what sort of righteousness is being spoken of, he seems to indicate that he believes it is a practical, ethical righteousness as it surely is in 1 Jn. 2:29; 3:7,10.[23] The clear portrayal of *dikaiosynē* in 1 John as an ethical righteouness is a problem for our view, but the case that we should not view *dikaiosynē* here with that meaning is made on stronger grounds than this parallel.

The first argument in favour of seeing *dikaiosynē* as forensic here is made from the context: as we now see, the other two objects of conviction are judicial. Many commentators of course see even more elements in this passage that are clearly forensic than we do.[24] With the legal background so prominent in the term *dikaiosynē* anyway, and in light of John's lack of use of the term and his incorporation of ethical righteousness into his concept of 'truth' (*alētheia*),[25] it is more natural to read the term here in terms of judicial righteousness.[26]

But how then can we speak of the world as possessing a judicial righteousness since it is already condemned (Jn. 12:31–32)? The views of Lindars, Hatch and others that here *dikaiosynē* means a verdict of innocent without any qualification falter on just this problem. But it is here that Carson's idea of the righteousness spoken of here as an *ironic* righteousness is so helpful. The Jews thought that forensic righteousness would be gained by keeping the law and that the final judgment would vindicate this brand of righteousness. But Jesus (and John, *cf.* esp. Jn. 1:17), while affirming the law is good in that it points to him (*cf.* Jn. 1:45; 5:39), also makes clear that he stands above the law and never makes fidelity to it the basis of God's judgment. The standard of judgment in John for right standing before God is strongly in terms of decision about him as Messiah (e.g. Jn. 3:18; 7:48–52; 18:31; 19:7).

Hence it is this wrong view of righteousness and the Jews' dependence upon it for salvation that the Holy Spirit (and the disciples with the Spirit's help) will continue to convince them of, just as Jesus has done while on earth. This view of the meaning of *dikaiosynē* in Jn. 16:8–11 is supported by two passages in Paul where he mentions a righteousness that is not adequate. In Rom. 10:3, the Jews have disregarded the righteousness that God displayed in Christ and have made their own, a righteousness that is based on law and not on the 'end' (*telos*) of the law, Christ (Rom. 10:4). Phil. 3:6–9 shows Paul recognising that he shared this same wrong view and considered himself 'blameless' before the judgment seat of God but now recognising that he must abandon *his* righteousness based on law for that which comes through faith in Christ. The parallel with the Johannine passage is striking because of Paul's owning of this false righteousness in the way we are arguing for John.

A last reason for seeing the *dikaiosynē* in vv. 8,10 as judicial is the *hoti* clause following it. Carson rightly points out, 'By his words and deeds, Jesus has set the world's self-vaunted righteousness against the backdrop of his own matchless righteousness and thereby brought home to the world the inadequacy of its own righteousness' and draws attention to the 'words and deeds' of Jn. 15:22,24: 'If I had not come and spoken to them, . . . if I had not done among them what no one else did, they would not be guilty of sin.'[27] As the world has looked for righteousness in obedience to the law and therefore needed Jesus' challenge to its wrong view of righteousness by confrontation with his words and deeds, now the Spirit will continue to convict it of the proper kind of righteousness by drawing attention to him as the truth-speaking and wonder-working Son of God.

What conclusions can we draw then about the presence or absence of justification in the forensic sense in the passage? Obviously, it is everywhere presupposed. We must be careful not to say that the passage *teaches* justification by faith. It is too scant in its teaching to make that claim, and that is not the focus of the passage anyway. Its teaching consists of truth about the Paraclete and his function, not about soteriology except in an indirect way. Nevertheless what it both says and implies about salvation demonstrates a similar conception of *dikaiosynē* to Paul's and can rightly be seen to fit perfectly with his doctrine.[28]

B. John 8:30

The occurrence of *dikaios* in Jn. 5:30 is more clearly in a forensic context than *dikaiosynē* in Jn. 16:8. Jesus' judgment is seen as 'just' because it is objective. This is shown both negatively in that Jesus is not seeking his own will or looking out for his own interests in his judgment, and positively in that he is judging according to the Father's will.[29] The context seems to be one of eschatological judgment, referring to a time in the future when Jesus will be the judge of 'those who did good things' (*hoi ta agatha poiēsantes*) and 'those who did evil things' (*hoi de ta phaula praxantes*).[30]

R. Brown translates *dikaios* as 'honest', comparing the use here with that of *alēthinē* in Jn. 8:16.[31] While the references to the Father's bearing witness to his testimony and the motif of judgment do provide important parallels to our passage, in Jn. 8:16 Jesus is portrayed as exercising *krisis* ('judgment') in a very different sense than in Jn. 5:30. In 5:30, he refers to his task as judge at the time of the resurrection of the dead when the dead will come forth from their tombs and will be judged (5:28–29). In 8:16, Jesus has just explicitly said that he 'is not judging anyone' and allows only for what would be the case if he were judging in a present sense of judging men's hearts and the truthfulness of their statements. 'Honest' probably does not catch the flavour of *dikaios* even in Jn. 8:16, as well as 'true' (as opposed to false) would; but in any case it leaves something to be desired as a translation for *dikaios* in 5:30.

There are many forensic terms and metaphors in the immediate context that point to the term's being understood here in a legal rather than cultic or moral sense. The witness motif is particularly strong in the passage; Jesus calls his Father (vv. 32,37–38),[32] John the Baptist (v. 33), his works (v. 36), and the Scripture (vv. 39–47) to bear witness to him.[33] The accusation motif (*katagoreō*) found in Jn. 5:45 parallels the judgment scene found in 5:27–28. And of course the fact that it is a just 'judgment' (*krisis*) makes it all but certain that the adjective describing this judgment should be understood in a legal sense.

The setting of the statement under discussion also confirms the judicial nature of the term here. In 5:18 we are told that the Jews were seeking 'all the more', i.e. more than simply for doing work on the Sabbath (v. 16), to kill Jesus because he was 'calling God his own Father, making himself equal with God'. The implication of the setting is that Jesus was doubly breaking the law as far as the Jews were concerned: once when he 'worked' on the Sabbath by healing the paralytic at the pool of Bethesda and encouraged the cured man to carry his mat (5:1–16), and a second time when he referred to God as *his own* Father.[34]

Despite this evidence, there are those who see here something less than a reference to Jesus as the Judge at the Great Assize. R. Schnackenburg argues that ' "Just" does not here mean merely that quality which all judgment ought to have (*cf.* 7:24); when Jesus pronounces judgment, it means something more. It is a true and effective judgment in accordance with the authority of God, who stands behind it (*cf.* 8:26). This confirms our interpretation that the reference is to Jesus' word, spoken here and now, which acts as judge over unbelievers.'[35] Schnackenburg argues that the verses preceding v. 30, i.e. 5:28–29, are indeed references to the future judgment, probably inserted by a later redactor, but that v. 30 returns to the present Jesus and his word which gives either life or death.[36]

Schnackenburg's argument mainly rests on two things: (1) the fact that the language of Jn. 5:30a is so similar to that of 5:19, where presumably the discussion is about the present work of the Father in revelation, and (2) the change back to the present tense in most of the verbs of Jn. 5:30.[37] In answer to the first, there is little argument that the parallel with v. 19 is a valid one to draw.[38] But it is incorrect to assume that present work is all that is being spoken of in v. 19; the statement of Jesus that he does what the Father does is not bound by any temporal sense at all and in fact seems to include past, present, and future activities. The continuing preservation of creation, God's 'work' during his Sabbath 'rest', is probably what Jesus refers to in v. 17 (see discussion above), and v. 21 seems to be referring either to past or to future resurrections by the Father. The explicit reference to future works in v. 20 seems to demonstrate with clarity that v. 19 cannot be limited only to present work. In fact, the parallel between v. 19 and v. 30 is probably best explained as an *inclusio*, stressing the links between the present and the future age brought about by the sending of Jesus.[39]

Similarly, the use of the present tense in v. 30 can just as easily be read as a futuristic present since Jesus has explicitly ruled out judgment for himself in the present age (Jn. 8:15). Schnackenburg is right in that 'just' does mean more than the quality of 'fairness' implied in Jn. 7:24 because behind Jesus' word is the authority of God. But this does not negate the fact that reference here is probably primarily to his eschatological word as Judge at the end of time.

We may now perhaps safely conclude that *dikaia krisis* is forensic in nature and occurs in a context of justice at the Great Judgment.[40] But what does this have to do with our pursuit of evidence for the doctrine of justification by faith in the Gospel of John? There is no clear statement of justification by faith, but several things point to a strong presupposition of that doctrine in the passage.

First, though the passage appears to be more Christologically than soteriologically oriented, soteriological motifs abound throughout, and their mere link with judgment, and just judgment at that, sounds a strong note. Themes such as revelation (5:17,20), the giving of life combined with the resurrection from the dead (5:21,25–26,28–29,39–40), the love of the Father for the Son (5:20) and the lack of love for God in the Pharisees (5:42), the mention of salvation and light (5:34–35) — all these are packed into the passage. But more impressive than the occurrence of any of these is the emphasis placed on belief in the passage. 'To believe' (*pisteuein*) occurs six times in the brief space from v. 38 to v. 47. Though the verb is used in the sense of accepting as valid the teaching of Jesus and not in the common Johannine sense of 'believing in Jesus', its very concentration is noteworthy. This is especially so since the matter of which Jesus is attempting to persuade them is in fact a soteriological one, i.e. coming to him in order that they might have life (v. 40).

Secondly, as is so often the case in John, here Christology serves soteriology. Stress in this passage is on Jesus' dependence on the Father, and the totality of this dependence is demonstrated in Jn. 5:30 in three areas: (1) his inability to do anything 'by himself';[41] (2) his judging only as he hears; and (3) his seeking not his own will, but the will of the Father. But this dependence serves Jesus' claim to be the just judge of the *eschaton*, the one who decides life and death (v. 29). Jesus as the giver of life is everywhere in the context, too (*cf.* 5:25,29,39–40,47), perhaps most strongly in v. 24 with its call to hear the word of Jesus and believe the Father and its promise to those who do that they will experience eternal life. In other words, the reason for Jesus' statements about himself in the passage is not simply to establish who he is *vis-à-vis* the Father, nor does it seem to be John's concern merely to clarify this relationship for his community. Jesus seizes the controversy concerning his statements about him and the Father and his actions on the Sabbath to exhort the Jews to listen to his word and to respond in faith.

Thus believing the Father and really hearing the word of Jesus about him as the worker of the Father's works (v. 20), as the giver of life (v. 21), and especially (for our purposes) as the judge whose word will call forth the dead at the end of time (vv. 28–29) is central to the soteriological message of John, and requires an assumption of justification by faith. The reference to *dikaia krisis* ('just judgment') arises out of that assumption and so bears witness to its place, however minor, in the soteriology of the Gospel.

C. John 7:24

The same phrase found in Jn. 5:30, *dikaia krisis*, occurs in Jn. 7:24, but in a different context. Here, rather than referring to the eschatological judgment, it is used of judging 'according to the Spirit and purpose of the Law'.[42] The judgment is the crowd's; they are asked by Jesus not to judge 'by appearances' (*kat' opsin*) 'but judge with righteous judgment' (*alla tēn dikaian krisin krinete*).

Whether or not this passage has any relevance to our discussion depends on the object of the judgment the people are being asked to render. Since there is no direct object of the verb *krinē* ('to judge') in the verse,[43] context must determine what that object is. Several possibilities obtain. If the object is Scripture, the law, or the crowd's interpretation of either, then the statement says very little, soteriologically speaking. If the object is Jesus, then in a sense parallel to that of Jn. 5:30, the passage might allude to an underlying presupposition of justification by faith. In fact the passage might carry something more than allusion and thus become even more relevant than the reference in Jn. 5:30 because here it is the audience, i.e. 'the multitude' (v. 20), doing the judging rather than Jesus. If there is a link between their judging Jesus 'justly' and having faith in him, then the relevance of the passage for our topic is obvious.

It seems unlikely that the reference here is merely to Scripture, law or their respective interpretations. Old Testament references to 'judging with a righteous judgment', while few, are nevertheless instructive. In Dt. 16:18f., the people are instructed to appoint judges who judge the people with righteous judgment. While such judgment would of course involve the judges' making proper interpretations of the law, the emphasis is on fairness and justice being practised in relation to the people (vv. 19–20).[44] In Zech. 7:9, the phrase occurs in a string of commands Yahweh had given to Judah, all of which are in accordance with the law, but none of which are purely casuistic. Instead they have to do with making personal ethical decisions about being kind and compassionate toward one's brother, not oppressing the widow and orphan, and not devising evil in one's heart against another (vv. 9–10). Isa.

11:3f. which may provide the best parallel to our present passage,[45] speaks of messianic judgment not being simply 'by what his eyes see, nor . . . by what his ears hear' (v. 3) but 'with righteousness' (v. 4), and his judgment is of the 'poor [and] . . . the afflicted of the earth' (v. 4). Thus, the Old Testament concept of judging with righteous judgment seems to pertain to making fair judgments about people and, further, acting rightly by them.

The immediate literary context also seems to steer away from this being a warning by Jesus to treat the law properly and toward its being a plea to judge Jesus fairly. In v. 20, the people accuse Jesus of having a demon because he has said that they seek to kill him. He then refers to 'one deed'[46] which he has done and at which they marvelled, and goes into a discussion that presupposes the accusation of violating the Sabbath work laws. Thus their judgment seems to be of him, though it is clearly based on a wrong view of the law. It is their accusation of Jesus as having a demon (and perhaps their duplicity in denying that anyone sought to kill him; *cf.* v. 25 where some of the people acknowledge that they knew there were some who were seeking him to kill him) that is condemned by Jesus as being 'superficial'.[47]

But is this plea of Jesus to judge him justly and not superficially a plea to believe in him as the one who justifies, or is it, as in other places in John, only a plea to believe his word and/or works? It is impossible to decide this question. It seems more than haphazard that, immediately upon this command of Jesus, people from the crowd begin to ask if he is the Messiah. In vv. 26–27, 'some of the people of Jerusalem'[48] are persuaded for a moment but then decide that since they know where Jesus is from, he must not be the Messiah. In v. 31 we are told directly that 'many of the multitude believed in him' on the basis of his 'signs', an apparent reference to the miracle at the pool of Bethesda discussed in vv. 22–23. From v. 37 to the end of the chapter, the discussion centres almost entirely around the question of who Jesus is, and more are portrayed as believing in Jesus, including officers of the temple and members of the chief priests and Pharisees.

On the other hand, the immediately previous context emphasises the teaching of Jesus and focuses on the question of how he obtained his education since he had not attended the rabbinic schools (*cf.* vv. 14–15). Jesus' response to the question is not that he is the Messiah but rather that his teaching is not his own but the Father's, and that anyone can know that it is the Father's and not his own, if he will but seek the Father's will (vv. 16–17). In the same discussion, Jesus states that Moses gave them a law which none of them follows, and it is from this reference that the later reference to the Sabbath controversy in vv. 22–23 seems to come by attraction. Thus it could easily be said that the statement of v. 24 is made by Jesus in order to encourage the crowd to accept his teaching, rather than being a call to faith, even though the following verses indicate that the effect was at least to cause people to consider Jesus' claim as Messiah, if not to bring them to faith in him.

In any case, the support here for an idea of justification by faith must be minimal at best. Though we have not discussed it here, it seems certain that we once again can see the term here as having forensic overtones.[49] But justification is accomplished by God, and in this passage, it is the crowds who are to judge Jesus. There may be an irony intended here in that the crowds are called upon to judge Jesus justly while he is the one who will someday judge them 'with righteousness',[50] but that seems oversubtle. It is probably better to say that this occurrence of *dikaios* provides only some linguistic support for what we have seen in Jn. 16:8,10 and Jn. 5:30.

D. John 17:25

The last use of a term from the *dikaio-* word group is found in Jesus' so called 'high priestly prayer' of John 17. Near the end of the prayer, Jesus addresses the Father as 'Righteous Father' (*pater dikaie*). As in Jn. 7:24, the reference appears relatively inconsequential, but once again the word 'suggests that the notion of vindication is present, which is suitable to the use of the Son of Man imagery in the preceding verse. The point is that Jesus' own cause is just, and therefore he makes his final appeal on the grounds of the Father's justice. The following words can then be expected to expose the justice of Jesus' cause.'[51] The assumption that the Father as just judge is being appealed to here, however, has not gone unchallenged and bears some discussion, however brief.

R. Schnackenburg challenges the notion that the reference here is to 'God's "just" rule, which hands the unbelieving world over to judgment'.[52] Rather, he sees Jesus' address as indicating 'God's "gracious" and good turning towards those who believe in Jesus', referring to 1 Jn. 1:9.[53] He bases this judgment on what he sees as an analogy with the attributive address in Jn. 17:11 where Jesus calls God 'Holy Father' (*pater hagie*) and

> because of the continuation in v. 26, which deals with the love of God in the disciples. The mention of the cosmos that has not known God has no value in itself. The connection between the statement about the world and that about the disciples by means of *kai . . . kai* forms a contrast, but, since nothing more is said about the world, but more is in fact said about the disciple, the latter's attitude of faith and acceptance of the one sent by God are clearly to be outlined more prominently so that the disciples will appear to be worthy of God's turning towards them in love.[54]

The first of these two reasons is based on the false premise that *hagios* is not an adequate parallel to *dikaios* when the latter is used in the forensic sense. But this is hardly true. Though it is largely a cultic, rather than a forensic, term, *hagios* nevertheless shares with *dikaios* a crucial aspect, that of separating the Father from mankind, both unbeliever and disciple. Only the Father is worthy of being addressed as the holy Lord of the cultus, and only the Father as righteous Judge of the earth. It is in this that the connection between the two exists.[55]

More substantive, perhaps, is the argument that the 'continuation' of the prayer after the address in v. 25 concentrates on the disciples and the love God will continue to show to them through the presence of Jesus (presumably through the Paraclete) among them (v. 26). But this is to assign too much influence to the address, and fails to see that the words 'Righteous Father' govern the thought only until the end of v. 25. The contrast is between the world which does not know the Father and is therefore condemned by the righteous Judge, and the disciples who know that the Father sent Jesus and are therefore acquitted by the righteous Judge.

Not only does the thought represented by the expression *pater dikaie* ('Righteous Father') end there; it probably began in, and is itself a continuation from, v. 24 where Jesus' desire is expressed that the disciples 'be with me where I am, and . . . see my glory'. Though the exegesis is by no means agreed upon, this wish is probably expressing something about the after-life[56] and therefore moves easily in the mind of Jesus into thoughts of judgment (especially when combined with thoughts of the world) and an address of the Father as *dikaios* in v. 25. Thus the most natural way to read *dikaios* in Jn. 17:25 is as a reference to the Father as Judge on the final day, though of course this reference should be regarded more as allusive than as making a strong statement.

What difference, then, does the occurrence of *dikaios* in Jn. 17:25 make for our investigation of justification in John? Very little; the word does not speak to soteriological concerns in this passage, but describes the Father. Perhaps, though, the small contribution it does make to our discussion is more significant than at first meets the eye; if what we have asserted about its meaning is true, i.e. that *dikaios* is here used with a forensic connotation and not an ethical or cultic one, then a startling fact emerges: *all* the occurrences of the *dikaio-* word group in the Gospel of John without exception carry the assumption of a forensic background.

The question asked at the beginning of this article, then, becomes even more demanding: does John, as he writes, bring with him a presupposition of justification by faith in the Pauline sense? Before we can answer this question, though, we must attempt to isolate some characteristics of the Pauline view of justification. Then we can use these as measuring sticks by which to measure two types of Johannine material: first, that which we have gleaned from these four passages; and second, such material as we can marshal from other passages in John which bear a relation to justification.

III. ELEMENTS OF THE PAULINE DOCTRINE OF JUSTIFICATION

Most New Testament theologies in this century have devoted a section to justification in the letters of Paul.[57] There seems little need to establish the importance of the doctrine for the apostle or to argue the case that he is its major exponent in the New Testament; these are well established and little-debated facts.[58] What is much more questionable is whether or not we can abstract categories from the Pauline idea that are sufficiently broad and useful to be used for purposes of comparison with John.[59]

At least a few things can be isolated from any view of Paul's understanding of *dikaiosynē*. G. Schrenk isolates what he calls the 'Main Elements in the Doctrine of Justification'[60] in Paul. Though the discussion is somewhat difficult to follow since he moves back and forth in his discussion between the simple *dikaiosynē* ('justification'/'righteousness') and *dikaiosynē theou* ('righteousness/justification of God'), he lists a number of elements of *dikaiosynē* in Paul, of which eight seem to be indisputably present.[61] They are certainly not all agreed upon by everyone in terms of their relative importance for our understanding of Paul's concept. Nor are they without a variety of nuances in the contemporary debate. But they are recognised by virtually everyone as essentially present in Paul's conception, and this is enough for our purposes.

The eight elements are these: (1) the term finds its understanding and message centred in the cross of Jesus Christ; (2) God both is and demonstrates righteousness; (3) justification is forensic; (4) *dikaiosynē* in Paul has the overtone not only of future justification before the judgment bar but also of a present gift 'both imparted and received'[62]; (5) *dikaiosynē* and *pistis* ('faith') are linked indissolubly such that, while *dikaiosynē* is not exclusively viewed by Paul in individualistic terms, it is a 'justifying action of God which seizes the individual'[63]; (6) *dikaiosynē* is seen as the object of hope as well as a present reality and 'impels to resolute action. . . . Paul never discusses the relation between justification and the last judgment. Yet the background of judgment remains, and the new assurance is characterised as a tireless pursuit of the goal. . . . This does not mean that assurance of salvation is either shaken or called in question. The point is that the thought of judgment serves as a powerful motive to obedience'[64]; (7) *dikaiosynē* and the Spirit are closely linked and make evident that 'justifying faith and union with Christ in the sense of identification with his destiny ("mysticism") are closely related'[65]; (8) justification leads to the reign of grace and is therefore the power of the new life. 'Thus, without any sense of difficulty or contradiction, the thought of pardoning and forensic righteousness passes over into that of righteousness as the living power which overcomes sin. The righteousness which is given commits to the living power of *dikaiosynē*.'[66]

How, then, do the Johannine passages containing the *dikaio-* word group relate to these eight elements?

IV.   COMPARISON OF JOHN AND PAUL

Of the four passages looked at above, clearly Jn. 16:8–10 and Jn. 5:30 are the most significant. Here the word-group, and hence the idea of justification, is more prominent than in the other two passages. Nevertheless, we will use information gleaned from all four passages to make our comparison. We will also use other passages in John on occasion to elucidate the connection between John on Paul on this topic.

(1) There can be little doubt that Paul centres the message of justification, and indeed of the *dikaiosynē theou*, ('righteousness/justification of God'), around the event of the cross of Jesus Christ.[67] It is true that Käsemann neglects the cross almost entirely in his famous essay on the righteousness of God in Paul, but even he admits that for Paul 'Christ is definitely not, as for instance, in Matthew's Nativity story, the second Moses; he is the second Adam and, in this role, brings in the new covenant and the new creation'.[68] As the first Adam brought sin and death into the world through the fall, so Christ brings justification 'by his blood' (Rom. 5:9). It is 'through one act of righteousness' (*di' henos dikaiōmatos*) that Jesus brings 'justification of life to all men' *eis pantas anthrōpous eis dikaiōsin zōēs*, Rom. 5:18). Though it is also true that focusing on this element of the *dikaiosynē* idea begs the question of Christology *vs.* soteriology (i.e. righteousness as an attribute *vs.* justification as an activity), there are few events in the New Testament that vie with the crucifixion for primacy when considering the unification of the person and work of Christ. Perhaps the unity of righteousness and justification is best found in this event, too.

It is instructive that none of the passages from John discussed above has much directly to do with the cross of Christ, though his death is prominently enough displayed as the means of salvation for the world throughout the Gospel.[69] In Jn. 16:8–10, the referent of *dikaiosynē* is an ironic forensic 'righteousness', i.e. verdict of not guilty, that the people believe they have on the basis of keeping the law. There is no direct mention of the cross in the passage, but the assumption of the death of Christ is everywhere in the background of the passage. From the reference to the greatest love one can have for one's brothers (15:13) to the references peppering the upper room discourse that say Jesus must go away or shortly will be with them no longer (Jn. 13:33,36–37; 14:2–5,18–19,25–31; 15:26; 16:4–33), the thought of the cross persists. There is a special concentration of this language in the immediate context of 16:8–10, of course, and it is difficult to miss a heavy emphasis on the death of Christ in the necessary reader-response to the passage. The reader knows perfectly well what the disciples do not know, i.e. that Jesus faces the pain and suffering of the cross and yet is lovingly preparing the disciples for his absence, while they alternate between confusion (16:17–18) and mistaken enlightenment (16:29–30) over what he means. This magnificent contrast keeps the cross at the forefront of the reader's mind without it ever actually being mentioned in the text itself. Thus the reference to *dikaiosynē* is made in a context heavily tied to the cross.

Reference to the cross in the context of the other passages is less apparent. Nothing in the verses surrounding Jn. 5:30 even suggests the cross, though there is reference in Jn. 7:33 to Jesus' brief sojourn with man, and the even more interesting tie of Jesus' just judgment (7:30) to the fact that the authorities are seeking to kill him (7:19–20,25–26). The word *dikaios* (righteous') in Jn. 17:25 appears in the high priestly prayer of Jesus which is dominated by the idea that Jesus is about to depart and be with the Father (17:1,5,11,13), again reminding the reader of the impending cross.

Thus, while we could not say that the idea of the cross is central to the usage of the *dikaio-* word-group in John, it is nevertheless interesting that, when the terms are used, the idea of the crucifixion is usually not very far away. Of course the terms are not used to discuss soteriology and so the cross is not tied to the justification of individuals in the Pauline sense; but we are concerned only to show that the idea is below the surface in John and readily accessible to him.

(2) The phrase *dikaiosynē theou* ('righteousness/justification of God') in Paul has often puzzled scholars, especially concerning the meaning of the genitive *theou* ('of God'). Is it perhaps an objective genitive which speaks of a righteousness that is acceptable to God but nevertheless is anthropologically approached because it is a gift that God has given to man? Is it a subjective genitive that points to a righteousness that is possessed by God and is demonstrated in Christ for the salvation of mankind but that as a gift to man can never be separated from the Giver? Is it some other genitival construction, signifying something else? We have neither the space nor the need to try to answer this question here; suffice it to say that for our purposes, we can point equally to *dikaiosynē* as proper to Christ, or, rather, to Christ as actually being the *dikaiosynē theou* (1 Cor. 1:30; *cf.* Rom. 5:10,17,21) and to the *dikaiosynē theou* as being something that God demonstrates to us concerning his own character (Rom. 3:25–26). We will look for this simultaneous attribute/function in John.

It is obvious that God, in the persons of both the Son and the Father, is viewed as being righteous. Jn. 16:8–10 does not emphasise this aspect of God's character because the righteousness alluded to in the passage is an aspect of humans, though the passage does appeal in a roundabout way to the world to act righteously and implies that God, and/or Jesus, is the standard by which that righteousness can be judged. Jn. 17:25 of course directly attributes to God the Father the characteristic of righteousness.

That God *acts* righteously is also obvious from the use of *dikaio-* words in John. Jn. 5:30 clearly makes both the judgments of the Father and the Son just: Jesus declares his own judgments to be just because he seeks the Father's will, implying that the Father's will is just, his judgments are just. As Jn. 16:8 speaks of the world's 'righteousness' and implies a contrast with the ontological righteousness of God, so Jn. 7:24 appeals to the world to judge with righteousness judgments, implying a contrast with the functional righteousness of God's just judgments. Thus both the ontological and functional righteousness of God, so important to the Pauline idea of justification, are also present in the concept of justice/righteousness that is present in John, pointing to a linking of the two, if ever so slightly, once again.

(3) There is little doubt that *dikaiosynē* has a background in the law courts, whether we are looking at it from a Jewish or a Greco-Roman perspective.[70] While in the Old Testament the idea of *sᵉdāqāh* goes beyond a formal, legal contract to a living, covenantal relationship between God and his people, it nevertheless does describe the legal situation of one being declared just or not guilty of crimes of which one has been accused (*cf.* Dt. 25:1). Thus any legal metaphors in John, especially those that speak of acquittal might be significant for our discussion.

It is now obvious that I believe John's view of *dikaiosynē* and related terms to be forensic. We should note that since the work of James Barr, language, especially individual vocabulary, can no longer be considered as having a static 'content'; context gives the full meaning of a term in any given passage and of a set of etymologically related terms in any given body of literature. But we have discovered in the exegesis above that John is remarkably consistent in his appeal to forensic categories when he uses this word group, and that consistent appeal says something significant about his acceptance of, or perhaps even appeal to, justification by faith as a means of being made right with God.

(4) *Dikaiosynē* is linked with *dōrea*[71] ('gift') at several crucial places in Paul. It is not going too far to speak of a relationship between the two at Rom. 3:23–26 and, especially, Rom. 5. Though *aphesis* ('forgiveness') is not actually mentioned, forgiveness or pardon is a good way to view this free gift aspect of justification: 'while we were yet sinners, Christ died for us' (Rom. 5:8; *cf.* also Rom. 8:1; Col. 2:13–14).[72] All have sinned according to Paul (Rom. 3:23), and the payment for that sin is death (Rom. 6:23), but God in Christ has exchanged our death for life and has given to us freely of his life eternal (Rom. 6:23; 2 Cor. 5:14–15). This gift of a pardon is so intensively stated in Paul that he says we not only no longer have our trespasses counted against us but we even *become* the gift of righteousness in him, i.e. Christ (2 Cor. 5:19–21).

The idea of justice underlying the Johannine use of *dikaiosynē* etc., does

not imply a *present* gift as the Pauline idea of justification often does. As we
saw earlier, the reference to Jesus' judgment in Jn. 5:30 seems to be to a time
of future judgment, not a present one. Indeed, the Johannine references bear
no resemblance to the ontological quality of righteousness which God
transfers to us in Christ, mentioned by Paul in Rom. 5:22, 2 Cor. 5:21 and
other places. Only in Jn. 16:8,10 might we argue that there is an underlying
irony as Jesus places that which the Jews think will bring them acquittal, i.e. a
righteousness based on works, over against the true righteousness that only
God can dispense.

But this is not to say, of course, that John has no sense of present gift,
already 'imparted and received',[73] in his soteriological scheme. In fact, Jesus
probably emphasises the free gift of the grace of God more in the Gospel of
John than in the Synoptic Gospels.[74] In the prologue, giving is put at the
forefront of the divine activity (and is connected intimately with having faith!)
in the crucial statement that '. . . to all who received him, who believed in his
name, he gave power [*edōken . . . exousian*] to become children of God (Jn.
1:12, RSV). Just a few short verses later, near the end of the prologue, the
gift of God's grace, present in Jesus, is highlighted again and this time as a gift
already received, at least in part. John refers to the 'grace upon grace' which
we have already 'received' from his fulness because, as opposed to the law
which was 'given' through Moses, grace and truth have come through Jesus
Christ (Jn. 1:16–17). The references could be multiplied far beyond the scope
of this paper.[75] The point, however, is that, though John has not connected
his use of the *dikaio-* word-group with the 'present gift' idea with which Paul
has connected it, the idea is nevertheless clearly and forcefully presented in
John in the soteriological framework he has constructed. Once again one
could say that he presupposes it in any view of justification that he
demonstrates.

(5) Perhaps the strongest verbal link of all between *dikaiosynē* and any
other signficant Pauline term is that between it and the *pistis/pisteuō* ('faith/to
believe') group. Though the actual phrase *dikaiosynē ek pisteōs* ('justification
by faith') does not occur as often as one might think, the two word groups are
linked over and over again in Paul. And they are linked in ways that make it
very difficult to distinguish categories that in some respects should be kept
separate for good theological reasons, the categories of the individual,
subjective justification of the believer and the objective divine act of
justification declared by God in the cross. As Schrenk puts it, 'The assertion
of faith as a condition is always closely linked with the most objective
declarations concerning the *dikaiosynē theou* ('righteousness/justification of
God'): Rom. 1:17; 3:22–28; 4; 5:1. The achievement and declaration of
salvation are never separated from the appropriation of salvation, because
the revealing action in question always stands in the I–Thou relationship . . .
The divine objectivity of salvation is thus the objectivity of a saving
relationship.'[76] Thus the activity of believing is never far from the idea of
justification in Paul.

Dikaiosynē is not linked with *pisteuō* ('to believe') in a believer in the
Gospel of John; the salvation attained by believing is most often eternal life,
not justification. In the two occurrences of *dikaiosynē*, though, in Jn. 16:8,10,
belief is prominent in the context as the world is convicted of its guilt/sin
because 'they do not believe in me' [*ou pisteuousin eis eme*]. With the forensic

view of righteousness that we have put forward above, the link is quite clear
in the passage: the world is condemned in Jn. 16:9 because they do not
believe in Jesus and, conversely in the next clause containing *dikaiosynē*, the
world's view of righteousness is shown to be wrong because Jesus' ascension/
exaltation proves his teaching to be right, i.e. the teaching that belief in him
brings eternal life.[77] Hence, though the focus of the passage is not on
soteriology but on pneumatology, its soteriological reference may be
justification by faith. At least it fits Paul's view very comfortably.

Similarly, in Jn. 5:38, the Jews are accused of not believing in the one
whose 'judgment is just' (5:30). They are judged by the Son because they do
not 'honour' the Son (5:22–23) and therefore do not honour the Father who
has given all judgment into the Son's hand. As we have seen, this judgment
seems to refer to the Great Judgment which Jesus will execute at the end. The
heavy concentration of *pisteuō* ('to believe') in the passage clearly links with
belief in him the 'good things' that Jesus is said to judge favourably in v. 29
Hence the connection between believing and accepting Jesus' judgment
makes justification by faith an almost necessary assumption underlying the
passage.

The distant echoes of justification by faith can even be heard in the context
of Jn. 7:24 and 17:25. Jesus' command to judge with just judgments (Jn. 7:24)
moves very easily and directly into soteriological questions about believing in
Jesus as Messiah (7:25–31), with some even believing in him. In Jn. 17:25,
Jesus appeals to the Father as righteous, in the midst of linking his continued
revelation of the Father (v. 26) with those who will believe in Jesus through
the message the disciples will preach (v. 20). Though the immediate context is
more important for our understanding of the forensic background of *dikaios*
in the passage, the reference to a righteous Father can also be said to occur in
a passage where the larger theme is prayer for all believers, present and
future.[78] Thus all four of the occurrences of the *dikaio-* word-group are in
passages with strong links to the *pist-* word-group and fit the Pauline linking of
the two very nicely.

(6) There is a double aspect to the gift of righteousness so that, even as we
state that *dikaiosynē* is present with us now, working in and through us, we
must acknowledge that Paul views it as future also, that 'we in the Spirit by
faith await the hope of righteousness [*dikaiosynē*]' (Gal. 5:5). As Käsemann
puts it, 'Thus, even the gift of the divine righteousness does not bring us to the
goal, but only sets our feet upon the road.'[79] Some believe that it is the
present aspect of the *dikaiosynē theou* ('righteousness/justification of God')
which separates Paul from the Jews of his day;[80] better put, the dual character
of God's righteousness, temporally speaking at any rate, is at least one of the
things that separates them. But whereas the Jew looked forward to a
judgment based on merit, Paul calls that judgment day a hope and looks
forward to the certainty of justification no matter what the charge brought
against God's elect (*cf.* Rom. 3:30; 8:33).

Judgment as a spur to obedience is only tangentially found in the idea of
justification assumed in John, but it is nevertheless there. Jn. 16:8–10 carries
the idea implicitly as the conviction that the Spirit generates in the world is a
personal one and implies that, if the 'world' turns to belief,[81] then it can be
saved. Jn. 5:30 intimately connects belief with obedience by its statement that
the just judgment of Jesus turns on hearing the word, believing in the one
whom the Father has sent and doing good (5:24,29), though of course the

justification here is implied rather than stated. Jn. 17:25, on the other hand, mentions nothing about obedience, unless the implied command for the disciples to preach the gospel is seen in v. 21, or the hard work of securing the unity that is given the disciples by Jesus is read into Jesus' statements in vv. 21 and 23. This is unlikely since Jesus is appealing to the Father to secure the unity that belongs to the disciples.[82]

Jn. 7:24 makes perhaps the strongest connection of all the passages containing the *dikaio-* word-group since it commands the making of just judgments in the context of a discussion about obedience to the law and the true understanding of Sabbath breaking (vv. 21–24). As we saw above, the discussion then goes on to involve questions of belief in Jesus as Messiah. Thus, while we would be very wrong to stress this aspect of justification as it seems to be assumed in John, we can nevertheless say that the connection is again strongly implicit and therefore fits well enough with Paul's view.[83]

(7) Though Rudolph Bultmann argued strongly for a highly individualistic view of justification in Paul, almost all New Testament scholars see at least some form of corporate or group aspect to the concept brought on particularly by the linking of being 'in Christ' and being made the *dikaiosyne theou* ('righteousness/justification of God') in him (2 Cor. 5:17,21). This group aspect flows largely from Paul's understanding that the covenant faithfulness of God has been manifested to his people Israel in his righteousness being given to the elect (Rom. 9–11). It has nothing to do with a covenant relationship with all creation, a view that tends toward a very un-Pauline universalism; nor does it teach a mystical union between God and man, except in the sense of the Spirit of God indwelling the individual on the basis of justification (*cf.* Gal. 3:2,5).

The sending of the Spirit of God is the main focus of the only passage in John to use the word *dikaiosyne* (Jn. 16:5–16); this key passage is a strong link between assumed Johannine justification and the doctrine taught by Paul. Of course, in 16:8–10, unlike the other parts of the discourse having to do with the Spirit (or Counselor, *parakletos*), Jesus speaks of the Spirit's challenging the world rather than guiding the disciples. But even this challenge is seen to benefit the disciples in some way (Jn. 16:7), perhaps solidifying them in that unity for which Jesus prays in ch.17. The 'world' which is challenged, i.e. convicted, and then turns to join the disciples will add to their numbers and convince them all the more of the truth of Jesus; the 'world' which does not turn will clarify the distinction between the disciples and itself, hardening the line which is already there in the earthly ministry of Jesus.

And this Spirit is clearly a Counsellor who comes from Jesus and the Father and sustains the disciples together in the Son. John 16 flows easily into John 17 and is linked with it through many motifs, but the one that is crucial for unifying the work of the Father, Son, Spirit and the disciples (both with Jesus and each other) is the motif of glory. In 16:4, the Spirit will bring glory to Jesus by 'taking from what is mine and making it known to [the disciples]' (NIV). In 17:10 the concept of shared possession, this time between the Father and Jesus, again results in glory to Jesus. Finally the unity of the disciples emphasised in 17:20–26 is connected to the glory which the Father has given the Son and which he has in turn passed on to the disciples (17:22,24). By now it will not have escaped our attention that the Father is described very easily as 'righteous' (*dikaios*) in the midst of this emphasis on unity. Thus the Pauline statement of oneness in Christ and its link to justification by faith is supported by the evidence that underlies two of the passages containing the *dikaio-* word-group in John.[84]

(8) Lastly, *dikaiosynē* is seen by Paul to be not only intrinsic to our salvation in the past but also that power to live life that saves us in the present and the future, too. This teaching is most clearly articulated in Rom. 5, but it is also evident in Phil. 3:7–14,16 and in Gal. 2:15–21. It is our slavery to *dikaiosynē* that leads to holiness and, paradoxically, frees us in Christ (Gal. 5:1–5; Rom. 6:17–19; 8:10). This comprehensive aspect of *dikaiosynē* is crucial for our investigation since it presents us with a broad understanding of righteousness or justification that extends throughout the entire soteriological process and thereby gives the idea a flexibility that might make it more legitimately accessible to Johannine categories of salvation.

If justification by faith underlies the Johannine teaching about salvation, that 'salvation' (to use a generic term) is certainly linked with a continuing power to live after the initial pardoning. The story of the woman at the well (John 4) and the dubious story of the woman taken in adultery (John 8)[85] serve as examples of the power of the eternal life Jesus gives to overcome sin in this life. The powerful statements of salvation contained in Jn. 1:12 and 16, 'believers' are 'the children of God' who have received 'one blessing after another' (1:16, NIV) from God, demonstrate even more clearly John's belief that salvation is accompanied by a power flowing from the sovereign oversight of a living Lord. This sanctification is implied strongly, too, in the Good Shepherd discourse of ch.10, especially in the statement that no one can take them (i.e. the disciples) out of the Father's hand (10:29). Lastly, the promises of the upper room discourse, albeit accompanied by commands, attest to the power that eternal life will have in the disciples after Jesus is gone and the Spirit is sent.[86]

But what of the passages containing the *dikaio-* word-group? Again, since the passages themselves are not clearly focused on the justification of sinners but only point to a conception of justification that John had, we should not expect to find much. Jn. 5:30 concentrates on the eschatological judgment and does not mention the power of present grace, though the ensuing verses and the discussion of salvation there might be said to fit into the larger framework of Johannine soteriology. Similarly, Jn. 7:24 contains no mention of sanctification. The work of the Spirit mentioned in Jn. 16:8–10 relates to the disciples in an oblique way, but there is no real statement there about the power for life that justification gives. Lastly, the work of the Father, not that of the disciples, is emphasised in unifying the disciples in John 17, and so it would be incorrect to speak of a linking of justifying grace and empowerment there. Since we have spoken only of an assumption of justification in John, and since the notions of power or transformation of life are clearly linked in John's Gospel to his own predominant salvific themes, it should not surprise us that this aspect of the Pauline idea of justification is not found in the Johannine passages containing the *dikaio-* word-group.

V. CONCLUSIONS

I have tried to discuss the idea of justification in the Gospel of John by the very limited means of looking at the passages where members of the *dikaio-*word-group occur and relating these and what they might indicate about justification to a synthesis of the Pauline conception. Several conclusions are immediately apparent.

(1) John does not have justification by faith at the centre of the *portrayal* of his soteriological scheme because he simply does not use the language of justification to describe the soteriological event as Paul does. Rather, such concepts as the giving of eternal life, and such metaphors as passing from darkness to light and the imparting of new wine, bread from heaven, life-giving water and sight to the blind, are used to describe salvation.

(2) There are indications, however, that John does assume justification in a forensic sense in many places in his Gospel, especially in the places where the *dikaio-* word-group is used. We have tried to show this from the way in which he uses the words themselves.

(3) We have looked at the idea of justification in Paul by means of eight different characteristics which seem to have a measure of agreement in the scholarly community. We have compared these with passages in John: those that are tied to John's use of *dikaiosynē*, etc., and to a lesser extent those that are linked to other Johannine soteriological themes. As a result, we have found grounds for saying that the idea of justification, while not *central* to John's thought, is nevertheless so often so close to the surface that it would be wrong to conclude it is not important to him. In seven of the eight categories we used as a test, we found links wth at least some of the passages that contain the *dikaio-* word-group, and in the eighth, we found strong links in many of the major passages in John addressing salvation.

More than this we really cannot say without a lengthy treatment of such Johannine concepts as witness, truth, and judgment among others,[87] looking to see what relationship they might have to Pauline justification. We have also not had the opportunity to see what, if anything, John might actually add to the biblical idea of justification through his scant treatment of it. But it does seem that we have the first elements of an answer to the questions that have been raised about the unity of the New Testament based on the lack of any statement about justification occurring in the Gospel of John. The New Testament's unity may be defended. Justification is in John.

8

'Justification' in the Epistle of James

RONALD Y. K. FUNG

Martin Luther's well-known dictum on the Letter of James, expressed in the Preface to his 1522 edition of the New Testament, was that it was 'a right strawy epistle' in comparison with the Gospel of John, 1 John, Paul's epistles (especially Romans, Galatians and Ephesians) and 1 Peter. Luther's verdict was partly based on his understanding that its teaching about justification was wholly incompatible with that of Paul. He is also on record as saying: ' "Faith justifies" [Rom. 3:28] stands in flat contradiction to "Faith does not justify" [Jas. 2:24]. If anyone can harmonise these sayings, I'll put my doctor's cap on him and let him call me a fool.'[1] Such a view of the relationship between James and Paul is still echoed today by not a few scholars, who speak, for instance, of James as vigorously disputing the *sola fide* ('by faith alone') which is the characteristic and decisive formula for Paul's doctrine of justification, and even nomistically corrupting the use or meaning of *dikaiousthai* ('being justified') by drawing works into it.[2]

But if on so fundamental a point as the believer's justification James and Paul are at cross-purposes, a question is raised not only about the unity of New Testament theology (would not 'theologies' then be a more appropriate word?) but also about 'a canon within the canon' (does James have a right to stand alongside Paul?). The topic of this chapter is therefore clearly important; a correct understanding of James's teaching on 'justification' not only is valuable in itself, but also will throw light on the larger questions of its relation to Pauline teaching and the place of the epistle within the canon.

Since the vocabulary of justification is, for all practical purposes, confined to the pericope 2:14–26,[3] we shall devote the major part of this essay to a detailed examination of that much-discussed and highly-disputed passage. We shall then try to show how the doctrine of 'justification' expressed therein fits into the teaching of the epistle as a whole. Finally, we shall bring the results of our study to bear on the question of the apparent conflict between James and Paul.

I. EXEGESIS OF 2:14–26[4]

A. Statement of Thesis (vv. 14–17)

From the man who shows favouritism while believing in the Lord Jesus Christ

(2:1–13) James now moves to the more general situation — but still the same phenomenon — of a man whose profession of faith is not borne out by his practice. The contrast in v. 14 is between a man's *claiming to have* faith and his *not having* 'works' (RSV) to match.[5] As suggested by the context, the works in question are 'deeds' of neighbourly love (15f., *cf.* 8) and other acts of obedience to God's will (21,25). As the man claims to have it, 'faith' (14a) probably denotes 'the fundamental attitude of the Christian adherent, which makes him a Christian';[6] but the faith which the man actually possesses is unaccompanied by deeds (14b) and, if it has any content at all, probably consists in mere intellectual acceptance of Christian dogma such as the tenet 'God is one' (19a, RSV).[7] The two rhetorical questions make it plain that 'such faith'[8] yields no profit (*cf.* RSV) for the man who possesses it: it cannot save him from the final judgment (*cf.* 13).[9] James plainly implies (a) that he does not regard such faith as the genuine article or its possessor a genuine believer,[10] and (b) that in his estimation a saving faith is an operative faith which shows itself in works. It should be observed in passing that in denying that a work-less faith can save, James does not thereby raise the question whether, let alone imply that, faith-less works can.[11]

To illustrate the uselessness of a barren faith, James in vv. 15f. introduces the comparable case of 'charity' which consists 'in word or speech' only and not 'in deed and in truth' (1 Jn. 3:18 [RSV], *cf.* 3:17). He pictures a Christian being 'ill-clad' (RSV) and in lack of 'food for the day' (NEB) and a fellow-Christian responding to the situation with a comforting formula of farewell ('Go, I wish you well') and a pious hope that the needy person will 'be warmed and filled' (RSV),[12] without making the slightest effort to provide actual relief. The stylised phrases in vv. 15–16a suggest that here we are not dealing with a concrete case from real life, but rather with a *comparison* contrived for purposes of illustration[13] which, nevertheless, reflects a real concern of James. His use of the rhetorical question, 'What good is it?', for the second time (thus forming an *inclusio* with v. 14a) effectively evokes the reader's ready assent that the 'charity' of this 'talking philanthropist' is totally inadequate and wholly ineffectual.[14]

This conclusion from the comparative material in vv. 15f., applied to the matter on hand (14), leads to the strengthened thesis of v. 17: 'In the same way, faith by itself, if it is not accompanied by action, is dead.' The word 'dead' possibly means 'barren, unfruitful' (*cf.* 20)[15] but more probably signifies the opposite of 'living', i.e. showing no sign that it is alive and real (*cf.* 26). As J. H. Ropes rightly remarks, 'The two things which are opposed are not faith and works . . . but a living faith and a dead faith.'[16] This dead faith is the merely claimed or professed faith of the man in v. 14; it is hardly worthy of the name of faith, any more than the merely professed concern of the Christian in vv. 15f. is worthy of the name of charity. The positive implication of all this is plain: a living faith will be seen to be genuine only when it is implemented in works.

We should note in passing that an alternative rendering, 'Even so faith, if it have no works, is dead in itself' (RV), has the advantage of keeping the final phrase in the Greek (*kath' heautēn*) in its original position, avoiding the repetition of the idea of 'not [being] accompanied by action' in the phrase 'by itself', and making it possible to understand James as moving 'onward from observation of phenomena to a judgment as to the cause' — a faith that 'does not lead to action' (NEB) is not only outwardly inoperative but also gives evidence thereby that it is dead 'in its very essence'.[17] Nevertheless, the usual rendering 'by itself' (also RSV, NASB; *cf.* AV 'being alone') should probably be retained, for two reasons: (a) it is supported by a similar sense which the Greek phrase (*kath' heauton*) has in the Septuagint (Gen. 30:40; 43:32; 2 Macc. 13:13), the New Testament (Acts 28:16; Rom. 14:22) and elsewhere;[18] (b) the main point of vv. 15f. is the uselessness of a charity consisting merely of fine words and devoid of practical action, so that what is suggested by the 'even so' (RV) at the beginning of v. 17 is the futility of a faith that 'is not accompanied by action' (thus 'by itself' rather than 'in itself'). On this showing, the tautology involved may be understood as being due to James's desire to emphasise the thought of ' "faith" in isolation' at the conclusion of his sentence (and paragraph).[19]

B. Two Rational Arguments (vv. 18–19)

The words 'But someone will say' in v. 18 simultaneously signal a new stage in the argument and introduce what is arguably the most difficult passage in the pericope. Two main questions arise in its interpretation: (a) Who is this 'someone'? (b) How far does his remark extend? These necessarily related questions will be dealt with together as we consider several proposals for their solution.

Some interpreters find it impossible to take v. 18b–c — 'You have faith and I have works' (RSV) — as an objection, since the objector would then be attributing faith to James and works to himself, which hardly fits the preceding context; he should rather have said, 'You have works and I have faith.'[20] They therefore take the adversative *alla* ('but') as having a strengthening force (= 'nay', 'indeed'; *cf.* RV 'yea') and the indefinite pronoun *tis* ('someone') as referring to a supporter of James's view, who champions his cause against the advocate of work-less faith (= the 'man' of v. 14).[21] On this showing the pronouns are consistently employed: 'I' is always James or his ally, and 'you' is always the opponent. But this *Sekundantenhypothese* (supporter-hypothesis) is beset with difficulties which render it untenable. For example:

(i) It is difficult to understand why James should introduce an imaginary supporter when he is quite capable of pleading his cause in his own name. 'To introduce an ally who disappears as sharply as he has appeared is an unlikely procedure for any writer, however modest.'

(ii) 'This introduction requires that the opening word be read "you *claim* to have faith", a nuance that James does not at all make explicit.'

(iii) To put the same objection in a different way, this interpretation 'might appear to attribute to James the acknowledgment that this man really has faith, when the aim of the previous verses has been to show that his faith is no faith at all.'

(iv) The *tis* ('someone') of v. 18 (who supports James) would be someone entirely different from the *tis* ('a man') of v. 14 (whom James argues against); such ambiguity is liable to be misunderstood by reader or hearer.

(v) It is surely more natural to take the *tis* of v. 18 by analogy with the *tis* of v. 14, as someone who represents a point of view that is opposed to that of *James*.

(vi) The interpretation under discussion robs the formula *all' erei tis* ('but someone will say') of its precise force: elsewhere it always introduces an objection and not a supporting argument (e.g. 1 Cor. 15:35; *cf.* Rom. 9:19; 11:19).[22]

In view of these difficulties, the supporter-hypothesis can hardly be maintained.

Of those interpretations which do give the formula (18a) its most obvious meaning, a widely accepted view is that in the objection, which consists of v. 18b–c only (as in NIV, RSV), the pronouns 'you' and 'I' do not refer to James and the objector respectively, but are equivalent to 'one' and 'another'; they are 'merely a more picturesque mode of indicating the imaginary persons'. In making the objector say, 'One person has faith, another has actions' (GNB = TEV, *cf.* NEB), James creates a strawman who advocates 'a *sophistic separation of faith and works*', regarded as of equal validity before God, and uses it as a foil against which to present his own view of the matter.[23] This interpretation, too, involves considerable difficulties:

(i) The use of *sy* and *egō* ('you' and 'I') for *heis* and *heteros* ('one' and 'another') is not sufficiently attested. To convey the latter idea, the natural expression would have been *hos/allos/heteros men* and *hos/allos/heteros de*.

(ii) In this interpretation, *sy* and *egō* in v. 18b–c mean 'one' and 'another,' but in vv. 18e–19a they have their normal signification; particularly glaring is the fact that the two instances of *kagō* in the same verse have different meanings, first 'and another' (18c) and then 'and I' (18e).

(iii) Even if the intention of v. 18b–c were to point out the equal validity of faith and works before God, it is doubtful that the objector, who is championing the cause of 'faith only', would have said 'You have faith and I have works' and not 'You have works and *I* have *faith*'.[24]

It is not surprising that one advocate of this interpretation is constrained to concede, 'This solution to the difficulty is adopted because it seems to make the best sense in context, not because it is entirely satisfactory.'[25]

The most satisfying solution of the *crux interpretum* is, to my knowledge, the one proposed by Heinz Neitzel.[26] There are two key elements in this proposal: (a) *sy pistin echeis* is to be taken as a genuine question from the objector, 'Do you have faith?'; (b) a colon is to be placed after *kagō* ('and I') as introducing the response of the author. Not the least merit of this interpretation is that the emphatic personal pronouns are given their proper force and *pistin* ('faith') and *erga* ('works') are appropriately attributed to the objector and the author respectively, as the following scheme (based largely on the RSV rendering) makes clear:

18a–b	But someone will say, 'Do you have faith?'
	(*Implication* = '*I have faith*, but you do not.')
c	and I [will say], '**I have works**.
d	Show me *your faith* apart from your works,
e	and I by **my works** will show you my faith.
19a	*You believe* that God is one . . .'

Two explanatory comments are necessary.

(a) Since in vv. 14–17 James appears to undervalue faith and demand only works, it would occur readily to the objector to doubt the presence of faith in the author: 'Do you have faith?' means 'You, you who speak thus of faith, do you have faith at all?'[27] This understanding of the words as a question casting doubt on the author's faith seems required by the fact that the author offers in v. 18e to 'show you my faith'. To the objection that the positive form of the question, being without the negative interrogative particle *mē* ('not'), is ill-suited to call in question James's faith,[28] it may be answered that questions about the presence or absence of a certain state of affairs which can be answered with 'yes' or 'no' do not require either in classical Greek or in the Koine an interrogative particle, since the inflection of the voice makes their nature clear;[29] a similar, expressive-of-doubt question like v. 18b is Pilate's question to Jesus: 'Are you the king of the Jews?' (*sy ei ho basileus tōn Ioudaiōn*; Mt. 27:11; parallels Mk. 15:2; Lk. 23:3; Jn. 18:33; BDF 277 [1] inserts parenthetically in explanation of *sy*, 'a man like you').

(b) *kagō erga echō* ('and I have works', RSV) is not, as such, the beginning of the author's answer to the objector's question. Just as the words 'and I will show you my faith' (18e) presuppose doubt regarding James's faith, i.e. it presupposes exactly the question 'Do you have faith?', so the words 'by my works' (RSV) presuppose that he *has* works — which is already expressed by the words 'I have works' (*erga echō*). These, then, are the words with which James's answer begins, and the word *kagō* ('and I') is the introduction to that answer.

Verse 18a–c is therefore to be punctuated like this: *all' erei tis· sy pistin echeis*; — *kagō* [sc. *erō*]· *erga echō*, and rendered as: 'But someone will say, "Do *you* have faith?" — and I [*sc.* will say], "I have works." ' In other words, the real parallelism (or antithesis) here is not between *sy* ('you') and *kagō* ('and I'), but between *pistin echeis* ('do you have faith?') and *erga echō* ('I have works'); and the *kai* ('and') in *kagō* binds the *egō* ('I') not with *sy* but rather with *tis* ('someone'). Taken in this way, the beginning of James's retort ('I have works') signifies that the question 'Do you have faith?' is wrongly put, since faith can only be inferred from works.

The ellipsis of the verb *erō* ('I will say') after *kagō* ('and I') is analogous to the omission of the verb 'he said' in reports of conversations, as in Acts 25:22; 9:5; 9:10f.; in the second and third of these examples the verb is omitted because it can be supplied from the foregoing. Just so, James avoids the repetition of the verb *erō*, 'not merely because the brachylogy works more elegantly, but rather because the main thing to him is to exploit his trump card "I have works" immediately and with force against the objection *pistin echeis* ["Do you have faith?"]'[30] That the direct speech follows immediately after *kagō*, without *erō*, is connected with the elementary principle that in reported speech in Greek, the verb which is connected with the person giving an answer practically never immediately follows the naming of the person, as examples from Plutarch and Epictetus also show; a few examples from these authors further show that the verb 'to say' is to be supplied from the preceding context, as in the NT instances already cited.[31]

If the objector's words consist only of the question 'Do you have faith?' and all the rest is spoken by James, the two sentences — 'someone will say . . . and I [will say]' and '[you] show . . . and I will show' — have the same syntactical structure: in both *kai* ('and') binds on the one hand the pronouns (subjects) *tis*, *egō* ('someone', 'I') and *sy*, *egō* ('you', 'I'), and on the other hand the verbs (predicates) *erei*, [*erō*] ('[someone] will say', ['I will say']) and *deixon, deixō* ([you] show', 'I will show'). Two good parallels to the structure of v. 18d–e are provided by Epictetus and Theophilus.[32] Thus 'the form of the verse [18] is in no way strange, but rather corresponds exactly to the style of philosophical dialogue (Plato) and popular philosophical diatribe (Epictetus, Plutarch). Moreover, it accords with the linguistic usage of the New Testament.'[33]

Faced, then, with the author's apparent depreciation of faith (14–17), the imaginary objector calls James's faith in question (18a–b). James's reply consists of three parts. *First*, he affirms that he has works (18c): since he has already made the point (by implication) that a living faith must of necessity be manifested in works (17), his affirmation amounts to saying that the works which he has are proof positive that he does have faith. *Second*, he proceeds with a logical argument which comprises a challenge (18d) and a counter-offer (18e): the challenge rests on the assumption that the existence of 'faith without deeds' is incapable of proof and thus implies that a work-less faith is no faith at all;[34] the counter-offer presents the obverse truth that works are the evidence of genuine faith, that faith will manifest itself in works.[35] Quite obviously James is contrasting *'two types of faith*, one of which claims to exist independently of works, the other producing works which demonstrate its validity', and here as in vv. 14–17 James 'affirms only the faith which unfolds itself in works'; his concern is not with 'faith and works' but 'faith in works'.[36]

The *third* part of James's reply consists in a second logical argument (19). The belief with which James credits the objector may be a belief in monotheism ('there is one God', also AV, NEB) or, more probably, a belief in the unity of the Godhead ('God is one', RV, RSV, NASB),[37] which is the fundamental formula of orthodox Judaism (the original *Shema'*, Dt. 6:4). In any case, the Greek construction used — *pisteueis hoti* ('you believe that') rather than *pisteuein* + dative, *en* or *eis*, emphasises intellectual acceptance rather than Christian commitment — indicates that the objector's faith is merely propositional.[38] In so far as the confession of God's oneness and uniqueness is part of true Christian faith, James's 'Good!' (the same Greek expression is rendered as 'you are doing right' in v. 8) may be 'not ironical', but in view of 'the sting in the tail' which follows, the words are made at least slightly ironical by the context.[39] For James goes on to draw attention to the fact that 'even the demons believe that [*sc*. God's oneness] — and shudder' (19b).[40] Their terror, due to their realisation of their fearful destiny of lostness before God, is a reaction well attested in the synoptic gospels when they come face to face with Jesus (Mk. 1:24; 5:7; Mt. 8:29).[41] No matter whether James intends to say 'even the demons believe' (also RSV) or 'the demons also believe' (NASB), the point of his reference to the demons appears to be that a faith that remains on the level of credal confession without corresponding conduct has no power to save either demon or man.[42] Thus the objector's implied position is reduced to absurdity, and v. 19 is an argument parallel to and serving the same function as vv. 15f., *viz*. supporting the original thesis of vv. 14,17 that faith without works is dead and has no saving power.[43] It is also an argument, by implication, in support of the point of v. 18 that genuine faith manifests itself in works.[44]

C. Two Scriptural Proofs (vv. 20–26)

Verse 20.[45] Still addressing the imaginary opponent of v. 18a, James now proceeds to reinforce his logical arguments (18f.) by adducing two biblical examples. The man is called 'foolish'[46] because he has divorced faith from works and fails to recognise[47] that 'faith apart from works is barren' (RSV). The word translated 'barren' (also RV, NEB; Gk *argos*[48] — literally 'workless', 'not at work' (Mt. 20:3,6) — means in this context (*cf.* 14) 'unproductive of the blessings of salvation'. The verse thus restates the point of the whole section in the form of an effective word-play: 'faith' that has no works does not work — it is dead (17) and does not save (14).[49]

Verse 21. This second, rhetorical question has the effect of an assertion[50] that 'Abraham our father[51] [was] justified by works, when he offered his son Isaac upon the altar' (RSV). The force of the aorist participle rendered 'when he offered' (also NIV, NASB) may be thus construed as temporal (*cf.* AV), or as explicatory (RV, NEB); in either case, the offering, though halted by God before it was consummated (Gen. 22:12), is presented here 'as a completed act in Abraham's intention'.[52] But whereas the offering of Isaac was a single act, James speaks of Abraham being justified by 'works' (plural). This could be an allusion to Jewish haggadic tradition in which the binding of Isaac forms the capstone of a series of testings of Abraham; in that case, 'James sees this one test as indicative of the whole; the pronouncement in the end [Gen. 22:12] is not the pronouncement on a single act alone, but on that act as the culmination of a series of works stemming from faith.'[53]

But it is preferable to regard the term 'works' as a plural of category, for the following reasons:

(i) The plural 'works' (Gk. *erga*) has already occurred no fewer than six times in the preceding verses (14a,17,18c,d,e,20), each time as a singular concept; i.e. the emphasis in the word is not on its plurality (at least two deeds) but on its character (deeds as action).[54]

(ii) It should be remembered that the offering of Isaac is referred to here in support of the thesis in v. 20 (and vv. 14–17) that faith without works is barren; in other words, 'the author speaks here [20–24] not as a defender of his [we should prefer to say "the"] slogan "works", but still chiefly as a critic of the slogan "faith without works" '.[55] So when he points out that Abraham was justified by 'works' he clearly intends Abraham to be taken as an example of 'faith *with* works', the term 'works' being used generically and subsequently illustrated by reference to the one act of the binding of Isaac.

(iii) 'As he [James] seems clearly to define Rahab's works in v. 25, so he may be taken to do so with Abraham in v. 21. . . . But the plural is really no more appropriate in the case of Rahab, for the reception and safe conduct of the messengers is a single event rather than two distinct events; and the use of *erga* in both examples surely derives from the contrast between *faith* and *works* throughout vv. 14–26, the language being imposed on both illustrations of the theme, rather than emerging from a strictly literal consideration of their context.'[56]

(iv) While James may have been acquainted with the Jewish tradition regarding Abraham's deeds of mercy, the text does not require the assumption that he has made use of it here; in fact, taking 'works' as a plural of category accords better with the most likely meaning of the term 'justified'.

This brings us to the most crucial question to be asked about this verse: In what sense is Abraham said to be 'justified' by works?[57] (1) Some maintain that the verb is here used with substantially the same sense as 'save' in v. 14;[58]

but such a sense of that verb, though it would fit the context ('barren' in v. 20 means 'unproductive of the blessings of eschatological salvation'), would be unparalleled in Scripture.[59]

(2) Many others, with or without seeing an allusion here to God's pronouncement on Abraham in Gen. 22:12, interpret the verb to mean that Abraham was declared righteous or 'approved by God as a righteous man by virtue of his deeds'; for him justification meant that 'his righteousness was not established [German *hergestellt*], but confirmed [*festgestellt*].'[60] This view is possible, but cannot be said to fit particularly well with, let alone be required by, the context (contrast the fourth view below; see also section II, [2] below).

(3) A related view takes James to be 'probably using *dikaioō* in a declarative sense, but . . . applying the word to God's *ultimate* declaration of a person's righteousness rather than [as Paul normally does] to the initial securing of that righteousness by faith'; James is then saying that 'Abraham did works and that these works were used as criteria in God's *ultimate* judgment over Abraham's life.' A considerable merit of this interpretation is that 'the use of *dikaioō* in this sense has ample precedent in the Old Testament, Judaism and the teaching of Jesus [Mt. 12:37], and it is held that 'James' frequent dependence on Jesus' teaching, particularly as found in Matthew, makes this reference all the more important'.[61] On the other hand, it is difficult to see either from v. 21 or from Gen. 22:12 that what the biblical author has in view is God's 'final justification' — the declaration of that 'verdict of innocence which is . . . associated with the last judgment';[62] and it is even more difficult to derive such a conclusion from v. 25 or the corresponding story in the Old Testament.

(4) The remaining option is to understand the term 'justified' in the more general, *demonstrative* sense of being vindicated, proved or shown to be just, as in Mt. 11:19; Lk. 7:35; Rom. 3:4; 1 Tim. 3:16. Now the Greek adjective for 'just' (*dikaios*) is used substantively in 5:16 ('a righteous man') to refer to any devout member of the believing community (*cf.* n.3 above), so that for Abraham to be 'shown to be just' means for him to be shown, by his action of offering up Isaac, to be a true believer. This interpretation accords well with God's pronouncement on Abraham's act of obedience in Gen. 22:12 ('Now I know you fear God'). The result is not vastly different if one proceeds from the English rendering of the Greek verb in question as 'vindicate', one meaning of which (latter word) is 'to make good a claim to':[63] for, in the light of James's basic thesis in this entire pericope, which is that genuine faith will manifest itself in works (*cf.* 17,26), the 'claim' in question can only be the claim (*cf.* v. 14, 'if a man claims') to have faith, so that for Abraham to be 'vindicated' by his action of offering up Isaac means that by that action he made good his 'claim' to believe in God, that the faith which he professed to have in God was proved to be genuine.[64] In view, however, of the strong hint provided by the use of the cognate adjective in 5:16, the other rendering, 'shown to be just/righteous', clearly seems preferable.

D. J. Moo has objected that 'this [demonstrative] meaning does not fit very well in James 2, where the question is not, "How can righteousness be demonstrated?" but, "What kind of faith secures righteousness?" '. But, as Moo himself reminds us, 'We should recall that it is the nature of Abraham's faith, a faith that is not "barren" (v. 20), that James wants to illustrate';[65] and it fits precisely this purpose for James to show that Abraham's faith was accompanied by works (22) which demonstrated that Abraham was a man of genuine faith (21). It is important to notice that having adduced the examples of Abraham and Rahab, James returns in the conclusion of the whole section (26) to the point of v. 17, which we have seen to be this: living faith manifests itself in works; this is also the point of v. 18, where James challenges the objector to '*show* me your faith without deeds' and promises in turn to '*show* you my faith by my works' (NASB; emphases added). All this emphasis throughout the section (17,18,26) on the necessity for faith to be demonstrated strongly supports the idea that 'James intends to say that Abraham was "shown to be just" by his actions.'[66] We are bound to conclude therefore that *dikaioō* in v. 21 is probably to be taken in a *demonstrative* rather than its more technical, declarative sense.

Verse 22. From the specific event of the binding of Isaac, which showed Abraham to be a man of genuine faith in God, James now elaborates on the relationship between faith and works in terms of a principle: 'You see that faith was active along with his works, and faith was completed by works' (RSV).[67] According to some interpreters, the faith of Abraham was 'only an assistance' in the attainment of the goal of approval by God as righteous;[68] but our exegesis of v. 21 has shown that the verb 'justify' there is not concerned with the question of forensic justification,[69] and the verb translated 'was active' is literally 'was working together with' (*synērgei*, imperfect), which should not be attenuated to the sense of merely assisting.[70] At the same time, to render the verb as 'was co-operating with' might carry the impliction that 'faith and works are thought of as two quite separate things existing independently of each other'; in view of the thesis that a 'without works' kind of faith is dead and useless (17,20) and that genuine faith manifests itself in works (18,21), it is more natural to render the first half of the verse as RSV (above) or NEB ('faith was at work in his actions') does, and to understand it to mean that 'Abraham's faith was the source and ground of his works, and his works the expression, the manifestation of his faith'.[71]

In the second half of v. 22, the verb (*eteleiōthē*) is better rendered 'perfected' (NASB) or 'made perfect' (AV, RV) than 'completed' (RSV) or 'made complete':[72] in 1:15 James has spoken of sin as 'full-grown' (*apotelestheisa*) when transformed into act and habit and in 1:4 of perseverance being made perfect by exercise. Here he speaks of faith being made perfect by works: just as a tree is made perfect by its fruits in that it attains its legitimate development in the bearing of fruits, which shows that it is a living tree, so faith is 'brought to due expression in appropriate actions', by which 'the integrity of [Abraham's] faith was fully proved' (NEB).[73] Thus both halves of v. 22 show that, as illustrated by Abraham's offering of Isaac, not only are faith and works inseparable, but faith 'constitutes the foundation but reaches fruition' in works.[74]

Verse 23. James sees in the union of faith and works manifested in Abraham's action (21f.) a fulfilment of Scripture (23a). The scripture quoted by James is clearly Gen. 15:6, which is also cited in the same form as here in Rom. 4:3 (*cf.* 4:9,22) and Gal. 3:6 (with *de* [untranslated] omitted): 'Abraham believed God, and it was credited to him as righteousness' (23b); but the significance of the quotation here is debated.[75] G. Schrenk says that 'according to 2:23 Abraham was justified before God by the imputation of a faith which found fulfilment in works' but adds that 'this view is nearer to the Jewish conception than that of Paul', especially since *'logizesthai* ['to be credited'] is here connected with human works and not with faith alone.'[76] What is latent in his comment becomes patent in the view of Dibelius-Greeven (and others), who are sure that James, like the Jews, understands the word 'righteousness' as 'an actual righteousness based on works' and the expression 'was credited' 'as proof of Abraham's righteousness by works'; at the same time, they find James's interpretation of Gen. 15:6 'not totally consistent', owing to 'the fact that James has introduced into the Jewish proof of Abraham's righteousness by works his own thesis . . . about the intimate connection between faith and works'.[77] What results then is that James believes that Abraham's justification before God is on account of both his faith and his works.[78]

Since in our view the 'justification' of v. 21 does not refer to a declaration *by God*, nor is the faith-works union in v. 22 spoken of in relation to such a declaration, we are bound to reject the above views in favour of the position that 'James quotes Gn. 15:6 for the same purpose as Paul does — to show that it was faith that secured Abraham's acceptance'.[79] In other words, *this* is the place, and the only place in the epistle, where Abraham's justification *before God* is mentioned; on this matter 'for James, no less than for Paul, the words of Gen. 15:6 . . . are decisive. It was by his faith that Abraham was justified'.[80]

Of the many explanations of the verb 'fulfil' in v. 23a, the one that commends itself to us as being most in accord with our exegesis of v. 23b and v. 21 is as follows: the 'sacrifice' of Isaac in Gen. 22:1–19 'explicates more fully the meaning of the statement about Abraham's faith' in Gen. 15:6, i.e. 'Abraham's faith (Gen. 15:6) was proven and more fully expressed by his act of obedience in the matter of sacrificing Isaac (Gen. 22:1–19)'.[81] On this showing, the word 'fulfil' does not bear the sense of the fulfilment of a predicted event, but the idea of 'confirming or showing to be true': in Abraham's offering of Isaac, the scriptural statement of Gen. 15:6 proved to be, or was confirmed as, correct.[82]

NIV, RSV, NEB and NASB correctly imply by their use of quotation marks that v. 23c is no part of James's quotation of Scripture, although in using the title 'God's friend' (*cf.* 2 Chron. 20:7; Isa. 41:8) James is probably 'echoing a familiar description of Abraham which ultimately has a scriptural background'.[83] And while the Old Testament nowhere indicates that the title was bestowed on Abraham during his lifetime, the intimate relationship indicated is clearly implied in God's words in Gen. 18:17 ('Shall I hide from Abraham what I am about to do?'), which were spoken well before the binding of Isaac in Gen. 22. It is more likely, therefore, that the title was added as indicating Abraham's complete acceptance by God[84] than that Abraham's privileged status as God's friend was a second result of the active 'co-operation' of faith and works in Abraham's life (the first being the 'fulfilment' of Scripture).[85]

Verse 24. James now reverts to addressing the readers directly (*horate*, 'You see', is plural) and summarises his discussion of Abraham (21–23) in the form of a theological principle — 'a person is justified by what he does and not by faith alone' — that is trans-temporal (note present tense 'is') and universal ('a person' = anyone). Precisely because this theological principle is derived from the example of Abraham, the term 'justified' must bear the same meaning here as it does in v. 21: a man is shown to be just, i.e. shown to be a man of genuine faith, by his works — the last word being for James a shorthand for 'deeds demonstrating faith'.[86]

D. O. Via asserts that 'Paul stands behind James's polemic in 2:24 because the expression *ek pisteōs monon* ['by faith alone'] is nowhere met in the whole literature of Judaism and earliest Christianity except in Paul.'[87] Strictly speaking, however, those words are not found even in Paul, for the word *monon* is missing in Rom. 3:28; 9:32; Gal. 2:16, and, indeed, are never added to any statement by Paul about justification by faith (even though the *sense* is implied, in contrast to 'works of the law' [RSV]).[88] It seems more likely, therefore, that the phrase 'by faith alone' is to be interpreted not with reference to Paul but *by its own context*: the term 'faith' here is a concession to James's opponents' use of words, being a reference to the merely verbal, falsely-so-called faith of vv. 14,17,19,20 (*cf*.26), while the word 'alone' means 'unaccompanied by works', so that the contrast in this verse, as throughout the pericope, is not between (genuine) faith (18e,22) and works but between ' "faith" without works' and 'works inseparable from and demonstrating faith'.[89] The final phrase of the verse means, then, that a merely professed faith which is unaccompanied by works can never show that a man is a real believer; only works can demonstrate the presence of genuine, and therefore (*cf*. v. 23) justifying, faith.

Summing up our discussion of vv. 21–24, we may indicate James's position on the relationship between faith, works and justification as follows: Righteousness (= forensic justification) is by faith (23); out of this arise 'works' that show ('justify' in the demonstrative sense, 24) that one is a real believer (and hence, *by logical inference*, justified in the forensic, declarative sense); or, as Buchanan puts it in his classic work on justification: good works 'are the effects of faith, and, as such, the evidences both of faith, and of justification'.[90]

Verse 25. 'In the same way' shows that the second biblical example is cited to make the same point as the first;[91] the 'works' (RSV) of Rahab showed that her faith in Israel's God was the genuine article, that it was the same justifying faith as that which Abraham had (*cf*. Heb. 11:31). James assumes that the readers already know the story of Rahab, who is both valued in Christian tradition as an example of faith (*cf*. Heb. 11:31; 1 Clem. 12:1,8) and lauded in Jewish tradition as the archetypal proselyte (*cf*. Josh. 2:9–11).[92] He does, however, specify the 'works' of Rahab: receiving the Israelite messengers and sending them out by another way (*cf*. Josh. 2:15f.), thus saving them from their pursuing enemies.[93] That James mentions the story of Rahab without elaborating on it (as he does the story of Abraham, 22f.) is probably due to the consideration that he has already made his argument clear in the case of Abraham. Some think that in juxtaposing Abraham and Rahab here James is merely following Jewish tradition, in which they already belong together in their character as ideal proselytes;[94] but the specific designation of Rahab as *the harlot* (even though it already appears in Josh. 2:2), in marked contrast with the description of Abraham as 'our ancestor', suggests rather that James intends Rahab as 'an extreme case, where, if anywhere, James's argument might seem to fail' (what good works could a pagan woman prostitute produce?), the two instances thus covering 'the whole wide range of possibilities'[95] and showing the theological principle of v. 24 to be universally valid.

Verse 26. This verse provides a supporting argument (note RSV 'for') for the implied answer to the rhetorical question of v. 25 — 'Yes, even Rahab was shown to be a genuine believer by her works' — as well as a final statement of the thesis of the entire pericope (*cf.* 17) with the aid of a second comparison (the first being in vv. 15f.): 'As the body without the spirit is dead, so faith without deeds is dead.' The comparison presupposes 'the popular view of the dichotomy of body and soul or life-spirit'.[96] Since James seems to be saying that 'works' (RSV) are to faith as the spirit is to the body, some interpreters have taken the trouble to defend the order body-spirit here: 'the FORM *of faith* without *the working reality* answers to the *body* without the *animating spirit.* does not follow that *living faith* derives its life from works, as the body derives its life from the animating spirit.'[97] Others maintain that the point of the comparison lies in the *unity* of faith and works: 'just as, when the spirit has departed from the body it is dead, so a man is inwardly dead if he has no "works" to show.'[98] It is to be observed that v. 26b forms an *inclusio* with v. 17, thus neatly tying vv. 18–26 together as a support for the main argument of vv. 14–17,[99] which is that saving faith is a living faith which manifests itself in works, which latter are the evidence of faith (18). This being the case, it is better to see the *tertium comparationis* as being the deadness of a 'faith' that is without works and the deadness of a body that is without 'breath' (NEB):

> As the body without breath is dead, so faith apart from works is dead. . . . Just as breath is the evidence, demonstration, proof of life in a human being, so works are the evidence, demonstration, proof of a living faith.[100]

To sum up, 2:14–26 can rightly be seen as a 'fuller theological treatment' of the theme mentioned in 1:4 and continuously discussed in 1:22–2:13, *viz.* 'the need for faith to be implemented in action.'[101]

II.   2:14–26 IN THE CONTEXT OF THE EPISTLE

The above exegesis has revealed two senses of 'justification' in James: (1) imputed righteousness (*dikaiosynē*) or forensic justification is attained as a gift by faith (23); (2) justification (*dikaiousthai*) in the sense of a demonstration of the possession of genuine faith is by works (21,24,25). We must now show how these conclusions are supported by the rest of the epistle.

A.   The Way of Salvation

(1) Although the specific terminology of justification is confined to 2:14–26, there are many indications elsewhere in the epistle as to the way of salvation. Against the backdrop of the universality of sin (3:2–12) conceived as transgression of the law (2:9–11; 4:17), the inexorable connection between temptation, sin and death (1:13–15), and the inevitability of judgment for sin (2:12f.; 3:1; 5:8f., 12; *cf.* 4:4,6), James presents salvation as a work and a gift of God, to be received by faith. Thus, God is a generous giver (1:5) who bestows grace on the humble and exalts those who humble themselves before

him (4:6,10). He is the source of all good gifts, supreme among which is the gift of spiritual life (1:17f.): the means of regeneration is 'the word of truth', *viz.* the gospel (*cf.* Eph. 1:13; Col. 1:5; 2 Tim. 2:15; 1 Pet. 1:23–25). Those who have thus been brought to life are exhorted to 'humbly accept the word planted in you, which can save you' (1:21). God is 'full of compassion and mercy' (5:11; *cf.* 3:17, divine wisdom is 'full of mercy'). The man who shows mercy has received mercy (2:13a; *cf.* Mt. 18:23–35), and will find again at the last judgment that 'mercy triumphs over judgment' (2:13b). The crown of life has been promised to, and will be received by, those who love God and have stood the testing of their faith (1:12). These references (especially 1:18,21) are sufficient by themselves to indicate that in James's view salvation is a gift of God and not the result of human works. Here, no less than in Paul, 'we have divine monergism in the work of salvation'.[102]

But a more striking parallel, specifically to Paul's teaching in 1 Cor. 1:26–28, is to be found in 2:5. Here we have the same agent ('God') performing the same action ('chose') on the same sort of people ('those who are poor in the eyes of the world', 'the foolish things . . . the weak things of the world . . . the lowly things of this world and the despised things') with the same goal in view: to be 'called . . . into fellowship with his Son Jesus Christ' (1 Cor. 1:9) is materially the same as being chosen 'to inherit the kingdom', a kingdom that is given by God to the poor in spirit (Mt. 5:3; Lk. 6:20; 12:32), entrance to which is effected by the new birth (1:18; *cf.* Jn. 3:3,5). This (being made 'rich in faith and heirs of the kingdom' [RSV]) is probably the 'high position' in which the brother in humble circumstances is to take pride (1:9). Now the appropriate human response to divine choice is faith — even faith 'in our Lord Jesus Christ' (2:1, NEB; *cf.* NASB, NIV). Thus 2:5 adds its significant weight to the other references to command agreement with the assertion that 'James clearly presents the same Gospel of salvation by grace through faith that Paul preaches'.[103]

One objection must be considered in passing. According to D. O. Via, 'there are real tensions between Jas. 1:19–27 and 2:14–26', for 'while in 1:19–27 salvation comes by receiving the word (hearing)', in 2:14–26 faith only 'contributes to justification' in that James is there 'calling for two kinds of co-operating responses — faith and works'. 'Consciously or unconsciously', Via claims, '[James] seeks to conform the word theology [of 1:18–24] to the works-faith theology [of 2:14–26]', but the two theologies 'are finally incompatible'.[104] However, Via's exegesis of 2:14–26 as teaching that faith and works are two co-working factors both necessary for justification[105] is to be questioned; if, as we have argued in section I, justification is here to be understood not in the forensic-declarative but in the probative-demonstrative sense, then Via's argument falls down. 'Works of the law would then be seen as following on from, rather than causing salvation'; moreover,

> as it is unnecessary to see 2:14ff. as suggesting works of the law as a condition for salvation, it is equally unnecessary to see a contrast between the passage and 1:18–24. Rather, we can use these verses to elucidate James's whole understanding of the law in relation to salvation. That is, throughout the epistle he is assuming that obedience to the law must follow on from salvation but does not give rise to salvation, which is God's gracious gift.[106]

To understand James, therefore, as teaching that forensic justification is a gift of God made available to faith (2:23) is fully compatible with his understanding of salvation as a gift of God to be received by faith.

B. Unity of Theme

(2) The Letter of James as a whole is best described as belonging to the genre of early Christian homily[107] rather than diatribe or paraenesis.[108] The author is obviously concerned to encourage the readers to live out their faith in practice and so, 'in spite of disconnectedness and in spite of borrowings, the epistle possesses a real unity derived from the persistence with which it puts the profession of Christians to the test'.[109] Thus, 1:3 may be said to sum up the underlying theme of the epistle in the phrase 'the testing of your faith', and patient endurance of the tests of faith is a theme that features prominently in both the first and the last chapter of the book (1:4,12; 5:7–11). In the bulk of the letter (1:19–5:18), we have virtually a series of exhortations to good actions which accord with Christian faith and warnings against wrong actions and attitudes which are incompatible with it. *Positively*, genuine obedience to God's word must issue in *action* (1:19–25, especially 22, 25); real religion manifests itself in *acts* of compassion towards the needy (1:27; *cf.* 2:15f.; 5:19f.); true faith must be accompanied by *deeds* (2:14–26), the truly wise person will by his good life show by his *deeds* in the meekness of wisdom, and true (heavenly) wisdom is characterised by, among other things, merciful and peaceable *conduct* (3:13–18, especially 13,17f.); genuine faith will constantly engage in the *action* of prayer (5:13–18; 1:5). *Negatively*, favouritism on the basis of social differences is a breach of the law of love and a practical denial of faith in Jesus Christ (2:1–13, especially 1,9); an unbridled tongue betrays a man's religion as worthless (1:19,26; 3:1–12); dissensions caused by evil passions (4:1–3), critical, condemning speech (4:11f.), presumptuous planning without reference to God (4:13–17), oppression of the poor by the rich (5:1–6) — all these are manifestations of that friendship with the world which is hatred towards God and requires repentance (4:4–10), and concrete illustrations of the evils that issue from the wisdom of the world (4:14–16).[110] James thus makes it abundantly clear that 'faith, love [2:15f.], wisdom, religion — all alike are spurious if they fail to produce the fruit of good works'.[111] It accords perfectly with this perspicuous, practical emphasis of the entire epistle to take the term 'justified' in 2:21,24,25 in the demonstrative sense of 'being shown to be just', i.e. shown to be a genuine believer.[112]

III. JAMES AND PAUL

As mentioned in the introduction of this essay, some scholars regard James as polemicising against Paul in 2:14–26. Thus, according to A. S. Geyser, Paul 'was the teacher with the uncontrolled tongue [*cf.* 3:1–12], and his was the teaching of a faith without works of Torah; which is a dead faith'.[113] Such a position has rightly been judged 'antecedently unlikely, since James was in accord with Paul's gospel (Acts 15; Gal. 2:1–10)',[114] which we have seen in section II to be the case. Moreover, 'as a reply to Paul's position James' argument totally misses the point; for Paul never contended for faith *without* works.'[115] The view under discussion is 'in fact impossible: the attitude James rejects (that faith takes the place of works in a person's life) is so clearly denied by Paul that it becomes unthinkable to suggest that he sets himself against Paul'.[116]

The majority view today regards James as correcting a misunderstanding of Paul's teaching without (most think) a knowledge of Paul's letters. Thus R. Bultmann's rhetorical question — 'Can the treatment of the theme "faith and works" in Jas. 2:14–26 be understood in any other way than that it is a debate against misunderstood ideas of Paul?' — finds its equivalent statement in, among others, Dibelius–Greeven, W. G. Kümmel, W. Marxsen, and J. A. Fitzmyer.[117] More specifically, James's polemic is said to be against a *slogan* ('faith alone') derived from the Pauline thesis of justification by faith without works.[118] In spite, however, of the wide support that it enjoys, the view under discussion has been met with the objections that 'James' treatment would not adequately clarify Paul's own teaching', and that 'it is scarcely probable that a writer intending to correct consequences drawn from St. Paul's teaching as to faith would have been content with such a far-off illustration [as the credal confession of 2:19]'.[119] More importantly, it is by no means certain that the final words of v. 24 are intended to counter Paul's doctrine of justification by faith (see our exegesis above); nor does James's use of the verb 'justify' necessitate the assumption of such an allusion, since the question of how a person is made right with God was already debated in Judaism,[120] and Jesus had already given his words on the issue (Mt. 12:37; Lk. 18:14). In short, the view under discussion is not without difficulties, and it is not required by the text itself.[121]

It is possible, then, to regard James as writing independently of Paul, i.e. without any reference to him.[122] Under this view, some hold that James is prior to Paul, on the grounds that 'the great probability is certainly from simple [the practical argument of James] to complex [the theological formulations of Paul], not the other way round', and that the evidence favours the supposition that Paul is acquainted with a perversion of James's teaching rather than that James is safeguarding a perversion of Paul.[123] This order is also favoured by the consideration that James's use of the verb 'justify' in the demonstrative sense suggests that the epistle was written 'at a very early time, before the controversy with the Judaizers had arisen and before the terminology had become fixed'; at the same time, 'some sort of acquaintance of one with the other's teaching would almost be expected, particularly since both Galatians and Acts point to the association of the two men'.[124] The upshot of our argument is this: James probably wrote before Paul, but acquaintance with Paul's teaching is not thereby excluded, nor is disagreement with it required; rather, 'James fights his battle in *his* milieu', 'against his *own* "sola fide" '.[125]

This brings us to our final question: How exactly is the apparent conflict between James and Paul to be resolved?

According to one interpretation, James is speaking of the justification of the righteous at the final judgment, which is on the basis of works, whereas Paul is concerned with the initial justification of the ungodly, which is by grace through faith.[126] We have, in our exegesis of v. 21, given our reasons for dissenting from this understanding of the verb 'justify' in James. Another view suggests that 'the difference between James and Paul is a difference of starting-point:. . . we are not saved *by* deeds [Paul's emphasis]; we are saved *for* deeds [James's]'.[127] This is correct only as far as the *verb* 'justify' is concerned (2:21,24,25); for James also makes reference to the initial, forensic justification of Abraham (v. 23, see above).

A better approach is to start with the fact that James and Paul are in different circumstances and address themselves to different, even opposite, problems:[128] against the reliance of Jews and Judaisers on obedience to the law (performance of 'works of the law' [RSV]) as the way of acceptance with God, Paul insists that justification is by grace through faith alone; against the 'lazy faith-quietism' of 'solifidians'[129] James insists that 'faith' without works is dead and that a living faith will manifest itself in works. Thus, 'they are not antagonists facing each other with drawn swords; they stand back to back, confronting different foes of the Gospel'.[130]

This difference in life-setting naturally gives rise to a different use of the same vocabulary. Here all the three key terms come in for consideration. (a) The verb 'justify' (*dikaioō*). If, as we have argued, this verb is to be taken in v. 21 in its *demonstrative* rather than declarative sense, then 'in James the accent would fall upon the *probative* character of good works, whereas in the Pauline polemic the accent falls without question upon the judicially constitutive and declarative'.[131] Whereas Paul is concerned with justification (Rom. 4:3,9), James (2:21) 'is concerned with the fruits of justification, the evidence that justification has taken place'.[132]

(b) The noun 'faith' (*pistis*). In the Pauline formula 'justified by faith' (Rom. 3:28) or 'by faith in Jesus Christ' (Gal. 2:16), the word 'faith' denotes an act of self-committal to Christ. James, too, knows such faith 'in' Christ (2:1) or in God as a means of access to God's blessings (1:6; 5:15) and as an object of trial (1:3). But in 2:14–26, James has in view two kinds of faith, the genuine (18b,e,22a,b; *cf.* 23b) and the spurious (14,17,18d,20,24,26; *cf.*19), and it is the latter only which he deprecates as dead and useless. His point seems to be that 'a faith that is alive gives evidence of being alive. If that evidence is absent, there is no reason for considering it alive'.[133] To the same effect Paul says that what matters is not circumcision or the want of it, but 'faith expressing itself through love' (Gal. 5:6).

(c) The term 'works' (RSV, Gk. *erga*). P. H. Davids maintains that Paul's 'works of the law' (*erga nomou*) 'are never moral prescriptions, but rather ceremonial rites added to the work of Christ. In James, *erga* [never *erga nomou*] are always moral deeds, especially acts of charity'; but D. J. Moo has rightly argued that 'both Paul and James are operating with an understanding of "works" that is basically similar: anything done that is in obedience to God and in the service of God'.[134] Their difference lies rather in the different contexts in which they speak of 'works': Paul denies any efficacy to pre-conversion works in the matter of justification, James affirms the absolute necessity of post-conversion works as evidence of justifying faith.[135]

The foregoing discussion warrants the conclusion that the apparent contradiction between James and Paul is just that — apparent, not real. 'While we must recognise that James has expressed his point of view in very un-Pauline language, yet the fact remains that he does not replace Paul's scheme of justification by another based on law-works.'[136] Indeed, not only has it been rightly said that James presents the active and Paul the passive side of the same thing,[137] but it should not escape notice that the two sides of the same coin are present in James 2:14–26 itself — *righteousness by faith* (23b) and *'justification' by works* (21,24,25) — with the result that he is at one with Paul in affirming forensic justification by faith and at one with Paul and the rest of the New Testament in insisting that 'the only faith worth considering is one which includes and produces the actual fruit of serious action'.[138]

IV. CONCLUSION

> Luther would have been right in saying that 'faith justifies' and 'faith does not justify' contradict each other flatly, *if* the substantive 'faith' and the verb 'justify' had the same meaning in the one proposition as in the other. But in fact James in this passage [2:14–26] uses neither term in the regular Pauline sense.[139]

In a similar vein Calvin had spoken of some who 'fall into a double paralogism, the one in the term *faith*, the other in the term *justifying*'.[140] By adopting this approach we have argued that there is absolutely no contradiction between James and Paul. Their relationship is in fact typical of the unity and diversity in the New Testament: unity without uniformity, diversity without opposition.[141]

By an act of divine providence, James was included in the canon with Paul, and both aspects of the truth — *forensic justification* (= righteousness) *by faith, probative 'justification' by works* — have been preserved for the guidance of the church in all ages. While James himself probably 'did not consciously write in order to refute Paul', his book nevertheless 'functions within the New Testament . . . as a means of preventing the misinterpretation and misapplication of Paul's teaching'.[142] Not only does James have a right to stand alongside Paul,[143] but, as R. V. G. Tasker observes, '[his] message sounds forth with special relevance' at certain times:

> Whenever faith does not issue in love, and dogma, however orthodox, is unrelated to life; whenever Christians are tempted to settle down to a self-centred religion and become oblivious of the social and material needs of others; or whenever they deny by their manner of living the creed they profess, and seem more anxious to be friends of the world than friends of God, then the Epistle of James has something to say to them which they disregard at their peril.[144]

9

Justification and Personal Christian Living

RUSSELL SHEDD

I. INTRODUCTION

The living heart of the gospel is the biblical doctrine of justification by grace through faith alone. Among God's gifts to men, none can compare with the good news that God freely justifies sinners who accept his pardon. This truth should provide, not only the secure foundation of salvation, but the proper incentive to sanctification. It has not always done so. Calvin said that 'justification is the main hinge on which religion turns'.[1] Luther incisively affirmed, 'The promises of God give what the commandments of God demand, and fulfil what the law prescribes so that all things may be God's alone.'[2] Nevertheless, however confidently these truths have been asserted, justification apart from works can disguise a fatal misconception. Throughout the church's history the demand for sanctification has often been lost owing to misunderstanding of justification.[3] The aim of this paper is to attempt to clarify the necessary implications of justification for the Christian's personal life.

II. PRELIMINARY CONSIDERATIONS

Jesus and the New Testament writers teach that God acquits sinners, as if to confirm their total innocence, yet denied the confidence of some contemporary Jewish leaders in merit.[4] All that sinners can hope to earn as a salary is death (Rom. 6:23). The righteous, on the other hand, will receive 'praise' (Rom. 2:29), 'honour' (Rom. 2:7) and the 'prize' (Phil. 3:14) from God in judgment. This sort of 'reward' is a gift (*praemium*), not a price or earned value (*pretium*), and it is proper to justification. No one can deserve it, nor does God owe it (Rom. 4:4).[5] But if human beings can add nothing to God's grace, why must the redeemed one day face judgment (2 Cor. 5:10)? If God makes over to believers all Christ's virtues and values, must the righteousness God imputes still be confirmed by holy living? Do believing in and submitting to the lordship of Jesus Christ negate the necessity of self-effort and discipline? Spurgeon attributed to faith the 'root of obedience', 'just as a captain trusts a pilot to steer his vessel into port . . . or a patient believes a physician, he carefully follows his prescription and directions.'[6] If all Christians did in fact display a serious desire to imitate and obey the Lord, there would be no need to raise the question. However, even an indulgent overview of the Christian world shows that for the majority heart submission to the lordship of Christ is the last thing to embrace.[7]

Is it possible to imagine the tax collector, a member of a notorious class of oppressors, going home justified but untransformed, after his prayer for mercy (Lk. 18:14)? Did his righteousness thereafter surpass that of the Pharisee (Mt. 5:20)? Zacchaeus' public declaration of his intention to reform drew a positive response from Jesus (Lk. 19:9), but what would Jesus have said if he had continued practising extortion and other wicked acts? Jesus preached, 'By their fruit you will recognise them' (Mt. 7:16).[8] How profoundly repentant was the crucified terrorist whom Jesus promised would accompany him to paradise (Lk. 23:40–43)?

That God desires that a practical holiness characterise his people, no one will doubt (Lev. 11:44f.; 1 Pet. 1:16). J. I. Packer writes, 'Holiness is commanded; God wills it, Christ requires it. Scripture prescribes it. A hurricane of texts and a barrage of theological arguments are ready to prove the point.'[9] But the question remains: If the justified must practise righteousness, if they must make a personal, conscious effort to obey and please God, how is the gift of grace free?

'The absence of justification as a theological category separate from sanctification is a dominant factor in shaping pre-Reformation spirituality.'[10] The Reformation theologians correctly faulted traditional Roman Catholic dogma for affirming that in justification God infused righteousness rather than declaring sinners to be righteous. But the promises of the new covenant go beyond God's merciful proclamation of absolution (*cf.* Heb. 8:12; Jer. 31:31–34). God also promised to 'put [his] laws in their minds and write them on their hearts' (Heb. 8:10). In keeping with these blessings, Jesus not only forgave the woman taken in adultery; he warned her to 'sin no more' (Jn. 8:11). More than a serious recommendation, the Scriptures present a demand for unqualified obedience to absolute demands that stem from an utterly whole-hearted allegiance to God.[11]

The centrality of justification affects the church's conception of her mission. Paul Tillich told an attentive audience in Edinburgh that the task incumbent upon Christians was to announce God's forgiving acceptance of sinners. For him, the good news the world needs to hear is, 'There is no condemnation.' God's love annuls the threat of his wrath.[12] Since Jesus Christ propitiated the sins of the whole world (1 Jn. 2:2), judgment has been eliminated and all things have been reconciled through him (Col. 1:20). By such truncated doctrine men and women are seduced into the quicksands of universalism.[13]

An offer of 'cheap grace', however, is not confined to universalists who deny God's ultimate condemnation of unrepentant sinners. An influential branch of evangelical Christianity teaches that submission to Christ as Lord is optional. To be saved one need do no more than trust him as Saviour. In their view, only those who already believe in the Saviour may acknowledge him as Lord.[14] Salvation is not contingent on obedience, for that would introduce 'works' as ground for regeneration. Claiming Paul's well-known reference to 'carnal' Christians for support (1 Cor. 2:15–3:4), they hold that he endorses the view that repentance which issues in practical life change is unnecessary.[15]

Another view, recently arisen in Brazil, understands regeneration so to empower Christians that they conquer sin and triumphantly celebrate salvation 'unto the uttermost' from the power of Satan and evil. Impeccability and the annihilation of the 'flesh' imply that sanctification has, like justification, become a free gift, received at the moment of exercising saving faith.

An intermediate position, common amongst some who embrace Arminian theology, fails to see justification as a once-for-all gift from God. If the Christian fails to live up to a minimal standard of righteousness, he incurs the penalty of salvation's loss. Repentance and reconciliation may restore the fallen to sonship again. Thus a Christian is directed to a subjective assurance which results in fear of damnation on the part of the morally sensitive and complacency on the part of the self-confident.

Such divergence of opinion amongst evangelicals makes it appropriate to explore the question of what God demands of his children. Any theology which separates the bent knee from the open hand in saving faith threatens the truth of the gospel. Faith entails commitment to Christ as a whole person, not to a particular role.[16]

If in the affluent Western church the main threat to biblical Christianity is the optional lordship of Christ — or, in C. Walsh's words, 'to vaccinate a man with a mild case of Christianity so as to protect him from the real disease'[17] — in the younger churches legalism is rampant. Some parts of the world swallow a gospel which has been described as 'truth without consequences', while in others justification is taken to imply complete victory over the tendency to evil within. By exploring anew the biblical relationship between justification and practical living, it is our hope that a more balanced view will emerge to illuminate our way. Much weight should be given to the teaching of Jesus in the Gospels. Evidence from Acts and above all from the Pauline Epistles will be added to provide the foundations for this study.

III.   THE UNION BETWEEN JUSTIFICATION AND PERSONAL LIVING IN THE TEACHING OF JESUS

While Jesus has left us no extended teaching on justification by faith, the kernel is there, even if it is constantly interwoven with other themes. Deeper than the necessary intellectual assent to truths regarding his person, Christ called men and women to follow him and trust him as their Lord. Such trust appropriates 'the life-power of the heavenly Christ'.[18] Many of the parables attest the sheer gratuity of the gift (e.g. the labourers in the vineyard, Mt. 20:1–16; and the parable of the prodigal son, Lk. 15:11–32). Jesus invited the weary to come to him for relief from the burden of sin and the struggle to fulfil the law's demands (Mt. 11:28–30). To accept his invitation meant reaching 'soul-rest' (justification?), along with the imposition of his yoke in discipleship, that is, following Christ in obedience. Bearing Christ's yoke involves learning from and obeying him. Similarly, the great commission calls for future generations of believers to observe all that Jesus taught his disciples (Mt. 28:20). No doubt included in the glad receiving of Christ as Lord was the reminder of Jesus' own insistence on repentance (Mt. 4:17; 9:13; 11:20; Lk. 13:3,5; 24:47 and elsewhere). Omission of repentance from the gospel may give a false signal, for when there is no radical change of heart, there can be no certainty that one has chosen the narrow way rather than the wide road to destruction (Mt. 7:13,14,21–23; Lk. 13:3,4).

If, as some evangelicals hold, faith is synonymous with repentance, how is intellectual assent to be distinguished from temporary following (*cf.* Jn. 6:66)? C. Ryrie identifies repentance with a 'change of mind in relation to Jesus of Nazareth as the Messiah. . . . Thus repentance as it was preached by the apostles . . . was in fact an act of faith in Jesus Christ who brought salvation to him that repents'.[19] But Jesus taught, 'A good tree cannot bear bad fruit' (Mt. 7:18). The source of the fruit must be supernatural, produced by birth from above, i.e. by the Spirit (Jn. 3:3,5,31), but made visible by acts of repentance and love of righteousness.

As for the wealthy ruler who expected Jesus would suggest some minor adjustments in his 'good' life, no way to eternal life was promised except by repentance. His avarice and self-centred independence held him hostage to his unregenerate life (Mk. 10:17–22). Jesus challenged him to keep the commandments (Mt. 19:17), yet compared the difficulty of a rich man gladly parting with his wealth to a camel traversing the eye of a needle.

To the expert in the Old Testament and its interpretation who came querying what he must do to inherit eternal life, Jesus asked, 'What is written in the law?' To his right answer that love for God and man is basic, Jesus replied, 'Do this and live' (Lk. 10:25–28). Since his self-confidence was not crushed by that seemingly simple requirement, Jesus recast it in the practical illustration of the 'Good Samaritan' followed by the imperative, 'Go and do likewise' (Lk. 10:30–37).

In the Sermon on the Mount, Jesus assesses all human righteousness or self-denial as unacceptable to God. Poverty of spirit that he rewards (Mt 5:3) is an internal condition necessary to any compelling sense of need for God's justifying grace. As the Pharisees' 'zeal for measuring up to standards did not produce the kind of life our Lord commanded' (Mt. 23:13–36),[20] so a true view of one's weakness and misery in sin will not create pride in one's performance of God's will. William Law had the heart of the matter: 'Since we neither are nor can be anything of ourselves, to be proud of anything that we are or of anything that we do . . . has the guilt both of stealing and lying. It has the guilt of stealing as it gives to ourselves those things (i.e. glory) which only belong to God. It has the guilt of lying as it is the denying of the truth of our state and pretending to be something we are not.'[21] Christ must be the mediator between God's demands and man's innate inability; therefore he is the 'goal' or 'end' of the law (Rom. 10:4).[22]

Despite the missing Pauline language of justification, the fundamental requirement of a faith commitment and consequent obedience is clearly taught. Both John the Baptist and Jesus proclaimed the atoning significance of Jesus' death (Jn. 1:29; Mk. 10:45). Jesus' baptism was appropriate or fitting to fulfil all righteousness (*dikaiosynē*, Mt. 3:15).[23] Jesus' baptism in water is cast in the role of a pre-enactment of his passion on the cross. His sinless life and expiatory death, as interpreted by Jesus, were integral parts of his archetypal baptism (Mk. 10:38; *cf.* Lk. 12:50).

For the Christian, baptism, like the cross, provides a life framework by initiating the believer in a realistic manner into the body of Christ (Gal. 3:26–28; 1 Cor. 12:13), as well as providing a model for his behaviour. Jesus' ultimate 'baptism' makes righteousness available to sinners, on the objective basis of Jesus' identification with those who have realistically 'washed' their sins away and trusted in him who took their place (*cf.* 2 Cor. 5:21). Through Jesus' baptism in blood (Lk. 12:50; Mk. 10:38) the sins he forgives are expiated (*cf.* Mk. 2:5). The sinful woman who washed Jesus' feet with tears and perfume was lovingly reassured, 'Your sins are forgiven' (Lk. 7:48; *cf.* v. 47; they were 'many'). Acquittal is grounded in Jesus' ransoming death (Mk. 10:45).

In a dramatic sign that inaugurated the first Christian passover, Jesus referred to his blood as the efficacious means of forming the New Israel by the establishing of the new covenant, 'for the remission of sins' (Mt. 26:28). All pardoned sinners are thus justified and included in the company of the redeemed. They are Jesus' 'little flock' to whom the Father is pleased to give the kingdom (Lk. 12:32). Jesus himself shepherds them, calling them by name and leading them out (Jn. 10:3). That means that they obey him.[24] They recognise his voice and follow him, but no one else (vv. 4,5).[25] A mutual knowing unites shepherd and sheep (vv. 14,17), comparable to the knowing which unites the Father and the Son (v. 15).

Jesus' mission to the world was one of seeking and saving the lost (*cf.* Lk. 9:24f; 13:3,5; chap. 15 [8 times]; 17:33; 19:10). The lost are called to believe, and follow Jesus. They are incorporated into his church (Mt. 16:18), grow out of the seed that died and germinated (Jn. 12:24) and become branches in him, the true vine (Jn. 15:1ff.). Disciples of Jesus demonstrate the reality of their faith by revealing character-traits produced by their 'in-Christ' relationship. Indeed, 'it would be a fatal mistake to think of holiness as a possession which we have distinct from our faith'.[26] Union with Christ and inclusion into the redeemed people, elements that are basic to justification, are a fundamental part of Jesus' teaching.

The practical implications of a disciple's vital relationship with Christ will weigh heavily in the judgment, and will certainly not be sidelined by a merely mental claim to saving faith in him (Mt. 25:31–40; 7:21,23). Because Jesus lives in and through his followers, they will show an unpretentious love for the needy. Practical expressions of love offered to hungry, thirsty, homeless, naked and sick fellow-disciples, signals that change of character (after all, they are 'sheep' and not 'goats') pursuant to justification. The good works they have done eloquently reveal their source and cause. They were done for Christ and it was he who prompted them.

John's emphasis on believing is somewhat parallel to the Synoptics' focus on following, cross-bearing and self-denial (Mt. 10:38; 16:24; Mk. 8:34; 10:21; Lk. 9:23; 14:27).[27] Faith and loyalty to Jesus' person is the goal of self-mortification. Without faith, denying oneself is of a piece with tithing, fasting and alms-giving that are pronounced hypocritical by the Lord (Lk. 18:12; Mt. 6:2). One must cut oneself free from all ties, even to one's own life,[28] to follow Jesus. In Stott's words, 'Every Christian is both a Simon of Cyrene and a Barabbas', escaping from the judgment Jesus bore for him, yet obligated to carry his own cross to follow him.[29]'

The trusting love which Jesus' disciples possessed during his earthly life provides a partial paradigm for future generations. Though physically absent after his ascension, Jesus remains present with all who believe and seek to obey him (Mt. 28:20; Jn. 15:8). Jesus replaced the model of man's obligation to observe the law, by the obligation to obey the will of God expressed in his own person. Paul is probably referring to this new obligation when he speaks of the 'law of the Spirit of life in Christ' (Rom.8:2). Peter would later urge his readers to accept Christ's suffering as a model (*hypogrammos*, 'copy', 'outline'; 1 Pet. 2:21). It is fully in accord with the historical fact that Christ died for our sins, that believers should die to sin and live for righteousness (1 Pet. 2:24). Imitation and obedience are implied in Jesus' sacrificial death for his own.

Jesus cannot be accused of ambivalence in regard to the implications of following him. Since he forgives, his disciples must do the same (Mt. 6:12–14). The parable of the unmerciful servant underscores that principle (Mt. 18:21–35). The king who forgives a debt so high that it surpassed realism, represents the Lord who in God's name has freely declared his followers' sins forgiven. Nevertheless, there is a condition, the very heart of the story. When the pardoned debtor refuses to show forgiving mercy to his fellow servant, the original obligation is reinstated, since he showed no change of heart. Jesus wished to convey with complete clarity that justification brings with it an inseparable requirement. The forgiven must forgive, otherwise saving faith is an illusion.

In John's account of the foot-washing (Jn. 13:1–17), an essential element in securing fellowship with Jesus is stressed. To Peter's objection, Jesus replies with the warning that if he fails to wash his feet, participation with and in his Lord is impossible (v. 8). But only washing of feet is necessary to restore the integral relationship of those who have been bathed (v. 10). It seems likely that Jesus referred to baptism and the Lord's Supper in calling attention to a complete and subsequent washings respectively.[30] Sin, represented by dirty feet, breaks spiritual communion. So Peter's request for Jesus to wash his feet amounted to a confession. When the community obeys the Lord's command to 'wash one another's feet', the three-way unity between the Head and Body as well as member with members is restored.

Jesus' teaching on the true vine in the upper room confirms what the 'footwashing' implies. Any so-called disciple ('branch') that bears no fruit will be removed by the Father (Jn. 15:2). The cleansing power of the word of Jesus (13:8) certifies that all except Judas are indeed clean (v. 3; 13:10f.). It is by maintaining fellowship, realised by confession and cleansing from sin, that branches maintain vital union with the vine, resulting in fruit production. Failure to abide in fellowship through trusting repentance causes withering, drying and final burning (v. 6). Loving obedience, by contrast, enables the disciples to bear much fruit by obeying Jesus' commands (vv. 8,10). The entire passage underscores what can be observed throughout the gospels: a life-transforming relationship with Jesus cannot fail to authenticate itself by visible evidence.

Jesus' new command that his disciples love one another should be considered 'a far more reliable measure of spirituality than our gifts or works'.[31] A deep concern for fellow-believers is neither optional nor a mere shibboleth. The Christian who lays claim to God's saving pardon, but does not love his brother as Jesus loved him, shows himself to be outside the orbit of the divine love (Jn. 13:34; 1 Jn. 3:10,14,18,23; 4:7,8,11,12,20; 5:1). Such love is quite different from the love depicted in secular Greek literature.

C. H. Dodd thought of it 'as an energetic and beneficent good-will, stopping at nothing to secure the good of its objects'.[32]

IV.   THE IMPLICATIONS OF JUSTIFICATION IN ACTS

Luke relates that Jesus only *began* his mission during his years on earth (Acts 1:1). Although now exalted to the right hand of God, he continues to act in his followers as they carry out their ministry in his name (3:12; 4:9f.). Jesus' name and power work effectively through the agency of the apostles. They are soon found proclaiming Christ's unique power to save sinners (4:12).[33] Healing bodies and justifying sinners demonstrate his power over the two ages. The risen Christ is lord over the fallen world and the world to come (2:36). If healings are no more than psychosomatic and short-lived, they can be compared to a 'salvation' that does not transform a sinner. It is like pronouncing a leper clean, who nevertheless dies of that dreaded disease. Spurgeon warns against a gospel that forgives the rebellion, but 'allows the rebel to remain an enemy to his King.'[34]

Evidence of the sanctifying power of the Spirit appeared in the earliest period of the church's life. Eager attention to the apostles' teaching, fellowship (*koinōnia*), love feasts, prayer, fear of the Lord, loving concern and sharing of possessions showed that Christ was fulfilling his promise to join with those who gather in his name (Acts 2:42–46; 4:32–37; Mt. 18:20). Joyful praise to God, sincerity of heart and enthusiastic sharing of the good news (2:46f.; 8:4) was a natural result of repentance and public commitment to Jesus' lordship in baptism (Acts 2:38–41).

Nor does Luke miss the characteristic element of joy that wells up in the hearts of those who know they have been forgiven (8:39). 'To be a sinner is to be lost; to be in Christ is to be saved, and that is a wonderful, joyful experience.'[35] The pervasive note of joy throughout the New Testament should remind us that grace (*charis*) and forgiveness (*charizomai*) and gift (*charisma*) are all branches that sprout from the common root *char* — from which also *chara* ('joy') derives.

Despite the pristine quality of the church's origins, it did not escape Satan's attack on the holiness of the fellowship. God, however, judged the hypocrisy of Ananias and Sapphira with summary deaths which struck great fear into the hearts of all (5:1–11). By tragic experience, the church learned that it was not a free-floating aggregation of adherents to the sect of the Nazarenes. Rather, it was a body subordinated to its divine head. Those early Christians concluded that he who added 'daily those who were being saved' (2:47) had the right to remove those who denied the faith in their deeds. The lesson is clear: free forgiveness offered through justification does not include a 'carte blanche' to sin with impunity. Thus God opposed the laxity some pursued out of their distorted vision of free grace, by instilling a holy awe that stimulates the pursuit of holiness (5:11; 2 Cor. 7:1).

Simon Magus, the powerful sorcerer of Samaria, chose to believe and accept baptism (8:13). Shortly, it became clear that his confession of faith was like the seedling that sprouts in rocky soil (*cf*. Lk. 8:6). Peter did not hesitate to condemn his life and his money to perdition. He urged Simon to repent in view of his heart condition, described as full of bitterness and slavery to sin (8:20–23). This episode shows that a confession of faith and baptism are not sufficient, in and of themselves, to guarantee the presence of justifying grace. Justification is a free gift apart from works, but God's gracious imputation of his righteousness and pardon of transgressions cannot be real if there is no accompanying evidence of holiness.

V. THE RELATIONSHIP BETWEEN JUSTIFICATION AND SANCTIFICATION ACCORDING TO PAUL

Paul's gospel affirms that God is both just and the justifier of sinners because of the substitutionary death and resurrection of Jesus Christ (Rom. 3:24–26; 4:25). Good works are unnecessary to justification because of God's righteousness imputed to all who by faith accept his gift (Rom. 4:1–17; 5:15–19). For Paul, justification meant a new relationship with God (Phil. 3:9), a new freedom from guilt and condemnation accompanied by a transformed obligation to obey God and a new empowering by the Spirit to attain the hope of the gospel. Objective historical events that transpired in Jerusalem in the first century have eternally validated the grounds of man's restoration.[36] The justified sinner need not fear condemnation (Rom. 8:1). He is also renewed internally according to the demand of God's holy law. Sin is not restricted to subjective guilt; it includes objective pollution.[37] When a sinner receives God's pardon, he stands before a holy Father who pledges himself to cleanse his stains. Thus sanctification draws upon God's way of changing the believer's consciousness of guilt, as well as making him good and enabling him to be good.[38] Paul would be in full agreement with the writer of Hebrews who states that the pursuit of holiness is mandatory (12:14). The absence of good works, therefore, is positive proof that any claimed justification is imaginary.

God is always the One who initiates. 'Human action, including even repentance and confession of sins, is not a work of man to bring about and initiate reconciliation, to which God reacts.'[39] Nevertheless, man must react in faith. He must either respond to God's loving action or stand in perpetual rebellion. But any salvation that is not worked out with fear and trembling (Phil. 2:12) is but a spurious deception.

Paul presents both justification and sanctification as positional: Christ is both our 'righteousness' (*dikaiosynē*) and our 'holiness' (*hagiasmos*, 1 Cor. 1:30). Seriously compromised Corinthians have been 'sanctified' (*hēgiasthēte*) as well as justified (*edikaiōthēte*, 1 Cor. 6:11). On these grounds, Christians are called 'saints' (Rom. 1:7; 1 Cor. 1:2; Eph. 1:1; etc.). They share in the holiness of Christ through the abiding presence of the Holy Spirit. They are accepted in the Beloved (Eph. 1:6), since Christ has perfectly kept the law, but not for himself alone, but for all who are in him (Rom. 8:4; 10:4).[40]

But if that faith relationship with Christ is missing, the law not only exposes sin, it incites it (Rom. 7:7,8), by inducing human pride and self-confidence, both nationally and individually. 'Rebellious instincts, latent or moribund in the soul are aroused by the "No" of the commandment.'[41] No less tragic, in Paul's view, is the Jewish confidence in a supposed national righteousness,[42] for it omits Christ, the centre, and stimulates glorying in human achievement.

Paul clarifies his doctrine by confessing his pre-Christian confidence. He wholly fulfilled his obligation to God, to his conscience and to his people in an extraordinary zeal for 'law-works'. Following his converting encounter with Christ on the Damascus Road, he renounced his former way so as exclusively to know and obey Christ (Phil. 3:7–10). The superb discipline produced by false striving and pride as a superior Pharisee was unmasked for what it was, the refined sin of self-righteousness, so odious to God, and consequently abandoned. The transformation was so radical that Paul the persecutor became Paul the evangelist, the author of 1 Corinthians 13. The old things had passed away, making way for the reality of the 'new creation' (2 Cor. 5:17). So he distinguishes carefully between the old 'letter' and the spirit of the law (2 Cor. 3:6). The indwelling Christ is indeed the 'hope of glory' (Col. 1:27). Over and above imputing his righteousness to sinners, God has poured out his Spirit on all who truly believe in Christ (Rom. 8:9) so that they might become Christ-like (Rom. 8:29).

Paul compares this transition from national pride and legalism to Christ, to a woman's release from her marriage vows on the death of her husband (Rom. 7:1–6). Having been freed from his enslavement to law, the Christian can and must transfer his devotion to Christ (Rom. 7:4).[43] Some passages in the epistles suggest that Paul thinks in terms of a new marriage to Christ, which inevitably will have ethical and spiritual consequences (2 Cor. 11:2; Eph. 5:25–29).[44] The new incentive to please God is not to be found in the fear of condemnation (Rom. 8:1), nor in the self-realisation of autonomous accomplishment (Phil. 3:3–6), but in the compelling love of Christ (2 Cor. 5:14). The divine love instilled in the hearts of believers by the Holy Spirit explains any propensity to do good on the part of God's children (Rom. 5:5). Still, 'no theologian or psychologist who has ever lived can find where man's choice stops and God's begins in this relationship.'[45]

Goppelt argues that the justification, sanctification and washing that had happened at the Corinthians' initial conversion 'might always happen afresh in faith'.[46] This would mean an approximation to the understanding of Augustine and his followers, that justification and sanctification are not really separate experiences but unified action of the Spirit as long as genuine faith is present.[47] It is doubtful if Paul ever uses 'to justify' for anything other than the *initial* step into the Christian faith. Even so, the concern of Goppelt, Augustine and others is to ensure the tightest connection between the initial step of faith and a life of growing holiness. And certainly if a person does not see God in a new way, nor perceive the glory and magnificence he had not seen before (2 Cor. 4:6)[48], the incentive to holy living will be absent.

Paul's understanding of the covenants also needed reappraisal. The threatening, powerless old covenant demanded an obedience no mere flesh could meet (Rom. 8:3). By contrast, the new covenant of the life-giving Spirit provides life (Gal. 5:25b), power and guidance (Rom. 8:13f.). Clearly, Paul saw the blessings of the new covenant as including both practical and imputed righteousness (2 Cor. 3:8f.).[49] 'So justification and sanctification are firmly linked together as the most essential blessings of the new order.'[50]

The perfect covering for transgressions is the highest blessing of justification. The essential faith of the heart then finds its proper expression in the confession of Jesus as Lord (Rom. 10:9–11). This trust calls for its sealing in baptism, signifying separation from the world and union with Christ in his vicarious death and resurrection. So the cleansed sinner is to give visible expression to his commitment to live for God rather than for himself (Rom. 6:3–7; Col. 2:12). Baptism, like faith, is an obedient response[51] to God's self-giving to sinners, and signals incorporation into Christ through the Holy Spirit (1 Cor. 12:13).[52] 'Justification, baptism into Christ and salvation history are all, it appears, inescapably correlated'.[53] Although Paul does not work out the specific connection between baptism and justification, 'nevertheless, baptism (with faith) is seen as the basis of a mystical or eschatological "being-in-Christ" (Rom. 6:3f.)'.[54]

Renunciation of the world's lusts is necessary (Tit. 2:13f.), that is, the removal of the unclean garments of the flesh, and putting on the new self, created to be like God in true righteousness and holiness (Eph. 4:23). Despite the supernatural reality of the event that unites the believer to his perfect Lord, washes away his transgressions and clothes him in righteousness, it does not annihilate his personal sinfulness. The redeemed believer cannot claim sinlessness, for he continues to share the common fallen nature of humanity even while he lives in Christ. Being in the Spirit, rather than in the flesh (that continuum of rebellion and cradle of sin)[55] can scarcely mean that he no longer stumbles (Rom. 8:12). The independent 'flesh' has no potential for pleasing God. Nevertheless Christians, renewed in mind and spirit, are able to receive God's grace (*cf.* 2 Cor. 8:1) and delight in God's law (Rom. 7:22). Indeed, they are obliged to 'work out [their] salvation with fear and trembling' (Phil. 2:12).

D. Wenham summarises the significance of justification and the believer's consequent inclusion in Christ:

> (1) To be in Christ means in some real sense release from slavery to sin and evil powers (e.g. Gal. 4; Rom. 6). (2) To be in Christ means having the Holy Spirit and his immeasurably great power at work in one's life (e.g. Rom. 8; Eph. 1). (3) The Christian is called to holiness and perfection (e.g. 2 Cor. 6:14–7:1; Phil. 3:12–14). (4) The Christian life should be a life of growth and is not a life of suddenly and finally achieved perfection (e.g. Phil. 3:12–14; Col. 1:10; Eph. 4:15,16). (5) Satan and the forces of evil continue active in their attacks on the believer after his conversion (e.g. 1 Thes. 3:5; 2 Cor. 12:7; Rom. 16:20; Eph. 6:11,12). (6) Our old sinful and weak nature does not disappear at conversion; it continues to be a threat to the believer (e.g. Gal. 5:16–26). (7) It is possible for the Christian to sin and indeed (to judge from the problems dealt with by Paul in his letters) it is common for Christians to sin. (8) Because of the preceding points the Christian life is a fight — against the flesh and the devil in the power of the Spirit. Vigilance and effort are called for (e.g. 1 Thes. 5:8–11; Rom. 13:12–14; Eph. 6:11–18).[56]

But the Holy Spirit does not live within as a spy; rather he acts as a collaborator who reminds us of our credit balance in Christ and encourages us to live in his triumph already accomplished for us.[57] Nevertheless, practice is the decisive criterion of eternal life and truth. The obstinate desire to pose a contradiction between Paul's theology of faith and James' theology of works is radically mistaken.[58] It is not by chance that Paul's letters culminate in lengthy admonitions. In rejecting works he renounces pride and self-justification. Not for salvation but issuing from the union of the believer with his Lord through the Spirit, holy works are the goal of the new creation (Eph. 2:8–10).[59]

VI. JUSTIFICATION MEANS LIFE IN CHRIST THROUGH FAITH

Justification must be received by faith. So too, by faith alone does the Christian live (Col. 2:6,7; Gal. 3:2–9). Union with Christ by faith initiates those who believe into the realm of the Spirit where true freedom reigns (2 Cor. 3:17). It is the Spirit who illuminates the law in the light of Christ, thereby transforming the perversion of legalism into genuine freedom.[60] In becoming members of Christ's body, believers are granted the possibility of obeying their Master's orders. Sin's compulsion, if not resisted and overcome, enslaves (Rom. 6:16). Sin, like a dynamic, demonic force, will bring believers back into its thrall if they do not, by faith, wage personal, continuous warfare against it (Gal. 5:16–26; Rom. 7:14–25). Paul warns the Galatians and the Corinthians that the battle can be lost (Gal. 4:11,19; 1 Cor. 10:1–13; 1 Cor. 6:14–7;1; 13:5).

Paul assures his Roman readers that there is no condemnation now for those who are in Christ Jesus, yet he is not loath to warn them that those who live according to the sinful nature (*sarx*) by following a fleshly mind-set (*phronēma*) will perish (Rom. 8:1–8). It is possible to detect an underlying appeal running through Romans 6–8, that calls the Roman Christians to seek the Spirit's power, renounce dependence on the flesh (human independent capacities), prone to egotism, self-indulgence and pride. The flesh can produce only 'works' that demonstrate their close alliance with Satan's hostility to God and his righteousness (Rom. 8:7; Gal. 2:19–21). The Spirit, on the other hand, produces fruit in keeping with God's character: love, joy, peace, patience, kindness, goodness, faithfulness, gentleness and self-control (Gal. 5:22–23). By battling against our Adamic nature and by faith laying hold of the Spirit, throwing open the door to his leading and power, we may progress toward the goal of righteousness in practical living (Gal. 3:3–5; Rom. 8:14).

When, motivated by pride, anyone attempts to establish his own righteousness rather than depend wholly on God's perfection offered by grace (Rom. 10:3,4), he or she succumbs to the flesh's insidious assault on the true faith that saves. Paul's affirmation, 'In my flesh dwells no good thing' (Rm. 7:18), expresses the redeemed sinner's cry of faith. Paul's thorn, a 'messenger of Satan', was eminently useful in convincing him of his need for sufficient divine grace and power to surmount his weakness (2 Cor. 12:9). Therefore, Paul delights in weakness because it annihilates the natural self-confidence of the flesh, even while he lays hold of Christ's power in the full assurance of hope (v. 10). Similarly, Paul claims that he has been 'initiated into the secret' (*memuēmai*) of eschatological power which produces continuous contentment, even as he depends on the power supplied by Christ to meet every challenge (Phil. 4:12f.).

Furthermore, Paul indicates that his past crucifixion with Christ persists as his present experience (Gal. 2:19f.) The ego ('I') has been killed in some spiritual or forensic sense, allowing Christ to live in its place. Yet Paul continues to live, a life of faith, yielding to the gracious will of him who died and rose again for him. This crucified life, no longer subject to the covenant of law, has a vitality that is maintained by faith in the living Christ. For this reason, it demonstrates in practice the blessedness of him 'who does not condemn himself by what he approves' (Rom. 14:22), as long as the rule of love for the brothers is not broken. To act independently, without faith — that is, to disregard the relationship that is completely dependent on Christ — means to act sinfully (v. 23). In a realistic way, justification by faith has altered far more than a believer's condition of guilt before God. It has raised him from death with Christ to a continuous faith-commitment to the Lord who orients his decisions by the Holy Spirit. By virtue of this relationship, Paul has escaped from the restraints of the law to come under Christ's lawful demand (*ennomos Christou*, 1 Cor. 9:21).

The fact that God has declared sinners righteous implies the cancellation of the obligation to produce law-works, for Paul must become 'like a Jew', under the law, to win those who are subject to the law, even as he must become as a Gentile to win those outside the law's jurisdiction.[61] Nevertheless, he does not launch out onto uncharted ethical seas without a compass. Recognising that he is Christ's slave, he has committed himself to observe Christ's will or law. Obedience to that law has become his goal and delight (Gal. 6:2; *cf.* Phil. 3:6–10). It is likely that he has Jesus' teachings in mind, received from the apostles and accompanied by the directives of the Spirit. The life of Jesus has also become his example, a model to follow (1 Cor. 11:1).

In addition to the 'law of Christ', Paul's opposition to moral wickedness can be attributed to his high view of God's perfection. God is righteous, therefore he hates and opposes all evil (Rom. 1:18ff.). All who call God their Father must therefore shun evil. God has imprinted his law on the human heart (Rom. 2:14–16). The ability to distinguish between right and wrong can best be explained by God's image mirrored in the human conscience, however distorted and indistinct it may have become through sin and deception (*cf.* Jer. 17:9). This universal law can be distilled into a single obligation, 'Love your neighbour as yourself' (Gal. 5:14).

Since the divine image has been perfectly reproduced in Christ, his life in and through the church means that it is being restored corporately in the fellowship of the church by the Spirit's power (Col. 3:10). Thus, in a very practical way, Paul's love for a brother prevents him from eating what he otherwise would be free to eat. His servant relationship to Jesus Christ and to the Community (2 Cor. 4:5) obligates him to avoid any action that might offend another's conscience or lead another into a compromising situation. Positively, Paul does all that is within his power to build up the faith of his spiritual children (1 Cor. 4:14–21; Gal. 4:19; Col. 1:28).

Saving faith must be energised by sanctifying love within the fellowship of the saints. The Christian does not act alone any more than a member of the human body can. Paul would have agreed with Wesley in denouncing 'solitary religion'. There is no holiness that is not essentially social.[62] Thus, the firstfruits of faith are compassion for the lost and needy, especially for the suffering members of the household of faith.[63] Thus Luther popularised the two-fold character of the truly justified, simultaneously as sinner and righteous. His Preface to the *Epistle to the Romans* has this gem: 'Faith is a living, busy, active, might thing . . . It is impossible for it not to be doing good works incessantly.'[64]

John fully endorses the Pauline dynamic conception of faith. 'Whoever claims to be dwelling in Christ, binds himself to live as Christ lived' (1 Jn. 2:6).[65] Not merely positionally does the believer enjoy the benefits of justification, but also as a way of life. So beyond confessing that Christ is Lord, he should exercise value judgments in the light of Scripture, and act upon them as the Spirit supplies the needed love and wisdom (Rom. 5:5, 8:5). 'Faith is morally vital by itself. It works "through love" (Gal. 5:6).'[66]

Jesus made seeking the kingdom a vital requirement for his followers (Mt. 6:33). The author of the epistle to the Hebrews warns his readers that neglect in pursuing sanctification will mean exclusion from the beatific vision (12:14). Paul expresses the pursuit of holiness as a straining to win the prize (Phil. 3:13,14). The unseen realities that faith seeks and longs for may bring suffering and affliction; still, the conflict with the unsubdued powers of the old age cannot becloud his vision of the 'eternal weight of glory' (2 Cor. 4:16). Consequently Paul wishes for a closer identification with his Lord's sufferings and death.[67]

VII. JUSTIFICATION AND PERFECTIONISM

Legalism demands that its followers obey an external code, but perfectionism is grounded in a skewed vision of the practical meaning of justification. A recent and influential movement in Brazil champions a view of sanctification that has proved to be both polemical and divisive.[68] The proponents of this doctrine teach that in the new birth the old nature has been annihilated. Crucifixion with Christ dealt a death-blow to the flesh. The 'old man' has been mortified and no more able to sin than a corpse. Divergent views are propounded. Some hold that the elimination of the old nature guarantees the impeccability of the twice-born. Others admit to the possibility of accidental or involuntary sin. Plausibility is gained for this teaching by defining sin as any voluntary transgression of God's known will.

Such a misguided understanding of the well-known proof-texts[69] cited in favour of total victory over sin has far-reaching consequences. The bulk of the New Testament is rendered inapplicable to the Christian's life. Scores of exhortations to pursue righteousness and modify behaviour become pointless (e.g. the Sermon on the Mount, the hortatory texts throughout the Bible). Christians are discouraged from repenting or asking for God's forgiveness. Self-examination becomes groundless, except to confirm or deny the fact of regeneration. Sins of omission need never be brought to mind if one believes that the new life within is nothing other than that of Christ himself, as Gal. 2:20 and 2 Cor. 5:17 are understood to teach (*cf.* Jas. 4:17).

Furthermore, it follows from the premise of the impeccability of the regenerate, that half of the church's mission is unnecessary. Sinless Christians scarcely need edifying. They may well dispense with the life-long process of learning to observe all that Jesus taught (Mt. 28:19,20).

Whatever the name given to perfectionism,[70] the consequences are similar. The seriousness with which Scripture confronts sin becomes dissolved into an opaque and spiritually irresponsible admission of mere mistakes. The biblical view of original sin as a condition, and sins as lack of conformity to God's law and a neglect of God-given obligations, are shunted aside. Sin must be confined to heinously wicked acts, the true signs of perdition. B. Waltke observes that the doctrine of eradication lacks 'conclusive biblical proof, has an unrealistic theological rationale, and leads to unedifying practical implications'.[71]

In perfectionism sanctification merges into justification. Nothing more needs to be done than to hammer into the heads of all who accept this viewpoint. 'Believe it, contrary to all internal doubts or external evidence.' But Matthew Henry put it succinctly, 'We shall never come to the perfect man till we come to the perfect world.'[72] Paul categorically denied that he had attained perfection (Phil. 3:12), and claimed rather to be the 'worst of sinners' (1 Tim. 1:16). This should convince us that 'The perfect Christian is the one who, having a sense of his own failure, is minded to press toward the mark.'[73] What is true of the individual is also true of the church. The gifts the risen, exalted Lord has bestowed on his people are intended to perfect the saints until (eschatologically) they attain the unity of the faith, the profound knowledge (*epignōsis*) of the Son of God, the complete (*teleios*) man, and mature stature measured by the fulness of Christ (Eph. 4:11–13).[74]

VIII. CONCLUSION

L. Goppelt has stated the argument of this paper succinctly:

> For Jesus the Law's validity and invalidity belonged inseparably together, and the first witnesses had correctly grasped this fact, so that, a conditional adherence to the Law was possible in the Church if one lived solely by repentance, i.e. if one no longer concealed oneself before God by means of the Law but rather surrendered oneself totally to that fellowship with God effected through Jesus.[75]

The pervasive peace which Christians enjoy by virtue of their having trusted in Christ as their perfect substitute and having shared in his Spirit, must not be obscured despite their stumbling and falling (Gal. 6:1,2; 1 Jn. 1:9–2:1). 'The radical significance of justification as the permanent resting point of our heart, must not be lost.'[76] Union with Christ is an objective reality. The relationship between Christ, the Shepherd, and his sheep, being a permanent, God-enacted one, bolsters an assurance as solid as his promise, 'I give them eternal life, and they shall never perish . . .' (Jn. 10:28f.).

On the other hand the certainty of faith's confidence in God and in a future destiny with Christ, must never encourage presumption. Complacency surely threatens evangelicalism at a profounder level than a groundless fear of perdition. Justification, understood as forgiveness past, present and future, produces what Theodore Beza called 'devil's logic'.[77] In such a context sin presents no real problem, since freedom from the law means freedom from moral obligation.[78] The claim that justification can be genuine without the confirmation of sanctification is a dangerous deception.

But neither antinomianism nor legalism reflect the Christian way. 'Law is needed as love's eyes; love is needed as law's heartbeat. Law without love is Pharisaism; love without law is antinomianism.'[79] When Christians congratulate their performance of religious duties however perfunctorily done; when earnest prayer and fellowship can be neglected without a pang of conscience; when the fate of the lost leaves them unmoved; when the wails of the suffering poor fail to stir them while they anxiously follow the vagaries of the stock market, it is time to re-examine the implications of the biblical doctrine of justification. If zeal for righteousness has cooled to become mere lip-service and the pursuit of righteousness a neglected hobby, there is danger that the broad way of destruction has replaced the narrow road that leads to life (Mt. 7:13,14). God told Ezekiel that he would be held accountable for not warning Israel's wicked men, whatever their judgment might be (33:8). Twentieth-century evangelicals must not ignore the signs of overconfidence in a presumed justification when sanctification is neglected. 'Make every effort to . . . be holy. Without holiness, no one shall see the Lord' (Heb. 12:14).

10

Justification and Social Justice

GUILLERMO W. MENDEZ

I. INTRODUCTION

For some Third World observers, to talk about social justice in so-called First World countries may seem irrelevant and redundant. After all, it is in the West that the great achievements in social affairs have taken place. Of course, this has not been accomplished without struggle, but democracy, abolition of slavery, labour rights, welfare programmes and human rights have come to fruition at least to some extent in the First World. Besides, the social issues discussed there are different. They centre on abortion, the homeless, drugs in the streets, education in the slums, and the like.

It is not the same in Third World countries.[1] These nations have high ideals but very poor performance. I suspect that my place of origin and residence are the main reasons why I was assigned this paper; and rightfully so, because in the Third World our perspective on the issues becomes painfully real. We have to struggle to distance ourselves from the subject in our ongoing effort to be objective. Yet it is our duty to think through these issues from a Christian perspective.

Furthermore, to relate justification to social justice might seem even stranger. Could this effort not have as its hidden agenda to politicise theology? Right from the beginning it should be made clear that to speak about social justice from an evangelical perspective is not to identify with a particular political position. Such an identification would be an oversimplification that would betray the biblical data, and could be made only if we wanted to say that the biblical texts dealing with the subject were also politically biased and favoured the right or left. Does that conclusion reflect a serious study of the Word of God? On the other hand, does our neglect of such subjects reflect a knowledge of the world we want to evangelise?

This paper has one key tenet: the doctrine of justification must be central to any biblical discussion of social justice. This premise can be seen in the following concepts:

(1) Justification, as the fruit of what Christ has done in our favour, serves as the basis for righteous living. Both the law of God and the gospel are expressions of God's justice. With justification the requirements of the law are met; and the gospel restores men and women from sin.

(2) The justified person is commanded to live according to God's character. In this effort the relationship of works to justification is not one of merit but of grace; this relationship is theocentric, not anthropocentric (Eph. 2:10). Justification is the true ground for righteous living; yet both believers and unbelievers, owing to sin, fail to live according to God's standard. Sin is a comprehensive reality that affects every human endeavour and area of life, whether individual or communal. Hence our need to talk about social justice.

(3) 'Social justice' is notoriously difficult to define. The justified person believes that the true source of justice is God, but the application of justice so understood to concrete human affairs is problematic. Theories of justice often can be partial and secularist. As Christians are continually confronted with relative ideologies, much clarification and investigation are needed to explore how to relate this theological perspective to modern realities.

(4) Christians face the challenge of living their faith in new and fresh ways to counteract a shallow, uncomitted 'believism' that does not properly reflect Christian ethics and theology. This type of 'cheap grace' has little to say to this world of injustice. Only the people of God who serve as sign of the kingdom of God can show the difference to the world.

(5) Justification from a soteriological point of view receives adequate treatment in other chapters in this book. Here we do not intend to repeat their work. Nor is it our intention to justify evangelicals at the level of praxis, that is, in what we actually do to serve the poor in concrete situations. This is an area of historical study that should be dealt with, but that I have decided to omit from this paper. The present chapter is more theological and philosophical in orientation.

II. JUSTIFICATION

I wish to begin by considering the relation of justification to Christian ethics.
'Salvation' is that all-encompassing term that refers to what God has done for the believer. Of course, in specific contexts the word may carry finer nuances, among which is eternal salvation after death. In Old Testament theology, however, salvation is more comprehensive than we might usually think. It is understood to include salvation from the *effects* of sin (1 Sam. 12:7–12; Ps. 40:10; 48:10; 51:14; 65:5; 72:1–4; 82:1–8; 145:5–7; Isa. 45; 24; 54:17).
It must be kept in mind that God's provision of salvation is expressly directed towards his enemies (Rom. 5:8). We are not to confuse God's justice with the expression of it. Rather, if the gospel is the greatest expression of God's justice, we must say that it certainly means far more than giving to each one what he deserves (Rom. 3:21–26). Human beings deserve judgment, yet a gracious God gives them forgiveness and salvation.

A. The Law and the Gospel

Basic to the idea of justification in any theological system is some position on the relationship between law and grace. We cannot understand the relation between the law of God and the grace of God, however, unless we view it in the context of sin. The law was given, in part, to restrict and direct men and women in the midst of pervasive evil in a wicked world. Law as a principle governing human endeavours was designed by God, at least in part, to counteract the presence of evil in all its manifestations.

We may think of justice as nothing other than righteous deeds that conform to God's written law. But God gives more than law: he gives the gospel. We find in the gospel a restoration from the sinfulness of sin. It is in the context of gospel proclamation that we read that the justice of God reveals itself (Rom. 1:17). The gospel embraces a moral standard that reflects God's justice and must be contrasted with all aspects of human life as they are exposed in Romans 1. Thus, the gospel must be understood to be the definitive contrast to the destructive effects brought about by sin. If the law of God is a gift of grace, a deterrent for sin, and a preparation and guide to Christ, then the gospel is the justice of God in its fuller expression as God replaces evil and establishes that which is good. So both law and gospel are correctives of sin and expressions of God's justice. We know we must preach that if sin and unrighteousness come through disobedience, justice can come only through the total obedience of our Lord and to our Lord.

B. Works and Justification

At least since Augustine, grace has been the basis of works for Augustinian and Reformed theology. This triumph of grace meant for Augustine that human beings are aided by grace to please God. Augustine believed in the preeminence of grace as a function of God's sovereignty, regardless of whether (as some think) he earlier also maintained that the works that originate in God's grace could in fact find their source in the believer's free will.[2]

The Reformation accentuated the emphasis on grace. The source of works lies solely in the grace of God, leaving the grace to live the Christian life as a consequence of salvation but never as the basis of it.

In Liberation theology we find a reversal of the Reformation in more ways than one. For one thing, 'Authentic love tries to start with the concrete needs of the other and not with the "duty" of practicing love.'[3] Here, there seems to be an optimism about the human capacity to love aside from duty. Love and duty seem to be free of coercion. For Gutiérrez, law 'is external coercion and, as such, is associated with the flesh and death'.[4]

> St. James can therefore say: 'So speak and so act as those who are to be judged under *the law of liberty*' (James 2:12). The Law of freedom, the law of the spirit, is the law by which will be judged the works without which faith is dead (James 2:14,26).[5]

It is true that his affirmations are balanced by a larger context of a treatment on grace. But what does 'the love of Christ compels us' imply, except the coercive force of Christ's example? Are not the law of the Spirit and the Word of God hortatory and coercive? See how v. 13 follows: 'judgment without mercy will be shown to anyone who has not been merciful' (James 2:13). So it seems that the gospel does include the idea of duty.

Secondly, for Liberation theologians, commitment to the poor is the 'first moment' in theology: 'the understanding of the faith appears as the understanding not of a simple affirmation — almost memorisation — of truth, but of a commitment, an overall attitude, a particular posture towards life.'[6] Praxis becomes 'the existential and active aspect of the christian life'.[7] Thus Gutiérrez can say that 'God is loved in the neighbour'.[8] But that is not exactly what Scripture says: love for one's neighbour whom we can see is a sign of true love towards God whom we cannot see (1 John 3:10).[9] In defining the qualitative leap of salvation Gutiérrez says: 'Man is saved if he opens himself to God and to others, even if he is not clearly aware that he is doing so. This is valid for Christians and non-Christians alike — for all people.'[10]

Clearly, in this view of praxis it is as important to liberate fellow-man as it is to please God. Indeed, the latter can be *defined* by the former. That is a negation of the Reformation and a step backwards towards an anthropocentric concept of justification. Moreover, from the perspective of the gospel this autosoterism is diametrically opposed to the cross of Jesus Christ.

Dr. Emilio A. Núñez clarifies what Reformation doctrine means for us regarding good works as the fruit of our salvation:

> According to Reformation Doctrine, the sinner is justified by faith alone, but the faith that justifies does not remain alone. It is not a sterile faith, and much less a dead faith. James' teaching (2:14–26) is in complete accordance with that of Paul, who affirms that we are not saved *by* good works, but that we are saved *for* good works which God has prepared for us (Eph. 2:8–10). These good works are the fruit of salvation, not the cause. They are not simply works that are liturgical in nature; they are closely related to our personal, family, and social life. The person who has been justified by having believed in Jesus continues demonstrating his faith, not only in words, but also in actions that glorify God and benefit his neighbour in society.[11]

If man is justified by God's grace, to dream that human institutions will reach justice apart from grace is a nonsense. Since it was not perversion of the environment that introduced injustice, then mere improvement of the environment will not take away sin and injustices in society.

C. The Nature of Sin

Since Augustine, our concept of sin has been more philosophical than biblical. Augustine almost denied ontological status to sin in his polemics against Manicheans, who made evil eternal and absolute. 'Evil is not a nature, but is rather the corruption of nature . . . it is not "something". . . . Evil is only a negation of good. . . . Evil is not a fiction of the intellect', but it is not a substance.[12] Here Augustine followed the path of neo-platonism, whose view was that evil is not a reality that exists apart from the One; rather evil is withdrawing from the One.[13] Thus, since the time of Augustine, many heirs of his theology take sin merely as a spiritual dimension.

We do not want to affirm that sin is a substance in any philosophical sense, but it is something more concrete than what our theology has made of it. Sin has a very concrete meaning in our world according to Johannine hamartiology. Satan is the head of a system that opposes God. This system includes the leader, the people and things — both good and bad — that are contrary to God (Jn. 12:13; 14:30; 16:11). Satan's influence on humankind is clear (8:44; 13:2,27; 1 Jn. 3:8; 5:19). It is no wonder that 'the wrath of God is being revealed from heaven against all the godlessness and wickedness of men who suppress the truth by their wickedness' (Rom. 1:18). Man's main problem is that he has exchanged the truth of God for a lie, since worship is due only to the Creator; but man through his distorted outlook prefers creatures and creation (Rom. 1:25). Even the concept of sin portrayed as 'missing the mark', though a good illustration, is not the only biblical idea for sin. The illustration of passively missing the mark can mean also actively hitting the wrong mark (Prov. 8:36). Thus, sin is far more than breaking the law. It involves everything that goes against God's justice and character.

This sinfulness also pervades God's people: 'for all of us have become like one who is unclean; and all our righteous deeds are like filthy garments' (Is. 64:6). The best of human achievements are like 'menstrual rags' in God's sight.

Sin affects the individual and everything he or she produces. Sin as the extravagance of human evil goes far beyond our comprehension. We prefer to talk about drinking, cheating and lying. Important as these are, God's justice cannot be limited to our micro-ethics. We must remember that, in the light of God's character, human institutions are not 'chemically pure'. Sin has left its deep impression in them and has moulded them to a certain extent.

Yet we evangelicals have had a poor vocabulary when it comes to social sin. We must widen and deepen our comprehension of sin as a concrete power with concrete expressions in the world — not only in the areas where we have learned to see it, but in many other human relations as well. We who claim to be biblical must see the variety of words and relations used for sin and through them recognise the different shapes of evil in our world.

D. Human Failure

Broadly speaking, the assumption of the Bible is that the various evils of society reflect a radical breach with God. This means that attempts to relate social problems and Christianity by merely righting social evils are inevitably superficial. From a biblical point of view, these attempts are doomed to fail because only the symptoms are dealt with. Yet this fact must not become an excuse for the Christian to ignore social ills; rather it is a warning that most attempts to pour all of the Bible's thought forms into addressing social ills are simply not radical enough. Appealing to the fundamental prophetic model corrects this basic error.

Both the lost and the redeemed need correction of their sin. The former many times admit the validity only of temporal solutions. The latter tend to deal exclusively with the spiritual. But in any case, it is not a matter of temporal priority; rather, it is a question of logical priority. In other words, if we must rebuke Christians who see Christianity exclusively in personal, privatised, and spiritual domains, we must also rebuke those who claim that Christianity's primary focus lies in the transformation of society, when that analysis does not deal with the fundamental question of sin, of evil in the human heart, of fundamental and radical rebellion against God.

III.   SOCIAL JUSTICE

In this section we want to establish God as our source of justice, hear the complaint of some Latin American exegetes, and then consider the concept of justice in economic terms, since economic factors are understood to be the crux of the matter in Third World countries. The relation of anthropology to theories of law and the place of the church as the source of Christian ethics are surveyed, and to this is added a brief section on history and the kingdom as the *locus* of justice.

The situation of poverty in the Third World could not be more tragic. Christian compassion should not ignore the needs of our world. To that effect, the Grand Rapids *Report on Evangelism and Social Responsibility* says:

> We are appalled to know that about 800 million people, or one fifth of the human race, are destitute, lacking the basic necessities for survival, and that thousands of them die of starvation every day. Many more millions are without adequate shelter and clothing, without clean water and health care, without opportunities for education and employment, and are condemned to eke out a miserable existence without the possibility of self-improvement for themselves or their families. They can only be described as 'oppressed' by the gross economic inequality from which they suffer and the diverse economic systems which cause and perpetuate it.[14]

To whom do we look in the midst of so much despair? Clearly, we must look to God.

A. God as a Measure of Justice

When we affirm that justice is an attribute of God, we are going back to the very basics. The definitions that see in the word 'justice' mainly a principle of rightly-ordered relations, can find strong support in pre-creation theology. The doctrine of the Trinity holds that God communicated and loved before the universe was brought into being. But beyond a purely relational definition, according to the Scriptures God is the measure of justice: he provides the real measure of what justice is. The non-theological use of the word *sed eq*[15] is a '*truthful* measure', a '*faithful* weight' (Lev. 19:36):

> The concept of righteousness [and righteous] . . . has never been easy to explain. However Hebrew usage helps us to define the concrete idea. In Deut 25:13–16 the law says, 'You shall not have in your bag diverse weights, a great weight and a small weight! But you shall have a perfect, a righteous weight.' There could not be a double standard for buying or selling; the Hebrew had to have a measurement to conform to the standard. He could not use a heavy weight on the scales to gain more, or a lighter weight to give less. So too in theological usage: that which is righteous conforms to the standard God has set up in Torah.[16]

Therefore, the idea of justice is to be right. The standard for justice is God's character, not human or political achievement. This fact illustrates that God's character provides the measure. He is just *par excellence*. For example, the king and the judge are called to rescue the oppressed and downtrodden (Pss. 72:1–4; 82:1–18). To do this is to participate in God's deeds of salvation from the effects of sin (Pss. 48:12–18; 140:12f; 146:7–10; Is. 1:17; Jer. 22:16), which is a foretaste of the coming eternal salvation. Here, mercy and grace seem to be part and parcel of God's justice (Ps. 145:7; Hos. 2:19). This has tremendous implications for Christian living. In New Testament theology the idea of social justice must be connected to the Old Testament view: '. . . a standard of justice is assumed and there is a clear differentiation between what is right and what is wrong.'[17] Commenting on Matt. 23:23 Mott says:

> Two aspects of this passage are noteworthy: (1) Jesus carries on the prophetic attack on the piety which leaves out social justice. (2) He clearly indicates the place of the Old Testament teachings about justice: they reflect the highest level of Old Testament ethics and are essential to his new order.[18]

God's creation was a just world with righteous people. His word, an expression of his character, was the governing factor; and his presence as a model for his people was the apex of the perfect world. The command to subdue the earth and exercise lordship over it has been interpreted as including human progress. Most do not see a problem with this. The problems seem to surface when the idea of wealth is also found in this command. Some insist that the idea of wealth is a post-lapsarian concept, and that wealth only emerged as an expression of greed. This view, of course, must be refined; otherwise, if wealth is due to greed, poverty becomes an ideal, very much as in monastic times. Then Third World nations are automatically pious, because they are poor, and it does not matter if they love God. Why then would they need liberation?

Wealth is not an ideal if it is based on greed. But at least we could agree that, as an administrator of the garden, Adam was a man immensely rich, and that the cultural mandate defined him and his wife as the stewards of the earth. If the fall had not occurred, some ask, would we have seen the development of a socialist or a capitalist Garden of Eden? So phrased, the question is highly speculative, and ignores the fact that all of our experiences of socialism and capitalism lie within a fallen order. Besides, might there not be other alternatives in an order without sin? Perhaps there would be some form of productive justice along with a limited administrator-owner concept.

What we must recall is that it was God who granted everything to the first couple, and this biblical datum is a first hint at distributive justice. He produced something to give to the ones he was going to create. Here compassion and care for the needy might be seen in a different light. Yet God also commanded Adam to work. Labour, hence production, is not a post-lapsarian curse, but rather is at the heart of the cultural mandate. Adam works not to achieve manhood but because he is man; his work seems to be a right and a duty because he is formed in God's image. We must affirm that both justice and justification come from God. They are realities revealed to us which find their full expression and content in who God is.

B.   The Wider Vs. The Narrower Definition

Here we must pay heed to the complaint of Third World exegetes whose contention is that we have not dealt properly with today's implications of justice. This battle between many Latin American exegetes and many of their counterparts in the North Atlantic countries rages over what we have called, for lack of a better expression, 'the wider *vs.* the narrower definition of justice'. It is strange for some theologians in Latin America[19] that a work such as Arndt and Gingrich's *A Greek–English Lexicon of the New Testament* 'fails to give "oppression" as a possible translation of *adikia* (unjustice)'.[20] They would argue that when we define 'injustice' mainly as 'a violation of the Law', as Kittel's *Theological Dictionary of the New Testament* does,[21] this wide definition has very little, if anything, to say about the concreteness of the unjust act outside the religious field of meaning.

Particularly, some wonder what was the meaning of social justice in New Testament times and what room there might have been for such an idea in the apostolic teaching. To put it bluntly, how does *dikē* ('justice') stand against 'dishonesty', 'immorality' or 'social injustice'? Costa Rican theologian Plutarco Bonilla charges:

> This problem (the translation of the New Testament and especially the epistles) shows that we have been reading Paul (and Peter), so to speak through the religious and ideological perspectives of the hellenistic world and not from the liberating perspective of the Old Testament (as it was put into Greek first in the Septuagint and later in the New Testament Writings).[22]

José P. Miranda goes a step further when he reworks the argument of the Epistle to the Romans in light of ἀδικια (adikia), understood as 'social injustice'. Regarding 1:18–3:20 he says: '. . . the justice of God is a new reality with social dimensions in human history.'[23] In fact, 'Paul's gospel . . . deals with the justice which the world and peoples and society, implicitly but anxiously have been awaiting'.[24] Thomas Hanks says:

> If we retranslate a Pauline epistle like Romans in the light of Pon's study [on oppression], we can see at once that 'oppression' may indeed be as fundamental to Paul's theology as it is to Jesus, Luke, James and the Old Testament. Then a basic text like Romans 1:18 might well read like this: For the wrath of God is being revealed from heaven against all violence (*asēbeia*) and oppression (*adikia*) of people who by their very oppression (*adikia*) of their fellows end up suppressing truth itself.[25]

Such a translation, of course, could make 'oppression' fundamental to Paul's theology, or biblical theology for that matter, but Hanks has not shown convincingly the biblical or linguistic basis for this translation.[26] This translation seems much too narrow in the context, although the Greek words may here include 'oppression' along with other forms of unrighteousness and injustice (*cf.* 1:19–32). Nevertheless, even if theologians in Latin America overstate their case, they are echoing real needs as well as the ideologies that emerge from them, and consequently they believe that the gospel has not been properly related to our context.

Here the discussion turns to theories behind economics.

C. Distributive Vs. Productive Justice

We need to overcome the false dichotomy between the distributive and the productive concepts of the justice. We understand by *distributive justice* that concept rooted in Byzantine ethics as put forward in Thomas Aquinas' commentary to Aristotle's *Nichomean Ethics*, which 'concerns the appropriation to individuals of what is "common" '.[27] This view posits an interpretation of reality that argues that the earth has plenty of goods. Those who have wealth do so because they have taken from the earth not only their share but also that which belongs to those who have not. Therefore, those who have must share their possessions with the poor. This concept of justice basically says: (1) to each according to his need; (2) to each according to his worth; (3) to each according to his merit; (4) to each according to his work.[28] This distributive practice will bring, it is claimed, social peace and justice to society. In extreme utopianism, this will bring a new order.

Behind the distributive theory of justice lies a certain concept of equality:

> When Aristotle in Book V of the *Nichomean Ethics* comes to grips with distributive justice, almost the first remark he has to make is that 'justice is equality, as all men believe it to be, quite apart from any argument'.[29]

Thus justice is to give to each one what is his due. The basic assumption is that the main concern of justice is to produce some sort of equality within the context of human needs.[30] Justice is identified with material equality and seems to be closely related to redistribution of wealth. In economics as in law, this quantitive sense has often permeated the concept of justice.[31]

Yet we find that equality and fairness are not traits of our present world. Wherever we turn in nature we find imbalance, unfairness and differences in resources, abilities, intelligence and possessions. That might indicate that equality is not an actual pattern in our world. We do not know if this is only the result of the fall or God's original intention. In Pannenberg's opinion, 'only a theory of justice can establish that inequalities among individuals are inescapable and determine which of these inequalities are justified (or at least tolerable)'.[32] Vlastos adds:

> . . . would anyone wish to say that there are no just inequalities? That there are no rights in respect of which men are unequal? One would think that this would be among the first question that would occur to equalitarians [sic], and would have had long since a clear and firm answer. Strange as it may seem, this has not happened.[33]

Nevertheless, it is legitimate to ask whether the church must exclusively choose mathematical equality to define justice, and whether or not it is sheer materialism.[34] Such is the question that must be put forward to Liberation Theology, since her economic analysis calls injustice all that is not economic equality.

On the other hand, the Bible points out the impossibility of expressing God's love without the consideration of concrete activity on behalf of fellow human beings (Ja. 2:14ff.; 1 Jn. 3:10ff.). Can we measure love in concrete actions better than we can justice? God is love and God is justice, and we cannot say that both categories are abstract unhistorical entities whose value lies precisely in their transcendent nature.

Yet surely our meagre projects of distributing goods are too narrow to represent fully God's purpose for humankind. God gave his Son, but he also placed demands on his children, and both are expressions of purposeful love. Just as God's purpose is not exhausted by giving alone, neither is justice exhausted by one type of action (that concerned with distribution of goods). Therefore quantitative categories, even though useful, should not be considered as the only standard. Critics of Aristotle and Aquinas note that they had little to say about the justice of producing wealth and creating economic development (possibilities which simply did not arise during their eras).[35]

In contradiction to the distributive viewpoint, *productive justice* is an interpretation of reality which says that human creativity, freedom for all, and controls over those who hold power will in fact produce a just society. Behind the productive theory of justice lies a sort of social agreement. In this notion of justice, the concept of sin has an important place. For Novak, 'The Jewish Christian notion of sin lay behind the fundamental division of systems, the division of powers in the political system.'[36] This means that one does not trust one person or institution with too much power.

Here the contention is that, given the proper restraints and morality, based on proper judicial, political, and ethical checks and balances, society will necessarily produce wealth for all.[37] Therefore, those who apply their inventiveness to hard work will benefit most. Only this approach, some believe, can bring social peace and prosperity to all.[38] The wealth accumulated will eventually reach everybody to a more or less just degree.

In practice, we discover that in most Third World nations the checks and balances and proper distribution of power are often lacking, and this results in gross injustices. Some are quick to maintain that at this stage capitalism is unworkable in Latin America since 'Latin American economies are not capitalist but pre-capitalist', and since in Latin America there is not 'a single capitalist economy'.[39] In addition, 'Monopoly' as a game of life exists even in those nations where proper checks and balances are legally in place. There we can find new forms of injustices, perpetrated not only by the very wealthy on the very poor, but by the very wealthy on the less wealthy.

In some Third World countries discussion centres on choosing the better alternative of these two theories of justice. Yet poverty reigns in those countries where, in theory, there is distribution of wealth as well as in those where productive justice is supposedly practised. In Latin America one finds gross injustices and a wide gap between the rich and the poor, especially since history and not hard work have made most of the continent's millionaires. For instance, the descendants of Spaniards and nobles from the last two centuries are, by and large, today's wealthiest people. Of course, there are some who have come from deep poverty to own small business empires or a reasonably large estate. Yet lack of education, sub-human living conditions and miserable salaries for most of the population make these very exceptional cases. Political ideologies are quick to point this out; but centuries earlier the Bible had already condemned greed and injustice in all spheres and systems, and its criticism of materialism seems applicable today (*cf.* Am. 1–2; Mic. 2,3; 6:6–16; Isaiah 5:10ff.).

Does the Bible opt for one of these positions? Distribution may seem to side with the Mosaic law and the prophets, while production perhaps appears to be presupposed creation theology and by Proverbs. Yet even from the distribution point of view, it is clear that having something to 'share' and distribute is a material impossibility without having anything to start with, or without having the means to produce wealth.[40] To say it boldy, some form of both production (Eph. 4:28; Pr. 10:4–5; 12:11; 24:30–34; Gen. 1:28–30, etc.) and distribution (Dt. 24:14–15; Amos 5:11–12; 4:1; 8:4–7; Is. 48:3,6,7; Mal. 3:5) is evident in the Scriptures, although not with the specific economic nuances that some theoreticians would claim today.

For instance, there are guidelines in Proverbs that underline a universal truth for any nation: 'justice makes a nation great' (Prov. 14:34). To pay fair salaries on time and without holding back what belongs to the worker is also biblical and pleases God. With a violation, ideally the judge and the court would come into play (Ex. 23:1–9; Mi. 7:3; Zech. 7:9; Am. 5:11–12; Ps. 22; 82). In this case a just settlement is demanded for those in need. On the other hand, the poor must be willing to work and go to the corners of the fields and reap (Lev. 19:9–10; 23:22). Nevertheless, in case of utter helplessness, the poor man must be the object of compassion from the rest of the people of God (Deut. 15:7,11).

The guidelines to evaluate distributive and productive justice should go far beyond the criteria of efficiency to meet the material needs of the majority. From a Christian perspective, room for spirituality, freedom and an adequate concept of history should also be borne in mind. Therefore the greatest demand for our philosophers and theologians is to go beyond the limits of productive and distributive concepts of justice, and develop something closer to revelation and to reality, much in the same sense as what was done in the eighteenth century by capitalist thinkers, when it was thought that distributive justice was the *ne plus ultra*. Yet today, it is probably fair to say that no one would argue over the *existence* of Aristotelian *suum cuique*, the concept of distributive justice; the problem in a capitalist or a socialist society is its *mechanisms*: state control or a free market? That is a question which today receives conflicting answers. And so we must proceed to deal with the greater theological concerns that are related to justice.

D.   Anthropology and Theories of Law

God created us 'in his image, according to his likeness'. Here we find the root of human moral ability. As is well-known, the interpretation of this phrase has a long history of disagreement, and biblical theology has hardly reached a consensus. At least, the ideas of administration, of producing life and of holiness, seem to be basic to its meaning. But human beings are fallen creatures. We were made in God's image but are now in every way tainted by sin.

Human beings created *imago Dei* ought to know what is fair in the administration of resources, what duties we acquire through procreation, and what dues we must pay to God. Christian theology contends that this is the basis of the shared moral sensibility of humankind. As a lawyer, H. L. A. Hart asks himself: 'Are they immutable principles which constitute part of the fabric of the universe, not made by man, but awaiting discovery by the human intellect? Or are they expressions of changing human attitudes?'[41] We Christians would answer 'Yes' to the first and put aside the conventional relativism expressed by the second. Yet *both* are true, although from different perspectives. Human beings express the *imago Dei* through a shared moral sensibility, and according to a higher morality we find within ourselves. In the past, theologians and philosophers have called the morality reflected in creation orders, and broadly perceived by humankind, 'natural law'. This view according to its critics is based on 'an older conception of nature in which the observable world is . . . proceeding towards a definite optimum state which is the specific good — or the end (τέλος, [*telos*] *finis*) appropriate for it'.[42] This concept is a theological and philosophical interpretation of the human desire to obey a higher hierarchy of values: God's (or nature's) law written on our hearts.

But a word must also be said about 'positive law'. Positive law is a nineteenth-century view that law and rights are no more than the product of the commands of a sovereign; or, for others, the result of judicial decision; negatively, 'that it is in no sense a necessary truth that laws reproduce or satisfy certain demands of [human/divine] morality, though in fact they have often done so'.[43] Recently this viewpoint has been interpreted with reference to a social dimension, or with reference to rules that can function only by way of a conventional morality.[44] This latter interpretation is also known as natural morality. This is an observation of reality that concludes that people of every culture seem to be concerned with morality, doing right, and ethics. Such a conclusion is only an observation of a given, and therefore does not pretend to legislate. Natural morality claims that what is right for each group may vary. It is a conventional ethic that projects what is acceptable to a group of people,[45] and justice, therefore, is a relative concept.

But here lies an important connection with John Rawls' theory of justice.[46] Should not justice be discussed according to a particular social system? Regarding a social theory of justice on which to base distribution, Panennberg says:

> The basic problem in this discussion seems to lie in the question whether such a theory should start with the assumption of the traditional social contract theory, the assumption of an 'original position' of isolated and equal individuals, or whether . . . the concept of justice must be developed in connection with a description of the social system and the hierarchy of its values.[47]

This provides us with a different set of questions. How does a social system develop a hierarchy within its values? Does not the concept of justice change from one social system to the other? Liberation theology assumes that all social systems agree on what justice is and should be, and hence does not define the term precisely.

1. *Justice as an Abstract Category.*

Liberation theologies not only separate the justice owed to human beings from the justice owed to God but they tend to subsume the latter under the former.[48] More importantly, the justice owed to human beings is tantamount to a particular transcendent ideology above all social systems.[49] Justice does not emerge from a particular social system, but rather it is severed from a social system and is reduced to the abstract construct of a political ideology.[50] Therefore God's justice is not the highest standard; revolutionary justice is. Once this theoretical move is made, the road is open to postulate that social justice is equivalent to the programme of historical praxis. But is justice really ever defined? If praxis is an open dialectical programme it seems that there is really not a final definition of justice. Unless we return to theological categories, such as the kingdom; or to ontological ones, such as God's person or the poor, the praxiological 'God's action' cannot define justice. God's action must be freed from the straitjacket of never-ending cyclical historical determinism.

The concomitant question is where we may find an operational measure of justice. Old Testament prophets clearly look to God for that standard. Contemporary prophets talk on God's behalf, but their system by necessity must conclude that the revelation is not directly applicable, nor specific enough to judge modern society. So they must find their measure of justice in a secular political ideology.[51] If, because of the theocracy, Israel's prophets could not resort to secular models to speak on God's justice, should theologians do it? Though times are different, does not the Word of God bind our opinion to determine what justice is?

Is it the aim of Liberation theology to provide secular society with a secular answer to its problems? Some answer affirmatively. Juan Luis Segundo talks about 'an undeniable linguistic fact: there exists one language for speaking of religious realities (sin, grace, etc.) and another for secular, earthly, or temporal realities'.[52] He goes on to say that Liberation theology makes use of the second language without abandoning its religious context. We must point out that as a secular answer to human affairs this position shows astuteness but, theologically speaking, is inadequate. The prophets of Israel did not try to secularise their answer to the point of changing the ontological status of the justice they were representing. That is particularly true even in times of gross materialism and unbelief, such as those under the ministry of Amos and Micah. Therefore we must go back to the Bible to learn who God is, what his demands are, and the basis from which he judges the human injustices of each and all social systems.

2. *Social System as a possible basis.*

We have mentioned that a social system can serve to some extent as the background to determine what justice is.[53] From a historical point of view, ethics and law emerged indirectly within particular social systems.

A social system is the compound interaction of traditions, laws, religious beliefs, political-economic structures, and rules of life shaped in a particular context. This social system produces a set of values of right and wrong. These values constantly interact with different world-views and, as a result, they are often reshaped.

Therefore for Job and Abraham uprightness was not a religious concept only, because part of the traditions, laws, and rules of life of their day taught them what was 'right'. Before Scripture was written there were concrete human relations and collections of laws which defined and legislated the 'just' actions of men, and gods that demanded and defended all that was 'good and just'.[54] When God's revelation about justice broke into history, therefore, it found concepts of justice, both religious and secular. Divine revelation was to shape the mentality of the patriarchs, and later of the nation; and to present to the world an order divinely established, where law and justice were to prevail by obedience to God's Word.

How was this applied? We must remember that the context in which God's justice was proclaimed was a *changing* context. Egypt, the desert, the promised land and captivity provided different obstacles and problems to the living out of God's justice. One might suggest that in some of these situations, God knew he could not require of his people what they were not able to give. For instance, God's revelation to the patriarchs does not emphasise social issues as does the law. Certainly the law is the basis for the prophets' preaching, but the materialism of their epoch makes social preaching reach its peak during their ministry. Failure and disobedience on social matters was treated differently from one epoch to another. There was some social teaching in every period, yet God's message emphasised it only when it became an acute problem.

In other words, it is not the case that God's justice was fully represented or almost fully expressed when there was silence on social issues. It means only that the social system of that period required *other* teachings and messages. God focused on the greatest needs; like a doctor, he gradually applied the appropriate medicine to the ignorance and sin of his people. But God's justice is far greater than the particular measure of justice in the social system in which it is proclaimed. To put it boldly: we are not saying that justice equals what a social system believes to be right, but rather that God's revelation is geared to the differing needs of particular social systems. In other words, in every case each social system will interact differently with revelation.

Although traditions, laws, religious beliefs, and political–economic structures may be common to various social systems, there is a different history behind each social system. For instance, what Old Testament Israel considered injustice, within the social system of Egypt, would be different in some ways from what 18th century Switzerland or 20th century South Africa considers injustice.

This poses two serious questions. First, are we not relativising justice when we make it equivalent to what a social system believes to be right? Second, and more serious, is not uniting justice to a social system actually a rationale for injustice? Would this not be an argument whose effect is to preserve the *status quo*?

In answer to the first question, it must be said that we have to establish a difference between God's justice, which is of the highest calibre, and the world's efforts. For instance, the matchless justice of God cannot find full expression in any social system or ideology in spite of the substantial progress made in some Western countries. Still, we must agree that the primitive social systems of the biblical world, where ideas of social justice were first proclaimed, have today — in some places and in some respects — been greatly surpassed. Therefore, far from relativising justice, we must anchor it in God's character and from there judge human motives, actions and structures.

This leads us to the answer to the second question: if God is the measure, we are not preserving the *status quo*, but actually prophetically calling for a fuller expression of the justice of God which is reflected dimly in all social systems. In some contexts a consideration of his justice has helped to produce more freedom, social improvement and peace.

In Old Testament Law, justice is closely related to social affairs. Details of social, political, economic, judicial and military life are treated in a way that leaves little room for ignorance of God's ideals. Clear demands are placed on Israel, since it is the nation under God's covenant, and God's precious possession (Ex. 19:1–6; Dt. 7:6–7). God demands obedience from his people, an obedience to be 'fleshed out' in justice (Am. 5:24; Mi. 5:8).

We know Yahweh is Judge of the whole earth (Pss. 9:4,8; 50:6; 96:13; 98:4; Jer. 11:20), and that the earth belongs to him (Ps. 24:1–2). Israel is to be witness of Yahweh's deeds among the nations (Ex. 19; Is. 49:6). This witness includes the preaching to Nineveh (Jonah). So it seems that God holds other nations responsible for their sins and unjustices (the 'don'ts' of the law; Am. 1–2), but nowhere are the specific positive ethics required of them ('do's') elaborated. There is no clear evidence as to how the other nations on earth should construct their social ethics. The role of the People of God was thus to be both a model and a messenger.

E.   The Church and Christian Ethics

'Discipleship' can be a mysterious and esoteric word. There is often among Christians a poor understanding of what it is and what its demands are. The proclamation of the gospel has been divorced from discipleship and the life of Christ. Confusion grows when it is popularly taught that our purpose today is to recreate the life of the early church.

What does following Christ mean? It is far more than the acceptance of the formulas we know today as evangelism. The end of Matthew's Gospel can help answer our query (Mt. 28:18–20). The final words of Christ deal with how to make disciples. The central command is 'make disciples'. This is to be accomplished by going, by baptising, and by teaching them 'all the things I have commanded you'. The teaching aspect is related to the content of the Gospel of Matthew, in which we find five discourses with recognisable didactic purpose. Christ himself modelled those teachings in his life. This makes the point of reference of discipleship not only Christ's teachings, but also Christ's life.

Of all the possible ways Christ had to further his cause, he chose one that was apparently powerless and harmless: he shared (more than 'teaching') his whole life with a band of poorly uneducated Jews. Yet this was the key to discipleship. Sharing, more than 'teaching', his life: showing what godliness means, illustrating God's priorities, humbly praying and depending upon the Father, choosing to oppose and counteract those institutions that claimed to represent God, and living in poverty.

Padilla captures this aspect of Jesus' life:

> Jesus' poverty is a hard historical fact unanimously portrayed in all four Gospels. In order to understand its significance, it must be viewed in the light of Jewish piety in Jesus' day, according to which poverty was often regarded as a curse and wealth was praised as evidence of God's favour. At the same time, however, it must also be viewed in its relation to what Martin Hengel has rightly called 'Jesus' free attitude to property', evidenced in Jesus' contact with well-to-do women (Lk. 8:2–3; *cf.* Lk. 10:38) and his willingness to attend banquets organised by the rich (Lk. 7:36ff; 11:37; 14:1,12; Mk. 14:3ff.) and to incur the label of 'a glutton and a drunkard' (Lk. 7:34). Obviously, Jesus was not a propounder of rigorous asceticism. With this qualification in mind, we still have to ask whether his willingness to defy Jewish piety by identifying himself with the poor, while at the same time maintaining a free attitude to riches, throws any light on the question of the kind of life-style which corresponds to the kingdom of God, or is Jesus' example at this point totally irrelevant to Christian discipleship?[55]

This is the life of Christ; this is the gospel of Jesus Christ. That is why Mark 1:1 says: 'The beginning of the Gospel of Jesus Christ': what follows are chapters relating not only what Christ said, but also how he lived.

Later, when the life of the church is described in Acts, we are told that they did things that could be described as a failure by some of us. Yet all was done in the spirit of the teaching and life of Christ. Padilla says:

> The common ownership of goods was one of the results of the outpouring of the Holy Spirit on the day of Pentecost. It was not an accomplishment made possible through human engineering but the outflow of spiritual life which welded the believers together in 'one heart and soul' (4:32).
>
> The sharing of goods was also practised by the Essenes, but in their case it was strictly enforced by law. By contrast, in the early community it was entirely on a voluntary basis. The sin of Ananias and Sapphira was not that they kept a part of the proceeds of the sale of their land for themselves, but that they brought only a part as if it had been all. Sharing was not compulsory; therefore, as Peter made clear, they did not have to sell their land, and after selling it, they were free to use the money as they wished (5:4). Private property was not totally eliminated (Mary the mother of John Mark, for instance, kept her house as a meeting place, according to 12:12), but it was made subservient to the needs of the whole community.[56]

The thirty-five miracles of Christ, besides being an attestation of his deity, are also parables that illustrate different aspects of God's salvation. These visual illustrations exemplify the prophetic tradition at its best. This says that salvation is wider than we sometimes think, and that what God does for human beings is a comprehensive work of re-creation.

Today the church has to rediscover the role of compassion as a means to illustrate in a fuller sense the different ways God works for human beings. We preach the gospel not only when we teach it in word, but also when we communicate it in deeds. Again Padilla clarifies how 'compassion' was administered;

> Concern for the poor in the primitive church is a normal aspect of Christian discipleship. Translated into action, it makes visible the life of the Kingdom inaugurated by Jesus Christ. Its root is neither in the idealisation of poverty nor in the desire to gain merits before God, but in 'the grace of our Lord Jesus Christ, that though he was rich, yet for our sake became poor, so that by his poverty you might become rich' (2 Cor. 8:9).[57]

From all this, it seems evident that it is in the intimacy of Christ's community, the church, that justice must be illustrated in Spirit, Word and action. But this life cannot remain within the confines of the church. The values here proclaimed sooner or later must touch the world for which they were meant. The Grand Rapids Report on Evangelism and Social Responsibility says:

> But the love of God cannot possibly be bottled up within the Christian community; it breaks out in compassion for the world. It yearns for the salvation of sinners, so that Christ's lost sheep may be gathered safely into his flock. It yearns also to alleviate the material needs of the poor, the hungry and the oppressed, so that if we close our hearts against the needy, we cannot claim that God's love abides in us (1 John 3:17). Love for God and love for neighbour belong inextricably together, as Jesus taught (Mk. 12:28–34; *cf.* 1 John. 4:19–21).[58]

F. Eschatology and History

Eschatology is the sphere where ultimately full justice will take place, yet we must be careful not to attribute moral value to eschatology itself. Such an error could go hand-in-hand with the soterism attributed to history by Marxist determinism, Darwinian evolution, and 'Yuppie' success and progress. History is the realm where moral value occurs, but is not the source of it. Salvation and goodness erupt from above and come from God. This contradicts a popular notion. Erazim Kohák says that 'ours is a time for which *later* has acquired a sense of *better* — while *better* has been drained of all meaning except that of *later*.'[59]

Human beings have placed their hope for a better world in the future. Time has powerfully bewitched us and promised a new world as if by the wave of a magic wand. In his eloquent evaluation of the loss of a proper understanding of eternity in the medieval church, Kohák says:

> . . . we could say that as the Church failed to make eternity real in time by addressing itself to the problems of desperate poverty, cruelty, and injustice which were the obverse of Rushkin's vision of the Middle Ages, humans turned their hopes to the future as a secular surrogate for eternity.[60]

Theologians have attempted to relate the kingdom concept to the struggle for a better society. Some see these two ideas as separate, unrelated realms, claiming that moral and political issues have nothing to do with the kingdom. For others, the two are so inextricably intertwined that there is no socio-political struggle where the kingdom is not fully at stake.[61] Still others see that humans are both political and religious beings and that there is moral value in proclaiming both the religious imperative and human morality. In the final analysis they cannot be separated, but rather find their true unity in God's creation and reign. Is this an attempt to reduce the secular issues of the world to the religious sphere? It may be so interpreted, but, after all, this is the difference between the effort to read reality from a Christian commitment and the effort to do so from an ideological one.

Justice is closely linked to eschatology in several ways. The pervasive presence of God's justice in the *eschaton* is the reality behind all present mirror-like human justice. The prophets announce a coming age where God's justice will prevail. But eschatology from a biblical perspective is not meant merely to inform. Its thrust is to encourage in times of calamity and to mould the ethics of the people. As the people awaited and envisioned a time of peace and justice within history, their present history was to reflect that moral value. But this was based on the presence of the God of history. Salvation and justice erupt as God intervenes in history. But history is also invaded by ungodly projects: hedonism, materialism, and ideologies are tools used by Satan to deceive humankind.

The church today must be an anticipation of God's kingdom. The promotion of categories such as peace, justice and joy in the Spirit is something that certainly begins with the preaching of the gospel, but it does not stop there. The time has come when the debate about justice must include not only the question of whether the definition of the term is mainly, say, relational, but also whether that concept has anything to say to socio-political structures, economics, and international relations. For of course all property, private or state-owned, every empire, personal or national, all wealth, individual or corporate, will be subjected to God's reign. And so it seems wise to find out if what we do today is in line with what he will do in the future, if what we do today will be destroyed as part of the evil he will eradicate when 'The kingdom of the world has become the kingdom of our Lord and of his Christ, and he will reign for ever and ever' (Rev. 11:15).

IV. CONCLUSION

(1) The justice of God is not a justice that remains an abstract construct. His justice is a model, a goal, a trajectory that begins with him, is shown in Jesus Christ, is modelled by his people and finds its final expression in the consummated kingdom of God. Therefore, the 'here and now' of God's kingdom seeks to express the justice of God in all human institutions. This is something the church must promote according to the vocations of her members.

(2) Sin is a harsh human reality. It is not true that changing human hearts will of itself necessarily produce a just world. Before this harsh fact we must widen our comprehension of the Church's mission in the following terms: (a) Rethink the whole of reality. Provincial perspectives do not allow one to see the needs of other 'worlds'. (b) Preach the whole counsel of God. We must announce that God is our true basis of justice. (c) Rediscover the place of justice in God's plan for the Church. Before the world's fragile sense of morality, we must seek moral leadership in society.

(3) God has imputed his righteousness to us, and this truth goes beyond what is offered in any merely philosophical or legal notion of justice. The justice of God granted to us is especially his justice in Christ. On the one hand, there is a gracious distribution of justice given to the one who believes. This is a reflection of distributive justice in so far as it is given to us freely in Jesus Christ. But on the other hand, justification demands a righteous life: an effort is required to influence and even to create political, economic, and jurisprudential institutions for the administration of justice where there is none. That creativity, promotion, and effort reflect productive justice.

(4) Justice must also be related not only to individual ethics, important as they may be, but also to the whole of human life — not least in those spheres that either make the practice of good more difficult and facilitate the preaching of the gospel, or *vice versa*.

(5) The situation in some Third World countries is such that when theologians go to the Bible they are looking for answers to some of the most basic questions in life. 'To eat or not to eat, that is the question.' Therefore, just as the Bible is a source of answers to the basic questions of life in the Western world, so theologians in the so-called Third World take it as their duty to look for answers for our context.

Sometimes the need to be specific calls for criticism of the Eastern and Western blocs of nations, whose history is linked to that of smaller and poorer countries. Theologians from these countries need to be ready to challenge the source and the methodology of some Third World theologies, but not to react adversely to their content merely because they sound new. The dialogue must be kept open, because, after all, the theological task is never complete; each generation asks a slightly different set of questions.

Theological systems take time to develop, and corrections have to be made along the way. To be involved in this process is the task of the whole body of Christ, based upon the written revelation of God. Here we must ask ourselves, 'What is the place of the church as the world's conscience, *vis-à-vis* other consciences in the world?' If the unredeemed, who do not know God's standards, proclaim high moral ethics by which most of them cannot abide, is it wrong for the church to proclaim God's character as a true measure of justice for all human activities? Is this not at least part of our pre-evangelism, and therefore part of our life?

11

Justification and Roman Catholicism

KLAAS RUNIA

I. INTRODUCTION

For the Reformers and those who stood in their tradition the doctrine of the justification of the sinner by faith alone (*sola fide*) was always of the utmost importance. In the Lutheran Reformation it was called 'the article upon which the church stands or falls' (*ecclesia stantis et cadentis ecclesiae*). Although Luther, as far as we know, never used this expression, it was certainly in agreement with his position. In the *Smalkald Articles* he wrote about the article on justification: 'Nothing in this article can be given up or compromised, even if heaven and earth and things temporal should be destroyed. On this article rests all that we teach and practise against the pope, the devil, and the world' (II,1). In other words, for Luther and his followers this article was 'a criterion or corrective for all church practices, structures, and theology'.[1] In the Reformed Reformation it was not different. Calvin called the doctrine of justification 'the main hinge on which religion turns'.[2] In our own day the Dutch Reformed theologian G. C. Berkouwer declares: 'The confession of divine justification touches man's life at its heart, at the point of its relationship to God; it defines the preaching of the church, the existence and progress of the life of faith, the root of human security, and man's perspective for the future.'[3]

It was at this very point that the conflict between Luther and the Church of Rome of his day came to a head. The Council of Trent emphatically rejected the view of justification as advocated by the Reformers. In the 'Introduction to the Decree' it spoke of an 'erroneous' doctrine which is disseminated 'not without the loss of many souls and grievous detriment to the unity of the church'. In Chapter VII of the Decree itself justification is described as 'not only a remission of sins but also the sanctification and renewal of the inward man through the voluntary reception of the grace and gifts whereby an unjust man becomes just'. In other words, justification is not a *declaratory* act on God's part, by which God declares the sinner who believes in Jesus Christ as his Saviour to be forgiven and therefore righteous in his sight, but Trent espouses a *transformationist* view: God's judgment is based on the transformation his grace has effected *in* the sinner. Justification thus is a part of sanctification and actually based on the renewal that has already taken place in man himself.[4] In some of the Canons of Trent the view of the Reformers is explicitly condemned. Here, for example, are four of the most important of them.

> 9. If anyone shall say that the sinner is justified by faith alone, meaning that nothing else is required to cooperate in order to obtain the grace of justification, and that it is not in any way necessary that he be prepared and disposed by the action of his own will — *anathema sit* [let him be anathema].

> 11. If anyone shall say that men are justified either by the sole imputation of the justice of Christ or by the sole remission of sins, to the exclusion of the grace and charity that is poured forth in their hearts by the Holy Spirit and remains in them, or also that the grace by which we are justified is only the good will of God — *anathema sit*.

> 12. If anyone shall say that justifying faith is nothing else but confidence in divine mercy, which remits sins for Christ's sake, or that it is this confidence alone that justifies us — *anathema sit*.

> 24. If anyone shall say that the justice received is not preserved and also increased before God through good works, but that those works are merely the fruits and signs of justification obtained, but not the cause of its increase — *anathema sit*.

It is no wonder that since Trent this sharp difference in the doctrine of justification was seen by both sides as one of the central aspects, if not *the* central aspect, of the conflict. So it was seen by all Lutheran and Reformed theologians of the 16th and 17th centuries. So it was clearly stated in all the Reformation confessions. Berkouwer notes that in the *Belgic Confession*, the *Heidelberg Catechism* and the *Canons of Dort* there is a 'striking harmony' on the central issue of the *sola fide*. He strongly rejects any suggestion of a difference between the Lutheran and Calvinist Reformation at this point.[5] The same position was taken by the Thirty-Nine Articles and the leading Anglican Divines of the 16th and 17th centuries.[6] But the Reformers and their followers were not the only ones to see the doctrine of justification as *the* locus of the conflict. For their part the magisterium of the Roman Catholic Church and all the leading Roman Catholic theologians of the Reformation period and of the following centuries maintained that the Reformation doctrine of *sola fide* was so one-sided that it constituted no less than a serious heresy. In fact, in 1653 the Roman Catholic Church again condemned certain Augustinian views, which were very close to the Reformation position and at that time were held by the so-called Jansenists. Sixty years later, in 1713, the Constitution *Uniqenitus* again condemned certain views held by the Jansenist Pasquier Quesnel. Among the condemned statements were the following:

> 10. Grace is the operation of the hand of almighty God, which nothing can hinder or retard.

> 13. When God wills to save a soul, and touches it with the inner hand of his grace, no human will resists it.

> 38. A sinner is not free, except to do evil, without the grace of Christ.

> 69. Faith, its increase, use and reward, is totally a gift of the pure liberality of God.

When at the First Vatican Council, in the session held on March 22, 1870, Ströszmayer protested against the notion that nearly all modern errors, such as rationalism, pantheism and materialism, were due to the 'revolution' of the Reformers, his last words were drowned out by the loud negative voices of the other council fathers.[7] As late as 1910 the notorious *Borromeo Encyclical* praised Carlo Borromeo (1538–1584), a contemporary of Trent, for his fight against those 'proud and rebellious men, enemies of the cross of Christ . . . men of earthly sentiments "whose god is their belly" . . . who were corrupters . . .'. By these evil men were meant the Reformers. Although there was some criticism of this encyclical within Roman Catholic circles, nearly all Roman Catholic theologians up to World War II were unanimous in the rejection of the Reformation understanding of justification as a complete misunderstanding of the biblical doctrine and they wholeheartedly defended the doctrine as defined by Trent.

II. A CLIMATE OF CHANGE

After World War II, however, an entirely new phase started. A new appraisal of the Reformers took place within certain sections of Roman Catholic theology. The Reformers were no longer seen as evil and licentious men, or as revolutionaries and heretics, but as pious men who really wanted to reform the church and earnestly tried to listen to the Scriptures.[8] As a matter of fact, the whole climate within the new Roman Catholic theology itself changed. It earnestly tried to get away from the scholastic methods of theologising which had dominated Catholic theology since the Middle Ages and made its own attempt to listen anew to Scripture itself. It also developed a new view of the church's dogma by emphasising the historical dynamics in its development and the historical, time-conditioned aspect in its formulations. These changes in the understanding of the Reformation, of the Scriptures and of the historical nature of the church's dogma also deeply affected the traditional view of justification.

As early as 1952 the Dutch theologian W. H. van der Pol, who after a study of Newman's doctrine of justification had entered the Roman Catholic Church and afterwards became professor at the Roman Catholic University of Nijmegen, denied that there was an essential difference between the Reformation and Rome concerning justification. After stating Paul's view in the following words: 'Without any merit on the part of the believer his sins are forgiven him and the righteousness of Christ is granted him in exchange, strictly through grace alone. For if there were any mention here of merits, grace would no longer be grace', he went on to say: 'This is precisely the doctrine of the Roman Catholic Church'![9] A little further he wrote: 'The *sola fide* as [sic] the Apostle Paul has in mind, in particular in his letters to the Romans and Galatians, is fully accepted by the Catholic Church.'

Van der Pol's views, however, did not make a great impact at the time. The real breakthrough came with the publication of Hans Küng's doctoral thesis on *Justification: The Doctrine of Karl Barth and a Catholic Reflection* in 1957 (ET in 1964). In this thesis, written under the supervision of Karl Barth himself, the young Roman Catholic theologian arrived at the conclusion that in principle there was no difference between the doctrine of justification of

Barth and that of the Roman Catholic Church. 'The time of antithesis is over.'[10] How was such a conclusion possible? Did Küng perhaps misinterpret Barth? No, for Barth himself said that Küng gave a correct interpretation of his view. The real clue was that, according to Küng, Protestant theology had continually misinterpreted Trent. Again and again Protestant theologians, including Barth himself, had interpreted Trent as teaching a synergistic doctrine of salvation. Küng denied this. According to him Trent, no less than the Reformation, maintained *sola fide*, by faith alone, and *soli Deo gloria*, to God alone be all glory (the titles of two chapters in Küng's book). The reason for all this misunderstanding (quite often also on the Roman Catholic side!) was that people on both sides of the conflict tended to forget that the statements of Trent were made in a polemical situation. They were directed against heresy or against views that were regarded as heresy and therefore the statements themselves were inevitably one-sided. Trent condemned the declaratory view of justification as found in the Reformers, because it did not realise that this declaration does include becoming righteous. On the other hand, the Reformers did not realise that the transformationist view of the Roman Catholic Church did presuppose the declaratory verdict of God.

How must we evaluate Küng's novel approach? It cannot be denied, of course, that throughout the centuries there have been many misinterpretations and caricatures on both sides.[11] But was it really *only* a matter of misunderstanding? Many Protestant and Roman Catholic theologians have taken issue with Küng at this very point. In his introductory letter to Küng's book Barth already expressed his serious doubts about Küng's interpretation of Trent. 'You can imagine my considerable amazement at this bit of news; and I suppose that many Roman Catholic readers will at first be no less amazed.' Barth cannot but wonder whether what Küng presents really represents the teaching of his church:

> If the things you cite from Scripture, from older and more recent Roman Catholic theology, from Denziger and hence from the Tridentine text, do actually represent the teaching of your church and are established as such, . . . then, having twice gone to the church of Santa Maria Maggiore in Trent to commune with the *genius loci*, I may very well have to hasten there a third time to make contrite confession — 'Fathers, I have sinned'. But taking the statements of the Sixth Session as we now have them before us — statements correctly or incorrectly formulated for reasons then considered compelling — don't you agree that I should perhaps be permitted to plead mitigating circumstances for the considerable difficulty I had trying to discover in that text what you have found to be true Catholic teaching? How do you explain the fact that all this could remain hidden for so long and from so many, both outside and inside the Church?'[12]

Likewise other Protestant scholars, such as G. C. Berkouwer,[13] Rudolf J. Ehrlich,[14] and Alister McGrath,[15] regard Küng's interpretation of Trent as 'incorrect and historically untenable'.[16] Several leading Roman Catholic theologians share this view.[17]

In spite of all this criticism Küng's book must be seen as a real breakthrough in the ecumenical study of the Reformation. It signalled a new way of approaching the centuries-old conflict. Other young Roman Catholic theologians took up the lead and tried to refine the argumentation used by

Küng. For instance, Otto Hermann Pesch wrote a work of over one thousand pages on the theology of 'Justification in Martin Luther and in Thomas Aquinas'.[18] His final conclusion was: 'Under the proviso that in all the questions stated here Thomas represents the doctrine of the Church and has been interpreted correctly, we must say that, although Luther's doctrine of the justification of the sinner does leave the territory of the theology of his own time and also of the preceding time, he nevertheless does not enter a new territory (*Neuland*) that the Roman Catholic theologian is forbidden to enter.' Although many Protestant theologians were deeply impressed by Pesch's study, they were not yet convinced that he had really proved that there was no essential difference between the Reformation and Thomas, still less Trent. Both G. C. Berkouwer and H. A. Oberman were of the opinion that also in the case of Pesch there was too much of an attempt to synthesise the two positions.[19] At the same time they did not deny that Pesch and his fellow-interpreters of Thomas and Trent had made a great contribution to a better understanding of the Roman Catholic position in the time of the Reformation.

In the final analysis, however, the correctness of either view cannot be determined by the research of the historians or by the interpretation (or re-interpretation) of the systematic theologians, but by the exegesis of Scripture. The decisive question is: Was Luther, when he appealed to the New Testament and in particular to the letters of Paul, right or wrong? It is interesting to note that in our day many Roman Catholic exegetes admit that Luther's interpretation of Paul's doctrine of justification *was* correct. The Roman Catholic scholar K. Kertelge admits that justification is 'the theological centre of gravity in the chief epistles of Paul' and constitutes his 'real theology'.[20] Likewise Hans Küng acknowledges that 'Luther with his chief statements on the doctrine of justification, with his *sola gratia*, his *sola fide*, his *simul justus et peccator*, is backed by the New Testament and in particular by Paul whose view is ultimate and decisive in the doctrine of justification'.[21] Many Roman Catholic scholars also recognise that Paul uses the term 'to justify' in 'a declarative, forensic sense'.[22] The Anglo-Catholic scholar N. P. Williams states that *dikaioun* as used by Paul means 'to deem, declare, or admit someone to be righteous, or in the right', and says on the basis of the terms used in Romans: 'It is thus the gateway to the Christian life, not a part of an event in that Christian life itself — a gateway which in the nature of things can only be passed once in a lifetime and once for all'.[23]

In the meantime there have also been developments on the other side of the fence. Unfortunately, we have to say here that among Protestants the doctrine of justification is no longer always recognised as *the* central and determinative theme in the Christian doctrine of salvation and the Christian life. Most disturbing and disquieting was the treatment of justification at the Fourth Assembly of the Lutheran World Federation, held in 1964 at Helsinki. In one of the addresses it was said that the Reformation witness to justification had been in the threefold 'Babylonian captivity' of 'doctrinalisation, individualisation, and spiritualisation' and should be freed from this captivity by focussing on the entire human race and on 'amnesty for all'. By this universalist tendency the *sola fide* was robbed of its intensely personal and determinative character. Particularly alarming was the fact that some questioned the contrast between forensic and transformationist views of

justification. 'The old alternative whether the sinner is considered justified
... "forensically" — or ... "effectively" — is begging the question', for
God's action brings about 'rebirth'. Another address insisted that 'the act
through which God forgives is at the same time that act through which God
renews'.[24] In the message of Helsinki we find a strong tendency to
accommodate the church's emphasis on and understanding of justification to
the needs of modern man. It says that the most burning question of modern
man is no longer about a gracious God, but about the meaning of life. We
read:

> Man of today no longer asks: How do I get a gracious God? He asks a much
> more radical and elementary question, he asks for God as such: Where are you,
> God? He no longer suffers under the wrath of God, but under the impression of
> God's absence; he no longer suffers under his sin, but under the meaninglessness
> of his existence; he no longer asks for the gracious God, but whether God really
> exists.

Apparently the drafters of this message had forgotten Karl Barth's prophetic
statement in Part IV.1 of his *Church Dogmatics*, written in 1953:

> Of all the superficial catch-words of our age, surely one of the most superficial is
> that, whereas 16th century man was occupied with the grace of God, modern
> man is much more radically concerned about God Himself and as such. As
> though there were such a thing as God Himself and as such! As though grace
> were a quality of God which we could set aside while we leisurely ask concerning
> His existence! . . . As though 16th century man with his concern for the grace of
> God and the right of His grace were not asking about God Himself and His
> existence with a radicalness compared with which the questioning of modern
> man is empty frivolity![25]

These two almost opposing movements — Roman Catholic theology
moving towards the recognition of the centrality of justification in the New
Testament, and Protestant theology (at least in some cases) moving away
from this centrality — show how much the doctrine of justification is caught
up in the turmoil of modern thought. Almost naturally this leads to the
question: how does the Reformation doctrine of justification fare in the
recent bilateral discussions?

III.   JUSTIFICATION IN RECENT LUTHERAN–ROMAN CATHOLIC DIALOGUES

In 1972 a statement was published by a Joint Study Committee, appointed by
the Luteran World Federation and the Secretariat for Promoting Christian
Unity. It is known as the *Malta Report*, since the final drafting was done in
San Anton, Malta, in 1971, and was published under the name 'The Gospel
and the Church'.[26] The section on justification was short. It did say that
'today . . . a far-reaching consensus is developing in the interpretation of
justification'. No grounds are given, nor do we get any indication why this
consensus is developing. Is it the result of a changing 'mood' in present-day
theology? Or is it due to a change in biblical and confessional hermeneutics?

Or is it perhaps due to a growing convergence in religious experience on both sides of the divide? We do not receive an answer to these questions. It is granted, however, that justification may indeed be seen as the general expression of the saving event and as an important expression of the centre of the gospel. At the same time it also admits that there is still much need for a fuller treatment of the subject and its implications.

This need was met in the dialogue on justification by a joint Commission of American Lutherans and Roman Catholics. The discussions on this topic started in 1978 and resulted in a very important 24,000 word statement, released in 1983 under the title *Justification by Faith*.[27] This document is a landmark in the dialogue between the Reformation and Rome. Alister McGrath, a specialist in the history of the doctrine of justification,[28] calls it 'by far the most important ecumenical document to deal with the theme of justification to date'. He is of the opinion that 'the analysis and conclusions of this document are reliable' and that 'it is, quite simply, a masterpiece'.[29]

After a short introduction the document deals with three topics: the history of the question; reflection and interpretation; and perspectives for reconstruction. It is, naturally, impossible to give a full summary of the document, since in its condensed form it contains a huge amount of information. We must, therefore, confine ourselves to some of the major points and findings. The Introduction mentions a 'christological affirmation' on which they are all agreed. Since both parties believe that 'Jesus Christ is the source and centre of all Christian life and of the existence and work of the church', they affirm:

> Our entire hope of justification and salvation rests on Jesus Christ and on the gospel whereby the good news of God's merciful action in Christ is made known; we do not place our ultimate trust in anything other than God's promise and saving work in Christ (16).

In all honesty they add that it does not mean that they have a full agreement on justification by faith, but 'it does raise the question . . . whether the remaining differences on this doctrine need be church-dividing'.

A. The History of the Question

In Part I they begin by stating that the controversy about justification is a typically Western problem. It was Augustine who in his struggle with Pelagius emphasised justification by grace alone. However, he took *justification* as meaning 'to *make* righteous' and thus developed the idea of justification as a *transformationist process* in man. While Augustine stressed the total need of grace on the part of human beings, his transformationist model allowed for growing speculation about the human role in the process. This led to various developments: (1) In the concept of grace all kinds of distinctions were made, gradually and increasingly leading to a discussion of the potentialities of human nature itself. (2) A doctrine of merit was developed, whereby a distinction was made between 'congruous' merit (a reward on grounds of fitness and based on God's generous character) and 'condign' merit (a reward due in strict justice to services rendered). While the latter was generally rejected, some theologians accepted the former. It was seen as a 'basis for a hope that God "does not deny grace to those who do what is in them" (*facientibus quod in se est Deus non denegat gratiam*)' (19). This 'doing what is

in oneself' could easily become a 'condition' which man had to fulfil in order
to receive grace. In fact, it became one of the reasons for 'the rampant
scrupulosity' of the late Middle Ages and was viewed by the Reformers as a
cause of the 'terrified conscience' (20). (3) In the doctrine of predestination
we observe in some medieval currents of thought a shift to the idea that God's
decree is based on the foreseen merits of man.

From all this it is clear that during the Middle Ages there were many
different schools of thought. Summing up their study of the post-Augustinian
developments the statement observes 'a bewildering variety', in which
Augustinian intentions are combined with emphases on the possibilities of
human nature itself. 'Everyone professed to be Augustinian and anti-
Pelagian, but there was little agreement on what these terms meant' (21).

Turning to the 16th century debate the document states that the Reformers'
appeal to Paul's doctrine of justification 'by faith apart from works of law'
(Rom. 3:28 RSV) was occasioned by two chief problems. The first was the
'rampant Pelagianism' that was noticeable in medieval trends both in popular
piety and in theology. Indulgences, with their practice of 'buying' salvation,
are mentioned in particular. The second (and perhaps major) problem was
the need to 'console terrified consciences'. Luther himself knew this from his
own experience. His question 'How do I get a gracious God?' was not yet
answered by Augustine's *sola gratia* [by grace alone], as long as the good
works still played a part in salvation. Listening to Paul he came to the answer
of *sola fide* [by faith alone]: we can trust in nothing but God's promise of
mercy and forgiveness in Jesus Christ. It is on the basis of the 'alien' or
'extrinsic' righteousness of Christ that God justifies, that is, *declares* the
sinner just. This justification is complete. The sinner is totally justified, even
though in himself he still is a sinner. Hence the famous phrase *simul justus et
peccator* [at the same time justified and a sinner]. This view of justification
meant an entirely new mode of thinking which was markedly different from
that of Augustine and medieval theology. Instead of a progressive transformationist model, based on God's gift of infused grace and of inherent
righteousness, Luther adopts an instantaneous and complete justification on
the basis of the *justitia aliena* (the 'strange' righteousness) of Christ.

Although in the ensuing controversies justification was by no means always
the central issue (*cf.* the censures passed by several theological faculties,
which centred on questions related to free will, the alleged sinfulness of good
works, penance, the value of indulgences, etc., rather than on justification
itself, 26), Luther's opponents realised full well that this new view of
justification touched the heart of the matter. In the *Confutatio* of the
Confession of Augsburg they described the doctrine of justification by faith
alone as 'diametrically opposed to the evangelical truth, which does not
exclude works' (29). All attempts to mediate between the two positions (as,
for instance, at the Colloquy of Regensburg, 32) were rejected by both
Luther and Rome.

Finally, in 1542 Pope Paul III decided to convoke a council, which
convened on December 13, 1545. The debate on justification started on June
22, 1546 and took nearly six months. The fathers of the Council knew full well
what they were doing. On June 21 Marcello Cervini (afterwards Pope
Marcellus II) reminded them that no preceding council had dealt fully with
this doctrine and that Luther's doctrine of justification by faith only was at the

root of most of his errors on the sacraments, the power of the keys, indulgences and purgatory.[30] The matter could not easily be decided, however, because there were different schools of thought present at the Council.[31] Some, such as San Felice, Bishop of La Cava, openly pleaded for the doctrine of justification by faith only. However, when in October a vote was taken on the question whether justification is inherent or imputed, the latter was rejected by a vote of 32 to 5. In other words, the Council opted for a transformationist view of justification.

This we clearly observe in the decree that was promulgated on January 13, 1547. The American document gives a fair summary of this decree that contains the official doctrine of the Roman Catholic Church on justification. The council reaffirms the unique role of Christ in our salvation. 'Nothing prior to justification', whether faith or works, truly merits the grace of justification. The preparation for justification is also a matter of God's predisposing grace in Christ. In other words, the Council sides with Augustine over against Pelagius, and with Orange II over against Semi-Pelagianism. However important this may be, it is not the end of the matter. For after this auspicious beginning it is added that the sinner is called to cooperate with this grace by not wilfully rejecting it. When this happens God's righteousness is infused (*gratia infusa*) into the sinner, whereby he is *made* righteous. All this is accepted by the sinner by faith (the council clearly teaches the primacy of faith!), but this faith is not living unless it is faith working through love. As a matter of fact, faith, hope and charity are infused at the same time. Thanks to this justification human beings are renewed and 'as faith cooperates with good works', they grow and are further justified. In other words, within the context of prevenient grace, there is room for (indeed, the necessity of) human activity and human merit. Whether the latter is a congruous or a condign merit remains unclear. Hence the many debates on this score after Trent.[32] Finally, to avoid the suspicion that this stress on faith and works might derogate from the saving power of Christ, the council declares at the very end of the last chapter: 'Far be it from Christians to trust or glory in themselves and not in the Lord (*cf.* 1 Cor. 1:31; 2 Cor. 10:17), whose bounty toward all is so great that he wishes his own gifts to be their merits'.[33]

It is evident that, in spite of the emphasis on the absolute need of grace, this is a view of justification distinctly different from that of Luther. It is therefore surprising that the document says: 'The Tridentine decree on justification, with its own way of insisting on the primacy of grace . . ., is not necessarily incompatible with the Lutheran doctrine of sola fide, even though Trent excluded this phrase' (35). I find this statement surprising, because Trent emphatically upheld the Augustinian and medieval tranformationist view, in which justification is virtually nothing but the first stage of sanctification[34] and in which therefore man, with his activity and good works, is included from the very beginning. For Luther, on the other hand, justification is nothing but the gateway to salvation, in which God does everything, declaring the sinner just on the basis of the alien righteousness of Christ, while the sinner has nothing but an empty hand (*sola fide*, by faith *alone*), in which he receives this gracious gift of God. Only after entering through this gateway is the sinner set on the road of sanctification and is he called to do the good works 'which God prepared in advance for us to do' (Eph. 2:10). How deep the difference between the two views runs, appears from the different perception of the assurance of salvation. For Luther this is included in the *sola fide* (if a person really trusts in this alien righteousness of Christ, he *is* at that very moment assured of his salvation). According to Trent this is impossible, and this conclusion is not surprising, for how can a person be sure of his salvation if this salvation depends on an inherent righteousness which can be lost through deadly sins, and partly also on the good works which have to accompany the grace given to him?

Another point at which the wide and deep gap between the two views becomes visible is the doctrine of the sacraments. For Trent itself there was a clear and inseparable connection between its own doctrine of justification and its doctrine of the sacraments. Not only was the latter the next subject for discussion and decision, but the Foreword of the Decree on the Sacraments begins as follows: 'For the completion of the salutary doctrine on justification . . . it has seemed proper to deal with the most holy sacraments of the Church through which all true justice either begins or, being begun, is increased, or being lost, is restored.' This inseparable connection is not surprising, for the council's view of the sacraments is also thoroughly transformationist. Accordingly we read in Canon 4 on 'The Sacraments in General': 'If any one shall say that the sacraments of the New Law are not necessary for salvation but are superfluous, and without them or without the desire of them men obtain from God *through faith alone*[35] the grace of justification, though all are not necessary for every individual — let him be anathema.' Likewise we read in Canon 8: 'If any one shall say that by the sacraments of the New Law grace is not conferred *ex opere operato* [through the act performed], but that *faith alone in the divine promise*[36] is sufficient to obtain grace — let him be anathema.' It is evident that the sacraments are necessary for obtaining justification, for it is by means of the sacraments that the grace of God becomes inherent in man, and only on the basis of this inherent grace is it possible for God to justify man.

B.   Reflection and Interpretation

In the second part of the American document, which is called 'Reflection and Interpretation', the question is asked whether these different patterns of thought should not be seen as, at least in part, complementary rather than necessarily divisive (49). The view taken is that the different patterns of thought are related to 'contrasting concerns'. Lutherans want to safeguard the absolute priority of God's redeeming word in Christ and therefore exclude all reliance on self for salvation. Catholics, while not rejecting the absolute priority of God's saving action, are generally more concerned with the efficacy of God's saving work in the renewal and sanctification of the creation. These different concerns lead to notably different patterns of thought and discourse. Lutherans, concerned with the sinner standing before God (*coram Deo*) and hearing at one and the same time God's words of judgment and forgiveness in law and gospel, focus all attention on this 'discontinuous, paradoxical, and simultaneous double relation of God to the justified', whereas Catholics, concerned with the renewal of the creation by God's grace, express themselves most easily in transformationist language which describes the process of renewal through God's infusion of saving grace.

At first glance this may seem to be a simple and straightforward description of the difference, the reader easily getting the impression that the difference is not much more than a matter of two sides of one and the same coin. The document, however, goes on and honestly shows that the difference goes much deeper than that. These two different concerns and their consequent different modes of thinking and speaking entail differences on many other points as well. Six of them are singled out: (1) The forensic nature of justification (50); (2) the sinfulness of the justified — the famous *simul justus et peccator* (at once justified and a sinner) (51); (3) the sufficiency of faith — *sola fide* (by faith alone), or *fides caritate formata* (faith formed by love) (52); (4) the concept of merit (54); (5) the concept of satisfaction, entailing such practices as the sacrament of penance, masses for special intentions, indulgences, and the doctrine of purgatory (55); (6) criteria for authenticity — when is a person authentically Christian? (56). In each case the different perspectives and interests are shown and an attempt is made to indicate that the other party shares the same concerns, even though they may be expressed and emphasised differently. After all this, it no longer surprises the reader that at the end of this section the document comes to the following conclusion.

> If this interpretation is correct, Lutherans and Catholics can share in each others' concerns in regard to justification and can to some degree acknowledge the legitimacy of the contrasting theological perspectives and structures of thought. Yet, on the other hand, some of the consequences of the different outlooks seem irreconcilable, especially in reference to particular applications of justification by faith as a criterion of all church proclamation and practice (57).

C. Perspectives for Reconstruction

In its third and last part the document looks ahead and tries to show ways of further rapprochement. It first points to a number of growing convergences and outright agreements in the exegesis of Scripture. In our day Catholics have also come to acknowledge that 'righteousness/justification is more prevalent in NT teaching than has normally been suspected in earlier centuries or among earlier commentators, and that it is an image of prime importance for our expression of the Christ-event or even the gospel' (58). It is also generally recognised that Paul was not the 'inventor' of the doctrine of justification, but that it is pre-Pauline in origin (60). It is true, however, that Paul, in his conflict with the Judaisers, did sharpen the meaning of the doctrine. Several other areas of convergence are mentioned as well.

The very last section, called 'growing convergences', begins with the candid admission that there are still considerable differences as to whether justification should be the criterion for the question of which beliefs, practices and structures are acceptable. Special mention is made here of purgatory, the papacy and the cult of the saints (69). Next, twelve material convergences are mentioned. In the fifth one we read: 'Justification, as a transition from disfavour and unrighteousness to favour and righteousness in God's sight , is totally God's work. By justification we are *both declared and made righteous*. Justification, therefore, is not a legal fiction. God, in justifying, effects what he promises; he forgives sin and makes us truly righteous.'[37] The twelve material convergences lead to two conclusions, which we shall quote in full.

The first conclusion begins with a repetition of the 'christological affirmation' which was mentioned at the beginning of the document.

> *Our entire hope of justification and salvation rests on Christ Jesus and on the gospel whereby the good news of God's merciful action in Christ is made known; we do not place our ultimate trust in anything other than God's promise and saving work in Christ.* Such an affirmation is not fully equivalent to the Reformation teaching on justification according to which God accepts sinners as righteous for Christ's sake on the basis of faith alone; but by its insistence that reliance for salvation should be placed entirely on God, it expresses a central concern of that doctrine. Yet it does not exclude the traditional Catholic position that the grace-wrought transformation of sinners is a necessary preparation for final salvation (72).
>
> It must be emphasised that our common affirmation that it is God in Christ alone whom believers ultimately trust does not necessitate any one particular way of conceptualising or picturing God's saving work. That work can be expressed in the imagery of God as judge who pronounces sinners innocent and righteous . . ., and also in a transformist view which emphasises the change wrought in sinners by infused grace (72).

D. Evaluation

It will be self-evident that it is not a simple matter to evaluate this document properly. It certainly will not do to dismiss it as unimportant, on the grounds that nothing will really change anyhow, as long as Rome does not officially retract or at least modify the decisions of Trent. However true it may be that the decisions of Trent on justification are still the official doctrine of the Roman Catholic Church, we should not underestimate the significance of the historical and exegetical research of recent years and of these serious and frank bilateral dialogues. We shall make a mistake if we think little of the convergences in the exegesis of Scripture. It is no small thing that many Roman Catholic exegetes acknowledge the centrality and the forensic nature of justification in the New Testament and particularly in Paul. It is no small thing either that historical research has shown that the interpretation of Trent is not as simple as has often been thought by both Protestant and Roman Catholic theologians. Apparently different interpretations are possible, some of which are much closer to the Reformation view than others. In addition, we should not forget, as G. Carey has rightly pointed out, that 'while it is true that the magisterium has not actually made any statements that indicate a change of heart in the Vatican, we must observe that it has also not uttered any statement which has condemned this shift in interpretation'.[38] We must also agree with him that all this recent research has 'uncovered layers of deep misunderstanding'.[39] Likewise G. C. Berkouwer points out that today it is generally recognised 'that the antithesis that Trent posits between itself and Luther proceeded from certain presuppositions about the Reformation and that these assumptions in turn played a large role in the Counter-Reformation'.[40]

On the other hand, we should also be careful and not conclude too hastily and too easily that all the differences of the past were nothing but *misunderstandings*. Undoubtedly, there were many misunderstandings, sometimes owing to the fact that 'what was central to the Reformers was often secondary to their opponents; perhaps neither side fully considered the claims of the other' (22). One such misunderstanding, for instance, was the Roman Catholic interpretation of the Reformation view of 'forensic' justification as a 'legal fiction', which had no ethical consequences whatsoever. Another misunderstanding is the charge by some Lutheran and Reformed theologians that Trent was nothing else than a repetition of the old heresy of Semi-Pelagianism. Yet it is hard to believe that the *whole* 16th century conflict was a matter of misunderstandings. Both sides were generally well aware of what the other side taught and believed.

The conflict was undoubtedly also more than a matter of *different concerns and patterns of thought*. We do not deny that there is some truth in this suggestion. It is a fact that 'many of the difficulties have arisen from the contrasting concerns and patterns of thought in the two traditions' (49). Yet to acknowledge this does not really solve the centuries-old conflict with its deep-seated differences. This already appears from the fact that it is impossible to telescope the two views and to unify them into a seamless harmony. I do not contend that the American report tries to do this. The participants in the dialogue were too honest to make such an attempt. Yet it cannot be denied that at times they too tend to harmonise various aspects of the two views, which in actual fact are irreconcilable. For instance, in the section on the biblical data they first admit that Paul in Gal. 2:16 uses 'to justify' in a declarative, forensic sense, but then immediately add: 'Yet since justification has not only a forensic sense but also represents God's power at work, sinners are "rendered righteous" (*cf.* Rom. 5:19); this involves righteousness both in an ethical sense and before God' (62). Protestant exegetes, such as Herman Ridderbos, maintain that in Rom. 5:19 'to justify' is used in a 'strictly' forensic sense. Käsemann speaks of an 'eschatological' righteousness. In the next paragraph Gal. 2:21 is quoted ('through faith, not through the law'), but then the writers immediately add: 'Faith is also something "which works itself out through love" (Gal. 5:6)', and conclude: 'Such an understanding . . . avoids much of the sixteenth-century acrimony over the interpretation of Gal. 5:6' (62). But this kind of argumentation is of no help whatsover; for it all depends on the context in which these phrases occur. In Gal. 2 Paul speaks about justification in the strict sense of the term and therefore emphasises the *sola fide* (by faith alone); in Gal. 5 he again speaks of justification which is imperilled when the Galatians think that in addition to Christ's work they also need circumcision and, consequently, the keeping of the law. Again Paul emphasises the need for faith in Christ, but now he adds that this faith does not disparage the keeping of the law, for it is 'a faith that works itself out through love'. At this point both Luther and Calvin also followed Paul. Neither they nor any of the other Reformers ever denied that the faith of justification issues in love. Calvin, for instance, quite clearly stated that 'it is faith alone that justifies, but the faith that justifies is not alone'![41]

Although we have to criticise the document on these points, we do not want to say that the authors are unaware of remaining differences. In fact, at several points they mention them quite honestly. They admit that, even though Catholics believe that God's saving will has no cause outside himself and that therefore salvation in its totality is unconditional, nevertheless they also believe that within this totality there are a number of elements, some of which are conditional upon others (50). They further admit that Lutherans think that the Catholic emphasis on the infusion of grace makes it difficult to express adequately the unmerited character of God's forgiving mercy (51). There is a different appreciation of sin in believers; Catholics continue to have difficulty in accepting Luther's *simul justus et peccator* (at once justified and a sinner) (51). There remains the difference about the nature of justifying faith. Is it *fides sola* (faith alone) or *fides caritate formata* (faith formed by love) (52–3)? Catholics still hold that 'the good works of the righteous give a title to salvation itself in the sense that God has covenanted to save those who, prompted by grace, obey his will' (54). Catholics also hold that the sufferings of penitent sinners and of the innocent can be prayerfully applied to beseech God's mercy and pardon (55/6). The document in all frankness states that further study on this last point is needed in order to determine whether and how far Lutherans and Catholics can agree on such points as the sacrament of penance, masses for special intentions, indulgences and purgatory (56). All these 'traditionally disputed doctrines' may indeed be very hard to accept for Lutherans and other churches of the Reformation, since they have no basis in Scripture. But do not these same doctrines also show that the real issue has not by any means been solved? For these doctrines are not accidental accretions but 'natural' consequences of the Roman Catholic doctrine of grace.

IV. ARCIC II

In Great Britain, too, there have been bilateral discussions, this time between Anglicans and Roman Catholics. Here, too, a statement on the doctrine of justification has been released, under the title *Salvation and the Church*.[42] Compared with the American document (which was used by the participants of ARCIC II [7]), the British document is much weaker. The title, of course, is already eye-catching: 'Salvation and the Church'. In the preface the two co-chairmen write that they had been asked to address themselves to the doctrine of justification, but they felt that this could be handled only in the wider context of the doctrine of salvation as a whole, which led to a discussion of the role of the church in Christ's saving work. Naturally, this extension entailed the risk that the study would not be really focused on the doctrine of justification itself. Unfortunately, this is what indeed happened. The section on justification itself again starts with the broader concept of salvation. The very first paragraph says that 'the Scriptures speak of this salvation in many ways' (15). The next paragraph explicitly mentions a wide variety of terms, starting off with the remark: 'Some terms are of more fundamental importance than others; but there is no controlling term or concept; they complement one another' (16). In this way justification becomes just one of the many terms used in the New Testament, and there is virtually no way left for giving it its special place as the gateway to the new life. In paragraph 15 the document states that 'justification and sanctification are two aspects of the same divine act'. Nowhere does it become clear that they are two clearly distinct acts of God. Continually the two acts are related so closely that they seem to be one. The difference between the Reformation view which is forensic and declaratory and the Catholic view which is transformationist is blurred all the time. Typical is a statement such as this: 'God's grace effects what he declares: his creative word imparts what it imputes. By pronouncing us righteous, God also makes us righteous' (17). It is therefore quite understandable that the document has been criticised severely by evangelical Anglicans.

This does not mean that there are no good points. McGrath rightly points out that the document assists us by summarising the main points of agreement between the churches, which were often obscured by controversy in the sixteenth and early seventeenth centuries.[43] It is helpful to have these misunderstandings clarified. But having enumerated these points of agreement McGrath has to admit that 'none of these points were actually the subject of real disagreement in the sixteenth century' and that the document 'appears somewhat reluctant to address the real disagreements which classical Anglican theologians perceived to exist between themselves and Rome'. This, of course, is a pleasant way of saying that the document contains no news and does not really help us to elucidate and overcome the existing differences!

On the basis of the document itself and of the articles mentioned in note 19 I feel obliged to make the following critical comments.

(1) It remains obscure what the real Anglican position is. In the note on page 10 of the document several Anglican divines of quite different theological colour are mentioned. Throughout the document the impression is given that Anglican theology stands somewhere between Reformation theology and Catholic theology and provides a *via media*.

(2) The agreements between the Reformation and the Roman Catholic Church are painted in such broad strokes that there seem to be hardly any real differences. Four difficulties are mentioned (the understanding of the faith through which we are justified; the understanding of justification and the associated concepts, righteousness and justice; the bearing of good works on salvation; and the role of the church in the process of salvation, 11ff.), but they are expressed in such a way that the conclusion is: they 'need not be matters of dispute between us' (13). In other words, the agreements are maximised and the disagreements are minimised.

(3) The historical part of the document must be severely criticised for this one-sidedness and incompleteness.[44]

(4) There is no clear distinction between justification and sanctification. It never becomes clear that 'although indissoluble, justification and sanctification are neither identical, nor simultaneous'.[45]

(5) Consequently there is no clear statement about the nature of justifying righteousness.[46] Is it the *justitia aliena* (strange righteousness) of Christ or is it an inherent righteousness? It is simply stated that the Reformers tended to follow the 'predominant' usage of *dikaioun* (the Greek verb) in the New Testament, which 'usually' means 'to pronounce righteous', while Catholic theologians and Trent followed the usage of patristic and medieval Latin writers, who translated *justificare* (the Latin verb) by 'to make righteous' (17). No choice is made! Hence the forensic nature of justification receives no special emphasis.

(6) The place of good works and of the concept of merit in the doctrine of salvation remains unclear.[47]

(7) In the final section on 'The Church and Salvation' there is no mention of

the ecclesiastical practices that follow from the Roman Catholic conception of grace and justification, such as indulgences, prayers for the dead, purgatorial penances, the cult of the saints, etc.[48]

(8) The statement makes no serious attempt to interpret any key passage from Scripture.[49]

In spite of all these weaknesses and shortcomings the document closes with the following conclusion:

> The balance and coherence of the constitutive elements of the Christian doctrine of salvation had become partially obscured in the course of history and controversy. In our work we have tried to rediscover that balance and coherence and to express it together. We are agreed that this is not an area where any remaining differences of theological interpretation or ecclesiological emphasis, either within or between our Communions, can justify our continuing separation. We believe that our two Communions are agreed on the essential aspects of the doctrine of salvation and on the Church's role within it (26).

In one way this conclusion surprises me; in another it does not. It surprises me that capable theologians and church-leaders can come to this conclusion on the basis of such scanty evidence. On the other hand, I am not surprised, because such a conclusion is possible only if one has not made a more profound and comprehensive study of this centuries-old conflict.

V.   EPILOGUE

Where do we stand today in the matter of justification? As we have seen before, the Lutheran World Conference of Helsinki was rather confused about the importance and centrality of justification for people of this day and age. Has the Roman Catholic Church also weakened its stand? Since Vatican I it is, of course, impossible for Rome to retract any official dogma of the church. But since the statement of Pope John XXIII, during the opening session of Vatican II, about the distinction between the substance of the faith, which is unchangeable, and the expression of the faith, which can be improved via more precise interpretation, there is the possibility for a further interpretation and even re-interpretation of Trent. Likewise it is possible to make clarifying additions. Some such additions have indeed been made by Vatican II (even though the doctrine of justification did not receive special attention). It broadened the definition of faith beyond the usual intellectual concept; it stressed the presence of Christ in the proclamation of the gospel; it emphasised that Christians should remember that their dignity is 'to be attributed not to their own merits, but to the special grace of Christ'. It also applied, at least to some extent, the *simul justus and peccator* (at once justified and a sinner) to the church itself, although at the same time it still put great emphasis on the role of the church and its sacraments in the doctrine of grace.[50]

We are also grateful that among many Roman Catholic theologians (especially the younger ones) there is a growing appreciation of Reformation view of justification. We should not underestimate the importance of this development. These theologians in many ways influence the thinking within their church, not only of the priests but also of many educated lay people. It is a matter for rejoicing that all kinds of misunderstandings have been removed and that many of the traditional caricatures (on both sides) have been recognised as such. Ecumenical dialogues, such as those between Lutherans and Roman Catholics in America, have proved to be very helpful on this score. No one can deny any longer that both the Reformation and Rome recognise that grace is indispensable for salvation. When McGrath says that all we have in common is an 'anti-Pelagian, Christocentric doctrine of justification'[51], he may be putting it too negatively and be minimising the common starting point. Wright rightly points out that Hooker already said that Catholic and Protestants were agreed 'that unto justice no man ever attained, but by the merits of Jesus Christ' and that Christ as God is the efficient cause and as man 'the meritorious cause of our justice'.[52] Likewise Berkouwer has pointed out that in the Roman Catholic doctrine of grace everything takes place within the circle of *gratia praeveniens* (prevenient grace). Even Trent said that we are justified gratuitously (*gratis*), 'because none of those things that precede justification, whether faith or works, merits the grace of justification, for "if by grace, it is not now by works", "otherwise", as the Apostle says, "grace is no more grace" (Rom. 11:6)'. This is also the reason why the American document can begin with its 'christological affirmation'.

And yet there remain deep-seated differences. They are not related to the starting point of salvation in grace, but to the *application* of this grace in the concrete life of believers. At this point there still is a wide and deep gap, in spite of all theological *rapprochement*. To this day Rome still retains its transformationist view of justification, together with the concomitant doctrines and practices. The significance of the latter for Roman Catholic faith and piety should not be underestimated. Steven Ozment, Professor of Ecclesiastic History at Harvard University, once listed the religious and social changes brought by the Reformation in 16th century Europe.

> Even in its most modest form the Reformation called for, and in most Protestant areas permanently achieved, an end to mandatory fasting; auricular confession; the worship of saints, relics, and images; indulgences; pilgrimages and shrines; vigils; weekly, monthly, and annual masses for the dead; the belief in purgatory; Latin worship services; the sacrifice of the Mass; numerous religious ceremonies, festivals, and holidays; the canonical hours; monasteries and mendicant orders; the sacraments of marriage, extreme unction, confirmation, holy orders, and penance; clerical celibacy; clerical immunity from civil taxation and criminal jurisdiction; non-resident benefices; excommunication and interdict; canon law; episcopal and papal authority, and the traditional scholastic education of the clergy.[53]

I do not wish to say that all matters in this list are connected with the Roman Catholic doctrine of grace, but it is obvious that a great many are. Some of them have even been sharpened in the centuries after Trent. We think in particular of Vatican I (and Vatican II!) on the infallibility of the pope, and of the mariological dogmas. Within the circle of prevenient and actual grace, man still plays an important role. The strongest evidence for this is perhaps found in the Mariology. The elevation of Mary simply underlines to what extent man is able to co-operate with God in the execution of his plan of salvation.[54] By its strong emphasis on justification as a forensic act of God, which can be accepted only by faith, the Reformation gave the death blow to all human co-operation at the very beginning of the application of salvation. Our salvation is entirely the work of God.

This does not mean that there is no place at all for human activity in salvation. In the first place the New Testament constantly sounds the call to *believe* in Jesus Christ. Undoubtedly this faith is not a 'work' in the sense that it adds anything to God's grace. As Calvin used to say, it is only the empty hand in which we receive his grace. But justification does not take place without this faith. At this very point we might well meet with *the* weakness in Karl Barth's doctrine of justification. Although he has written many beautiful pages on justification in his *Church Dogmatics*, and although he fully subscribes to the Reformation doctrine of *sola gratia* (by grace alone) and even to *sola fide* (by faith alone), it nevertheless is striking to note that in the fourth volume of his dogmatics he refuses to call justification 'the article by which the church stands and falls'.[55] To be sure, he does not deny that 'there never was and never can be any true Christian church without the doctrine of justification'. Yet at the same time he states that 'it relates *only to one aspect* of the Christian message of reconciliation'.[56] What then is the article by which the church does stand and fall? The answer is: 'the confession of Jesus Christ, in whom are hid all the treasures of wisdom and knowledge'. Naturally, it is hard to disagree here with Barth. Who would like to deny that Christ is the 'basis and culmination' even of the doctrine of justification? We may not forget, however, that Barth has his own particular view of Christ's place in God's plan of salvation. According to him everything has actually been decided already in all eternity, namely, in the election and rejection of Jesus Christ, who is the beginning of all God's ways and works. From all eternity the entire creation stands in the light of God's grace in Jesus Christ. Hence the 'objectivism' we find in Barth's doctrine of grace. The only real difference between the believer and the unbeliever is that the former knows about grace, while the latter does not (yet) know.[57] Here justification is essentially nothing but a new insight, by which the sinner recognises and admits his 'actual' situation. It is, so to speak, a transition on the *cognitive* level: from not-knowing to knowing. For Luther — and here he most certainly follows Paul — justification is an *existential* transition, in which the sinner *really* and *actually* moves from guilt to acquittal, from being under God's condemnation to being in God's favour. Rightly Berkouwer has pointed out that Barth does not take sin and unbelief seriously enough, as appears from his speaking of the 'ontological' impossibility of sin and unbelief.[58] According to Barth, in Jesus Christ the possibility of unbelief is 'rejected, destroyed and set aside'.[59] This does not mean that Barth therefore denies the necessity of faith. But this necessity, too, is of an 'objective' nature. In fact, it has already taken place in the election of Jesus Christ. The necessity of faith in man is actually nothing but the repetition of that eternal decision. Berkouwer rightly asks whether Barth in this way does not 'relativise' the human decision of faith.[60] He finds it striking that neither Scripture nor the Reformation knows Barth's problem. Fully acknowledging the sovereign action of God in his justifying of the sinner, they also take man very seriously in his unbelief and therefore call him most earnestly to faith. To put it in biblical terms, Paul did not say to the

Philippian jailer: 'You *are already saved* in Christ; therefore believe in him', but: 'Believe in the Lord Jesus, and you *will be saved*, you and your household' (Acts 16:31). Indeed, faith is an indispensable necessity in the miracle of justification.[61]

But we must also stress that this faith never remains alone. In his Homily 'Of the Salvation of Mankind' Cranmer already stated it very clearly: 'Faith doth not shut out repentance, hope, love, dread, and the fear of God, to be joined with faith in every man that is justified; but *it shutteth them out from the office of justifying*'. Likewise Hooker said: 'We by this speech (faith alone justifieth) never meant to exclude either hope or charity from being always joined as inseparable mates with faith in the man that is justified; or works from being added as necessary duties, required at the hands of every justified man; but to show that *faith is the only hand which putteth on Christ unto justification*'.[62] The elimination of all human cooperation precisely at this point gives the sinner the greatest joy and gives him *assurance* of his salvation.

It is no wonder that exactly at this point Trent rejected the view of the Reformers. In chapter IX of the Decree of Justification the Council not only described such an assurance as 'boasting' and as a 'vain and ungodly confidence', but also stated unequivocally that 'no one can know with the certainty of faith, which cannot be subject to error, that he has obtained the grace of God'. And in Canon 16 it says: 'If any one shall say that he will for certain, with an absolute and infallible certainty, have that great gift of perseverance even to the end, unless he shall have learned this by a special revelation — *anathema sit* (let him be anathema).' This view is a necessary inference from the Roman Catholic view of justification, because of its inclusion of the idea of human co-operation. As soon as an element of synergism, however small, enters into the doctrine of grace, there is no room left for the Reformation concept of the assurance of faith.

Because Luther and the other Reformers placed all their faith in the declaratory act of the justifying God and rejected any possibility of human co-operation at *this* point, they had a firm basis for assurance. Because man's salvation in no way rests on anything he himself does, not even on his faith, but rests solely on that wonderful *justitia aliena* (strange righteousness) of Christ, such a man may know for sure that his sins are truly forgiven and that, in spite of the sinfulness that remains in him, he will never fall out of the hand of this gracious God. 'At once justified and a sinner' is not a Lutheran one-sidedness, but it touches the very heart of salvation. *Solus Christus* (Christ alone), *sola gratia* (by grace alone), and *sola fide* (by faith alone) belong together in an unbreakable unity, and because of this unity the last word is and remains: *soli Deo gloria* (to God alone be the glory)!

12

Justification by Faith: Its Relevance in Hindu Context

SUNAND SUMITHRA

Hinduism is primarily a religion of duty. The word for 'religion' in Indian languages is *dharma*, which also means 'duty personified'.[1] The duties envisaged consist of religious (ritual, sacrificial) or social (customary, traditional) demands, but hardly any ethical obligations. Hence, though the terminology of justification is not found in the index of any Hindu scriptures, yet justification would be universally understood by Hindus to mean that one stands justified before the whole of society if one has done one's duty or what is socially appropriate. For, as is often repeated, Hinduism is not a religion. Well-known recent Hindu thinkers (such as Radhakrishnan, K. M. Panikkar, Hireyanna, Das Gupta, Aurobindo Ghosh) refer to it as Hindu*dom* or Hindu*ity*, thus defining Hindu*ism* as a way of life rather than a system of *beliefs*.[2] By the fifties books published by the government of India were already promoting the view that Hinduism was basically a social system, namely, that of the *varnashrama dharma*, the system of castes[3] and the all-pervading teaching of *Karma-samsara*: that one reaps what one sows, and that this reaping is experienced in a series of births.[4] Transmigration or metempsychosis is the great bugbear, the terrible nightmare, of Indian philosophers and metaphysicians. All their efforts are directed to getting rid of this oppressive scare. The question is not: What is truth? The one engrossing problem is, rather: How is a person to break this iron chain of repeated existences?

The doctrine of transmigration strengthens the sociology of castes. Observe in the following citation the use of the adjectives 'pleasant' or 'stinking' to describe human conduct, rather than 'good' or 'bad', even though the purpose is to match an adjective for the word 'womb':

> Accordingly, those who are of pleasant conduct here — the prospect is, indeed, that they will enter a pleasant womb, either the womb of a Brahman, or the womb of a Kshatriya, or the womb of a Vaishya. But those who are of stinking conduct here — the prospect is, indeed, that they will enter a stinking womb, either the womb of a dog, or the womb of a swine, or the womb of an outcast.[5]

These two aspects of Hinduism — the caste-system, emphasising social obligations, and the teaching of *karma* that we reap the fruit of our actions in a series of births — constitute the essence of Hinduism, whether it be called a religion, culture, social structure or whatever, and have strengthened the hold of *duty* on the Indian mind for thousands of years. And in the process, the doctrine that a person is justified by works *alone* — doing what is required of him — has taken away, for the most part, the joy of living, especially as it took away the possibility of faith in a personal, benevolent deity, for a very long time.[6]

Since the Hindu sacred literature is vast and of varying quality and authority, we need to be selective in establishing the Hindu approach to justification. Hence, instead of quoting numerous Hindu thinkers, it is adequate and safer to go back to the roots, the Hindu *sriti* ('revelation'). Thus we first proceed to study the question of man's justification before God in the most important scriptures of Hinduism, comparing that with what the Bible has to offer, along with its relevance for the Hindu mind; and finally end with outlining the task of the Indian church relating to the issues and needs thus raised.

I. THE HINDU QUEST

Every Hindu strives to achieve four goals: *dharma*, the fruit of having discharged all duties; *artha*, progress in material wealth; *kama*, the satisfaction of earthly desires; and *moksha*, deliverance from bondage to the cycle of births and deaths. It is significant to notiee that none of these, the highest goals in human life, has any god-reference. The first three, relating to duty, desire and wealth, are to be accomplished in the social plane one is born in; while to achieve the last, *moksha* (deliverance), several ways are possible, according to different personalities. These ways are known as *margas*[7] ('ways'), whose number varies: *Karmamarga*, the way of works (*Karma* means work as well as the fruit of work — literally, 'action'); *Gnanamarga* (the way of wisdom; however, not intellectual wisdom, the Hindu thinkers are always quick to point out, but rather the divine, superior or intuitional wisdom); and *Bhaktimarga* (the way of loving devotion). It is hardly necessary to point out that these ways are human achievements, assuming human capability. Those who follow the path of *Karmamarga* are expected to meet all the requirements: celebrating the regular *pujas* (worship rituals) of the various deities; keeping the holy times and seasons; making pilgrimages to the numerous holy places; giving the prescribed offerings, gifts and sacrifices; taking the necessary vows; and so on. All these are performed as part of one's caste duties; even renunciation or alms-giving takes place not so much out of a necessity for self-discipline or pity for human misery, but out of a sense of duty, particularly as Brahmins are often the recipients of the alms or gifts. By performing these duties one increases *punya* (the balance of good deeds, or superergism), while their neglect increases one's *papa* (the term Indian *Christians* use for sin in almost all languages), balance of evil deeds.

To grasp the way in which Christian theology uses the term justification, to mean that those who trust in Jesus Christ are declared righteous by and before God, we must think through three basic theological components: (1) the nature of the *justifier* — i.e. the nature of God; (2) the *need* for justification — or the nature of sin; and (3) the nature of the *justified* — i.e. the nature of man. Similarly, we must address ourselves to these components of Hindu thought, if we are to understand what bearing justification might have in a Hindu context.

A. Doctrine of God

For a theological analysis, undoubtedly the most important references are the *Rigveda*, the *Gita* and the *Upanishads*; we may consider these as representative of all the Hindu scriptures.[8]

Hindu thinkers admit that *Rigveda*, the oldest of the four *Vedas* and the most venerable of all Hindu scriptures, does not provide a coherent picture of God for us. In this collection of (mostly ritual) prayers to different deities, there is clearly a polytheistic approach to the divine; but one also finds there monotheism[9], henotheism, and pantheism. What is basic to the rigvedic doctrine of God is that behind every activity in the universe there is a deity, thus giving rise to the three tiers of gods, belonging respectively to *dyuloka* (heavens, the celestial realm — sun, moon and stars); *antarikaloka* (atmospheric space — rain and thunder); and *bhuloka* (earth — rivers, mountains). Obviously the powerful natural phenomena have been personified into gods. The Hindu pantheon is undeniably anthropomorphic. Max Mueller is right when he says:

> The gods worshipped (in the *vedas*) as supreme by each sect, stand still side by side. No one is first always, no one is last always. Even a god of a decidedly inferior and limited character assumes occasionally, in the eyes of a devoted poet, a supreme place above all other gods.[10]

It is necessary to note that in *Rigveda* itself there is a deep dissatisfaction with these poly-pantheistic tendencies. Thus we read, 'They call him Indra, Mithra, Varuna, Agni and he is heavenly nobly-winged Gerutman; to what is One sages give many a title.'[11] On account of this, *Rigveda* often repeats *neti, neti* (god is not this, not that — in other words, God is unknowable).

This agnostic approach was further developed in the *Upanishads*, making the understanding of the supreme 'god' (*Brahman*) a full-fledged philosophical agnosticism. The most positive knowledge of the supreme god, *Brahman*, is expressed in the famous words, *tat tvam asi*,[12] 'Thou art that' (that is, everything is *Brahman*). Thus *Brahman* is the absolute, indefinable being. Some *Upanishads* describe this ultimate being as *saccidananda*, that is, self-existent (*sat*), conscious/intelligent (*cit*), and blissful (*ananda*).[13] There is an interesting hymn in the *Rigveda* to the 'unknown god', *Ka* (meaning 'Who?', which affirms that 'he is the God of gods, and none beside him'.[14]

We can briefly summarise the various Hindu concepts of God as follows: Though the gods originated in the personification of natural phenomena, thanks primarily to upanishadic philosophical influence contemporary Hindus generally think of the supreme god in impersonal terms as *Brahman*, yet worship the personified deities according to their traditions and needs. There is a very great hunger in the Hindu scriptures to know the supreme god: each of the polytheistic names seems to be a desperate but earnest attempt to identify that particular deity with the supreme God, an attempt doomed later to be found wanting and hence discarded or replaced by another — a truly amazing search.[15] We may briefly note here in passing that such a search for God is an evidence of lostness — or of seeking, but not finding.[16]

B. Doctrine of Sin

The vedic concepts of sin contain three main elements, clearly demonstrating that a non-biblical concept of God in the Vedas leads to non-biblical concepts of sin:

(1) *Sin as darkness*. In the thinking of the rigvedic seers darkness was identified with sin, which later developed into sin as *avidya* (ignorance): 'Aditi, Mithra, Varuna, forgive if however we have erred and sinned against you. May I obtain the broad light free from peril; O Indra! Let not darkness seize us.'[17] Note the assured confidence that one can be sinless.

Thus, *knowledge* was the one object of supreme value, the irresistible means of realising one's ends, particularly in the *Upanishads*. This idea of the worth and efficacy of knowledge is expressed again and again throughout the *Upanishads* not only in connection with philosophical speculation, but also in the practical affairs of life. So frequent are the statements describing the invulnerability and omnipotence of the one who is possessed of this magic talisman, the intuitive knowledge of the *Brahman*, that *ya evam veda* ('he who knows this') becomes the most frequently recurring phrase in all the *Upanishads*.

> . . . verily, even if one performs a great and holy work, but without knowing this, that work of his merely perishes in the end. One should worship the Self alone as his [true] world. The work of him who worships the Self alone and his world does not perish.[18]
>
> He who knows that wonderful being *Yaksha* as the first born — namely, that *Brahma* is the real — conquers these worlds. Would he be conquered who knows thus that great Spirit as the first born — namely, that *Brahma* is the real?[19]
>
> He who knows *Brahma* as the real, as knowledge, as the infinite . . ., he obtains all desires.[20]
>
> Verily, indeed, even if they lay very much on a fire, it burns it all. Even so one who knows this, although he commits very much evil, consumes it all and becomes clean and pure, ageless and immortal.[21]

(2) *Sin as disease*. Some other prayers portray sin as something physical, which like disease can spread from person to person (through the medium of another man or even a god; or it can be passed on from the father to the son, so that it may crop up amongst relatives like any other physical characteristic). This 'sin' can be carried away: 'If by address, by blame, by imprecation we have committed sin, awake or sleeping, all hateful acts of ours, all evil doings may Agni bear away to distant places.'[22] This sin can be removed like some disease or dirt, washed by water, and purified by fire. By prayers, offerings, magic formulae (*mantras*) or rituals (*samskaras*) one can remove the wrath of the offended deity; but the inner disposition of sin remains untouched. It is also possible that the sinner is not conscious of it. This last understanding has given rise to the Aryan belief that sin can therefore be committed unwittingly even when one is asleep.

In other places the prayer is for freedom 'from sin as from a bond that binds me';[23] 'on every side, dispel all sin'.[24]

(3) *Sin as moral deformity*. But there are also several Vedic passages where sin is conceived as a moral lapse, so that the one who prays is under a burden of guilt for having committing it:

> What, Varuna, hath been my chief transgression, that thou wouldst slay that
> friend who sings thy praises? Tell me, Unconquerable Lord, and quickly sinless
> will I approach thee with mine homage. Free us from sins committed by our
> fathers, from those wherein we have ourselves offended . . . Not our own will
> betrayed us, but seduction, thoughtlessness, Varuna! Wine, dice, anger.[25]

It is important to notice two aspects of this vedic morality. Positively, a
careful study of the passage reveals that sin is really a violation of an accepted
custom; once he knows the appropriate thing to do, the worshipper has the
capacity to become sinless before the deity. Negatively, unlike the biblical
doctrine, sin here is not against any deity. The 'five-fire doctrine' runs: 'The
plunderer of gold, the liquor drinker, the invader of a teacher's bed, the
Brahman killer — these four sink downward in the scale, and, fifth, he who
consorts with them.'[26] Here also killing *per se* is not evil, but the killing of the
Brahman; adultery *per se* is not evil, but adultery in the teacher's bed (who is
always a Brahmin); and so on. The accomplice to these offenders is also a
sinner — that is, once again most of morality is governed by the accepted
social norms, rather than having a superhuman or divine sanction. The roots
of such an ethical theory lie in a peculiar Vedantic understanding of God and
the human person. In the *Brihadaranyaka Upanishad* we read, 'Not for the
love of the wife is a wife dear, but for the love of the Soul is a wife dear.'[27]
   In the Gita, this 'supra-ethical' vision of life is expressed thus:

> From whom proceeds the activity of all beings, and by whom all this is pervaded,
> worshipping Him through one's *Swadharma* [one's own morality — i.e., the
> requirements of one's caste; some liberal Hindus interpret this to refer not so
> much to the caste-system as to the different psychological temperaments of
> human beings], a man attains perfection. Better one's *Swadharma*, though
> defective, than another's duty, apparently well performed. Doing the duty
> ordained by one's nature, one incurs no sin. One should not . . . relinquish the
> duty born of one's nature, although it may be attended with evil.[28]

Hindus call such an approach supra-ethical because each individual has his
own 'morality' (*swadharma*) to keep; there are no constraints from a
universal code of conduct.
   Yet behind the morality of Rigvedic hymns lies the root idea of *rita*, and
without a grasp of this seed concept it is impossible to understand the third
concept of sin in the *Vedas*. The frequency of the usage of the term in the
Rigveda is next only to the names of most popular gods, *Agni* and *Indra*. *Rita*
literally means 'the course of things', thereby having the derived meanings of
law, order, customs and ethical behaviour. The *Rigveda* describes the world
of experience as the reflection or shadow of *rita*. *Rita* is the established root of
the world, of the sun, moon and stars, morning and evening, day and night;[29]
or simply, what scientists call 'the laws of nature'. In the course of time, *rita*
came to mean the moral laws governing actions of human beings, the cosmic
moral order. Though it is not clear whether *rita* is a self-existing moral order
or is established by gods, it is *rita* which forbids or positively commands the
actions of men. Every Indian aspires, in all his rituals, prayers and worship of
gods, to attain to this *rita* — doing *nature's* will, a strange parallel to the
biblical understanding of doing *God's* will. There was a time in India when
the Brahmins (the priestly caste) rose to power, when the rituals attained

great significance and power even over gods, so that a sacrifice or ritual became *ex opere operato*, without any essential link with the deity in whose honour it was being offered. Thus the priest became all-powerful. What mattered was the *way* in which the sacrifice/ritual was conducted: even a slight lapse in performing it brought a curse upon the worshipper, while the proper conducting of the ritual brought even gods trembling to the worshipper's feet.

Particularly in the period of *brahmanas*, when the priest became all powerful, *rita* came to mean the ritual order of sacrifices, giving the priest who performs sacrifices, the Brahmin, absolute power in society. In our time, *rita* is practically replaced by the more concrete concept *dharma* (which means right, justice, virtue, duty). If *rita* stands for the uniformity of nature, *dharma* stands for

> all those ideals and purposes, influences and institutions that shape the character of man both as an individual and as a member of society. It is the law of right living, the observance of which secures the double object of happiness on earth and salvation. It is religion and ethics combined.[30]

Beyond this, the essence of vedic morality consists in the proper observance of rituals. *Rita*, (universal) law, controls the whole universe, including gods. Obviously there is some tension at this point (not to say a contradiction) between the universal morality (*sanathana dharma*) and caste-morality (*swadharma*). The power of the priests (*Brahmins*) was absolute in that even gods were goverened by *dharma* and *rita*. It is for this reason that guilt among the Hindus owes more to breaking the tradition than to contravening a god's command. More precisely, a Hindu is affected not so much by inner guilt as by social shame.[31] This also explains why the priestly class, the Brahmins, are greater than *Vedas*, and so have absolute control over society. Thus the main burden of *Manudharmashashtra*, the 'ethical' code of *manu* (undoubtedly the most important of all Hindu moral codes) as well as of the *Bhagavadgita* is conformity to the social, traditional duties.

As philosophical speculation gained precedence over ritual, priestly practices, sacrifices and works of merit towards hypostatised divinities became, in the light of the metaphysical knowledge, futile. Hence, religious piety was renounced as unnecessary, and the knowledge of that fact, or metaphysical knowledge in general, replaced ritualised religion in fundamental worth. It was such knowledge alone that rendered efficacious any religious and meritorious act which anyone, for the sake of conformity to popular custom, chose to perform:

> . . . if one offers the *agnihotra* (fire) sacrifice without knowing this that would be just as if he were to remove the live coals and pour the offering on ashes [i.e., utterly worthless]; but if one offers the *agnihotra* sacrifice knowing it thus his offering is made in all worlds, in all beings, in all selves.[32]

Here the possession of metaphysical knowledge actually cancels all past sins and even permits the knower unblushingly to continue in what seems to be much evil, with perfect impunity, although such acts are heinous crimes and disastrous in their effects upon others who lack that kind of knowledge.

> He, however, who has not understanding, who is unmindful and ever impure, reaches not the goal, but goes on to reincarnation. He, however, who has understanding, who is mindful and ever pure, reaches the goal from which he is born no more.[33]

In the above quotation, knowledge, mercy and purity are equated with one another.

> The knower of the bliss of Brahma is saved from all fear and from all moral self-approach. . . . Such a one, verily, the thought does not torment: 'Why have I not done the good? Why have I done the evil?' He who knows this, saves himself from these [thoughts]. For truly, from both of these he delivers himself — he who knows this![34]

> . . . people say, 'By offering with milk for a year one escapes repeated death' — one should know that this is not so, since on the very day that he makes the offering he who knows escapes repeated death.[35]

It is important to note that the doctrine of *karma* in the last of these quotations (relating to 'repeated death') is not found in *Rigveda*.

Thus different periods developed different understandings of sin and its solution, and consequently also different theological systems. When sin was viewed as ignorance, the solution propounded was the acquiring of the *Brahma-gnana*, the intuitive knowledge of *brahman*, *viz. Gnanamarga*, as in *Vedanta*. Taking sin as a failure in ritual duties, the solution was conceived as action and obedience, i.e. *Karmamarga*, as in *brahmanas*. And taking sin as moral lapse led to loving devotion to a particular deity, generating the *Bhaktimarga*, as in *Bhagavadgita*.[36]

C. Doctrine of Man

Owing to the great significance given to *rita* (the order of the universe), human freedom, which potentially contradicts such an order, belongs more to the 'fall' than to 'nature' (more precisely, the image of God; in Hindu terms, ignorance and knowledge).[37] Further, owing to the fact that the concept of *atman* ('Soul') was seen as identical with the *Brahman* himself, any 'original sin' is impossible. Hence Vivekananda could say that the greatest sin is to call man a sinner.

The Hindu striving is therefore for this self-realisation, which is at the same time god-realisation, i.e. to *know* this ontological identity with divinity. One can speak neither of imputation nor of impartation, but of identification. The relationship is mystical rather than forensic.

This gnostic concept of human personality is expressed in Hindu scriptures in various ways:

> As the sun, the eye of the whole world is not sullied by the external faults of the eyes, so the one Inner Soul of all things is not sullied by the evil in the world, being external to it.[38]

Gita accepts that a 'man' verily constituted of his faith, and he is what his faith is . . . But man's faith is determined by the dominance of one or the other of the three qualities (*gunas*) of nature: tendency to do good for others and to depend on god (*sattwa*), the tendency to self-glorification (*rajas*) and the tendency to do evil (*tamas*).

Elsewhere the human Self is called 'the bright, the bodiless, the scatheless, the sinewless, the pure unpierced evil'. There is also a trace of a deterministic concept of personhood in some places:

> A person is made (not of acts but) of desires only. As is his desire, such his resolve; as is his resolve, such the action he performs; what action (*karma*) he performs, that he procures for himself.[39]

This strange combination of an 'agnostic' view of God (that God is essentially unknowable) and a 'gnostic' understanding of man (that Spirit is good and body is evil) is possible only in Hinduism.[40]

Knowledge and renunciation are the major ways to escape the *karma samsara*, and 'grace' was added only later. With the rise of philosophical/ religious speculation, moral and religious actions were spurned more and more. The moral distinctions do not benefit the man who has metaphysical knowledge. 'By tranquility of thought deeds, good and evil, one destroys! With soul serene, stayed on the Soul, delight eternal one enjoys!'[41]

In general the controlling idea of all Hindu religion is a 'justification' by knowledge as achievement — or works, in Christian terms. The possessor of knowledge is freed even now from all his evil deeds as well as from the later results of the metempsychosis, or transmigration, from doing any deeds at all:

> . . . by knowing what is therein, *Brahma* knowers become merged in *Brahma*, intent thereon, liberated from the womb [i.e. from rebirth];[42] 'By knowing God there is a falling of all fetters; with distresses destroyed, there is cessation of birth and death';[43] 'but they who seek the *atman* by austerity, chastity, faith and knowledge . . . that is the immortal, fearless, that is the final goal, from that they do not return'.[44]

There is also a peculiar justification of this *Gnanamarga*, *viz.* that precise knowledge is possible because of speech: 'Verily, if there were no speech, neither right nor wrong would be known, neither true nor false, neither good nor bad, neither pleasant nor unpleasant. Speech indeed makes all this known'.[45] Here there seems to be a confusion between 'form' and 'content' of knowledge.

Later, however, the opposition to the supremacy of such knowledge became very strong, giving rise to another line of salvation, however small or neglected — that of 'grace'.[46] The apprehension of the speculative knowledge of *Atman* by means of human knowledge is opposed by the doctrine of *Prasada*, or 'grace', in *Kathopanishad* II.20 (the first mention of grace in Hindu scriptures) and with a slight verbal change in *Shwethasvatara Up.*, III.20: 'through the grace of the creator he beholds the greatness of Atman'. It is by means by this grace, according to *Shwethasvatara* I.6, that an individual obtains release from illusion and reaches immortality: 'In this *Brahma* wheel the soul flutters about thinking that itself and the actuator are different. When favoured by him, it attains immortality'. 'This Soul is not to be obtained [i.e., realised] by instruction, nor by intellect, nor by much learning. He is to be obtained only by the one whom he chooses, to such a one that Soul reveals his own person.' The last sentence is an interesting parallel

to Paul's understanding of God: 'I will have mercy on whom I will have mercy
. . .' (Rom. 9:15).

II. THE RELEVANCE OF THE DOCTRINE

The biblical concept of justification is rooted in its teaching of God, that he is
one, creator, sovereign, holy (wholly other) and merciful. As such, the stress
is not on what a human being can do — for the Bible portrays people as
incapable of pleasing God — but on what God *is* and *has done* for us. Thus
justification turns on the restoration of a relationship with God — a god-
reference missing in the Hindu concepts of sin — and not a quality in man.
Being holy, God demands that his norms be met; where they are not met,
there is a penalty.[47] Since he is the one sovereign Lord of the universe, not
least because he is its creator, his verdict holds. If his verdict is acquittal, that
verdict stands, even if the whole universe condemns. Hence the Bible says
that he is the justifier of the sinner. This biblical view of justification does not
mean that evil is too strong for God. Moral evil is not a substance, as is
sometimes suggested by the Hindu scriptures,[48] but is finally a broken or
tarnished relationship with God. Being merciful, God works out the way to
justifying a person by paying all his penalty himself. Here God's grace is free,
but not cheap. Thus the doctrine of justification comes as a strong corrective
primarily to the Hindu doctrine of God. Those coming to believe in Jesus
Christ from a Hindu background have a crucial re-orientation to undergo
when they read what the Bible says about God.

Once the doctrine of God falls into place, other aspects of Christian
theology are more easily discerned. Only because of the biblical understanding
of God does Christian theology portray human beings as created in the image
of God, yet sinful; as created, sinless, yet now fallen. In justification, this
original worth of a person is restored. Such a person is 'saved', for now he or
she is accepted before the most sovereign Lord, and so can walk the earth
with head held high. When the faith of the individual is the sole means by
which grace is received, human beings are credited with a distinct personhood
unknown in the Hindu pantheistic concept of the self. Just as children who
have received the discipline and generous love of good parents display a
certain carefree happiness, so also those who have received God's free offer
have a buoyancy in life unknown in Hinduism. Indeed if sin had been
condoned, human worth would have been destroyed;[49] but since human
beings are pardoned by the substitutionary death of Christ, the very Son of
God, their worth is real and measured before God by the inestimable value of
the Son. There is also *spontaneous* praise and gratitude to God — not as a
duty or appeasement, or out of fear. The truth that a person's justification
before God is effected *once* and is neither repetitious nor continuous is a
thrilling discovery for Hindus to make.

Clearly, the doctrine of justification reflects what one thinks of human
beings. This individualistic concept of man, as 'the alone with the Alone',
appeals very much to Hindus, surely reflecting the Hindu hunger for the
Christian sense of personal worth. Does this mean that the doctrine of
justification does not have any concern for others, that it is not tied to a
practical display of sanctification that includes love as the fruit of faith?[50]

Hardly. For justification also means that since God is no respecter of persons, all human beings are treated as equals — cancelling all the caste and other forms of discrimination human beings have invented for their own vested interests. Hence one's love for those belonging to one's own caste broadens to include the outcaste, the marginalised and the poor, once it is understood that all human beings enjoy the privilege of having been formed in God's image.

On this basis, a genuine fellowship also becomes possible, a fellowship never possible in the Hindu social structure of castes. Often the needy and the suffering are deliberately ignored by Hindus for the simple reason that if less needy people were to attempt to alleviate such sufferings, they might be found working against their own *Karma*, against *rita* or *dharma*. But under God's grace there is no place for holier-than-thou attitudes. This change of attitude leads a converted Hindu to a concern for the outcaste, the marginalised and the poor.

On the other hand, Hindus rightly ask if God is just in reckoning the fruit of one to another, as he does when he applies the fruit of Christ's death to my sins. Does not such a view support the Roman Catholic idea of supererogation?[51] Even in Ezekiel we read the sarcastic words of the Jews, to the effect that the fathers have eaten sour grapes and the children's teeth are set on edge. But that is exactly the answer to this objection. As Stanley Jones rightly says, in our social life (as family, tribe, nation) each of us automatically reaps the fruit, not only of our own doings, but also of others who are in influential roles. If the father is a drunkard, the children do not have enough to eat or to study; if the ruler of the village or nation is rash, the citizens reap the consequences too. Thus, being united to Christ, it is legitimate that believers also reap the fruit of his death for themselves.

Perhaps more than any other biblical doctrine, it is justification which brings Hindus to Christ. Hinduism is, as we saw at the beginning, primarily a religion of duty; justification wrought by God's free grace can be enormously appealing. Still it is necessary to explain that to believe in Jesus Christ as one's personal Saviour is also to confess that he is the Lord of all of my life. The implications of this Christological emphasis for mission among Hindus is clear: if Jesus is the only way, and if I am prompted by the love of God shed abroad in my heart, I am under constraint to share him with others. Hindus reject the uniqueness of Christ more than any other Christian truth; for the same reason, witnessing comes to Hindu converts rather slowly. It is the focus on the sufficiency and grace of Christ (*cf.* Jn. 1:17; 1 Cor. 1:30–31) that wins release from such bondage.

Equality of all before God eliminates any distinction in intrinsic worth among Christ's disciples. True human unity is possible only under the gospel — the unity of all believers. Only because God has forgiven me can I really and freely forgive others from my heart. Because of the one simple way of salvation, belief in Jesus Christ, the different Hindu ways of salvation (*Karmamarga, Gnanamarga, Bhaktimarga*) all become irrelevant, and the unity of the disciples of Christ is thereby enhanced.

III.   THE CHURCH'S TASK

The biblical doctrine of justification profoundly challenges Hindu understanding, especially the Hindu understanding of God. The church needs to be sensitive to the three-fold change a Hindu convert faces in this regard, *viz.* (1) he begins to see God as one, creator and absolute sovereign of all the universe, over against the polytheistic framework to which he was earlier accustomed; (2) God becomes a personal being with whom human beings can have a personal relationship, in contrast to ideas of the ritual control of gods or appeasement by gifts and sacrifices; (3) God is not only quantitatively different from human beings and from the universe, but qualitatively different too: the Wholly Other — which undermines the monistic tendency to identify self, world and *brahman*.

Correspondingly, the church needs to nurture the new convert in these areas: (1) in the area of his or her dependence on a benevolent, personal, merciful God; (2) in the continuing need to differentiate communion with God from an ontological identification with god(s); and (3) in the need to submit totally to him as to the absolute sovereign, not out of duty, but by way of his claim over the individual, as that person's Creator — the experience of joyful obedience.

Such a relationship with God is not one of manipulation or mystical union, but one of responsible communion. The way in which the pastor and the elders of the church deal with divine things makes a lasting impression on the convert's picture of the nature of God — in handling worship, sacraments, prayer, mentioning his name, the Bible, and the like. The church's activities must manifest the biblical understanding of God as *holy love*. Deification of man is the ultimate goal in Hinduism — which for the same reason also amounts to the humanisation of god. Martin Luther's *simul justus et peccator* (at once justified and a sinner), emphasising the *relationship* between God and man, avoids both, and gives a proper emphasis to the doctrine of God. The consummation of this imputation of righteousness to the believer occurs of course in its ultimate impartation at the resurrection, in the blessed life of eternal communion with God; life this side of the resurrection is a foretaste of that.

A Hindu is accustomed to *doing* religious things, much more so than a Christian. In consequence, justification through faith alone, without active participation in worship, witness and service, may mean for him a change in lifestyle from hectic ritualistic duties to freedom from any duties. The biblical emphasis on justification by God's grace fosters neither indolence nor antinomianism. A Hindu convert needs to be taught that what the Spirit has worked *in* his heart, he must now work *out* by way of Christian conduct. Too often churches in India do not encourage participation by the new converts in the churches' various programmes. This makes the convert think of Christian faith as more internal and individual than social in its implications. It is therefore crucial to emphasise the importance of the *church* to a Hindu convert. The biblical teaching that we need one another, since Christ is building his church and not just individual believers, and has mandated the church/congregation as the locus for many good works, can prevent many a former Hindu from becoming an inactive or fruitless member. The mandatory character of a Christian's participation in the programmes of the church, as opposed to tithing or the like, must constantly be emphasised.

On the other hand, Christian unity, worship, witness, and service can be hard for a Hindu convert to grasp fully at the beginning of his Christian life. The rigid caste distinction (which is actually the only universal distinctive of all shades of Hinduism) is a habit hard to overcome in pursuing the Christian ideal of full fellowship based only on the common bond of faith in Jesus Christ and the resultant indwelling of the Holy Spirit in each believer. Corporate worship in the churches is far different from the Hindu 'alone with the Alone' type of worship. All-embracing Hinduism is hardly a missionary religion, and so to witness that Christ is the only answer is harder for a Hindu convert than we can imagine. And finally, having been brought up in the universal doctrine of *Karma* the convert from Hinduism finds any service springing from motives of compassion and gratitude extraordinarily difficult. The church needs not only to sympathise with the slowness of converts in digesting these cardinal elements of the gospel, but must evolve programmes which will enhance these values amongst new converts.

The teaching and practice of caste distinction lies at the heart of Hinduism. Birds of the same feather flock together, and so for practical reasons, because some kind of bonds come into play when churches are planted, certain associations are inevitable. For example, those belonging to a factory or other institution, or those living in one geographical area, or speaking one language, may more easily join together in some meaningful church activity. But it is another thing to say that caste should become the basis of church planting, as some are advocating. Precisely because caste has been for millennia the great curse of Indian civilisation, it must be avoided as the controlling principle of homogeneity. Priority of ethnicity, in my opinion, is more harmful in India for church planting than is any other error. The voting pattern of church elections, the social and ecclesiological intercourse (including marriages, and patterns of employment, leadership, education and other benefits, etc.) show that castes are still a dominant factor for Christians in India, simply because in early missionary work they were at least condoned. If those who brought the gospel to India could not grasp the seriousness of this evil, contemporary Indian Christians at least should leave no stone unturned in plucking this evil out of all Christian teaching and conduct.

13

Justification by Faith: Its Relevance in Islamic Context

CHRIS MARANTIKA

It is not righteousness that you turn your face to the East and the West; but righteous is he who believeth in Allah and the Last Day and the angels and the Scripture and the Prophets; and giveth his wealth, for love of Him, to kinsfolk and to orphans and the needy and the wayfarer, and to those who ask, and to set slaves free; and observeth proper worship and payeth the poor due. And those who keep their treaty when they make one, and the patient in tribulation and adversity and time of stress, such are they who are sincere, such are the God-fearing (*Surah* 2:177).[1]

This Qur'anic verse and many others demonstrate that justification by faith through grace in the death of Christ is an absolute contradiction to the Islamic mind. Good works save a person from the damnation of evil. 'Salvation', therefore, 'is attained by all who submit to Allah, that is, live according to His rule as revealed by Prophet Mohammed.'[2]

This 'rule' is divided into two main parts, *viz.* the principle of faith (*Iman*) and the practice of faith (*Din*).

The first part consists of six main beliefs to which every good Muslim should adhere. They are:

(1) belief in one absolute and sovereign God (Allah);
(2) belief in an angel who is next to Allah and who intercedes for men;
(3) belief in the Holy Qur'an, as a direct revelation from Allah to Prophet Mohammed, and henceforth the basis of all Muslim teaching;
(4) belief in the Prophets of Allah;
(5) belief in judgment, paradise and hell, where Allah will give all men their eternal reward or punishment;
(6) belief in the divine decrees.

The second is *Din*, the practice of faith, consisting of the five pillars of Islam. They are:

(1) the recitation of confession of faith (*Shahadat*),
(2) the observance of prayers (*Salat*),
(3) the obligatory contribution (*Zakat*),
(4) an obligatory fasting for those who are adults and physically fit, in the month of Ramadhan (*Saum*), and

(5) a pilgrimage to Mecca at least once in a lifetime in a certain month of the year (*Hajj*).

These practices have to be performed through strict and tedious minutiae of prohibitions, procedures and processes, so that by the time one finishes practising the *Din*, generally one feels a great satisfaction because of one's accomplishment in finishing the task of being submissive to the God of Abraham, and therefore one becomes a very settled Muslim, a Muslim who has resigned his will to God and who continues to strive after righteousness.

The discipline in such repeated religious activities is so strenuous that for many it creates guilty feelings and is tiresome, but without providing assurance or confidence regarding the prospect of salvation. The biblical concept of justification can fully serve as good news to relieve such men and women from the burden of Islamic laws as well as from inadequate righteousness, faith and obedience to that law.

I.   RELEVANT APPROACHES

At the outset, some principles constraining evangelism amongst Muslims should be laid down, in order to undergird the discussion of justification by faith through grace in Christ in the Islamic context. Otherwise one's proclamation of justification may backfire and severely limit the testimony of words and deeds.

We should note the reminder of one of God's faithful servants to the Muslims, Christy Wilson. He said: 'The era of the great Muslim controversy has passed; it has gone into the limbo of things that are past.'[3] He emphasises the fact that in order to win a hearing amongst Muslims, one should (1) avoid arguments; (2) have a solid and steady faith; (3) be ready to give answers; (4) live a holy life filled with the Spirit.[4] Similar emphasis was voiced by David Penman, Archbishop of Melbourne who concluded, after becoming a missionary to Pakistan and Lebanon, 'I do not believe there is any other way than through the hard discipline of sitting where he sits and grappling with the issues that form and create his faith.'[5]

Two approaches have too frequently been practised in the past. *One* is the aggressive argumentative approach, which usually appeals to the Occidental mentality. The *second* is the pietistic, passive approach, which is usually appealing to the Oriental mind-set, but ineffective. Other approaches that persuade the Muslim hearer, but minimise the tension, should be developed. Several approaches have been found fruitful. These are not mutually exclusive.

One is the *positive apologetic* approach. This approach requires that the points of convergence between Christianity and Islam be emphasised so as to capture the hearing and imagination of Muslims. A syllogism to support the deity of Christ that reflects this approach is as follows:

Major premise: The only eternal person is God.
Minor premise: Christ is eternal.
Conclusion: Therefore, Christ is God.[6]

The concept of the eternal existence of Christ, as a starting point leading toward a persuasive presentation of the total Christ, is one aspect of Christian faith that can be discussed with Muslims without much tension. Even though the concept of the Scriptures, God and Christ are the most discussed and distorted messages of Christianity by the Qur'an and by Muslims, there are several aspects of these messages that can be discussed in a positive apologetic to present the comprehensive message of the Bible, including the gospel of Jesus Christ. These elements include:[7]

(1) *Concerning God*:
    (a) God as a transcendent, immanent personality;
    (b) God as a living, loving, caring Father (his activity in creation, history and redemption);
    (c) God's master plan for the world.
(2) *Concerning Christ*:
    (a) Christ, the Word of God (his eternal nature);
    (b) Christ, the Spirit of God;
    (c) Christ's holiness (his holy life);
    (d) Virgin birth (miraculous birth of Christ);
    (e) Christ's miracles;
    (f) The Son of Man concept;
    (g) The biblical presentation of Christ as Prophet;
    (h) Judgment to come by Christ;
    (i) Angels' words concerning Christ;
    (j) Christ as King (*Mahdi*), and the kingdom to come;
    (k) Figures relating to Christ, such as the Good Shepherd, the True Vine, etc.
(3) *Concerning the Scriptures*:
At this point, it should be noted that the doctrine of the inerrancy of the Scripture becomes of utmost significance. Since Muslims, who comprise one-third of the Asian population, believe that the Qur'an is inerrant because it is the Book given by the inerrant God, to appeal to the Muslim with an errant Bible is like waving the white flag of surrender before the battle even begins.

A second is an *indirect polemic* approach, which aims to build a presentation of the Christian message so that it attacks false teachings indirectly, without mentioning any name or group or institution, government or religion. Attacking polygamy, for instance, can be activated with emphasis upon the original master plan of a happy home. Using the principles of marriage in Genesis 1 and 2 (the pre-Fall period) will put Christian teaching on a superior footing to Islamic teaching, and therefore win a hearing. In the area of Christology, one can develop positively the fact that Christ is not a man promoted to the status of God, but the God of the universe, who took human form (Philippians 2) to visit his creation. The emphasis upon God, who was the Initiator of the incarnation, should dominate the Christian mind in the Islamic context. Another intriguing aspect of the message of Christianity that implicitly attacks Muslim teaching is Matthew 22:21, where our Lord laid down practical instruction on the relationship between the Kingdom of God and the governments of this world.

The third important approach is the *persuasive presence*. This means that a believer should make his or her presence felt in a positive, constructive and creative way in the community, with a high sensitivity to the open doors all around. Through prayer, assembly, education, health and social projects, Christians create an openness to the minds and lives of Muslims; and with extreme sensitivity, such Christians live and speak out their faith.

A testimony given by a young Muslim convert explains why this approach is very significant:

> I was born to very devout Muslim parents. My grandparents made the pilgrimage to Mecca twice. And since I was a child I had been brought up to become a faithful Muslim girl.
>
> For high school education, I attended Immanuel High School, a school started by the ETSI (Evangelical Theological Seminary of Indonesia), near my community. At this school I was taught Christianity, twice a week, an hour each time. In addition to this, I attended Christian fellowship conducted by the school every Saturday. I began to lose interest in my former religion. Instead, every night before I went to bed I read the Bible that was given to me by my teacher. In a Bible camp held by the school, I accepted Jesus as my Saviour and Lord. On March 5, 1985, I was baptised in a local church nearby. And through the ministry of ETSI students, my father also accepted Christ two years ago.[8]

Evangelicals are known for their heavy emphasis on persuasion but are lacking in the area of making their presence felt and accepted. Ecumenicals are known for their emphasis on presence but are lacking in the area of persuasion. Should the two approaches be put together with balanced emphasis, which might be called the *persuasive presence* approach, penetration of the Islamic community and mind would be more successful.

The fourth important factor in our approach is an *appropriate attitude*. Scripture provides guidelines to stances that have to be acquired in any attempt to present the message to Muslims. There must be the kind of attitudes which while still maintaining aggressiveness in evangelism, at the same time maintain peace and tranquility, and therefore win the heart and hearing of Muslims. God says, 'Sanctify Christ as Lord in your hearts, always being ready to make a defence to every one who asks you to give an account for the hope that is in you, yet with gentleness and reverence . . .' (1 Peter 3:15). This passage emphasises three things. We must: (1) sanctify Christ in heart and mind; (2) share Christ in any situation at any moment that presents itself; (3) show sensitivity and soberness to the people as a part of the presentation of the gospel.

In 1984, WELCOME (World Evangelical–Lausanne Consultation On Muslim Evangelism) called for a new appreciation of Muslims. In an open letter to Christian churches, they stated:

> Testimonies from around the Muslim world indicate that when Muslims are truly loved by Christians, they may prove to be far more receptive to the good news of Jesus Christ than any one ever dreamed. Whether we have initially perceived Muslims as friends, neighbours or enemies, is irrelevant. Jesus asks us to reach out in love to Muslims at home and abroad. . . . Without in any way condoning sin or compromising the Gospel, we may be able to disciple Muslims in their own cultural milieu.[9]

Fifth, one must approach Muslims with *relevant thought patterns*. Missiologists have classified human mentality into three categories.[10] One is the rational–logical pattern of thought, dominant in the Western world. A second is the imaginative-mythological pattern of thought, most relevant to Africans and Latin Americans; and the third is the intuitive–meditative–mystical pattern of thought dominant in Asia.

Indonesia, which comprises the largest Muslim group in the world, possesses the third pattern of thought with a little combination of the second pattern. The message presented should appeal to the intuition and the imagination of the people. The Christian message of God's actions in history, because of his love and care for humankind, will appeal to this kind of mentality — if presented with a story-telling appoach.

Finally, our approach must take into account the *relevant social structure*. Each culture has been shaped by at least four social structures. There is the structure of the relationships between the individual and society. In addition, one must be sensitive to family structures, community structures and the tribal structures of society.[11] Each group in each Islamic country should be studied to determine what structure is the most desirable to the people. The evangelistic effort and the formation of the church should be patterned accordingly.

With these guidelines in mind, we now proceed to discuss the subject of justification by faith. The most relevant message here is the sovereignty of God.

II.   JUSTIFICATION AND THE SOVEREIGNTY OF GOD

A sovereign act of God to declare a man's righteousness is of course not completely foreign to the Muslim mind.[12] From *Surah*, *Al-Fatihah*, the Opening Chapter of the Qur'an, which is most exalted by the Muslims, one can see that all of God's activities are based upon his personality, the All-Merciful and the All-Compassionate, Lord of All-Being, the Master of the Day of Doom. But the reason for God's blessings (vv. 6,7) is a person's right paths and prayers.

The sovereignty of God in the biblical concept of justification should be greatly emphasised to convince Muslim hearers and believers in Muslim countries concerning the initiator of salvation, God himself. Out of his sovereign will, he declares a person to be righteous. In some Christian circles, the discussion of justification by faith frequently overlooks the fact that justification is the initiative of God. It is God who justifies the ungodly. The emphasis of this aspect of justification in some countries in Africa and in Indonesia has reinforced their national philosophy.

Muslim scholars think of the sovereignty of God as generating not a passive relationship between a human being and the Divine will, but an active relationship that includes the power to choose.[13] They assign to moral freedom and human responsibility the main reason for one's service.

This moderate view, as opposed to the traditional view of extreme predestination (based upon *Surah* 67), seems to move to a more balanced view of the biblical teaching of the sovereignty of God and the responsibility of man. The verses which strongly emphasise both factors are *Surah* 58:1,2:

> Blessed is He in whose hand is the sovereignty, and He is able to do all things, Who hath created life and death that He may try you, which of you is best in conduct and He is the mighty, the forgiving.

However, this implies that the sovereign acts of God to save a person depend upon that person's excellence in performance of good works. A synergistic approach to righteousness is suggested here, contradictory to the Christian doctrine of justification.

The constant uplifting of this aspect of the biblical concept of justification, namely, God's sovereign act to declare a person righteous, will present an opening for the gospel in Muslim contexts. It has to be proven that God's action, including the provision of a Saviour, the preparation for the arrival of the Saviour, the sacrifice of the righteous Saviour, the proclamation of the good news of righteousness by faith, and the ethical removal of condemnation in the Day of Judgment, is all God's sovereign act. This point of contact should invite more curiosity in the prospect of discussing justification by faith.

Another important divine attribute that should be strongly emphasised in the Islamic context is God's grace. Divine acts that declare a person righteous are based upon his grace. As *Al-Fatihah* indicates that he (God), Who is the Master of the Day of Doom, is the All-Merciful and the All-Compassionate (vs.1), it should be clearly expounded that justification is an act of the *sovereign God* based upon *his grace* to declare a person righteous.

In his study of the Qur'anic concept of mercy, Muhammad Al-Nawaihi, a Sufi and a professor at the American University in Cairo, testifies:[14]

> I discovered that the Qur'anic verses which speak of mercy, forgiveness and allied meanings, outnumber their opposites (punishment) in the ratio of more than two to one . . . From my subsequent studies and meditations, I became even more convinced that the ideal relationship between God and man, as depicted in the Qur'an, is that of mutual love. The greatest reward that the Qur'an holds out to men is God's love; the greatest punishment is God's displeasure. In this I am by no means original; this is exactly what had been asserted by our great Sufist mystics.

One should be cautioned, however, that the expressions 'All-Merciful' and 'All-Compassionate', which are translated from the phrase *rahmaanir-rahiim*, do not carry the meaning denoted by the biblical concept of *charis* ('grace'). The closest biblical equivalent is the Old Testament word *ḥēn*, which in most instances denotes the act of a superior in presenting something, usually material blessings, to an inferior. The superior and the inferior are totally separated from one another. The intimate relationship bound up with the special covenant of grace reflected by the Old Testament word *hesed* (often rendered 'mercy') is not carried by this phrase in the Qur'anic chapter of *Al-Fatihah*. The special meaning of *charis* in the New Testament, where the person of Jesus is the central point, is of course rejected by Muslims.

Caution should also be exercised so that Christians do not depend on the Qur'an and other elements of Islam to explain the concept of God. As it has been rightly observed,

> Depending on the teaching of the Qur'an to explain God is like raising a white flag of surrender before the enemy. Acknowledging those elements which are

similar in both religions is an honest approach. One can communicate the Gospel by beginning with elements of Christianity known to the Muslim, and going from there to the presentation of the Gospel and its challenge to accept Christ as Saviour and Lord.[15]

The desire of Muslims for a personal knowledge of God presents an avenue for the gospel-bearers to present a theocentric message of the Good News of Jesus Christ. The understanding of the divine Person, both transcendent and immanent, and the divine plan and purpose, will prepare the way for a clear understanding of the message of Christ as Saviour.

This conclusion is clearly supported by the excellent work of Harun Hadiwiyono, President of Duta Wacan Seminary in Yogyakarta, Indonesia, and a Christian expert in the area of world religions. In 1973, he produced a theological treatise entitled *Iman Kristen (Christian Faith)*,[16] an excellent study that is the result of twenty-five years of teaching theology and world religions.

In its four hundred pages, seven familiar theological themes are discussed under the headings 'The Revelation of the Lord God', 'The Teaching Concerning the Lord', 'The Teaching Concerning the Work of the Lord God as Creator, or God as Creator', 'The Teaching Concerning the Work of God as Saviour', and 'The Teaching Concerning the Work of God as Redeemer'. Christ is discussed in the book in relation to these subjects. Basically, Hadiwiyono has shown that the message which breaks through to the mentality of the Muslim is a theocentric message.

What is lacking in the book is an expositional and exegetical approach to the concept of God. The treatise appeals to human reasons, but lacks power to convince the human heart. What is needed now is a biblical-theological approach to God's person, purpose and work.

The presentation of the biblical God, emphasising such aspects of his person as his holiness, his oneness, his greatness and his uniqueness, will put Muslims face to face with God, whom they fear. Coupling this with an emphasis on individual sins will make Muslims see themselves as all of us must ourselves — as filthy and helpless beings. As Calvin has stated:

> Suppose we but once begin to raise our thoughts to God, and to ponder His nature, and how completely perfect are His righteousness, wisdom and power — the straight edge to which we must be shaped. Then, what masqueraded earlier as righteousness and was pleasing in us, will soon grow filthy in its consummate wickedness. What wonderfully impressed us under the name of wisdom, will stink in its very foolishness. What wore the face of power will prove itself the most miserable weakness. That is, what in us seems perfection itself, corresponds ill to the purity of God.[17]

III. JUSTIFICATION AND FAITH

Faith (*Iman*) to a Muslim is not a matter for argument. Islam's basic creed is probably the most decisive, clear and simple doctrinal statement ever written in any religion. The Muslims, the masses and the leaders, know that it includes the principles of faith (*Iman*) and the practice of faith (*Din*), as mentioned earlier in this paper.

The only similarity between Christianity and Islam in this regard, however, is in the word 'faith'. Both Muslims and Christians use the word to explain their relationship with God. The difference, however, lies in the content of faith. The object of Christian faith is Jesus Christ, who is the atoning grace for justification; while *Iman* and *Din*, which are good deeds, become the objects of righteousness in Islamic faith.

The *Kalimah Shahadat*, which is the first point of *Din*, functions as the cardinal principle of *Iman*, and also a linking between *Iman* and *Din*. In addition it functions as a formula for profession of faith when a newcomer chooses to embrace Islam.

The process and procedures of practice are the most difficult to follow. The demands for discipline are such that when a person is able to perfect his practice, he has become involved in a repetition of activities which not only bring peace of mind, but also steep an adherent in Islam through experience, so that he is able to refute and reject any other religious ideas foreign to *Iman* and *Din*. This is probably the main reason behind the minimal success the church has experienced in her effort to reach Muslims. Not many Muslims who embrace high Islam are among converts to Jesus Christ.

The vigorous demands for adherents to follow the rules and the regulations, while still being uncertain of one's righteous standing before God, have forced some to follow the extremist line, while others have chosen to leave Islam. The reason a Muslim village turned to Christ in a very fanatic Islamic district in Java was that there had been an attempt to force Islamic dress code, such as is practised in Arabia. This kind of imposition should lead many to consider the grace of God in Christ as truly good news, should it be presented in a manner that is fitting to the frame of mind of a Muslim.

The aspect of certainty inherent in the Christian concept of justification can serve as a vehicle to the understanding of the total Christ. It comes as truly good news because it is by faith, which assures one's standing, and not by works which leave one still uncertain about the results. Compensation, however, should be provided in order that after accepting this standing before God, the new Muslim convert can have a grip on something that is not too far from his or her past religious practices, such as set praying for three times a day (rather than the usual Muslim practice of five times a day).

IV. JUSTIFICATION AND JESUS CHRIST

The object and the content of saving faith in Christianity is the person and the finished work of Jesus Christ on Calvary as the substitutionary sacrifice for sin. This view conflicts with Islam. The question, therefore, is how the great grace of God in Christ can be understood and accepted by the Islamic mind.

Muslims accept that Christ is the most holy and powerful of prophets, even though they deny his Lordship. Bey Arifin, in his book, *Maria, Yesus dan Mohammand*, writes: [18]

> In this situation, under the open sky, without companion except for faith and obedience, the long awaited hour arrived, a baby was born, a baby who will become the *holiest* and *the most influential* man [*translation and emphasis mine*].

Concerning his power, Harbullah Bakry writes:[19]

> By the permission of God, the prophet Isa performed many miracles to prove
> his status as prophet. For instance, he raised the dead, gave life to birds made of
> clay, healed the deaf and blind, and told what was in a person's house. Also by
> the permission of God, he brought food from heaven to be eaten by many
> Israelites [*translation mine*].

Christ's wonderful characteristics of holiness and marvellous power, fully
acknowledged by the Muslims, can serve as meeting points of thought that
bearers of the gospel can make use of to explain his right to impute
righteousness to those who receive him as personal Saviour. These are
elements in the concept of justification that can attract the attention of Muslims.

When explaining Christ's mission the role of the angels in Christ's birth,
death and resurrection should also receive much emphasis. This is especially
true during Christmas and Easter seasons. The strong emphasis in Islamic
thought on angels, one of the six tenets of Islam, serves to give approval to
Jesus' status as the Messiah of God. An accurate exposition of what the
angels said about Christ in the Gospels will make the message of justification
by faith more desirable. Only a holy mediator can bring a human being before
the holy God.

The rejection of the death of Christ by Islam has to do mainly with the
uniqueness of his death. Muhammad and his followers believed that Christ, as
a holy prophet, could not have suffered and died in the way he did. Internal
evidence in the Qur'an itself is not consistent concerning this matter.[20] But
the most difficult truth to get across is the fact that he rose from the dead.
There are four popular theories used by Muslims in their attempt to prove
either that Christ did not die (but God strengthened him and restored his
life), or that he died and his body disappeared. These theories of Christ's
death are the Judas' kiss theory, the swoon theory, and the stolen body and
the miraculous disappearance theories.[21] The first two attempt to prove that
he did not die; therefore, Jesus' atonement for sin, as held by Christians, is
not valid. The last two theories attempt to prove that he was not raised from
the dead, so that he is not Lord at all. Denial of Jesus' death and resurrection
is the constant aim of Islam. The fact is that if he was not crucified, and if he is
not risen from the dead, then the Christian message is unreliable and
undesirable. Uniting the message of Christ's death and resurrection in an
Islamic context is a 'must' task.

This quotation from the Qur'an sheds light on the confusion:

> And because of their saying: We slew the Messiah, Jesus Son of Mary, Allah's
> Messenger. They slew Him not, nor crucified, but it appeared so unto them; and
> lo, those who disagree concerning it are in doubt there; they have no knowledge
> thereof, save pursuit of a conjecture; they slew Him not for certain. But Allah
> took Him up unto Himself. Allah was ever Mighty, Wise.[22]

These and similar verses were adopted from various late New Testament
pseudepigraphical writings, often tinged with Gnosticism. Attacking the
credibility of such books will be very appropriate. It is an indirect polemic
against Islamic inconsistency.

Concerning Christ's mission, the Qur'an seems to come quite close to the biblical truth. He came to bring the good news (*Injil*), to confirm the *Torah*, to reveal God's wisdom and wonders, to demonstrate mercy, and to teach prayer and almsgiving. Should the death of Christ be explained in the light of his mission, it may become more attractive to a Muslim. And since the emphasis in Islam is that Christ carried that mission to the people of Israel, strong emphasis should be placed upon the universality of Christ's mission, including his death on Calvary. This kind of discussion will make the Christian message of justification by faith more appealing. It prepares Muslims for further examination of the Scriptures.

The most appealing message to the Muslim community is the concept of Christ as the Word of God. An exegetical exposition of this presentation of Christ from the Bible will appeal to the mind-set of many Muslims. In fact, the proclamation of the gospel, building from this aspect of Christ's personality as *Kalimahtullah*, will draw much attention to the gospel of salvation in Christ. As the *Logos* concept successfully served to bridge the gap between the idea of divinity and matter in the thinking of Greek knowledge-seekers, it will do the same to bridge the gap in the mind-set of Muslims, who are occupied by the tension of choosing between the transcendent God of Islam and the immanent, ultimate reality of Hinduism, Buddhism and mysticism.

A Muslim scholar who actively led the movement of Muslim young people to halt the expansion of Christianity in Indonesia decided to read the Gospels carefully so that he might intelligently attack Christ and Christianity. When he came to John 1:1, he marvelled at the 'the Word of God', which is also a phrase used by the Qur'an to refer to Christ. And after pondering verses 14 and 18, he accepted Christ as Lord and Saviour. His conversion created so much tension and attracted so many other Muslims to Christ that finally he was imprisoned. At the trial he defended himself and was released. He is one of the most sought-after evangelists in Indonesia today. He has also spent one year in Egypt to explore the possibility of sending missionaries with Islamic background from Indonesia to that country.

Certainly the bearers of the gospel can proceed from these points of agreement to the further message concerning the Word of God: Christ is 'the light of life' (John 1:4), 'the light to every man' (John 1:9, *cf.* 9:5), and the conquering 'Word of God' (Rev. 19:12). In short, it must be said that in presenting the gospel to Muslims, a Christian should put emphasis upon biblical messages about Christ that centre on the person, purpose and plan of God, and on the idea that Christ is the Word of God. These truths will often open up the mental channels of Muslims and prepare them to accept the challenge of the Good News. The concepts of the Trinity and the Son of God will not unlock the mind-set of the Muslims to the gospel of Jesus Christ. The presentation of these truths should be delayed.

Many of the elements of the doctrine of 'Isa Almasih as Man' ('Jesus the Messiah as Man') which are held by the Muslim come very close to biblical teaching. They can be used as points of entrance to the Muslim mind. Such elements include: (1) the miraculous virgin birth; (2) the holy and perfect life of Jesus Christ; (3) the concept of Christ as a prophet of Allah; (4) the concept of the Son of Man. Careful presentation of these aspects of Christ will put Christ in the position of a 'trustworthy' mediator beteen man and God.

The bearers of the gospel should begin with Christ as a perfect human being, then lead to his missionary call, and finally treat his relationship with God. This will run parallel to a theocentric approach that makes the starting point God himself — the person, purpose, plan and programme of God. This will make the gospel presentation more intelligible and appealing to the Muslim mind. Whether Muslims receive or reject the gospel, they will do so intelligently.

The presentation of Christ as Messiah should be closely tied to the purpose and plan of God in the Old Testament. The parables, especially from the book of Matthew, can be expounded to present Christ's universality and Christ's saviourhood. A presentation of both the historical particularity and racial universality of the relevance of Christ from the book of Matthew, and similarly the particularity and the universality of the redemptive plan of God from the Old and New Testaments, will help open the door to the gospel of salvation in Christ.

No doubt the Muslim community has come to grips with the idea that Jesus Christ is the Saviour of the Israelites, as explained by Harbullah Bakry. What is lacking is an understanding of the universal aspects of his messiahship. The bearers of the gospel must therefore develop the biblical messages related to the larger scope of the story of the Messiah. For instance, one must expound the coming of the Magi, the account of which is found only in the book of Matthew (Matt. 2:1–12), despite the fact that this is distinctly a book for Jewish readers. Matthew also includes the names of the two non-Jewish women in Jesus' genealogy (1:5); Jesus' warning that the Jews would be shut out of the Kingdom because of their unbelief while others from all parts of the world would enter (Matt. 8:10–12); and the prophecy that the Messiah would declare judgment to the Gentiles and that the Gentiles would hope in him (Matt. 12:18–21). Matthew also relates a parable spoken by Jesus to the Jews, who because of their unbelief would be supplanted by others who were faithful (Matt. 21:33–43). And the strongest evidence of all is the fact that the declaration of God's grace for the Jews and the Gentiles alike is entrusted to the church (Matt. 16:18; 18:17).

To begin with the particularistic aspects of Christ may well win the attention of Muslims. This can be tied to well-accepted notions: Isa Almasih (Jesus the Messiah) as the prophet, Isa Almasih as the fulfilment of the Old Testament anticipation, and Isa Almasih as the Son of Man will be interesting subjects to put the Muslim's thoughts in motion. The biblical, theological presentation of these aspects may finally lead to his universal relevance. Then the bearer of the gospel may present the clinching message of the Good News: 'Christ died for all'.

The definiteness of salvation in Christ and the corresponding emphasis on assurance may also win a hearing with the Muslim. The obscurity of salvation within Islamic faith creates eagerness for something more definite from the most gracious God. In addition, presentation of Christ as the Living Water and the Liberator of the human soul may cause the Muslim to take notice.

In short, it can be said that Muslims, who comprise the second largest religious group in the world, have been prepared to hear the message of definite assurance of salvation. They have tried to do good works, but they are uncertain about their safety in the sure life beyond. The Christian message of assurance in Christ for the life to come is well suited for their desperate hearts. The bearers of the gospel will do well to draw the Muslim's attention to an elaborate and convincing presentation of the biblical message of assurance for the life to come in Jesus Christ.

V. JUSTIFICATION AND SIN

Christian emphases that are acceptable to the ears of the Muslims include the message of Christ's call for repentance from personal sins and his warning of judgment on those who do not repent of their sins. Sins of idolatry, ungratefulness, disbelief, injustice, and specific daily sins are interesting subjects to the Muslim. The most rejected aspect of sin is original sin. Discussion of this should be delayed to later times of encounter, possibly after conversion. Sin is sin, a rebellion against God, whether it is understood as original sin or individual sin, and Christ died for sinners; and in the presentation of the gospel in a Muslim context, the witness needs to say more about personal sins. A theological, biblical approach to individual or personal sins will win the hearing of Muslims and should prepare them for the challenge of repentance of their sins and the acceptance of the Lord Jesus Christ as their Redeemer.

The hesitancy on the part of Muslims to discuss personal sins in detail springs from a disturbed conscience. Like all other human beings, they are frequently conscious of their personal sins, which may take a variety of forms and which have expressed themselves in their daily life by their failing to conform to the character of God. Many also recognise their inability to cope with sin's bondage. Their hearts cry for deliverance. Their traditional religion has not given them the answer. They are waiting for the solution.

The bearers of the gospel need to speak specifically concerning sin and all of its expression as it relates to daily life, and present them with the gospel which is the power of God for salvation (Romans 1:16) to all men, including Muslims.

Four components of personal sin should be especially emphasised, as they will build bridges and prepare the way for the Muslim to accept the message of salvation in Christ. They are: (1) all forms of idolatry; (2) ingratitude to God; (3) unbelief and injustice; and (4) sins of adultery, anger and murder.

The message that emphasises the holiness of God, individual sins and judgment to come will create a desperate need for Christ as the Saviour who provides a definite salvation.

VI. JUSTIFICATION AND JUDGMENT

The judicial act of God to remove the curse of sin, as maintained by the Christian doctrine of justification in the present life, is not in agreement with Islamic belief. The Qur'an does not focus much attention on present forgiveness. Its concern is with the life hereafter. Its main objective is right standing before God in the future.

Muslims acknowledge the reality of hell, into which a sinful man will enter as a logical necessity of his evil actions. 'We cannot avoid it' because even 'our various organs will bear witness to the wrong we have done in this life.'[23]

However, Muslims contend that hell will serve as 'purgatorial treatment' that will operate a cleansing process to purify the sinful person. It is 'like a mother who brings her child willingly to a surgical operation to free his body from the wounds from which he is suffering, though the operation will be a most painful one'.[24] The curse of sin is something that can happen in the future only.

Islam, however, strongly emphasises the need for repentance, as stated, for instance, in these Qur'anic verses:

> Forgiveness is incumbent on Allah only toward those who do evil in ignorance (and) then *turn quickly* (*in repentance*) to Allah. They are those toward whom Allah relenteth. Allah is ever Knowing, Wise. The forgiveness is not for those who do ill deeds until, when death attendeth upon one of them, he saith: 'Lo! I repent now'; nor yet for those who die while they are disbelievers. For such we have prepared a painful doom.[25]

This repentance will assure a person of the divine forgiveness, as Bey Arifin observes:

> Whatever great and thick sin of a man, if he asks forgiveness and repents with all his heart, and feels ashamed totally, with fears and trembling, not only God will forgive him, but even man will surely forgive that man . . . By the will of God also, his sin that filled the space between earth and heaven, will be forgiven.[26]

The emphasis on repentance *in life now* will not produce certainty in righteousness, as declared by these verses from *Surah Al-Tahrim*:

> O ye who believe! Turn unto Allah in sincere repentance! It may be that your Lord will remit from you your evil deeds and bring you into gardens, underneath which rivers flow, on the day when Allah will not abase the Prophet and those who believe with him. Their light will run before them and on their right hands; they will say: Our Lord! Perfect our light for us and forgive us! Lo! Thou art able to do all things.[27]

Strong emphasis on repentance now, as the negative aspect of conversion, and on the assurance of right standing before God in the day of judgment, will expose the superiority of the Christian message. The confusion in Muslim minds stems from the uncertainty of salvation even after hard works on earth.

The return of Christ as a just King to put an end to the world and to build and to rule a Kingdom of peace and prosperity is a Christian message that Muslims hear with sympathy. This message may serve as a point of contact to win the hearing of the people and, therefore, expose them to the gospel of salvation in Christ. Moreover, the millennial kingdom expected by some Muslims is based upon hearsay and doubtful sources. Therefore the clear presentation of the prospect of the consummation, based upon written revelation, may win their hearing. The relevant points to emphasise are: (1) that today's generation is moving toward the end of this age, leading to climactic chaos; (2) that Christ will come back as the Judge; (3) that every person needs purification in anticipation of that event; (4) that Christ will establish and rule over a peaceful and prosperous Kingdom.

These emphases sometimes win the hearing of Muslims. Muslim authors do not write much to refute these notions. They do not sense a need to attack these aspects of Christian thought.

That the message of the coming of Christ as Judge has won the hearing of many Muslims could be seen in the ministerial experience of the present writer in over fifty evangelistic series in Indonesia. One approach that has brought many people to Christ is the series titled 'Di Depan Meja Hijau Allah' ('Before the Green Table of God'), based upon Romans 14:12, which says: 'Each of us will give an account himself to God'. The green table is Indonesian slang for the court. Usually many have cried before the sermon ended. The ones who have responded to the appeal to trust Jesus have usually done so with cries of relief.

In June 1976, when the same sermon was delivered at Gereja Baptis Indonesia Kebayoran Baru, Jakarta, forty people trusted Jesus Christ as their Saviour. In the meeting in Gereja Baptis Jatinegara, Jakarta, on June 12, 1976, a Muslim lady in her fifties, the wife of a former ambassador during Sukarno's reign, rushed forward with tears saying, 'Am I too late? Am I too late?'

In July 1976, the entire congregation of about two hundred in attendance, of which about one third were not professing Christians, registered the commitment of their lives to Christ when that sermon was delivered at Gereja Baptis Karang Anyar Gunung, Semarang. A Muslim man in the community, who had put much pressure on the church, and his Christian wife, attended meeting with six of his neighbours. They all put their trust in Jesus without hesitation. However, when the same message was delivered in June, 1976 in Gereja Baptis Baitlahim, Bandung, West Java, no converts were reported.

The audiences of the two churches in Jakarta and the one in Semarang consisted primarily of Christians with Islamic background and their Muslim visitors. Here the response was overwhelmingly favourable. The church in Bandung consisted of an audience mostly of Chinese background. The response to the same message was less than enthusiastic.

The following testimony, written by Pastor Maryono, who is a Muslim convert from Trenggalek, East Java, reveals that the message of divine judgment strikes home with Muslims. He writes:

> One day a pastor preached a sermon based upon Romans 6:23. He repeatedly emphasised that the wages of sin is death, and only by the grace of God through His Son can we be saved. The message made me tremble. For the first time I realised *the horror of the judgment of my sins, and eternal punishment in hell.* When the invitation was given, I stepped forward and accepted Christ as my personal Saviour and Lord.[28]

Maryono identifies two important emphases that captured his attention: first, 'the horror of the judgement'; Second, the focus on personal or individual sin as seen in the emphatic phrase 'eternal punishment in hell'. These are messages that may serve to open many Muslims to the gospel of Jesus Christ.

Another example of the effect of an emphasis on judgment related to justification by faith in Christ among the Muslims can be seen in the testimony of Abubakar, a devout Muslim from Sultanic background who trusted Christ in 1983.

While I was devoting my time to the study of the Qur'an, I came across *Surah Almaidah* 46 and 47, where it says that the Torah and the Gospel are given as a light to the believers, and those who do not believe in the Gospel shall be punished. I was startled with the fact that many qur'anic verses had been misinterpreted to us by my religious teachers. But the answer came when I read Hadits Sohih Muslim No. 100, where it says, 'Muhammad said: in the name of Allah, *Isa* the Son of Mary will come and will become the most righteous Judge.' Even though I tried to forget the subject and intensified my prayer life, the fear of the judgment by Isa [Jesus] haunted me every day. I began to read the Gospels and quietly attended a church. I trusted Jesus and was baptised in 1983. In 1984, after reading the entire Bible, I felt the urgency to share the good news with fellow Muslims. I am now preparing myself to become a missionary to the Middle East.[29]

VI. CONCLUSION

Justification by faith in the biblical sense is a message that can win a hearing among Muslims. The emphasis, however, should strongly be on the side of divine acts based upon Allah's sovereign and gracious nature. Human beings should respond with faith. Personal sin and judgment by Christ should receive due attention. The object and content of faith should be clearly elaborated because of the deep differences between Christian faith and Islamic faith. What Muslims reject is the death of Christ for the atonement of sin, as a remedy applicable to all humankind. With solid historical facts to back up the message, Christian witnesses may make some impact on Muslims.

Finally, however, after all attempts have been made to present clear, relevant, challenging and biblical messages about Christ, whose death on the cross paid the penalty of sin that God might justify believing sinners, one must sit back and wait to observe the working of the Holy Spirit in convicting and redeeming those whom God 'in love . . . has predestined to the adoption of sons . . . to the praise of the glory of His grace' (Eph. 1:5,6 NASB). Total dependence upon the work of the Spirit to convict, to anoint, and to regenerate lost Muslims is indispensable.

14

Justification by Faith: Its Relevance in a Buddhist Context

MASAO UENUMA

I. INTRODUCTION

One of the crucial issues for human beings is to find a way to accept themselves. This is known as salvation in a general religious sense. In Christian belief, acceptance of oneself is secondary to being accepted by God. And so the doctrine of justification is a crucial and vital point in Christian thought because it describes what our salvation is based on. In Christian thought *God* has initiated our salvation. The faith that brings us to salvation is a result of the grace of God manifested in Jesus Christ. We Christians hold that Jesus Christ is the mediator between the righteous God and humankind, and the means of our justification. Whatever diversity of opinion exists among Christians over the doctrine of justification, there is widespread agreement as to its importance.

It is the task of this paper to compare the Christian doctrine of justification with whatever is parallel in Buddhism. This raises an initial question about Buddhism, *viz.* 'Is there any concept of salvation in Buddhist teaching?' It is tempting to conclude that there is no positive idea of salvation in original Buddhism; there is certainly nothing akin to Christian justification. The central goal of Buddhism is enlightenment, which means an understanding of emptiness. By this understanding one will be detached from this world. In emptiness there is neither attainment nor non-attainment.[1] The world which the Buddhist envisions as salvation is not a positive construction or a metaphysical reality. The enlightened have to accept the idea that everything is empty and that there is nothing that human beings can rely on or attach themselves to.

It is perhaps impossible to compare this original idea of emptiness with the Christian doctrine of justification because there seem to be no parallels between the two. But there is one sect of Japanese Buddhism that is considered to have a belief structure somewhat similar in its doctrine of justification. In this regard, this sect is not only different from original Buddhism but also from other kinds of Japanese Buddhism (like Zen). This sect, called Jodoshin Shu (True Sect of the Pure Land), originated from Jodo Shu (Sect of the Pure Land). These two sects are quite similar in their teaching, but the former is particularly distinctive in its idea of faith. Together the two sects constitute one of the major groups in Japanese Buddhism. And so I intend to focus this paper on a comparative study of the Christian doctrine of justification and this particular type of Buddhism.

Jodo Shu was founded by Genku-Honen (1133–1212) and Jodoshin Shu was founded by Shinran (1173–1262) who was Honen's pupil. The development of these sects constituted a turning-point in religious history in Japan, because they opened up an easier way of salvation than the earlier forms of Japanese Buddhism, such as Esoteric Buddhism and Zen Buddhism, with their principle of self-attainment. These earlier forms of Buddhism insisted that a person should redeem himself by his own efforts, by his striving after a higher morality, mystical absorption, and contemplative meditation. In this sense they adhere to the original principle of Buddhist teachings, that is, attaining Buddhahood by one's own effort.

Honen substituted for this difficult path a much easier way of salvation. Amida–Buddha became the central figure. In spite of sharp opposition from other sects, Honen taught that a man has to put all his trust not in his own strength, but in that of another, Amida. Shinran sharpened Honen's teaching by making available this faith in Amida to everyone, even to women. He went so far as to teach that this faith is ultimately a gift of Amida.

It is not difficult to see that these sects have certain similarities of belief to the Christian doctrine of justification. These similarities have caught the attention of some theologians such as Karl Barth. He considers this structure of thought in these two related Buddhist developments in 12th and 13th century Japan (the same period as the lifetime of Francis of Assisi, Thomas Aquinas and Dante) to be 'the most adequate and comprehensive and illuminating heathen parallel to Christianity, . . . not to Roman or Greek Catholicism, but to Reformed Christianity, thus confronting Christianity with the question of its truth even as the logical religion of grace.'[2] Barth accepts that there is a formal similarity and takes the Japanese 'Protestantism' of Honen and Shinran seriously. He even says that the Roman Catholic St. Francis Xavier, who was the first Christian missionary to live in Japan (1549–1551), 'thought that he recognised in Jodoshin Shu the Lutheran heresy'.[3]

This formal similarity has been developed more fully by Japanese theologian Seiichi Yagi, who emphasised the similar work and role of Christ and of Amida–Buddha in relationship to the believer. Christ and Amida–Buddha are both considered to be the Saviour, calling men and women to believe in them. In this sense they are both the object of faith and the subject of faith. Yagi compares Shinran with Paul and John: 'In both Shinran and John, the transcendent (the Saviour) speaks to us, calls us, through the event in which he created the ground of our salvation, and demands our response. When we respond to this call in the decision of faith, the Saviour who called us becomes the object of our faith. But the believer becomes in his faith conscious that it is the Saviour who gave him the very faith, that it is the Saviour who acts when he, the believer, believes. In this sense the object of faith is at the same time the subject of faith.'[4]

Yagi also detects a similarity in the respective status of Christ and of Amida–Buddha. The Saviour Christ can be viewed in three aspects: Christ exalted, Jesus on this earth, and the Logos before the incarnation. Christ as Logos appeared as Jesus through the incarnation and works now in heaven in the make of his resurrection and exaltation. Yagi feels that this movement is well described by Paul in Philippians 2:6–11: 'Who, being in very nature God, did not consider equality with God something to be grasped, but made himself nothing, taking the very nature of a servant, being made in human likeness. And being found in appearance as a man, he humbled himself and became obedient to death — even death on a cross! Therefore God exalted him to the highest place and gave the name that is above every name, that at the name of Jesus every knee should bow, in heaven and on earth and under the earth, and every tongue confess that Jesus Christ is Lord, to the glory of God the Father.'

These three aspects of Jesus Christ are said to correspond to the doctrine of the Three Bodies of the Buddhas, which is called the doctrine of the Trikaya. Nirmanakaya is the Buddha's tranformed earthly body; Samkhogakaya is the shining body of his glory which only the awakened one can see; Dharmakaya is the body of the teaching, presenting the embodiment of the one truth which illuminates the whole world and lets the world appear — again, only for the awakened — as the no-thing-ness in which samsara and nirvana coincide. Amida–Buddha corresponds to the exalted Christ. Dharmakaya corresponds to Logos. Nirmanakaya, embodied by Hozo, corresponds to Jesus. Yagi explains this correspondence succinctly: 'For Chinran Samkhogakaya comes from Dharmakaya and reveals the former, just as in the case of John, where Christ is called the Son of God and reveals God (John 1:18, 14:9)'.[5]

It is apparent that this formal similarity does not denote a substantial similarity. There is a quite different concept of the meaning of salvation, though both make faith significant for salvation. The role of the Saviour — whether Christ or Amida–Buddha — is actually quite different in the two cases, because of this substantial difference in the very meaning of salvation, as will be shown later on. Moreover it is possible to argue for the superiority of Christianity by demonstrating a superiority of Christ over Amida–Buddha. Even Karl Barth could not find any other unique characteristic that showed Christianity to be the only true religion, apart from the name of Jesus Christ. He says: 'Only one thing is really decisive for the distinction of truth and error. And we call the existence of Jodoism a providential disposition because with what is relatively the greatest possible force it makes it so clear that only one thing is decisive. That one thing is the name of Jesus Christ.'[6]

It is not the task of this paper to examine the meaning of the name of Jesus Christ for Karl Barth. Rather the purpose is to make clear the relevance of the Christian doctrine of justification by faith in the context of a type of Buddhism which at certain points has a formally similar structure of salvation to that of Christianity. For this purpose it might be proper here to study what Shinran says about his own salvation, and then compare it with what the Bible says about the meaning of salvation.

One more thing should be mentioned about this similarity, *viz*: the possibility of a historical connection between Christianity and Buddhism. Some have speculated that there must have been some Christian influence on Buddhism through the Nestorian mission, since Amida–Buddha had been preached in China since the seventh century. Barth also admits the possibility of this connection.[7] From the eighth century onwards, Amida–Buddha has been preached in Japan. This historical connection has to be studied separately, but the possibility would have to be taken seriously when the doctrine of justification is preached in the context of a religion that has a similar teaching, as in Japan.

II.   THE DOCTRINE OF PURE LAND BUDDHISM

Shinran was born in Kyoto in 1173, and became one of the young monks at Mount Hiei when he was nine years old. Mount Hiei was the centre of the Tendai sect where Shinran's master, Honen, also studied. He had left six years before Shinran arrived. Shinran studied widely and deeply, and found that all the doctrines he met with in the various branches of the Tendai philosophy were holy and pure, but they did not satisfy him. He was taught that one had to recite the name of Amida and walk around the image of Amida without ceasing for ninety days, and then the shining Amida would appear to him and he would never forget. But his training, and the books he read, failed to give him what he wanted. At last, before an image of Kannon in the Rokkakudo or 'Hexagonal Temple', he heard a voice. In the Tendai sect Kannon and Amida were both worshipped and considered to be the embodiment of the ideal Buddha. As he knelt before the image, the answer came to him in the shape of a vision of Kannon. The vision said, 'Go to Genku [Honen] . . . and he shall teach you.' So Shinran went to Honen and became his most distingushed disciple.

Honen was disappointed with the Tendai teachings that salvation had to be attained by one's own power. He emphasised Buddha's grace, that is, 'another power', in which one can obtain salvation by faith. For Honen faith and Buddha's grace had to work together to attain salvation. Faith is recognised as a meritorious work necessary for salvation. However Honen did not deny that other meritorious works were possible. Shinran was very devoted to Honen because he said, 'As far as I am concerned my sole reason for repeating the Nembutsu [Amida] lies in the teaching of the good man who made me understand that the only condition of salvation is to say the Nembutsu . . . I should never regret it even if I were to go to Hell by being deceived by Honen Shonin.'[8] But Shinran differed from Honen in that he could not accept the idea of any meritorious works being necessary for salvation. For him, even faith was not a meritorious work. Only Buddha's grace would bring salvation. The various sayings of Honen and Shinran reveal this difference. Honen says, 'Even a bad man will be received in Buddha's Land, how much more a good man!' Shinran turns it into, 'Even a good man will be received in Buddha's Land, how much more a bad man!'

The teachings of both Honen and Shinran were so opposed to those of traditional Buddhist sects that they were exiled from Kyoto to the countryside. That caused the diffusion of their teachings into other areas of Japan. Many accepted their teachings because of social, historical and political difficulties. And their influence has been widely felt throughout the following centuries even up to the present.

Shinran was the first monk to have a family. He did this as a living testimony because he regarded celibacy to be a sign of lack of absolute trust in Buddha's grace. For him no sin was an obstacle to salvation through grace. In this sense Shinran is considered to be a religious reformer in Buddhism just as Luther was a Protestant reformer. Shinran died in 1262 at the age of ninety. This was fifty years after his master Honen had died in 1212 at the age of eighty. There are two major books on Shinran's teachings. One is called *Tainnisho*, and the other is *Kyogyoshinsho* or 'Doctrine, Practice, Faith, and Realisation'. The former is not his own writing. Some time after his death Yui

Embo, who was one of his immediate disciples, wrote a collection of his sayings in order to put an end to misunderstandings of his teachings. But the latter title, published in 1224, was a collection of 143 passages from various works such as the Avatamsaka and Nirvana sutras which, in Shinran's opinion, justified his views. It is regarded as the fundamental textbook of the Shinshu sect.

As we have seen, Shinran spent twenty years at Mount Hiei in the Tendai sect attempting to achieve his own salvation by his own works and efforts. During this time, he did not attain enlightenment, but recognised more deeply his own lust. He was in despair that he would have to go to hell because no work could make him enlightened. It is said that he was especially disturbed by sexual lust. He confessed in both books that he was full of sin and lust, and that they were rooted very deeply in him.

This confession has its parallels in what Paul expresses in his epistles. Paul recognised that neither regulations nor works could control human sensual indulgence. He says: 'Such regulations indeed have an appearance of wisdom, with their self-imposed worship, their false humility and their harsh treatment of the body, but they lack any value in restraining sensual indulgence' (Col. 2:23). In another confession in Rom. 7 he cannot help admitting that the sin living in him causes him to do what he does not want to do. 'For in my inner being I delight in God's law, but I see another law at work in the members of my body, waging war against the law of my mind and making me a prison of the law of sin at work within my members' (Rom. 7:22,23). Paul admits that there is no way we can stop himself from committing sin because sin lives in him very deeply. His final confession is: 'What a wretched man I am!' (Rom. 7:24).

This recognition of sinfulness by Shinran and Paul led them to put their trust in an absolute 'other'. Faith connects this absolute 'other' and the believer. In other words, the meaning of faith had to be carefully formulated to make effective the merit or grace of the absolute 'other'. In this sense both Shinran and Paul carefully define the role of faith to make clear how the grace of the absolute 'other' works on the believer, and how the believer is led to faith.

After Shinran left Mount Hiei he went to Honen and discovered the new teaching about Amida–Buddha. Amida means 'infinite light' or 'infinite grace', including its infinity with respect to space and time. Therefore it is eternal and everywhere without darkness. Amida is the shining body of Hozo the Bodhisattva, the latter being the name given him during his sojourn on earth as a man. Shinran explains this relationship of Hozo the Bodhisattva and Amida as follows:

> Hozo the Bodhisattva, in the days of his humiliation, being in the presence of the Tathagata Sejizaio, examining the degree of excellence of the Paradise of all the Buddhas, the causes of their formation, and the angels and men in them, made his great Vow and proclaimed his mighty Oath, which he meditated and selected for the space of five long Kalpas; and he repeated the Vow of announcing his Holy Name, Amida, in all the Ten Quarters. Universally doth he send forth his endless, boundless, all-pervading, unrivalled, supreme Light, his Light of Purity, of Joy, of Wisdom, His changeless, unconceivable, unexplainable Light, brighter than the brightness of Sun or Moon. His Light illuminates worlds

more numerous than dust, and all sentient creatures enjoy it and are illuminated thereby.[9]

Amida–Buddha was worshipped in the Tendai sect where Shinran studied for twenty years. But eventually this became the central Buddha figure through which salvation was considered to be brought to man. This understanding of Amida as boundless and surpreme Light means that Amida shines by itself and illuminates all creatures. In this concept of Amida is seen a formal similarity to the idea of the Logos in John's Gospel: 'Through him all things were made; without him nothing was made that has been made. In him was life, and that life was the light of men. The light shines in the darkness, but the darkness has not understood it' (1:1–3).

When Amida–Buddha is defined as boundless and supreme Light, the definition leads to the idea that salvation is dependent on illumination by this Light. Shinran uses this as the starting point to explain whence and how salvation comes. He says: 'The Light of the Divine Heart which has taken hold of us, illuminates and protects us continually, and dispels the darkness of Ignorance.'[10] He illustrates this illumination by comparing it to the light shining under a cloud. 'It is true that the dark mist of covetousness and passion constantly overhangs the sky that is above the believing heart. Yet though the sky above may be constantly overcast, beneath the cloud it is light, there is no darkness.'[11]

From this perspective Shinran focuses on an explanation of how salvation comes from Amida–Buddha itself. He says that the merit of Amida is bestowed upon the believing heart. This bestowal is called *Eko*. Originally the word referred to a bestowal of man's meritorious works upon Buddha. But Shinran reversed the direction and made the merit flow from Amida to the believer instead of from the believer to Amida. Shinran qualifies this *Eko* as *Tariki Eko*, that is, a bestowal of another's power. It is 'a Vow to the Salvation of Men through the Faith in Another's merits which Amida bestows upon us'.[12]

Shinran presents two different kinds of *Eko*. One is 'the Grace of new birth into Paradise', and the other is the grace by 'which we can return to Earth to aid our fellow-beings'. Both of these types of grace are 'a gift which we receive through the Buddha's power'.[13] Shinran takes this to be what is essential in the teaching of Jodoshin Shu. In the first paragraph of *Kyogyoshinsho* he says: 'In presenting the basic principles of Jodoshin Shu in general there are two kinds of *Eko*. One is a new birth into Paradise, and the other is a return to the earth'. Here is seen a clear teaching about the *Eko* of a new birth into Paradise in the *Kyogyoshinsho*. He primarily explains the first kind of *Eko* because he thinks that the second kind comes forth naturally as the result of the first kind. Therefore the point is that the gift of Buddha's grace makes possible the new birth into Paradise. This is the way Shinran explains the principal method of salvation through Amida-Buddha.

Shinran also explains the reason why Amida-Buddha possesses this grace that is able to reach down to people and save them. Amida is supposed to be the shining Buddha that Hozo the Bodhisattva became when he entered into Nirvana. This Hozo the Bodhisattva made sixty-eight vows, and in forty-eight of them he particularly requested Buddha to save the people. In the eighteenth vow he asked for the salvation of all people suffering from sin and lust. He says: 'Even if I could become Buddha, if all the other people who put their trust in Buddha from their heart and wanted to go Paradise, and who made the request ten times, and even then they were not allowed into Paradise, I would not want to become Buddha.' This is called the vow of vows. On the basis of this vow Hozo was elevated to the position of Amida–Buddha, and became the law of the Pure Land. This vow is the means by which the salvation of Hozo also becomes the salvation of all other people, because this vow was accomplished when he became Amida-Buddha. Therefore this vow is the means of grace for all people. The Light of Amida is able to shine over all the people. In this sense Amida-Buddha has a causal ability to save the people. *Eko*, the way of salvation from Amida, is now effective.

Shinran then goes on to explain the role of human beings in this process of salvation. The *Kyogyoshinsho* is composed of four parts — Doctrine, Practice, Faith, and Realisation, and these constitute a literal translation of the title. In the first part of the book Shinran explains the significance of *Eko* and the reason why salvation comes from Amida, as has been discussed above. In the second and third parts he explains practice and faith and their relationship to salvation. Finally in the fourth part he describes the happiness and joy which come as the result. This part will not be dealt with in this paper as it is not related to justification.

In the first sentence of the second part Shinran says, 'When we discuss the merit of bestowal for the new birth to Paradise, there are two ways to achieve it. They are a great Practice and a great Faith.' Practice, Shinran says, 'is to recite the name of the great Thathagata of Boundless Light'. This is not a contemplative recitation but a vocal recitation. If it were contemplative it would resemble the recitation of Esoteric Buddhism and Zen Buddhism. This would then again become the practice of one's own power. What Shinran means is simply a vocal recitation of the name of Amida, that is, a recitation of this name by mouth. Adherents repeat *Namu Amida Butsu*, which is composed of six Chinese characters and means 'going back to Amida–Buddha', or 'Amida–Buddha is coming back'. This recitation of six Chinese characters in itself is effective because the name of Amida has the power to illuminate people. Indeed, salvation becomes available to anyone who recites this name. In this sense the sects of Jodo and Jodoshin are considered an easy way to attain salvation in comparison with Esoteric Buddhism and Zen Buddhism.

The role of this recitation differs for Shinran and his master Honen. Honen thinks that the recitation is essential for entrance into the Pure Land. By contrast, Shinran thinks that faith is essential for salvation. For Shinran this practice itself originates in the vow of grace of Amida. If one recites the name of Amida, it is actually the means of appropriating the grace of Amida, from whom faith itself comes. Shinran focuses on the point that Amida has made a vow for the people. Therefore when Honen says that Buddha will answer if recitation is performed, Shinran counters by saying that even if human beings do *not* perform this recitation, Buddha will always keep his vow toward them. This is integral to Shinran's understanding of what faith is.

At the beginning of his discussion of faith, Shinran says:

As I reverently consider the nature of the outgoing movement of Amida's merits

[*Eko*], I find that there is a great faith, and as to this great believing mind I make this declaration . . . it is the miraculous act of longing for the pure and loathing the defiled . . . it is the true mind as indestructible as a diamond; it is the absolute faith cause leading to the realisation of great Nirvana, . . . It is the ocean of faith of Suchness and One Reality. This mind indeed is no other than the one that is born of Amida's Vow.[14]

For Shinran, Amida's outgoing merit and a great faith are almost identical. This bestowal of merit upon the believer by Amida is called Tathagata, which means literally 'thus come'. Therefore Amida is called Amida the Tathagata, which means that Amida comes to the believer. Faith corresponds with Amida's bestowal.

Based upon this understanding Shinran makes a firm statement about faith. He says, 'If a man enters into this Faith, he will acquire the merit of the Great Ocean of Divine Treasures, and will certainly be admitted to the Great Company of the Saints, in the present life.'[15] He says again, 'The effective cause whereby we are justly determined to be born in the Pure Land, is only the believing heart'.[16] Then on the basis of this faith and the gift of Buddha's power, Shinran says, 'Wherefore, if we, blind and sinful persons, arouse this believing heart, we can perceive Nirvana in this life.'[17] This is the way to salvation 'without fail'. Thus when grace or mercy and faith coincide, salvation is brought forth. But it also means that man goes away from evil or passes out of it. 'When we have made Faith our own, and have received a sight of the great mercy and a thought of pious joy, we pass away sideways from the five evil spheres of life.'[18] Shinran does not mean by salvation that there is no more evil, but means that way of 'cross-wise going-out' through the merits of the great Fundamental Vow is opened up for the believer. Shinran clearly states that 'we turn just as we are with our sins and lusts upon us, towards Nirvana'.[19] Salvation is not salvation from sin and lust, but a by-passing of evil and entering into the Pure Land in an unchanged condition.

Shinran recognises the difficulty of exercising faith: it is the turning point in the relationship between the grace of Amida and the believing heart. How is sinful man able to believe in this grace? Shinran says, 'For sentient creatures, who are heretical, evil, and proud, to believe and accept the practice of Amida's Fundamental Vow, is indeed a hard matter; there is nothing harder than this.'[20] Faith is the most difficult matter that Shinran himself has ever encountered. He confesses that it is hard to explain how belief in Amida occurs. He thinks that this is so mysterious that it is almost impossible to explain the reason, process and meaning. He uses the illustration that Amida is like a medicine that is the antidote to all poisons. When faith is understood as being a gift from the object of faith, it is always difficult to explain its relationship with the subjective will of the believer. This difficulty again has its parallels in the Christian doctrine of justification by faith.

Shinran asks himself again how one can have this faith in and of oneself, since it is the gift of Amida-Buddha. He thinks that it is a natural process derived from the ultimate and formless reality which is Nirvana. This natural mode is called *tathata*, and is the mode of the believing heart. It means literally 'suchness'. The believing heart is able to accept everything as it is, but the unbelieving heart always wants everything as it wishes. This mode, *tathata*, is a motionless tranquil world, but going out from it is a movement which is called *tathagata*, meaning 'thus come'. Hence come faith and salvation to man. Shinran thinks that this brings great joy.

III. RELEVANCE OF THE CHRISTIAN DOCTRINE OF JUSTIFICATION

The structure of faith in the Pure Land sect has been claimed to be quite similar to that of the Scriptures. In the structure of the faith propounded by Shinran, the relations amongst the believer, the object of faith and the salvation that is the result of faith, could be said to be much more similar to the Protestant faith than to the Buddhism from whence it sprang. These structural and formal similarities, it is often thought, betray a psychological similarity between exercising faith in the Pure Land sect and doing so in Christianity. There would then be no psychological difference between believing in Amida-Buddha and believing in Jesus Christ. Some, of course, go further, and insist that the faith is the same, and the truth is the same, and that it is only arrived at by a different way. An old Japanese poem says that there are many ways to go to the top of the mountain, but that the moon which everyone sees from the top is the same.

This psychological similarity has raised a missiological question. How should the Christian faith be preached to those who have this outlook? This missiological question embraces a theological question, *viz.*: how can the relevance of the Christian doctrine of justification by faith be demonstrated in a Buddhist context? The answer to this question lies in the substantial elements that sustain the doctrine of justification. These are God, humanity, and Christ. The Christian doctrine of salvation differs from the Buddhist teaching about salvation in its understanding of these basic elements, and an examination of this difference will give insight into the missiological task.

It is apparent that there is no clear concept of justification in Shinran's teaching because there is no clear concept of righteousness, although there is a clear consciousness of guilt. The doctrine of justification in Christianity presupposes the concept of the righteousness of God. The righteousness of God is an essential aspect of the Gospel. 'For in the gospel a righteousness from God is revealed, a righteousness that is by faith from first to last' (Rom. 1:17). The righteousness and holiness of God are evident in the relationship between God and man. God is the Creator of the whole universe, and the Lawgiver who maintains a righteous and holy relationship with man. This relationship is defined by the law that God has established.

Because of this law established by God the righteousness of God gives rise to the wrath of God when the law is not kept. 'The wrath of God is being revealed from heaven against all the godlessness and wickedness of men who suppress the truth by their wickedness' (Rom. 1:18). The righteousness of God and the wrath of God are expressions of the character of God in relation to human beings. The doctrine of justification thus originates in the character of God and the law established by God.

J. I. Packer also emphasises these presuppositions as being the basic principles which uphold the doctrine of justification. 'Protestants of today are accordingly disinclined to take seriously the uniform biblical insistence that God's dealings with man are regulated by law, and God's universal relation to mankind is not that of Father, but of Lawgiver and Judge.'[21] Packer contends that law is established by God for the purpose of maintaining a righteous relationship with human beings — indeed, that this is the uniform biblical principle. Therefore divine wrath directed against human sin is another principle which the doctrine of justification presupposes. Packer continues: 'Reformation theologians have always believed this; first, because the Bible teaches it, and second, because they have felt something of the wrath of God in their own convicted and defiled consciousness.'[22]

The solution to the conflict between the righteousness and wrath of God is the death of Jesus Christ, God's only Son. The full meaning of the death of Christ is a Christological issue which is beyond the scope of this paper and has to be examined in detail separately. But from the standpoint of justification, the least that must be said is that because of Jesus' death, sin and guilt have been imputed to Christ and the righteousness of God has been imputed to the believer. In this sense Christ's death is substitutionary. Packer sees this substitutionary satisfaction as being one more 'given' in the doctrine of justification. 'Salvation in the Bible is by substitution and exchange: the imputing of men's sins to Christ and the imputing of Christ's righteousness to sinners.'[23] This revelation of righteousness through Jesus Christ is a basic biblical teaching. 'God presented him as a sacrifice of atonement, through faith in his blood. He did this to demonstrate his justice . . . he did it to demonstrate his justice at the present time, so as to be just and the one who justifies the man who has faith in Jesus' (Rom. 3:25,26).

The elements which sustain the doctrine of justification are the basic principles which also constitute the whole structure of Christian theology, that is, God, humanity, and Jesus Christ. These substantial elements make the Christian faith different from other religious forms even though they may claim similarity to it. In an examination of the history of Buddhism it has been conjectured that the formal structure of the Christian faith was adopted into Pure Land Buddhism through Nestorian influence in China in the 7th and 8th centuries. This alleged adoption of the formal structure of Christianity has never been disclaimed by any Buddhist sects. Rather, the teachings of Shinran have penetrated into the hearts of the people because of their emphasis on simple faith in Amida–Buddha. This teaching has actually become part of the mental structure of the people, who have then been influenced by it subconsciously. Therefore there needs to be a clear proclamation of the *distinctiveness* of the Christian gospel to those people; otherwise the gospel will simply be absorbed into this mentality and disappear. Shusaku Endo, in his novel *Silence*, refers to this mentality as a big swamp, which indiscriminately accepts anything into itself and makes it disintegrate.[24]

The relevance of justification in a Buddhist context cannot be taken for granted. The full meaning of the doctrine of justification can be understood only when the substantial elements sustaining it are fully proclaimed and taught. The God of the Bible is the Creator of heaven and earth, and the One who judges according to the law he has established. Two points have to be emphasised when the gospel is preached in a Buddhist context. One is that God is ontologically transcendent. God has created all creatures, therefore he is not a part of this world and is qualitatively different from it. This is an important point to make clear in a pantheistic context like Pure Land Buddhism. God cannot be absorbed into any culture, but God is above culture and can change it. The second point is that this transcendent God has established a law between himself and mankind. This law is characterised by the righteousness and holiness of God. Therefore when this law is broken God will react with his judgment and wrath.

These points are essential teachings of the Bible. In the first few chapters of Genesis God is revealed as Creator, Lawgiver, and Judge. These aspects should be clearly proclaimed and taught to people who have a Buddhist background. God should never be identified with Buddha. The biblical teaching regarding God himself is not always well emphasised when Christ and salvation through him are preached. Whenever the gospel is presented the aspects of God as Creator, Lawgiver, and Judge have to be made clear. Then the necessity of Christ as Mediator will be understood more easily. If these truths are not stressed, no difference will be seen between Christ and Amida–Buddha.[25]

The necessity of Christ is also understood when the concept of sin is made clear. In Shinran there is a strong consciousness of sin and guilt, but there is no clear idea about what sin is, where it originates, why we sin, how it comes to be present in us, and what the result is. Biblical teaching always makes clear that sin is related to the law of God. Sin is in one way or another a revolt against God's law. Shinran has a clear consciousness of sin and guilt, and knows that it can never be removed by human effort. Therefore he emphasises the necessity of faith, especially faith in the mercy of Amida. There can be doubt about the sincerity of Shinran's faith, but that does not lead to salvation. Shinran cannot explain why and how salvation occurs through faith in Amida–Buddha. He just says that the mercy of Amida comes upon the believing heart. This ambiguity comes from lack of a clear concept of sin and lack of a clear understanding of what salvation is.

As we have seen, Shinran is very conscious of sin and guilt. Therefore there is little need to emphasise these. But the origin, cause and result of sin need to be made clear, and the means of salvation from it. The substantial elements which sustain the doctrine of justification, that is, God as Creator and Lawgiver, the human predicament, and the historical Jesus, all have to be understood in order to have clear understanding of salvation through Christ. If any of these elements is not taken seriously the actual meaning of justification fades away. Instead of a clear understanding of salvation from sin and Satan, a psychological reinterpretation will take place, which will be no different from the original Buddhism.

In this study of the relevance of justification in a Buddhist context, the decline of the doctrine of justification in recent theological discussion is of considerable significance. Because of this the popular perception of the line between Christianity and Buddhism has become less distinct, as is evident in recent mutual encounters of the two. J. I. Packer indicates that neglect of the doctrine of justification began during the last century, and emphasises the necessity of renewal of this doctrine. 'If all we knew of the church in the past century was that it had neglected the subject of justification in this way, we should already be in a position to conclude that this has been a century of religious apostasy and decline. It is worth our while to try to see what has caused this neglect, and what are the effects of it within Protestant communities today; and then we may discern what has to be done for our situation to be remedied.'[26]

Packer sees this situation as resulting from neglect of 'the historic understanding of the inspiration and authority of Holy Scripture'[27] in modern Protestantism. The relativising of scriptural authority has brought a decline in 'the uniform biblical insistence that God's dealings with man are regulated by law, and that God's universal relation to mankind is not that of Father, but of Lawgiver and Judge'.[28] The basic structure of the doctrine of justification has collapsed with the fall of scriptural authority. Packer concludes that 'thus modern Protestantism really denies the validity of all the forensic terms in which the Bible explains to us our relationship with God'.[29]

G. C. Berkouwer also discusses this weakening of the doctrine of justification and suggests the cause lies in problems raised by dialectical theology. 'The dialectical theology has raised acute problems concerning the relation between justification and sanctification, and therewith between faith and justification, problems that had not been seriously entertained for a century.'[30] Modern Protestantism has done away with a clear distinction between God and man, and has attempted to deal with God and man within the same dimension. The transcendent God has been denied along with his character of righteousness and holiness. The forensic nature of the relationship between God and man has been neglected. Modern Protestantism has reinterpreted all the basic theological issues.

Thus the decline of this doctrine in the mainstream of contemporary theological discussion has paralleled the decline of the authority of the Scriptures and of basic biblical teachings. On the other hand modern theology sees this decline in a positive way because it then allows for more common ground in the encounter between Christianity and Buddhism. W. Pannenberg interprets the doctrine of justification as having brought the believer into a constant consciousness of sin and guilt. 'In the perspective of a purely forensic conception of justification, therefore, believers must turn again and again beyond themselves in their concern for their salvation, and thus continue to relate to themselves as sinner.'[31] The preaching of the law and judgment of God only produces a guilt consciousness. Pannenberg takes seriously the claim of Nietzsche and Freud that Protestant pietism has brought about a penitential mentality. He therefore thinks that the doctrine of justification has brought about an 'ununified mentality' because of repeated preaching that induces guilt.

Hence Pannenberg takes Buddhist spirituality seriously because he thinks that 'Buddhist teaching does not first of all urge the individual to confess to being a sinner, responsible for the miserable condition of his or her life and its social context',[32] and 'in many ways, the Buddhist teaching about the human self seems more realistic than the dominant Western ideology of individual freedom'.[33] To those suffering from this ununified mentality or unauthentic self caused by guilt consciousness, Pannenberg thinks that 'Buddhist spirituality seems remarkably relevant to the spiritual needs of the alienated human individual in modern secular society'.[34] However, Pannenberg does not try to reconcile Christianity with Buddhism; rather he sees this Buddhist teaching as presenting a serious challenge to Christianity. Pannenberg believes that the teaching of Jodoshin is essentially no different from original Buddhist principles, even though he knows that Karl Barth recognises a superficial similarity between this form of Buddhism and Protestant belief. He views Buddhism in general as being a criticism of Christianity because

Buddhism, he thinks, focuses on the experience of the human self which could be damaged by the forensic concept of justification. Pannenberg feels that this criticism is valid because of his own idea that justification is not the central issue, while transformation is. This in turn arises from his Christology, an issue which will not be dealt with here. This concept of transformation fits in more easily with the Buddhist concept, hence he takes it more seriously.

From the biblical standpoint, transformation into the likeness of Christ is based upon the whole work of Christ — his incarnation, cross and resurrection. Justification is based mainly upon Christ's redemptive work on the cross. Thus transformation is predicated on justification by faith in the same way that the resurrection is predicated on the death of Christ. This relationship between justification and transformation needs to be investigated more thoroughly in a separate context, and is beyond the scope of this paper.

However, Pannenberg's basic problem is his denial of the teachings of Scripture that support the forensic concept of justification. When Scripture is accepted in its entirety the forensic concept of justification must be taken seriously. The basic elements of biblical teaching — God, humanity and salvation — sustain this doctrine of justification. Although Pannenberg remarks that the forensic idea of justification has given believers a constant consciousness of sin and guilt, it does not necessarily follow that Buddhism can satisfy the spiritual needs of human beings. Rather it should be remembered that the biblical teaching of justification provides a total way of salvation for human beings because human beings are justified only before God. For Shinran salvation is not salvation from sin and lust, but just a passing away sideways into the Pure Land where human beings are accepted in their sinfulness. Shinran tried to solve this human predicament but was forced to conclude that human sin and lust remain as such even after we have seriously sought for salvation, because Shinran did not know any God who could deliver us from our sin.

It should always be remembered that there is no solution to guilt consciousness in Buddhism because there is no way of being forgiven by 'Absolute Other'. In Buddhism the solution to guilt consciousness can only be found by invoking the name of Amida. But this solution is not based upon historical reality, only upon an interpretation of the story of Hozo the Bodhisattva. The law given by God and the death and resurrection of the historical Jesus are the crucial points which make justification by faith different from Shinran's teaching.

Recent Buddhist influence in the West, and its manifestations in the New Age movement, may be an indication to Western Christianity that there are some areas in which its own message is deficient or not being proclaimed in its fulness. That does not mean that Buddhism can fill any vacuum which Christianity might have left. Rather, it means that Christian perspectives should be widened and deepened whenever they face a different context.

Notes to Chapters

NOTES TO CHAPTER 2

1. *Apology of the Augsburg Confession* (1531) 4:2, cited by John Reumann, *'Righteousness' in the New Testament: Justification in the United States Lutheran–Roman Catholic Dialogue* (Philadelphia, 1982) 3. See Roland H. Bainton, *Here I Stand: A Life of Martin Luther* (New York, 1955) 50.

2. See N. T. Wright, 'Justification', *NDT* 361. Note the view of Georg Strecker, a participant in the Malta Report, who 'regards justification as a mere polemical doctrine against Paul's opponents not repeatable today' (John Reumann, *op. cit.*, 5 n. 2).

3. See John Reumann, *'Righteousness' in the New Testament*, 41, 42, 103. See also the survey by Peter T. O'Brien in this volume.

4. Cited by Stephen Motyer, 'Righteousness by Faith in the New Testament', in J. I. Packer, ed., *Here We Stand: Justification by Faith Today* (London, 1986) 33. Motyer suggests that neither Paul nor any other New Testament author would immediately use the language of justification, as Cranmer does, to state the heart of the gospel.

5. Richard Hooker, 'A Learned Discourse of Justification', *Of the Laws of Ecclesiastical Polity* (Everyman Edition) 17 (cited in C. Fitzsimons Allison, 'The Pastoral and Political Implications of Trent on Justification: a Response to the ARCIC Agreed Statement *Salvation and the Church*' [*SLJT*, 31:3 (June 1988)]).

6. *Salvation and the Church: An Agreed Statement by the Second Anglican-Roman Catholic International Commission*, ARCIC II (London, 1987) 26.

7. John C. Cooper, 'Justification', in William H. Gentz, ed., *The Dictionary of Bible and Religion* (Nashville, 1986) 567.

8. The development of the doctrine in the theology of the Reformation has been traced in: Reumann, *op. cit.*; Peter Toon, *Justification and Sanctification* (London, 1983); and especially in Alister E. McGrath, *Iustitia Dei: A History of the Christian Doctrine of Justification*, vol. 2 *From 1500 to the Present Day* (Cambridge, 1986).

9. Rom. 2:16; 16:25; 2 Tim. 2:8. The meaning is not different when Paul says 'our gospel': 2 Cor. 4:3; 1 Thess. 1:5; 2 Thess. 2:14.

10. F. J. Foakes Jackson & Kirsopp Lake, eds., *The Beginnings of Christianity: Part I, The Acts of the Apostles*, vol. V (Grand Rapids, reprint 1966) 74–96.

11. James I. Packer, 'Justification', *IBD* 842f. See P. T. O'Brien's discussion, in this volume, of the question of the centrality of justification in Paul's theology.

12. Meredith G. Kline, *The Treaty of the Great King* (Grand Rapids, 1963).

13. Herwi Rikhof, *The Concept of the Church: A Methodological Inquiry into the Use of Metaphors in Ecclesiology* (London, 1981).

14. Gerhard von Rad, following the hypotheses of source criticism, alleges that

God was not spoken of as King in Israel until the Israelite kingship was established. He says, 'As is only natural, references are first found only after the rise of the empirical monarchy: Nu. 23:21; Dt. 33:5; 1 K. 22:19 and Is. 6:5 are among the earliest.' (*Cf.* '*melek* and *malkûth* in the OT' under '*basileus*' etc., *TDNT* 2.568f.) In addition to the references from the Pentateuch cited by von Rad, we might note the use of the verb in the song of Moses (Exod. 15:18). Since, as von Rad says, the term 'king' was applied to the gods in all the ancient Orient, why should its use in Israel await the establishment of its own national kingship? Note that the institution of the political kingship is described as Israel's rejection of the divine king. God says to Samuel, 'It is not you they have rejected as their king, but me' (1 Sam. 8:7). Perhaps the reserve in the use of king as a title for God in the Pentateuch points to the superior force of the divine names. God is not just heavenly royalty, but reveals himself by name as the personal Lord of the covenant. The concept of 'judge' is more fundamental than king, is rooted in an earlier social structure, and serves to define the main function of a king (1 Sam. 8:15). God is the judge of all the earth, and of his people in particular (Gen. 16:5; 31:53; Exod. 5:21; Deut. 32:36; 1 Sam. 2:10; 24:12,15).

15. Joachim Jeremias, '*poimēn*', *TDNT* 6.486.

16. An Old English verb, 'rightwise', to put in the right, has fallen into disuse.

17. Does the 'justice' rendered to the poor and needy go beyond distributive justice? McGrath (*Iustitia Dei* 1.8) claims that it does, and that the *ṣᵉdāqāh* due to the poor is 'just' because it restores 'a right order of affairs' violated by the existence of poverty. This assumption seems unnecessary. In the Mosaic law, the poor are seen as victims of injustice. Just judgment redresses their wrongs and delivers them from unjust oppression (Exod. 23:6,7). The person of the poor is no more to be respected in judgment than the person of the rich (Lev. 19:15).

18. The Hebrew idiom for the comparison, literally 'righteous and good from him', has the sense of 'righteous and good as seen (judged) from his state' (KB, 536).

19. McGrath, 1.23.

20. McGrath, 1.12.

21. The adjective *nāqî*, often translated 'innocent', means 'not chargeable'. Usually what is not charged is a sentence of guilt, but it may be another obligation (1 Kings 15:22). The expressions for 'declaring righteous' or 'clearing' are often used in association with the term *rîb*, a law-case, and *mishpāṭ*, judgment (Deut. 32:4; Job 9:2; 13:18; 29:14–17; Ps. 43:1).

22. John Reumann takes issue with Luther and with recent authors who find similarity between the Pauline conception of faith and that found in Hebrews (Reumann, '*Righteousness' in the New Testament* 23). The language is surely similar (Heb. 11:7). It is true that Hebrews reflects the Old Testament view of faith in the promises of God. Paul makes the meaning of looking to God for salvation more explicit, but his doctrine, too, is drawn from the fundamental nature of faith in the sovereign, saving God.

23. The Hebrew term '*ābad* means to serve in the sense of working for someone (sometimes as a slave), but also to serve in a cultic sense (as to speak of a 'service of worship'). God commands Pharaoh to let his people go that they may serve in both of these senses: enter into covenant with him as his servants, and worship him (Exod. 3:12; 8:1).

24. Francis I. Anderson, 'Yahweh, the Kind and Sensitive God', in P. T. O'Brien and D. G. Peterson, eds., *God Who Is Rich in Mercy* (Grand Rapids, 1986) 41–88.

25. Gerhard von Rad, *Old Testament Theology* vol. 1 (New York, 1962) 247, 378, 379). G. M. Butterworth calls attention to von Rad's contribution: 'Justification in the Old Testament', in J. I. Packer, ed., *Here We Stand: Justification by Faith Today*, 17f.

26. David Peterson, *Hebrews and Perfection: An Examination of the Concept of Perfection in the 'Epistle to the Hebrews'* (Cambridge, 1982) 167.

27. John Murray has shown the need of distinguishing between biblical passages that speak of sanctification in terms of the ongoing process and those that speak of an

initial 'definitive' sanctification, accomplished in Christ's death and resurrection and received by faith. (*Collected Writings of John Murray*, vol. 2: *Systematic Theology* [Edinburgh, 1977] 277–293). Murray distinguishes 'definitive sanctification' from justification as well as from regeneration. The distinction is important, yet we must also recognise that the biblical language of cultic holiness may include what justification properly isolates, the status aspect of those who have been declared to be acceptable to God.

28. To some extent Jewish writers had already used universal language in describing the blessings of the latter days, following the lead given by the prophets. 'Therefore with an oath He promised him "To bless the nations in his seed"', to multiply him "as the dust of the earth", and to exalt his seed "as the stars"; to cause them to inherit "from sea to sea, and from the River to the ends of the earth" ' (Ecclesiasticus 44:21). See the citation from *Mekilta* 40*b* in C. E. B. Cranfield, *Romans* (Edinburgh, 1975) 1.229.

29. The NIV translation 'this is their vindication from me' is reasonable, since the context speaks of judgment against the enemy. In the light of the broader context, however, the broader term may be preferred (*cf.* Isa. 54:14; 53:11).

30. For this translation, see Henri Blocher, *Songs of the Servant* (Leicester, 1975) 64.

31. Blocher, *op. cit.*, 72, 73.

32. Artur Weiser, '*Pisteuō*' etc., in particular 'B. The Old Testament Concept', *TDNT* 6.187.

33. Weiser, *ibid.*

34. The article by Weiser was cited above. See the later article and bibliography by Alfred Jepsen in *TDOT* 1.293–323.

35. Jepsen lists Gen. 15:6; Exod. 4:31; 14:31; Ps. 106:12; Jonah 3:5; Ps. 119:66; (*cf.* 116:10; 27:13), and, in another form, Exod. 19:98; Isa. 7:9; 2 Chron. 20:20; Isa. 28:16; 43:10. He does not list passages where the lack of faith is mentioned, *e.g.* Num. 14:11.

36. See Weiser's article, cited above.

37. Jepsen calls attention to this use of *bātah* in Pss. 13:5; 25:2; 26:1, 28:7; 31:7, 14; 52:8; 55:23; 56:3,4, 11; 86:2; 143:8; 71:5.

38. Rudolf Bultmann, '*pisteuō*' etc., in particular 'C. Faith in Judaism', *TDNT* 6.198. Bultmann emphasises the use of other terms than *'āman* in the Psalms to express trust, and the fact that only *'āman* terms are translated by *pisteuō* terms in the LXX.

39. *Ibid.*

40. 'To believe' (*'āman*) is to be firm in. The verb is repeated in this verse. If Ahaz will not make himself firm in the Lord, he will not be made firm. Weiser takes the 'establishing' of the second clause to be establishment in existence, actualising (*ibid.* 189). He takes faith to be 'the condition of existence'. While this may be too existential an interpretation, the necessity of faith is surely asserted.

41. 'But the NT gives a legitimate development of the prophet's thought through the medium of the LXX translation, *pistis*' J. B. Taylor, 'Habakkuk, Book of', *IBD* 2.597.

42. Keeping the clause 'the Son of Man who is in heaven' as original, although it is missing in early manuscripts. See Bruce M. Metzger, *A Textual Commentary on the Greek New Testament* (London, 1971) 203f.

43. N. T. Wright, 'Justification', *NDT* 359.

44. The Old Testament identifies the kingdom of God with his righteous rule. The announcement of the kingdom is therefore the announcement of God's saving righteousness. There is no reason to question the authenticity of Matthew's reporting of this teaching of Jesus on the grounds of redaction criticism. See the discussion in John Reumann, *'Righteousness' in the New Testament*, 125–135.

45. See the strong defence of this in Herman Ridderbos, *The Coming of the Kingdom* (trs. H. de Jongste; Philadelphia, 1962) 285–333.

46. Ridderbos, *ibid*. 253. He defends the translation 'faith' rather than 'faithfulness' in the light of such sayings as Matthew 17:20.

47. See Reumann, *ibid*. 27–40.

48. Literally, 'made alive in the spirit'. The reference is to the resurrection of Christ's body as a new and spiritual reality.

49. See Reumann, *ibid*. 28 n. 41.

50. See the careful exposition of Romans 10:4 in C. E. B. Cranfield, *Romans* 2.515–520. Cranfield concludes that Paul's meaning is that Christ is the goal of the law, although he finds this to be closely related to Christ's fulfilling the law. 'The righteousness to which the law was summoning them was all the time nothing other than that righteousness which God offers to men in Christ' (p. 520). This does indeed imply that Christ is made to us righteousness because he is the righteous one.

51. Herman Ridderbos, *Paul: an Outline of His Theology* (trs. J. R. De Witt; Grand Rapids, 1975) 192.

52. Friedrich Büchsel argues against the locative use of *en* in the formula *en Christō*: ' "In Christus" bei Paulus', *ZNW* 42 (1949) 141–158.

53. When Paul speaks of the 'obedience of faith' (Rom. 1:5; 16:26) he uses the noun form of the verb translated 'hearken' in Romans 10:16 (ASV). The 'hearkening' of faith is the receiving and appropriating of the offer of the gospel; it includes the committal of trust. It should not be misunderstood in a way that would overthrow Paul's emphasis on the distinctiveness of faith. Faith, by its very nature, is not an achievement but the opposite. In Romans 10:20 the term *apeithounta* also describes distrust. See BAGD p. 639 2a: The verb *peithō* in the second perfect with a present meaning, when used with the dative can approach the sense of 'believe in', a sense that it also approximates in the LXX. See also BAGD p. 82, *apeitheō*, 3.

54. Some of the phrasing of this section has been taken from a paper prepared as a study at Westminster Theological Seminary, Philadelphia, 'Westminster Statement on Justification' (May, 1980).

55. The doctrines of the last judgment and of the deliverance and justification of believers are regularly set together in the New Testament, and not only in Paul's writings (John 5:24, *cf*. v. 29; Rev. 22:11, 12, *cf*. vv. 14, 17; Acts 10:42, *cf*. v. 43; 2 Cor. 5:10, *cf*. v. 19, 21; 1 Pet. 4:19, *cf*. 2:23).

56. Charles H. Cosgrove rightly holds that 'justification in Paul belongs not only at the beginning of life in Christ but also at its final consummation' ('Justification in Paul: A Linguistic and Theological Reflection', *JBL* 106 [1987] 653). He fails to recognise, however, how fully Paul identifies the Lord's present verdict of justification with the final verdict. He takes Paul's use of 'justify' in 1 Cor. 4:4 in an absolute sense, rather than as an evaluation of his stewardship, and deals with 1 Cor. 3:15 (certainly relevant) in a puzzling way. In exegeting Romans 8, he well emphasises the suffering servant theme as applicable to Christians (and the apostle), but seems to miss the climactic force of Paul's argument ('justified' in v. 30) and the importance of Christ's death and resurrection in v. 34. The exegesis of Rom. 5:10 is the key to Cosgrove's position. He misconstrues Paul's position when he says, 'Past justification provides neither the grounds of exemption from future wrath nor the model for such exemption' (p. 667). Justification does not provide the grounds for exemption from wrath. It *is* exemption from wrath. The grounds are in Jesus Christ, and Paul regularly joins the death and the resurrection life of Christ precisely to affirm that salvation is complete.

57. The Council of Trent, in its Canons on Justification, did not substitute works for faith, but held that works must be added to faith. It rejected the 'faith alone' formula and anathematised all who would not agree that justification once received is preserved and increased in the sight of God through good works (Session VI, January, 1547; *cf*. Henry Bettenson, ed., *Documents of the Christian Church* [London, 1943] 366).

58. William Hendriksen describes the gaining of Christ as a 'life-long activity'

(*Exposition of Philippians* [Grand Rapids, 1962] 164 n. 145). Even if the aorist subjunctives are so understood, their final reference is to the end.

NOTES TO CHAPTER 3

a. (Since the publication of his major work, *Paul and Palestinian Judaism* (Philadelphia/ London, 1977), E. P. Sander's influence on Pauline studies has been so phenomenal that a separate essay, by Dr. P. T. O'Brien, is largely devoted to interacting with him.)

1. By 'Jewish' is meant intertestamental categories highly influenced by the Old Testament.

1a. We here use the term 'Judaisers' as it is commonly used in contemporary discussion of the problems Paul faced along these lines, even though the term had different connotations in the first century.

2. We have in these verses an example of the remarkable change that had come about in Paul's own scale of values as a result of his faith in Christ. As a Christian he considered all these things (see vv. 4b–6) as refuse, but he knew only too well how much they meant to his erstwhile companies in Pharisaism.

3. See G. F. Moore, *Judaism in the First Centuries of the Christian Era* (Cambridge/ Harvard, 1927) 482f. for references.

4. *Ibid.* 495.

5. *Ibid.* 494.

6. Jub. 23:10.

7. Sir. 44:20; Jud. 8:26; 1 Macc. 2:52; Jub. 6:19; 18; 21:2, etc.; 4 Macc. 16:20; Syr. Bar. 57:1ff.

8. *Aboth* 5:3; *sif. Dt.*, 32 on 6:5.

9. G. F. Moore, *op. cit.* 232.

10. G. E. Ladd, *A Theology of the New Testament* (Grand Rapids/London 1974) 368.

11. E.g. F. Mussner, *Der Galaterbrief* (Freiburg, 1974) 80.

12. So H. G. Wood, 'The conversion of St. Paul. Its Nature, Antecedents and consequences', *NTS* 1 (1954–55) 276–282 (281).

It is contended by some scholars on the basis of Acts 26:14 that even while he persecuted the church, Paul had a guilty conscience because he had begun to suspect that the Christian case was true after all. This is not a necessary interpretation of this passage and actually conflicts with the general thrust of the three accounts in Acts of Paul's confrontation with the exalted Lord. It has been pointed out by other scholars that 'kicking against the goads' was a well-known expression in the Greek world for opposition to deity. Here in Acts 26:14 it draws attention to Paul's realisation that his persecution of the church was, ultimately, opposition to God himself. See R. Longenecker, *The Ministry and Message of Paul* (Grand Rapids, 1971) 32.

13. It is significant that Paul makes little, if any, distinction between his 'conversion' and his 'call to be an apostle to the Gentiles'. Indeed, the purpose clause in Gal. 1:16 reflects his conviction that the 'revelation of Jesus Christ' to him laid an obligation on him to preach the gospel to the Gentiles. Therefore, Paul's emphasis on the grace of God not only reflects his personal experience of God's grace but is directed against the Jewish emphasis on works of the law and human achievement.

14. The term 'salvation history' 'focuses on the thought that the unifying theme of Scripture is the history of God's saving acts, first in Israel under the old covenant and then in Christ who brings about a new covenant relationship between God and man. This in turn points to the Parousia and the culmination of history. Salvation history is seen as the key to the meaning and course of secular history' (*NIDNTT* 1.59).

15. So e.g. H. Ridderbos, *The Epistle of Paul to the Churches of Galatia* (London, 1954) 124.

16. *Ibid.* 123. This is the traditional interpretation of this text, but it has been vigorously challenged in recent times. See e.g. D. P. Fuller, 'Paul and "The Works of the Law" ', *WTJ* 38 (1975) 33; *Gospel and Law* (Grand Rapids, 1980) 88–105. However, Fuller's interpretation as well as other recent alternative interpretations are unconvincing. See T. R. Schreiner, 'Is Perfect Obedience to the Law Possible?' *JETS* 27 (1984) 151–160; *idem*, 'Paul and Perfect Obedience to the Law', *WTJ* 47 (1985) 245–278 (253–60), where he critiques E. P. Sanders's interpretation of this verse in *Paul, the Law and the Jewish People* (Philadelphia, 1983) 17–23.

In Gal. 3:13 the apostle states that in order to redeem us from this death-curse, Christ 'became a curse for us'. This must mean that Christ's identification with man's sin extended to bearing the penalty that is pronounced against it. See further L. Morris, *The Cross in the New Testament* (Grand Rapids, 1965) 222f. This verse is closely paralleled in 2 Cor. 5:21, where Paul speaks of Christ 'being made sin for us, so that in him we might become the righteousness of God'. Barrett says, '[Christ] came to stand in that relationship with God which normally is the result of sin, estranged from God and the object of his wrath'. He adds, 'We, correspondingly and through God's loving act in Christ have come to stand in that relation with God which is described by the term righteousness, that is, we are acquitted by his court, justified, reconciled' (*The Second Epistle to the Corinthians* [London, 1973] 180).

17. E. de W. Burton, *A Critical and Exegetical Commentary on the Epistle to the Galatians* (Edinburgh, 1921) 166. An examination of Rom. 1:17 where Paul cites Hab. 2:4 again supports this interpretation. A major point of interpretation in this text is the meaning of the phrase *dikaiosynē tou theou* in the first half of the verse. There are two important considerations that favour taking *theou* as a subjective genitive and *dikaiosynē* as a reference to God's activity: (1) both in the Old Testament and in late Jewish apocalyptic writings the righteousness of God refers to God's activity in salvation and in faithfulness to his covenant and his creation; (2) in the context in Rom. 1 *theou* as subjective genitive occurs in v. 16 and v. 18, and in both these verses the reference is to God's activity. Moreover, there is a clear parallelism in structure between v. 17 and v. 18. This latter point is certainly significant. However, with regard to (1) it ought to be said that far more important than the usage of the phrase in the Old Testament and late Judaism is the usage of Paul in the rest of Romans and in his other letters.

There are several texts in the Pauline letters in which *dikaiosynē* refers to man's righteous status received from God. In Phil. 3:9 'a righteousness of my own' is contrasted with 'that [righteousness] which is through faith — the righteousness that comes from God'. Similarly, in Rom. 10:3 Paul contrasts 'the righteousness of God' with 'their own [righteousness]', which suggests that the reference is to the status of righteousness that God offers rather than to God's righteous activity. Thus NIV translates: 'the righteousness that comes from God'. In Rom. 5:17 there is a reference to 'the gift of righteousness' which is closely associated with 'God's abundant provision of righteousness' and must mean man's righteous status that is bestowed on him by God.

However, perhaps the most serious problem with interpreting *dikaiosynē theou* as a reference to God's activity in Rom. 1:17 is the phrase that follows: *ek pisteōs eis pistin*. Cranfield rightly says: 'It is extremely difficult to see how *ek pisteōs eis pistin* can at all convincingly be shown to be a natural expression for Paul to have used, if he meant by *dikaiosynē theou* God's activity' (*Romans* 1.98).

On the other hand, the structure of the argument of the letter supports taking *dikaiosynē theou* in Rom. 1:7a as a reference to the righteous status bestowed by God. Similarly, since the citation from Hab. 2:4b is in confirmation of what he has just said, it is almost certain that *ek pisteōs* is to be connected with *ho dikaios* rather than with the verb (see Nygren, *Romans* pp. 85ff. for a detailed argument).

18. See E. P. Sanders, *Paul and Palestinian Judaism* 483.

19. See A. Oepke, *Der Brief des Paulus an die Galater* (Berlin, 1957) 79.

20. So Ridderbos, *Galatia* 124.

21. *Cf.* Lk. 7:39; Jn. 8:42; 9:33 for a similar grammatical construction.

22. D. Guthrie, *Galatians* (London, 1969) 111.

23. So most commentators; *pace* Cranfield, *Romans* 1.291–92, who insists that the reference is merely to the undisputed fact that the law was given at a later date than that of Adam's fall, i.e. in the time of Moses.

24. E.g. Ecclus. 5:5f.

25. For the relation between what Paul says in Rom. 2:1–16 and his doctrine of justification through faith see Cranfield's discussion in *Romans* 1.151–53; also W. G. Kümmel, *The Theology of the New Testament* (ET, London, 1974) 228–32.

26. See Moore, *Judaism* 1.277.

27. See e.g. 2 Esdras 3:33f. where the writer insists that although the Jews have not done perfectly, they have as a nation done better than others.

28. H. J. Schoeps, *Paul. The Theology of the Apostle in the Light of Jewish Religious History* (ET, Philadelphia, 1961) 187.

29. *Ibid.*

30. See D. A. Carson, *Divine Sovereignty and Human Responsibility* (Atlanta, 1981) which traces the development of merit theology in the Intertestamental Jewish literature (pp. 41–121).

31. Monotheism necessarily implies that salvation in the divine intent must be universal.

32. Cranfield, *Romans* 2.507f.; R. Badenas, *Christ the End of the Law* (Sheffield, 1985) 104f. rightly draw attention to the fact that Paul says 'law of righteousness' and not 'righteousness of law' or legal righteousness. The significance of this is that, for Paul, the righteousness that the law prescribed is precisely the righteousness that is offered to believers. Paul reproaches Israel not for pursuing this righteousness, but for pursuing it 'as if it were by works'.

33. The phrase 'righteousness of God' appears twice in this verse, and one of the points of interpretation is whether the phrase means the same thing in both instances. Cranfield, *Romans* 2.515 assumes it does, and clarifies the meaning as 'God's proffered gift of a status of righteousness' (*contra* several commentators who understand the phrase as referring to God's redemptive activity). The explicit link between righteousness and faith in the wider context (*cf.* 9:30, 32 and 10:4) suggests that Cranfield's interpretation of the phrase is right at least in the first instance. A further point of interpretation is what is meant by Israel seeking to establish 'their own righteousness'. Cranfield explains this as 'a righteous status of their own earning', but the strong emphasis in the wider context on true righteousness being available to all — that is, both Jews and Gentiles — suggests that 'their own righteousness' connotes rather an understanding of righteousness that is the exclusive prerogative of the Jews. (See G. E. Howard, 'Christ the End of the Law', *JBL* 88 [1969] 331–37 [336]). There is general scholarly consensus that Israel's 'not submitting to God's righteousness' must refer to the Jewish rejection of the Messiah. *Cf.* Cranfield, *Romans* 2.515; Badenas, *op. cit.* 110.

34. E. Käsemann, *Commentary on Romans* (ET, Grand Rapids, 1980) 282–83, accepts this meaning only.

35. So e.g. Cranfield, *Romans* 2.515–20; Badenas, *op. cit.* 112ff.

36. So F. F. Bruce, *Romans* (London, 1963) p. 203 and several other scholars. This is vigorously opposed by Cranfield and Badenas. There are, however, a number of passages in the Pauline epistles that could be understood to mean that in Christ the law has been superseded and Cranfield's attempt to interpret all these passages otherwise (*ibid.* 852–61) is unconvincing. It is much more natural to understand Paul to be saying that 'with Christ the old order of which the Law formed part, has been done away, to be replaced by the new order of the Spirit' (so Bruce, *ibid.*).

37. *Cf.* G. E. Howard, 'Christ the End of the Law', 336.

38. In interpreting Rom. 10:5–8 one must remember that Paul consistently denies

that there are two kinds of righteousness — legal righteousness and faith-righteousness — but contends rather that even in the Old Testament, true righteousness is attained by faith. In other words, Paul is not setting Deut. 30:11–14 against Lev. 18:5, but rather interpreting Lev. 18:5 in the light of Deut. 30:11–4. He argues that the righteousness required by the law is actually attained only through faith that issues in righteous living. See D. Fuller, *Gospel and Law* 66–70.

39. The expression 'reckoned as' simply expresses the idea that a certain thing is valued at a certain value or credited to a person, without implying that such valuation was otherwise than according to the fact. 'Reckoned as righteousness' meant that Abraham's faith was counted to his credit 'with a view to the receiving of righteousness' rather than that faith was reckoned to him as equivalent to righteousness. So e.g. M. Black, *Romans* (London, 1975) 76.

40. So E. Käsemann, 'The faith of Abraham in Romans 4', *Perspectives on Paul* (ET, London, 1969) 85.

41. *Cf.* E. E. Ellis, *Paul's Use of the Old Testament* (London/Edinburgh, 1957) 126, who points out that the stress of Paul's quotations is not upon predictive prophecy as it is usually understood, but upon the application of principles enunciated in the Old Testament. These principles are viewed as realised or fulfilled in a special way in the Messianic Age ushered in by Christ's resurrection.

42. V. Taylor, *Forgiveness and Reconciliation* (London, 1946) 47.

43. Käsemann, 'The faith of Abraham in Romans 4', 92.

44. J. Murray, *The Epistle to the Romans* (Grand Rapids, 1973) 151.

45. On this see Kümmel, *Theology* 200–203.

46. So e.g. C. H. Dodd, *The Meaning of Paul for Today* (London/Glasgow, 1958) 121–22. He is followed by V. Taylor, *op. cit.* 58.

47. See J. B. Lightfoot, *St Paul's Epistle to the Galatians* (London, 1865) 149.

48. *Cf.* R. Bring, 'Preaching the Law', *SJT* 13 (1960) 21. *Pace* Cranfield, *Romans* 1.383f.

49. *A Commentary on the Epistle to the Romans* (London, 1957) 157.

50. It is appropriate to comment briefly on why the 'righteousness' terms appear to be tied up to Romans and Galatians. On the one hand, Phil. 3:9 indicates that Paul's doctrine of justification by grace through faith was implicit in his Damascus road experience. It is through that experience that he came to realise the inadequacy of law-keeping as a way of gaining God's acceptance. In Galatians Paul deals with a situation that had arisen because certain opponents had convinced some of his new converts to Christ that they needed to keep the Jewish law and be circumcised. Paul uses the doctrine of justification through faith as his weapon to contend with this situation. However, it is clear from Romans that the doctrine cannot be dubbed as merely 'polemical doctrine'. There is general scholarly consensus that in Romans we have 'Paul's exposition of "his" gospel to the Gentile churches' (C. K. Barrett, *Romans* 7). Therefore it is only to be expected that justification by grace through faith would be a dominant theme in this epistle.

NOTES TO CHAPTER 4

1. So M. T. Brauch, 'Perspectives on "God's righteousness" in recent German discussion', in E. P. Sanders, *Paul and Palestinian Judaism* (London, 1977) 523–542, esp. 532. I am indebted to Brauch's discussion as well as that of M. L. Soards, 'The Righteousness of God in the Writings of the Apostle Paul', *BTB* 15 (1985) 104–109. Note also the histories of interpretation in P. Stuhlmacher, *Gerechtigkeit Gottes bei Paulus* (Göttingen, 1966) 11–73, and C. Müller, *Gottesgerechtigkeit und Gottes Volk. Eine Untersuchung zu Römer 9–11* (Göttingen, 1965).

2. N. T. Wright, 'The Paul of History and the Apostle of Faith', *TynB* 29 (1978) 61–88, esp. 61, with particular reference to the debate between K. Stendahl and E.

Käsemann over the relationship in Paul's thought between the doctrine of justification and salvation history.

2a. The writings of E.P. Sanders have stimulated recent research into the sociological aspects of justification, particularly with reference to the Jew-Gentile question in Galations and Romans. Space has prevented me from interacting with this area which has developed apace since this paper was first delivered in November, 1988.

3. M. T. Brauch, in *Paul* 523–542, esp. 524.

4. Although described somewhat imprecisely as an objective genitive, it has been more accurately termed a genitive of authorship.

5. M. T. Brauch, in *Paul* 525; *cf.* P. Stuhlmacher, *Gerechtigkeit* 19–23.

6. R. Bultmann, *New Testament Theology* 1 (London, 1951) 276; *cf.* M. L. Soards, *BTB* 15 (1985) 105.

7. R. Bultmann, *Theology* 1.285.

8. Like a divine property or characteristic of a Greek god (*cf.* M. L. Soards, *BTB* 15 [1985] 105).

9. E. Käsemann, *New Testament Questions of Today* (London, 1969) 168, 173, 175f., 180f.

10. E. Käsemann, *Questions* 180.

11. M. L. Soards, *BTB* 15 (1985) 105.

12. E. Käsemann, *Questions* 182.

13. E. Käsemann, 'Justification and Salvation History in the Epistle to the Romans', *Perspectives on Paul* (London, 1971) 78; *cf.* M. L. Soards, *BTB* 15 (1985) 106.

14. M. T. Brauch, in *Paul* 527.

15. M. T. Brauch, in *Paul* 528–529. Käsemann (*Questions* 182) speaks of being 'obedient to the divine righteousness'.

16. C. Müller, *Gottesgerechtigkeit.*

17. M. T. Brauch, in *Paul* 531.

18. P. Stuhlmacher, *Gottesgerechtigkeit* 175, cited by M. T. Brauch, in *Paul* 532.

19. P, Stuhlmacher, *Gottesgerechtigkeit* 98; *cf.* M. T. Brauch, in *Paul* 531–532.

20. M. T. Brauch, in *Paul* 533.

21. P. Stuhlmacher, *Gottesgerechtigkeit* 227, cited by M. T. Brauch, in *Paul* 533.

22. In *Reconciliation, Law & Righteousness. Essays in Biblical Theology* (Philadelphia, 1986) 68–93.

23. P. Stuhlmacher, in *Reconciliation* 68 (his emphasis).

24. P. Stuhlmacher, in *Reconciliation* 78.

25. P. Stuhlmacher, in *Reconciliation* 81.

26. K. Kertelge, *'Rechtfertigung' bei Paulus. Studien zur Struktur und zum Bedeutungsgehalt des paulinischen Rechtsfertigungsbegriffs* (Münster, 1967).

27. K. Kertelge, *'Rechtfertigung'*, 305. *Cf.* M. T. Brauch, in *Paul* 533.

28. K. Kertelge, *'Rechtfertigung'* 112–160.

29. M. T. Brauch, in *Paul* 536; *cf.* K. Kertelge, *'Rechtfertigung'* 127.

30. K. Kertelge, *'Rechtfertigung'*, 157f.

31. R. Bultmann, 'δικαιοσύνη θεοῦ', *JBL* 83 (1964) 12–16.

32. C. E. B. Cranfield, *The Epistle to the Romans* 1 (Edinburgh, 1975) 99. He argues (p. 97) that 'θεοῦ [*theou*] is a genitive of origin and that δικαιοσύνη [*dikaiosynē*] refers to man's righteous status which is the result of God's action of justifying'.

33. H. Conzelmann, 'Die Rechfertigungslehre des Paulus: Theologie oder Anthropologie?' *EvT* 28 (1968) 389–404. Note M. T. Brauch, in *Paul* 537–539.

34. M. T. Brauch, in *Paul* 538.

35. G. Klein, 'Righteousness in the New Testament', *IDBS* (Nashville, 1976) 750–752.

36. E.g. R. B. Hayes, 'Psalm 143 and the Logic of Romans 3', *JBL* 99 (1980) 107–115, and M. L. Soards, 'Käsemann's "Righteousness" Reexamined', *CBQ* 49 (1987) 264–267.

37. K. Stendahl, now printed in his *Paul Among Jews and Gentiles* (Philadelphia, 1976) 78–96.

38. As part of Stendahl's reply, in *Paul* 131 (*cf.* 129–133), cited by N. T. Wright, *TynB* 29 (1978) 63.

39. Note the helpful treatment of the debate between Stendahl and Käsemann in N. T. Wright, *TynB* 29 (1978) 61–72.

40. S. K. Williams, 'The "Righteousness of God" in Romans', *JBL* 99 (1980) 241–290.

41. J. Reumann, *'Righteousness' in the New Testament* (Philadelphia, 1982) 66, has entered the caveat: 'in our opinion not every use of *tou theou* need be uniform after *dikaiosynē*; each passage must be judged for itself in context'. While this is certainly possible, Williams' case for the subjective genitive, understood along the lines of God's faithfulness to his covenant promises to Abraham, makes sense out of many Pauline texts.

42. Although not strictly part of this debate, the work of J. A. Ziesler, *The Meaning of Righteousness in Paul. A Linguistic and Theological Enquiry* (Cambridge, 1972), ought to be noted. Ziesler argues that the verb *dikaioō*, to 'justify', was used relationally in Paul, often with the forensic meaning 'acquit', but the noun *dikaiosynē* and the adjective *dikaios* have behavioural meanings. In Paul's thought Christians are both justified by faith and also righteous by faith. However, the distinction Ziesler draws between Paul's use of the verb on the one hand, and the adjective and substantive on the other, has been seriously questioned both linguistically and exegetically.

43. As M. T. Brauch, in *Paul* 539, calls it. Note his summary discussion, pp. 539–542, to which I am indebted.

44. E. Käsemann, *Questions* 180. It is perhaps not insignificant that Käsemann, who has been criticised for blurring the distinction between creation and new creation in his treatment of righteousness, has expressed the later developments of his understanding of power in socio-political categories.

45. R. Y. K. Fung, 'The status of justification by faith in Paul's thought: a brief survey of a modern debate', *Themelios* 6 (1981) 4–11.

46. The names of W. Wrede, W. Heitmüller and A. Schweitzer particularly stand out. Fung included H. J. Schoeps, C. H. Buck, K. Stendahl, W. D. Davies, E. P. Sanders and G. Strecker in his survey of more recent scholars who regard Paul's doctrine of justification by faith as being of secondary importance.

47. G. Bornkamm, *Paul* (London, 1971), 115–117, 152; *cf.* R. Fung, *Themelios* 6 (1981) 9.

48. K. Kertelge, *'Rechtfertigung'* 286, 295–306; *cf.* R. Fung, *Themelios* 6 (1981) 9.

49. R. Fung, *Themelios* 6 (1981) 10.

50. K. Kertelge, *'Rechtfertigung'*, 295, cited by R. Fung, *Themelios* 6 (1981) 11.

51. Note the treatment by C. J. A. Hickling, 'Centre and Periphery in the Thought of Paul', *Studia Biblica* III (Sheffield, 1978) 199–214.

52. J. Reumann, *Righteousness* 106–107.

53. *ST* 42 (1988) 55–68.

54. H. W. Boers, *ST* 42 (1988) 62.

55. H. W. Boers, *ST* 42 (1988) 63.

56. R. Fung, *Themelios* 6 (1981) 9.

57. *Cf.* H. W. Boers, *ST* 42 (1988) 57.

58. For a discussion of the meaning of 'content criticism' and its use, see R. Morgan, *The Nature of New Testament Theology* (London, 1973) 42ff.

59. R. P. Martin, *Reconciliation. A Study of Paul's Theology* (Atlanta, 1981) 75;

note his discussion, pp. 71ff., and the recent treatment by B. Ehler, *Die Herrschaft des Gekreuzigten. Ernst Käsemanns Frage nach der Mitte der Schrift* (Berlin, 1986) 279–342.

60. G. Maier, *The End of the Historical–Critical Method* (St. Loius, 1977), 40, with a response by P. Stuhlmacher, *Historical Criticism and Theological Interpretation of Scripture* (Philadelphia, 1977), 66–71; *cf.* J. Reumann, *Righteousness* 181–183.

61. H. Küng, 'Der Frühkatholizismus im Neuen Testament als kontroverstheologisches Problem', in *Das Neue Testament als Kanon: Dokumentation und kritische Analyse zur gegenwärtigen Diskussion*, ed. E. Käsemann (Göttingen, 1970) 175–204, esp. 199.

62. R. P. Martin, private paper.

63. R. P. Martin, *Reconciliation* 5.

64. R. P. Martin, 'Reconciliation in Paul', *Theology, News and Notes* (1985) 9.

65. P. Stuhlmacher and H. Class, *Das Evangelium von der Versöhnung in Christus* (Stuttgart, 1979) 17, 44; and P. Stuhlmacher, 'The Gospel of Reconciliation in Christ — Basic Features and Issues of a Biblical Theology of the New Testament', *HBT* 1 (1979) 161–190, cited in J. Reumann, *Righteousness* 111 n. 117.

66. Cited by J. Reumann, *Righteousness* 111.

67. *Cf.* J. Reumann, *Righteousness* 111.

68. R. P. Martin, private paper.

69. R. P. Martin, private paper.

70. R. P. Martin, *Theology, News and Notes* (1985) 16.

71. Note, for example, his remarks in *Reconciliation* 80.

72. R. P. Martin, *Theology, News and Notes* (1985) 15. It is not necessary to conclude, with Martin, that in Romans Paul expressed dissatisfaction with the forensic–cultic imagery of justification when seeking to universalise the scope of Christ's saving deed for Gentiles and thus formulated his gospel for Gentiles in terms of reconciliation. It is doubtful whether the argument from Romans supports this contention, while Gal. 3, with its message about Gentiles inheriting the covenant promises made to Abraham, speaks in terms of justification (vv. 6–9) and receiving the Spirit (v. 14).

73. Further research may well demonstrate that the 'in Christ' motif, like 'reconciliation', is a more comprehensive category (note the eschatological dimension at Phil. 3:9), with justification by faith alone the fundamental blessing focusing particularly on the point of entry into this new relationship. At Phil. 3:9 Paul refers to his supreme goal in terms of his full participation in Christ. The manner in which he will be found in Christ fully is as one who has now (and will continue to have until the final day) that righteousness which comes as a gift from God.

74. J. I. Packer, 'Justification', *NBD* 684.

75. See his detailed references, *NBD* 684.

76. So J. D. G. Dunn, 'The New Perspective on Paul', *BJRL* 65 (1983) 95–122, esp. 97.

77. J. D. G. Dunn, *BJRL* 65 (1983) 98.

78. E. P. Sanders, *Paul and Palestinian Judaism* (London, 1977) 543, R. H. Gundry, 'Grace, Works and Staying Saved in Paul', *Bib* 60 (1985) 1–38, esp. 5. I am particularly indebted to Gundry's insightful treatment.

79. E. P. Sanders, *Paul and Palestinian Judaism* 550.

80. R. H. Gundry, *Bib* 60 (1985) 13.

81. E. P. Sanders, *Paul, the Law, and the Jewish People* (London, 1985) 140; *cf.* R. H. Gundry, *Bib* 60 (1985) 13.

82. E. P. Sanders, *Paul, the Law, and the Jewish People* 44.

83. E. P. Sanders, *Paul, the Law, and the Jewish People* 44f., his italics.

84. E. P. Sanders, *Paul, the Law, and the Jewish People* 140.

85. *Cf.* N. T. Wright, *TynB* 29 (1978) 78: 'the tradition of Pauline interpretation has manufactured a false Paul by manufacturing a false Judaism for him to oppose'.

86. After his discussion of Paul's charges against the Jews in terms of boasting, breaking the law, and relying on the law and circumcision as badges of national privilege (Rom. 2; *cf.* Rom. 9–10), N. T. Wright concludes (*TynB* 29 [1978], 81–84, esp. 83): 'Paul's criticism of Judaism . . . was on target'.

87. R. H. Gundry, *Bib* 60 (1985) 6f. *Cf.* J.E. Davidson, 'The Patterns of Salvation in Paul and in Palestinian Judaism', *JRS* 15 (1989) 99–110, esp. 111–113.

88. E. P. Sanders, *Paul and Palestinian Judaism* 543.

89. *Cf.* Gal. 3:3; 5:4, 7, etc.; Rom. 6–8; 11:20; 15:18, etc.

90. R. H. Gundry, *Bib* 60 (1985) 9.

91. R. H. Gundry, *Bib* 60 (1985) 12.

92. E. P. Sanders, *Paul, the Law, and the Jewish People* 140.

93. This is a lame conclusion and draws attention to a significant weakness in Sanders' reconstruction; *cf.* N. T. Wright, *TynB* 29 (1978) 81.

94. E. P. Sanders, *Paul, the Law, and the Jewish People* 44f. (Sanders' emphasis). For a critique of Sanders' view regarding the possibility of fulfilling the law in Paul see T. R. Schreiner, 'Paul and Perfect Obedience to the Law: An Evaluation of the View of E. P. Sanders', *WTJ* 47 (1985) 245–278.

95. R. H. Gundry, *Bib* 60 (1985) 17 n. 43.

96. R. H. Gundry, *Bib* 60 (1985) 13.

97. E. P. Sanders, *Paul, the Law, and the Jewish People* 36–38.

98. R. H. Gundry, *Bib* 60 (1985) 19.

99. See R. H. Gundry, *Bib* 60 (1985) 8–38, together with the further bibliographical details.

100. R. H. Gundry, *Bib* 60 (1985) 37f.

101. Note C. H. Cosgrove, 'Justification in Paul: A Linguistic and Theological Reflection', *JBL* 106 (1987) 653–670, esp. 653f. The amount written in this century on the twin themes of justification and judgment is vast, as K. P. Donfried's bibliography (see following note) up to 1976 shows.

102. K. P. Donfried, 'Justification and Last Judgment in Paul', *ZNW* 67 (1976) 90–110; *cf.* his slightly shorter article of the same title in *Int* 30 (1976) 140–152.

103. K. P. Donfried, *ZNW* 67 (1976) 98.

104. K. P. Donfried, *ZNW* 67 (1976) 102.

105. K. P. Donfried, *ZNW* 67 (1976) 102.

106. E. Synofzik, *Die Gerichts– und Vergeltungsaussagen bei Paulus* (Göttingen, 1977) 152–154; J. Reumann, *Righteousness*, 82–83.

107. R. H. Gundry, *Bib* 60 (1985) 35.

108. *Cf.* N. M. Watson (see following note) 209–210, who states: 'I question . . . whether Sanders does justice to the eschatological finality of Paul's message of justification'; and C. H. Cosgrove, *JBL* 106 (1987) 654.

109. N. M. Watson, 'Justified by Faith, judged by Works — an Antinomy?' *NTS* 29 (1983) 209–221.

110. E. Synofzik, *Die Gerichts– und Vergeltungsaussagen*, and W. Joest, *Gesetz und Freiheit: Das Problem des Tertius Usus Legis bei Luther und die neutestamentliche Paraenese* (Göttingen, 1961).

111. N. M. Watson, *NTS* 29 (1983) 216.

112. N. M. Watson, *NTS* 29 (1983) 217.

113. *Cf.* C. H. Cosgrove, *JBL* 106 (1987) 653.

114. K. R. Snodgrass, 'Justification by Grace — to the Doers: an Analysis of the Place of Romans 2 in the Theology of Paul', *NTS* 32 (1986) 72–93.

115. K. R. Snodgrass, *NTS* 32 (1986) 86.

116. My colleague, Glenn N. Davies (*Faith and Obedience in Romans* [Sheffield, 1990]), while not primarily concerned with justification by faith in relation to judgment according to works in Romans, nevertheless makes a significant and distinctive contribution to this issue. From the letter to the Romans he points out that God has always required of human beings, both before and after Christ, an obedience to his

will which arises from faith in him. Rom. 1:18, Davies argues, is not describing the universal condemnation of all mankind but only of the wicked. Rom. 1:18–3:18 does not refer to the sinfulness of all human beings, but is stating that sinfulness is spread indiscriminately among both Jews and Gentiles. With Snodgrass he agrees that God grants eternal life or salvation to those who live obediently in accordance with the revelation they have received. Rom. 2:12–16 affirms that the doers of the law, especially Gentiles, will be accounted righteous before God. This is not a doctrine of works righteousness (vv. 12–16 are dealing with judgment according to works), but a description of those who, by doing the good, show that their obedience is the direct result of the activity of God. The paragraph proleptically makes statements of past fact from the standpoint of the last judgment (*cf.* 2:6–11). Davies' distinctive contribution, however, is that Paul's words include all who exercise faith in God, before and after Christ's coming. But since Paul has not developed the Christian gospel at this stage of the argument, it is difficult to see how Christians could be in the forefront of his thought. One cannot really exclude a primary reference to OT believers in 2:6–11.

117. K. R. Snodgrass, *NTS* 32 (1986) 83.
118. C. H. Cosgrove, *JBL* 106 (1987) 654.
119. C. H. Cosgrove, *JBL* 106 (1987) 660.
120. C. H. Cosgrove, *JBL* 106 (1987) 670.
121. H. Ridderbos, *Paul: An Outline of His Theology* (Grand Rapids, 1975) 180.
122. Note the discussion of H. Ridderbos, *Paul* 178–181, esp. 180.

NOTES TO CHAPTER 5

1. See, for example, D. A. Carson, *Matthew*, EBC, vol. 8 (1984) 41–49. See also Benno Przybylski, *Righteousness in Matthew and His World of Thought* (Cambridge, 1980) 160–170.
2. Przybylski, *Righteousness* 1–12.
3. *Cf.* Carson 224–226, who points out that if the Pharisees were *perfectly* righteous, it would be incoherent to demand a righteousness greater than theirs. Compare Walter Grundmann, *Das Evangelium nach Matthäus* (THNT; Berlin, 1971) 271, where he points out that those who are righteous in a cultic sense place themselves against the mercy of God and become his enemies. See also John Calvin, *Calvin's New Testament Commentaries*, vol. 1, *Matthew, Mark and Luke*, tr. A. W. Morrison; e.d. D. W. Torrance and Thomas F. Torrance (Grand Rapids, 1972) 265: 'We are asked to rebut the pride and hypocrisy of the scribe. The grace of Christ is only of benefit to us when we are conscious of our sins and come to him, groaning under their weight'. *Cf.* Bo Giertz, *Evangelium Enligt Matteus* (Stockholm, 1978) 74: the one who claims to be righteous has no need for the gospel. Similarly, Sverre Aalen, *Matteusevangeliet* (Oslo, 1971) 171, labels this righteousness relative. By contrast, the poor are given the righteousness of the kingdom.
4. Przybylski, *Righteousness*, 85. See pp. 80–87. *Cf.* Robert Banks, 'Matthew's Understanding of the Law: Authenticity and Interpretation in Matthew 5:17–20', JBL 93 (1974) 226–242.
5. Martin Luther, *Luther's Works*, vol. 21, *The Sermon on the Mount and the Magnificat*, ed. Jaroslav Pelikan (St. Louis, 1956) 73.
6. Calvin, 182–183.
7. Grundmann, 151–152. *Cf.* also Gerhard Maier, *Matthaus–Evangelium*, Teil 1, Teil 2 (Stuttgart, 1979–80) 1.150; R. C. H. Lenski, *The Interpretation of St. Matthew's Gospel* (Minneapolis, 1943) 213–216.
8. C. H. Windisch, 'Die Spruche von Eingehen in das Reich Gottes', ZNW 27 (1938) 163–192.
9. *STR–B* 1.251–252.

10. We agree with Przybylski (p. 87) that perfection is required, but not that this perfection was achieved or fulfilled by the conduct of the disciples. Similarly, the mandate to observe everything that Jesus commands is not met very satisfactorily when we consider the requirements of entering the kingdom. Carson (pp. 146–147) is right when he argues that the new righteousness outstrips the old. Robert H. Gundry, *Matthew: A Commentary on His Literary and Theological Art* (Grand Rapids, 1982) 13, is right when he points to the righteousness as that which is stipulated by the demands of God and his law. But it is not clear what he means by 'more righteousness'. Sigurd Odland, *Fortolkning av Matteus Evangelium* (Oslo, 1942) 90, sees this righteousness as the fulfilment of the law; but in that case, what did the disciples need? Floyd F. Filson, *The Gospel According to St. Matthew* (London, 1960) 84, 90–91, and Lenski, *op. cit.*, point out the relationship between the relationship of faith and that of life. George Eldon Ladd, *A Theology of the New Testament* (Grand Rapids, 1974) 103–129, emphasises that the righteousness in the Sermon on the Mount if the gift of God. So also Fritz Rienecker, *Das Evangelium des Matthäus* (Wuppertal, 1969) 54–56.

11. Przybylski, 86–87.

12. *Ibid.*

13. Carson (pp. 160–162) gives a good survey of interpretations of 5:48. Aalen (p. 129) discusses the *teleios* in terms of a complete heart. D. A. Frøvig (pp. 228–229) thinks in terms of a wholehearted commitment, the highest evidence being love for one's enemies. Odland (p. 106) argues that the perfection in view is likeness to the Father in his love towards all people. Compare Gundry, pp. 99–100; and Calvin, p. 200, for whom the perfection must be understood primarily in relation to the standard set out.

14. Maier 1.189.

15. Rienecker, 66–67.

16. Grundmann, 179–190.

17. Ladd, *op. cit.*

18. G. Campbell Morgan, *The Gospel According to Matthew* (London, repr. 1976) 58.

19. Gundry, 388–390.

20. Lenski, 746–757; Frøvig, 494–499.

21. Carson, 350–351; compare 160–162.

22. Rienecker, 263–266.

23. *STR–B* 1.814–817.

24. Maier, 1.538–540.

25. Grundmann, 373–374.

26. Carson, 186–187.

27. Filson (p. 105) argues for the sinfulness of all men according to Matthew 7:11. Similarly Grundmann, 225. Maier (1.163–164) affirms the same on the basis of Matthew 5:27. It is impossible, he says, to fulfil the law on the basis of man's heart (*kardia*): the evil is endemic to man's fundamental being. The demands of Jesus cry out for the compliance of the entire heart.

28. Maier, 1.60–61 (on 3:15); and 1.163–164 (on 5:20).

29. Lenski, 124–128.

30. Gundry, 50.

31. Carson, *passim.*

32. Grundmann, 97–98.

33. Rienecker, 39–40.

34. Carson on 5:15.

35. Grundmann on 5:17.

36. *Ibid.*

37. Carson, 433.

38. Frøvig, 510–512.

39. Przybylski, 89.

40. Przybylski, 90–91. Compare David Hill, *Matthew* (NCB; Grand Rapids, 1972) 145, etc. He argues that the righteousness of life is in agreement with the will of God; obedience and trust lie at the heart of this righteousness. See also R. T. France, *Matthew* (TNTC; Grand Rapids, 1985) 142–142; similarly, Lloyd-Jones, 459, 461.

41. Carson, 181–182.

42. Odland, 124–125.

43. Frøvig, 258–263.

44. Gundry, 118–119.

45. Calvin, 223–224.

46. Luther, 203.

47. Donald Guthrie, *New Testament Theolgy* (Leicester, 1981) 100, 496–497.

48. Grundmann, *op. cit.*

49. Ladd, 79, 85.

50. Aalen, 149; *cf.* Filson, 101, 102.

51. Maier on 6:33.

52. Lenski, 285–286.

53. Lloyd-Jones, 459–461.

54. Przybylski, 96–98; *cf.* also Hill and Gundry *in loc.*; see also Filson, 77–78.

55. Carson, 134; compare Przybylski, Hill, Strecer and Ridderbos (references in Carson).

56. Maier, 1.114–116.

57. Calvin, 172–173 (on verse 10).

58. Maier 1.124–128; *cf.* Aalen, 105–107, and Lenski, 194–196; *cf.* Luther, 26–50.

59. Maier, 150; Aalen, 118; Lenski, 213–216; Carson, 146–147; Przybylski, 80–87; Ladd, 79; Guthrie, 100, 496, 678, 897.

60. Aalen, 224.

61. Gundry, 439–440; Odland, 292; Carson, 457; Frøvig, 535; Hill, 202–203; Filson, 233–234; France, 313.

62. Guthrie, 605.

63. Grundmann, 470–471.

64. Lenski, 854–858; Maier, vol. 2, *in loc.*; Rienecker, 292–295; Ladd, 74.

NOTES TO CHAPTER 6

1. See, e.g., the full discussion of D. A. Carson, 'Unity and Diversity in the New Testament: The Possibility of Systematic Theology', in D. A. Carson and John D. Woodbridge, eds., *Scripture and Truth* (Grand Rapids, 1983) 65–95, and the literature cited there.

2. Almost certainly the friend and co-worker of Paul mentioned in Col. 4:14; 2 Tim. 4:11; Phm. 24. For a thorough defence of this traditional identification, see E. E. Ellis, *The Gospel of Luke* (NCB: London, 1966) 40–52; *cf.* I. Howard Marshall, *The Acts of the Apostles* (Grand Rapids, 1980) 44–46.

3. See Ellis, *Luke* 62, and I. Howard Marshall, *The Gospel of Luke* (Exeter, 1978) 39.

4. See, e.g., W. W. Gasque, *A History of the Criticism of the Acts of the Apostles* (Tübingen, 1975) and the survey in E. Haenchen, *The Acts of the Apostles* (ET, Philadelphia, 1971) 14–51. In the continuing fluctuations and variations where a critical position often supplants its predecessors, there has been one constant: the claim that, considered historically, Luke-Acts is more or less unreliable. Particularly in this century, with the emergence of form and redaction criticism, the conclusion often reached is that both Luke (along with the other Gospels) and Acts are so heavily overlaid with tradition and/or editorial shaping that such genuine historical reminiscence

as the text may contain can be uncovered only by careful and arduous critical sifting. We will have occasion, in passing, to interact with specific critical viewpoints.

5. See especially the helpful discussion of I. Howard Marshall, *Luke: Historian and Theologian* (Exeter, 1970) 13–76; *cf.* E. F. Harrison, *The Apostolic Church* (Grand Rapids, 1985) 19–40; M. Hengel, *Acts and the History of Earliest Christianity* (ET; Philadelphia, 1979) 3–49, 59–68.

6. Conveniently summarised in one paragraph by H. Seebass, 'Righteousness', *NIDNTT* 3.361.

7. Strictly speaking, unless I have overlooked something, there is none. Closest are the section on Luke–Acts in J. Reumann, *'Righteousness' in the New Testament* (Philadelphia, 1982) 135–143, and P. H. Menoud, 'Justification by Faith According to the Book of Acts', *Jesus Christ and the Faith* (ET, Pittsburgh, 1978) 202–227; *cf.* F. F. Bruce, 'Justification by Faith in the Non-Pauline Writings of the New Testament', *EQ* 24 (1952) 66–71. There are numerous relevant materials in various commentaries, New Testament theologies, and monographs and articles on Lucan theology, but they are not substantial.

8. See, e.g., H. Ridderbos, *The Coming of the Kingdom* (ET; Philadelphia, 1962) 3–60; G. E. Ladd, *A Theology of the New Testament* (Grand Rapids, 1974) 34–210.

9. G. W. H. Lampe, 'The Holy Spirit in the Writings of St. Luke', in D. E. Nineham, ed., *Studies In Luke–Acts* (Oxford, 1955) 192.

10. See, e.g., J. D. G. Dunn, 'Spirit and Kingdom', *ExpT* 82 (1970–71) 36–40, and I. H. Marshall, 'The hope of a new age: the kingdom of God in the New Testament', *Themelios* 11/1 (Sept. 1985) 10, and the literature cited there.

11. N. Geldenhuys, *Commentary on the Gospel of Luke* (Grand Rapids 1960) 641; *cf.* Marshall, *Luke* 904.

12. In v. 8 'you', at least proximately, is not all believers indiscriminately; 'the apostles' (v. 2) is its concrete antecedent.

13. The link between John's baptism and Christian (water) baptism is that the one anticipates, the other looks back on the finished work of Christ and its benefits.

14. *Cf.* J. D. G. Dunn, *Baptism in the Holy Spirit* (Naperville, IL, 1970) 10–14.

15. Dunn, *Baptism* 13.

16. *Cf.* Marshall, *Luke* 150–51; Ellis, *Luke* 91; Dunn, *Baptism* 23ff.

17. 'Free from all taint of sin' (by virtue of his Spirit-worked conception); so Geldenhuys, *Luke* 77.

18. 'It refers especially to the infliction of punishment associated with the wrath of God' (Marshall, *Luke* 831, with the citation of numerous pertinent Old Testament passages); *cf.* 831f. for a defence, on balance, of the originality of vv. 43–44.

19. *Cf.* Marshall, *Acts* 69.

20. S. Farris, *The Hymns of Luke's Infancy Narratives* (Sheffield, 1985) 139, who also calls the phrase 'a favourite of Luke's'.

21. See, e.g., Marshall, *Historian* 92–94, and his development of subsequent chapters of the book around the theme of salvation; similarly, R. F. O'Toole, *The Unity of Luke's Theology* (Wilmington, DE 1984) goes so far as to argue that God as the bringer of salvation to his people is Luke's main, unifying theological theme.

22. N. B. Stonehouse, *The Witness of Luke to Christ* (Grand Rapids, 1953) 76; *cf.* Marshall, *Luke* 177–178.

23. Marshall, *Luke* 184 ('possible'); even more tentatively, J. A. Fitzmyer, *The Gospel According to Luke* (AB 28; Garden City, NY, 1981) 533.

24. *Cf.* Ridderbos, *The Coming of the Kingdom* 211–232. This entire section ('Remission of Sins') repays careful reading.

25. Marshall, *Luke* 213.

26. Ellis, *Luke* 106.

27. The literature on the origin of this term, the background and meaning of its usage in the Gospels, including the question of its authenticity as a self-designation on the lips of Jesus, is voluminous. Marshall (*Luke* 215–216) and Ellis (*Luke* 105–106), in

their comments on v. 24, provide brief overviews of the debate. For more extensive surveys, see, e.g., Ladd, *Theology* 145–158, 244–246; L. Goppelt, *Theology of the New Testament* 1 (ET, Grand Rapids, 1981) 178–193; I. Howard Marshall, *The Origins of New Testament Christology* (Downers Grove, IL, 1976) 63–82; D. Guthrie, *New Testament Theology* (Downers Grove, IL, 1981) 270–291. See also, S. Kim, *The 'Son of Man' as the Son of God* (Tübingen, 1983), especially 72–73, 99–102.

28. Most likely in view here is 'the generic, although not necessarily personal, relationship between sickness and sin' (Ellis, *Luke* 104); rather than specific sins that cause the paralytic's condition, in distinction from others, and must be forgiven before he can be healed; *cf.* 13:1–5.

29. Marshall, *Luke* 308.

30. Mentioned by Fitzmyer (*Luke* 686), who himself adopts the evidential view; *cf.* Marshall, *Luke* 313.

31. See Fitzmyer's helpful survey of the Lucan usage of faith, repentance, and conversion (*Luke* 235–239); *cf.* Goppelt, *Theology* 133.

32. See, e.g., Goppelt, *Theology* 1.127–128 and the literature cited there; *cf.* 34–35.

33. Effectively worked out by Goppelt, *Theology* 1.135–136.

34. E.g. the classic statement of A. Harnack, *What Is Christianity?* (ET, New York, 1957) 19–78.

35. So, e.g., Goppelt, *Theology* 2.282–284; *cf.* the helpful treatment of L. Morris, *New Testament Theology* (Grand Rapids, 1986) 187–190.

36. See above, n. 24 and G. Vos, *The Kingdom and the Church* (Grand Rapids, 1958 [1903]) 60–61.

37. Goppelt, *Theology* 1.132.

38. *Cf.* H. Ridderbos, *The Speeches of Peter In the Acts of the Apostles* (London, 1962) 5–11; Harrison, *The Apostolic Church* 26–33.

39. So, e.g., J. M. Bassler, 'Luke and Paul on Impartiality', *Bib* 66 (1985) 546–552.

40. See the helpful treatment of G. Davies, 'When was Cornelius saved?', *RefThRev* 46 (1987) 43–49. Highly problematic, in my judgment, is the use of this passage made by C. H. Kraft, *Christianity in Culture* (Maryknoll, NY, 1979) 253–257.

41. Bruce, *Acts* 492.

42. Literature on the *Paulusbild* in Acts is voluminous. Current debate, complicated and often convoluted, is usually traced back to the 1950 German original of the article of P. Vielhauer, 'On the "Paulinism" of Acts', in L. E. Keck and J. L. Martyn, eds., *Studies in Luke–Acts* (Nashville, 1966) 33–50; *cf.* Haenchen, *Acts* 112–116 and the survey of F. Plümacher, 'Acta–Forschung 1974–1982', *ThR* 49 (1984) 153–158. See the helpful lecture/article of F. F. Bruce, 'Is the Paul of Acts the real Paul?', *BJRL* 58 (1975–76) 282–305 (p. 305: 'Yes; he is the real Paul, seen in retrospect through the eyes of a friend and admirer, whose own religious experience was different from Paul's and who wrote for another public and purpose than Paul had in view when writing his letters.').

43. *Cf.* J. Murray, *The Epistle to the Romans* 1 (Grand Rapids, 1959), 348–353; J.A. Ziesler, *The Meaning of Righteousness in Paul* (Cambridge, 1972) 128–130, 141.

44. Its authenticity as the teaching of Jesus is widely acknowledged, although some scholars raise questions about vv. 9 and/or 14b, e.g. E. Linnemann, *Jesus of the Parables* (ET, New York, 1966) 64, 146; *cf.* the response of Marshall, *Luke* 678

45. Fitzmyer, *Luke* 1183.

46. So J. Jeremias, *The Parables of Jesus* (ET, 2nd rev. ed.; New York, 1972) 139–140 (n. 38).

47. *Cf.* Morris, *Theology* 155. In Heb. 2:17, its only other New Testament occurrence, the verb is applied to Christ's propitiatory activity as high priest. *Cf.* Rom. 3:25; Heb. 9:5; 1 John 2:2; 4:10.

48. J. Jeremias, *The Central Message of the New Testament* (New York, 1965) 70.

49. So Murray, *Romans* 1.352.

50. H. Ridderbos, *When the Time Had Fully Come* (Grand Rapids, 1957) 48–49.

NOTES TO CHAPTER 7

1. We have limited ourselves in this discussion almost entirely to the Gospel. I have done this because space considerations preclude major discussion of justification in the Johannine Epistles, to say nothing of the Revelation.

2. The very important verb (for Paul at any rate) *dikaioō* ('to justify') does not occur at all in John. *Dikaiosynē*, the noun normally translated 'justification' or 'righteousness', occurs twice in the same passage at Jn. 16:8,10. The adjective *dikaios* is found at Jn. 5:30; 7:24 and 17:25. Other less frequently used words belonging to the group (such as *dikaiōme, dikaiōs, dikaiōsis*, etc.) are not found at all.

3. As far as I know, the most recent discussion of this problem is found in Stephen Motyer's Tyndale New Testament Lecture 1987 entitled 'Righteousness in John and Paul: Diversity and Unity' (unpublished). Probably the two most important recent discussions of the translation of the word in these verses are found in D. A. Carson, 'The Function of the Paraclete in John 16:7–11', *JBL* 98 (1979) 547–566, and B. Lindars, 'Δικαιοσύνη in Jn. 16:8 & 10', in A. Descamp and Andre de Halleux, eds. *Mélanges Bibliques en hommage au R. P. Béda Rigaux* (Gembloux, 1970) 275–285.

4. Almost all the Protestant systematic theologies have a lengthy discussion of justification, and New Testament theologies regularly give the idea prominence as well. *Cf.* e.g. A. Richardson, *An Introduction to the Theology of the New Testament* (New York, 1958) 232: '. . . the justification theme is virtually peculiar to St. Paul, although the basic idea which Paul is expounding by means of it is fundamental to the whole NT and was first enunciated by Jesus himself'.

5. *Cf.* e.g. the introduction of the paper by R. Gaffin in this collection.

6. James Barr, *The Semantics of Biblical Language* (Oxford, 1961) made a deep impact on all succeeding biblical exegetes with his stress on doing theology based on understanding biblical concepts apart from merely trying to do word studies. In his 1969 'Postscript and Retrospect' he lauded the fact that 'the popularity of "word studies" and the lexically-based approach to theology has greatly waned' (*Biblical Words for Time* [London, 1969], 171).

7. R. P. Martin may be guilty of this in his insistence on reconciliation as the central motif in Paul's soteriology when *katallagē, katalassō* and *apokatallassō* occur a total of twelve times in Paul and then in a total of only five passages. *Cf.* P. T. O'Brien's paper in this collection, p. 69ff.

8. There is of course great debate today over the meaning of justification for Paul. *Cf.* e.g. the appendix by M. T. Brauch, 'Perspectives on "God's righteousness" in recent German discussion', in E. P. Sanders, *Paul and Palestinian Judaism* (Philadelphia, 1977) 523–542 for a discussion of at least the German debate over the different emphases claimed by New Testament scholars today for Paul's use of the phrase *hē dikaiosynē tou theou*. *Cf.* also of course the paper by P. T. O'Brien (pp. 000–000) for the broader discussion of justification/righteousness in Paul generally.

9. The word occurs three times in 1 Jn. at 2:29; 3:7, 10.

10. Carson, 'Function', 547. While a full investigation of the passage would no doubt be a useful exercise, it would also be somewhat redundant in that the passage has been well researched by Carson, and I find I am in agreement with him on so many points that it would be counterproductive to restate the evidence and the arguments for the answers to many of the difficulties in the passage. I do have substantial disagreements with him at some very important points, and those I will argue in some detail, but what follows will be briefer than it might have been because I will often recite the conclusions that are argued much more fully in his article.

11. Carson, 'Function', 558.

12. Carson, 'Function', 561–562.

13. Carson, 'Function', 564–565.

14. Carson, 'Function', 558–560.

15. B. Lindars, *The Gospel of John* (NEB; London, 1972) 502.

16. Lindars, *John* 502.

17. *Cf.* R. Schnackenburg, *The Gospel according to St. John*, 3 vols. (ET, London 1968–82) 3.128–129.

18. This judicial view of *hamartia* ('sin') would be strengthened even further of course if we were to find a judicial aspect of *elengchein* ('conflict') in the passage; but we, like Carson, do not (*cf.* discussion, above). The objective judicial 'conviction' of the world does not come in this passage at the point of the Spirit's *elengchein*. It is referred to in the content of all three objects as we shall see, but the three events of the judgment of the world in John are the rejection of the Son (*cf.* e.g. 3:17–19; 9:39), the cross (e.g. 12:31–32) and the final judgment (e.g. 5:21–29). The two definitions of *hamartia* as personal sin and judicial guilt, while clearly different in content, are not different in an objective/subjective sense. Both are personal; my definition sees the guilty verdict as very definitely the world's possession. Of course the verdict is meted out by God, but it is felt by the world under the Spirit's conviction. If this is true, can the conviction of the true cause of that conviction, i.e. the sin of the world, be far behind?

19. Carson, 'Function' 561.

20. Technically, it mentions the sentence or punishment of the devil, that he 'will be cast out' (probably of his office as prince of this world, *cf.* C. K. Barrett, *The Gospel according to St. John* [London: SPCK, 1978] 427). This results from his being judged. It is not a point of major importance in that the forensic link is already there in the passage in a more important way with the mention of the judgment of the world, i.e. the world's judgment by God/Christ in the cross.

21. *Cf.* Lindars, *John* 503.

22. *Cf.* Carson, 'Function', 559–560.

23. Carson, 'Function', 530, n. 36.

24. *Cf.* e.g. Lindars, *John;* R. Bultmann, *The Gospel of John: A Commentary* (ET, Oxford, 1971); Schnackenburg, *John*; Barrett, *John, ad loc.*

25. *Cf.* Lindars, *John*, 502–503.

26. *Cf.* also W. F. Hatch, 'The Meaning of John XVI, 8–11' *HTR* 14 (1921) 103–105.

27. Carson, 'Function', p. 562.

28. It is important to note here that I am not saying that John *got* the doctrine from Paul. In fact I think that unlikely in that to make that claim would be to imply that John has here invented this saying and assigned it to Jesus, a claim that has little merit on any grounds. Jesus is the author of the statements in Jn. 16:8–11 and is making them from the framework of his own understanding of his death and of belief in him for salvation.

29. *Cf.* B. F. Westcott, *The Gospel According to St. John* 88, who calls this 'absolute justice' because it is reinforced both negatively and positively.

30. Jn. 5:29. See the discussion below for the argument that the Great Judgment is not in view here. To say that this is 'eschatological' judgment is not to exclude the idea that a realised eschatology of sorts is in view in vv. 25–30. Here we have a clear example of the 'already but not yet' eschatology of the New Testament. The hour is both coming and present (v. 25) and, though I will stress the future aspect in this discussion in order to refute the views of Schnackenburg and others, that should not be taken as evidence that I believe the passage speaks only of future judgment.

31. *Cf.* Brown 1.215. Brown opts for the textually less certain *alēthēs* in the passage.

32. *Cf.* Brown 1.224. The cryptic 'another' *allos* of v. 32 cannot be John the Baptist because of v. 34. Whether it is the Spirit (*cf.* Jn. 15:26) is an open question, though vv. 37–38 and Jn. 8:17–18 seem to point to the Father as the most likely candidate.

33. It is instructive that *martyreō* ('to bear witness') and its cognates are found eleven times in the short space of Jn. 5:31–39.

34. The uniqueness of Jesus' claim is probably what is at issue here, not the fact that God was called Father by Jesus; *cf.* L. Morris *The Gospel according to John* (Grand Rapids, 1971) 310, esp. n. 47. In the light of v. 17 and the reaction recorded in v. 18, Brown is probably correct in thinking that the problem goes beyond a simple claim to equality, to a violation of the rabbinic notion that only God could work on the Sabbath: 'In particular, as regards men, divine activity was visible in two ways: men were born and men died on the Sabbath . . . For the Jews the Sabbath privilege was peculiar to God, and no one was equal to God (Exod. xv.11; Isa. xlvi.5; Ps. lxxxix.8). In claiming the right to work even as his Father worked, Jesus was claiming a divine privilege' (Brown 1.217). *Cf.* TB, *Taanith 2a.*

35. *Cf.* Schnackenburg, 2.468, n. 103.

36. *Cf.* Schnackenburg 2. pp. 117–118.

37. *dynamai, akouō, krinō, estin,* etc.

38. *Cf.* also Brown, 1.219 for the striking parallels between 5:26–30 and 5:19–25.

39. *Cf.* Brown 1.219.

40. I did not discuss the obvious parallel to *dikaia krisis* ('righteous judgment') found in Jn. 7:24 because I will be treating that passage below.

41. R. E. Brown, *The Gospel according to John*, 2 vols. (AB; Garden City, 1966–70) 1.213. The clause is *Ou dynamai egō poiein ap'emautou ouden*, and has been translated several ways. *Cf.* NASB: 'I can do nothing on My own initiative'; RSV: 'I can do nothing on my own authority'; NIV: 'By myself I can do nothing'. The double negative, though common enough for John, can be said to stress Jesus' inability.

42. F. F. Bruce, *The Gospel of John* (Basingstoke, 1983) 177.

43. *Dikaia krisis* is a cognate accusative and not a true direct object.

44. The 'words of the righteous' referred to in Dt. 16:19 are of course not Scripture or the law but rather the true testimony of righteous witnesses or the accused.

45. This is acknowledged by many commentators, e.g. Barrett 321; Brown 1.313; Lindars, 292.

46. Presumably the healing of Jn. 5:1–15 since the following verses bring up the question of healing on the Sabbath. It is this and other oddities in the text of chapter seven that make Bultmann and others hypothesise that chapter seven immediately followed chapter five in the original Gospel. Some of these objections are dealt with by Brown, 1.315–318. He describes the various scenes of chapter seven as having 'a certain rambling unity' (Brown 1.315).

47. Bultmann 278; R. H. Lightfoot, *St. John's Gospel: A Commentary* (Oxford, 1956) 179.

48. Presumably part of the multitude who had accused him of having a demon in v. 20. These were residents of Jerusalem, whereas the crowds at the time of the Feast of Tabernacles were largely composed of visitors. *Cf.* Brown 1.313.

49. *Cf.* Schnackenburg, 2.135.

50. *Cf.* the brief discussion of Isa. 11:3f. above.

51. Lindars, *John* 532. *Cf.* also Barrett 514: 'It [*dikaios*] is significant here because it is by God's righteous judgment that the world is shown to be wrong, and Jesus and the disciples right, in their knowledge of God.'

52. Schnackenburg, 3.196.

53. Schnackenburg, 3.196.

54. Schnackenburg, 3.196.

55. Note also various occasions in the New Testament when *dikaios* and *hagios* or cognates are quite naturally linked in descriptions: e.g. Rom. 6:19; 7:12; 1 Cor. 1:30.

56. Even Schanckenburg sees a reference to the after life here ('Now his will is turned towards their union with him in heaven and their fulfilment beyond this world in the vision of his glory'), denying any reference to the parousia here but strongly claiming that '. . . the only possible conclusion is that attention is directed here to the fulfilment of believers after death' (3.195).

57. *Cf.* e.g. two such different theologies as those of R. Bultmann, *Theology of the New Testament* (New York, 1951) 1.270–285 and L. Goppelt, *Theology of the New Testament* (Grand Rapids, 1982) 2.135–142.

58. Though Paul uses the *dikaio-* word-group relatively infrequently outside Romans and Galatians, there is a scholarly consensus that the idea is central to his soteriology both because of his heavy emphasis on it in those epistles and because of the key passages in which he mentions it in his other writings. It is also true that he is clearly the chief exponent of the idea in the New Testament.

59. Of course we are not advocating that *every* element we might discern is present *every* time Paul might use the term but rather that these elements are present often enough to allow us to speak of them as major aspects of Paul's concept.

60. This is part of the title of a major section in his discussion of Paul's use of *dikaiosynē*. *Cf.* G. Schrenk, *TDNT* 2.203ff.

61. Though these eight ideas occur in Schrenk's section on *dikaiosynē* they cover thought common to the ideas shared by the whole word-group well enough to be useful. Since John does not use the verb *dikaioō* and only sparingly uses the adjective *dikaios*, basing our thought on ideas common to *dikaiosynē* becomes even more hermeneutically justifiable.

62. G. Schrenk, *TDNT* 2.205.

63. G. Schrenk, *TDNT* 2.206.

64. G. Schrenk, *TDNT* 2.207–208.

65. G. Schrenk, *TDNT* 2.208.

66. G. Schrenk, *TDNT* 2.209.

67. *Cf.* e.g. Rom. 3:25; 5:9; Gal. 2:21.

68. ' "The Righteousness of God" in Paul', in E. Käsemann, *New Testament Questions of Today*, (London, 1969) 178.

69. *Cf.* for instance the dramatic identification of Jesus by John the Baptist near the beginning of John: 'Look, the Lamb of God, who takes away the sin of the world!' (Jn. 1:29, NIV). For further discussion of the cross in John, *cf.* D. Guthrie, *New Testament Theology* (Leicester, 1981) 449–460 and L. Morris, *The Cross in the New Testament* (Exeter, 1965) 144–179.

70. *Cf.* G. Schrenk, *TDNT* 2.193, 195–196; H. Seebass, *NIDNTT* 3.353–356.

71. *Dōrēma* is also found at Rom. 5:16.

72. *Cf.* W. G. Kümmel, *The Theology of the New Testament* (Nashville, 1973) 193.

73. G. Schrenk, *TDNT* 2.205.

74. By my count there are fourteen separate passages relating to divine giving in the Synoptics. In John there are nineteen; chapter 17 alone records thirteen uses of the verb *didōmi* ('to give').

75. We should perhaps mention the famous gift-to-the-world verse, Jn. 3:16; the gift of eternal life found in the narrative of the woman at the well (4:10, 14); and the bread of life discourse (6:32–33, 51).

76. *TDNT* 2.206.

77. In fact, even the objective/subjective duality of Pauline *dikaiosynē* may be hinted at in Jn. 16:8 as the ironic 'righteousness' of the world takes on a sort of double nuance standing between the subjective 'guilt' and the objective 'judgment' of vv. 8–10. I would not want to press this except to say that, though the *hamartia* ['sin'] of v. 8 is forensic, it is not the *verdict* of guilty that rests upon the world as a result of God's action. This, too, is their possession but is stated in the *krisis* of Jn. 16:8. Rather, the *hamartia* of v. 8 is the guilt, i.e. the personal sense of being declared guilty that the verdict, i.e. the judgment, brings about. Hence it is subjective, i.e. personally felt, whereas the *krisis* is objective, i.e. personally understood. As we argue above, all three elements of which the Spirit convicts the world in vv. 8–10 are their possession, but I think it is proper to speak of an objective/subjective duality relating to an objective understanding/subjective feeling duality that seems present in the verses as well.

78. Note the section heading in the NIV: 'Jesus Prays for All Believers' (vv. 20–26).

79. 'Righteousness', 170.

80. *Cf.* e.g. Schrenk, *TDNT* 2.196–197, 207. Of course, Sanders disagrees and sees the differences between Paul and Palestinian Judaism to be in terms of 'the meaning of "righteousness", the role of repentance, the nature of sin, the nature of the saved "group", and, most important, the necessity of transferring from the damned to the saved'. *Cf. Paul* 548.

81. The fact that the world is addressed as 'they' in Jn. 16:9 shows that individuals are being discussed, and 'worldly' individuals are always fair game for repentance in John, e.g. Nicodemus in Jn. 3 and the woman at the well in Jn. 4.

82. When Jesus prays that their unity be brought to completion he uses the divine passive *ōsin teteleiōmenoi eis hen* (17:23), emphasising God's activity, not the disciples' obedience.

83. Of course we cannot say Paul *stresses* the connection between faith and obedience. The controversy over faith and works continues to rage too strongly in too many minds for this to be said. For a contrary view, *cf.* John Barclay, *The Obedience of Faith* (Edinburgh, 1988).

84. There is no reference to the Spirit or to his unifying work anywhere in the contexts of Jn. 5:30 or Jn. 7:24, unless one stretches the 'context' of Jn. 7:24 all the way to Jn. 7:37–39, certainly an unwarranted move.

85. Though I do think it unlikely that this story was in the original text of John, it is surely noteworthy that early church teachers thought it consonant enough with the teaching of Jesus in the rest of John to include it in the manuscripts they did.

86. Jesus' breathing of the Holy Spirit upon the disciples, whatever else it means, must imply also this sense of confidence in the ministry of the Spirit in preserving and using the disciples because of its linking with the sending of the Son by the Father. *Cf.* Jn. 20:21–23.

87. These are suggested because of their use in the realm of legal metaphors.

NOTES TO CHAPTER 8

1. See W. G. Kümmel, *The New Testament: The History of the Investigation of Its Problems* (ET, London, 1973) 23f. and 26 respectively, with 411 n. 15.

2. So, respectively, F. Hahn, 'Taufe und Rechtfertigung' ['Baptism and Justification'], in *Rechtfertigung* (*Fs.* E. Käsemann), ed. J. Friedrich, W. Pöhlmann and P. Stuhlmacher (Tübingen and Göttingen, 1976) 95–124 (97), and W. Schrage, 'Die Frage nach der Mitte und dem Kanon im Kanon des Neuen Testaments in der neueren Diskussion' ['The Question about the Centre and (about) the Canon in the Canon of the New Testament in Recent Discussion'], in *Rechtfertigung* 415–442 (427).

3. Here the verb 'justify' is used in the passive (*dikaiousthai*) three times (vv. 21, 24, 25, see RSV) and the noun 'righteousness' (*dikaiosynē*) occurs once (v. 23). Elsewhere in the epistle the noun occurs twice (1:20; 3:18), both times in the sense of the righteousness of life which God requires (G. Schrenk, *TDNT* 2.200, *TDNTA* 172); the cognate adjective *dikaios* ('righteous') is used substantively twice (5:6 [see RSV], 16) as a generic collective term for, respectively, the righteous sufferer and any devout member of the believing community (J. Reumann, *'Righteousness' in the New Testament* [Philadelphia and New York, 1982] 150f. [§269]).

4. A helpful analysis of the structure of this passage in Greek is provided by W. Nicol, 'Faith and Works in the Letter of James', *Neot* 9 (1975) 7–24 (7–11, esp. 8). A more elaborate analysis of the form of the passage as reflecting 'a "step parallelism" with multiple stanzas' is offered by G. M. Burge, ' "And Threw Them Thus on Paper": Recovering the Poetic Form of James 2:14–26', *Studia Biblica et Theologica* 7 (1977) 31–45 (35f.; quotation from 34).

5. Such a gap between profession and practice is characteristic of the Jews (*cf.* Mt.

3:7–10 and parallels; Rom. 2:17–24). Some maintain that no emphasis is to be laid on the word 'claims' or 'says [RSV]' (e.g. E. H. Plumptre, *The General Epistle of St. James* [CBSC; Cambridge, 1915] 70), which is taken by R. Walker, 'Allein aus Werken. Zur Auslegung von Jakobus 2,14–26' ['By Works Alone. On the Interpretation of James 2:14–26'], *ZTK* 61 (1964) 155–192, (165 n. 29) to describe 'the solemn, positive confession of the believer'. On the other hand, C. E. B. Cranfield, 'The Message of James', in *The Bible and Christian Life. A Collection of Essays* (Edinburgh, 1985) 151–175 (165) finds in the wording 'if a man says he has faith' (RSV) — in contradistinction to the hypothetical expression 'if a man has faith' — 'the clue to the understanding of the section'. That the word 'claims' should be emphasised is favoured by the contrast between saying and not doing (v. 16a, b) in the comparison which follows.

    6. J. H. Ropes, *The Epistle of St. James* (ICC, Edinburgh, 1978) 203.

    7. J. B. Mayor, *The Epistle of St. James* (Grand Rapids, 1954) 216 rightly distinguishes two meanings of the word 'faith' in James: faith as 'the essence of Christianity' (e.g., 2:1) and 'empty profession of faith' (2:14ff.). Strictly speaking, however, the change of meaning begins not with v. 14a but with v. 14b: *cf.* M. J. Townsend, 'Christ, Community and Salvation in the Epistle of James', *EQ* 53 (1981) 115–123 (121). Nicol, 'Faith and Works', 16 maintains (wrongly) that 'in our pericope "faith" must mean true faith' (*cf.* n. 44 below); similarly, F. Mussner, *Der Jakobusbrief* [*The Letter of James*] (HTKNT 3rd ed.; Freiburg, 1975) 129f. D. O. Via, Jr., 'The Right Strawy Epistle Reconsidered: A Study in Biblical Ethics and Hermeneutic', *JR* 49 (1969) 253–267 (256) erroneously attributes to *James* the understanding of the world 'faith' or 'believe' (vv. 14, 19) as 'the intellectual acceptance of monotheism'. Walker, 'Allein aus Werken', 189f. argues unconvincingly that 'faith' in 2:14ff. is to be understood 'passive-nomistically as Christian devotedness to the law'; for a critique see Nicol, *art. cit.*, 11–14.

    8. If the RSV rendering is preferred, it should probably be understood as meaning: 'Can his faith save *him*, being such as he is?' (Plumptre 70); *cf.* C. F. D. Moule, *An Idiom Book of New Testament Greek* (2nd ed.; Cambridge, 1968) 111. In any case, the article in *hē pistis* (lit. 'the faith') is clearly anaphoric ('that faith': RV, NEB; MHT 3. 173); the AV rendering, 'can faith save him?', is completely misleading.

    9. The use of *mē* ('not') in the second question — which might be paraphrased as 'That sort of faith cannot save him, can it?' — indicates that a negative answer is expected (*cf.* n. 50 below). The verb *sōzō* ('save') similarly denotes deliverance at the last judgment in three of its other four occurrences in James (1:21; 4:12; 5:20); in 5:15 it means 'to make . . . well'. *Cf.* W. Foerster, *TDNT* 2.996.

    10. According to C. Burchard, 'Zu Jakobus 2.14–26' ['On James 2:14–16'], *ZNW* 71 (1980) 27–45 (33f.), the man in v. 14 is a new Christian who does not have 'the gift of works' (because the community has failed to instruct him along the lines of v. 12) and therefore thinks that 'in his case faith suffices [for salvation]'. The expression 'the gift of works' crops up repeatedly in Burchard's article (32, 33, 35, 36, 37, 41); the notion of works as a *gift* is derived by analogy with Burchard's interpretation of the illustration in v. 26 (faith and works are the two elements which constitute Christian existence just as body and spirit constitute physical existence, 31f.), but this would seem to be a misapplication of the comparison in v. 26, so that neither the expression nor the idea of 'works as a gift' has a firm basis in the text.

    11. T. Lorenzen, 'Faith without Works does not Count before God! James 2:14–26', *ExpT* 89 (1978) 231–235 (231*b*). Burchard, *art. cit.* 33 points out that in no sentence in our pericope is 'works' the grammatical or logical subject. G. Braumann, 'Der theologische Hintergrund des Jakobusbriefes' ['The Theological Background of the Letter of James'], *TZ* 18 (1963) 401–410 (404) rightly observes that the epistle by no means thinks of summoning the readers to 'deeds without faith'; the purport of the exhortations is to put before the readers 'deeds based on faith'.

    12. This rendering (*cf.* AV, RV, NASB) rightly takes the verbs *thermainesthe* and

chortazesthe as passive rather than middle ('keep warm and well fed'; *cf.* NEB). The issue makes no difference, however, to the *point* of the comparison which is brought out in v. 17.

13. So, e.g., M. Dibelius — H. Greeven, *James* (Hermeneia; Philadelphia, 1976) 153. On the other hand, J. Schneider, *Der Briefe des Jakobus, Petrus, Judas und Johannes* [*The Letters of James, Peter, Jude and John*] (Göttingen, 1961) 19 thinks that the case is 'certainly not invented, but rather confirmed by definite, ever-recurring experiences.'

For the possible significance of the change of subject from 'one of you' (v. 16a) to the plural 'you' (v. 16b [NASB]) see, on the one hand, Mayor 98 and, on the other hand, R. V. G. Tasker, *The General Epistle of James* (TNTC; London, 1957) 64; D. E. Hiebert, *The Epistle of James. Tests of a Living Faith* (Chicago, 1979) 180.

14. While this is the primary or even exclusive meaning of 'good' within the sense of the comparison, the attentive reader will not miss a connection with the spiritual 'good' of v. 14: empty words will bring no profit either to the person in need or to the 'talking philanthropist' himself (the expression is from Mayor 216). *Cf.* D. J. Moo, *James* (TNTC; Grand Rapids and Leicester, 1985) 103.

15. E.g. Dibelius–Greeven 153 with n. 25. Burchard, 'Zu Jakobus 2:14–26', 35 gives the word the unlikely meaning of 'being devoted to eternal death'.

16. Ropes 207. S. Laws, *The Epistle of James* (HNTC; San Francisco, 1980) 122 concurs.

17. Quotations from, respectively, R. Johnstone, *A Commentary on James* (Edinburgh, 1977) 187f.; W. E. Oesterley, 'The General Epistle of James', *EGT* 4.385–476 (455a).

18. See BAGD 406 (s.v. *kata* II 1 c). *Cf.* Dibelius–Greeven 153f.

19. *Cf.* J. Zmijewski, 'Christliche "Vollkommenheit". Erwägungen zur Theologie des Jakobusbriefs' ['Christian "Perfection". Reflections on the Theology of the Letter of James'], *SNTU* 5 (1980) 50–78 (57).

20. The words *pistin* ('faith') and *erga* ('works') are in fact transposed in the 9th-century Latin Codex Corbeiensis (Corbey MS); their inversion was suggested by O. Pfleiderer at the end of the 19th century as a conjectural emendation. See, e.g., H. Neitzel, 'Eine alte crux interpretum im Jakobusbrief 2:18' ['An Old crux interpretum in the Letter of James 2:18'], *ZNW* 73 (1982) 286–293 (287 with n. 6).

21. E.g. J. B. Adamson, *The Epistle of James* (NICNT; Grand Rapids, 1976), 124f.; Mussner 137f.

22. For these objections *cf.* respectively, (i) Laws 123; (ii) Moo 104f.; (iii) Tasker 65; (iv) Neitzel, 'Eine alte crux', 288; (v) Zmijewski, 'Christliche "Vollkommenheit"', 59; (vi) Dibelius–Greeven 150.

According to another (unconvincing) interpretation, the *tis* here (18) is the representative of a 'works-only' position who now engages in a fictitious dialogue with the first *tis* (14), the representative of a 'faith-only' position; James does not identify himself with either of these *one-sided* positions; just as in vv. 14–17 he mentions and rejects the one, so now in vv. 18–21 he will describe the other, only to reject it a few verses later (22ff.): so Zmijewski, *art. cit.*, 59f. with n. 56, 61. It is extremely doubtful, however, whether the formula 'but someone will say' can be taken in any other way than as introducing an opponent *of James*.

The view that the words of the opponent — perhaps, 'What's the use of works without faith? This is the chief item and this I have' (Schneider 19), or 'I have faith; you have no doubt only works, where have you your faith?' (H. Windisch, *Die Katholischen Briefe* [*The Catholic Epistles*; HNT; 2nd ed., Tübingen 1930] 17) — have for some reason dropped out of the text is rightly dismissed by H. Balz and W. Schrage, *Die 'Katholischen' Briefe* (Göttingen, 1973), 31 as 'a violent measure and too hypothetical'.

23. E.g. Ropes 209 (whence the first quotation); Dibelius–Greeven 150f. (point [2]), 155f. (third quotation from 156). In the view of A. Schlatter, *Der Brief des*

Jakobus [*The Letter of James*] (Stuttgart, 1956), 192–194 the pronouns can be taken in their natural senses since the objector is a Jew who opposes works to faith as of equal validity as a ground for hope of obtaining divine grace.

24. For these objections *cf.*, e.g., C. E. Donker, 'Der Verfasser des Jak und sein Gegner. Zum Problem des Einwandes in Jak 2. 18–19' ['The Author of James and His Opponent. On the Problem of the Objection in Jas. 2:18–19'] *ZNW* 72 (1981) 227–240 (230); Neitzel, 'Eine alte crux', 288f.; Adamson 136.

25. Laws 124. The exegesis proposed by Donker, 'Der Verfasser des Jak', 230–239, in which the objection (from a Paulinist) extends to the end of v. 19 and the author's response begins with v. 20, appears to us unnatural and contrived, particularly the suggestion that v. 18b — to be read as a question — is to be understood as conditional and v. 18c is not to be taken seriously: 'If *you* have faith then *I* have works' means, '*You* can appeal to your having faith as little as *I* can appeal to my having works.' The allegation that (the objector charges that) in vv. 14–17 the author fails to distinguish two concepts of faith (correct faith and alleged, false faith) goes directly against our exegesis of those verses.

Another view which similarly regards the objector as speaking in vv. 18f. and James as replying in vv. 20–23 is propounded by Z. C. Hodges, 'Light on James Two from Textual Criticism', *BS* 120 (1963) 341–350 (especially 347–350). This view rests on the substitution of *ek tōn ergōn* ('by [your] works') for the better attested and more difficult reading *chōris tōn ergōn* ('without deeds', v. 18b) and is, if for no other reason, to be rejected.

26. Neitzel, 'Eine alte crux' (see n. 20 above), especially 289ff.

27. *Ibid.* 289 (citing H. von Soden).

28. Ropes 212; Dibelius–Greeven 157.

29. Neitzel, *loc. cit.* (with reference to BDF §440.1).

30. Neitzel, *art. cit.*, 290f. (quotation from 291), with reference to Bl.–D. §480.5 (=BDF §480(5))..

31. *Ibid.* 291f. Neitzel (292) gives reasons for rejecting the punctuation — which is also mentioned by Dibelius–Greeven 157 only to be dismissed — which would interpret *kagō* 'both times [18c, e] as an introduction to the author's answer'.

32. *Ibid.* 292f. (with reference to Dibelius–Greeven [154f. n. 29]).

33. *Ibid.* 293. The above reasoning (under [b]) more than suffices to answer the objection of Moo 105 that '*kagō* ("and I") is a very unusual way to introduce an answer to a question and the entire phrase seems redundant'.

34. *Cf.* e.g., H. P. Hamann, 'Faith and Works: Paul and James,' *LTJ* 9 (1975) 33–41 (35).

35. *Cf.* L. Goppelt, *Theology of the New Testament*, 2 vols. (ET; Grand Rapids, 1981–82), 2.209. Walker, 'Allein aus Werken' (see n. 5 above) 172, in stating that '*works are the reality which constitutes faith*', goes beyond the warrant of the text: he speaks of there being no 'faith *without works*' but 'faith *from works* (Glauben *aus Werken*)'; but the phrase used by James here is not *ek tōn ergōn* ('from works') but *ek tōn ergōn mou* ('from my works'), and it is not used adjectivally with the noun 'faith' but adverbially with the verb 'I will show' (*deixō*).

36. Quotations from, respectively, Martin in R. A. Martin and J. H. Elliott, *James. I–II Peter/Jude* (Minneapolis, 1982) 31 (*cf.* 28); H. Preisker, *TDNT* 4.726, and 727 n. 18. B. Reicke, *The Epistles of James, Peter, and Jude* (AB 37; Garden City, 1964) 32f. holds that v. 18 'seems to presuppose an agreement between a Christian missionary and a Gentile regarding his acceptance of the Christian religion on particularly favourable terms'. But this interpretation is unconvincing.

37. This rendering presupposes the most probable reading *heis estin ho theos*, in which *heis* ('one') is separated from *ho theos* ('God') by *estin* ('is'). On the textual problem here *cf.* B. M. Metzger, *A Textual Commentary on the Greek New Testament* (London and New York, 1971) 681.

38. In its original intention, of course, the *Shema'* is 'no mere intellectual

conviction' (E. M. Sidebottom, *James, Jude and 2 Peter* [NCB; Grand Rapids and London, 1982] 44), but as used here by James it is probably meant to state 'the content of the "faith without works" which is in question' (Dibelius–Greeven 158).

39. *Cf.* Laws 126 (whence the quotations), and Mayor 100; Ropes 216, respectively. Others think that the commendation itself is ironical (e.g. Balz-Schrage 31) or strongly so (e.g. Moo 106).

40. The word translated 'shudder' (*phrissein*, a NT *hapax*), properly 'to bristle', is used of the physical signs of terror (*cf.* Dan. 7:15), especially of the hair standing on end (e.g. Job 4:14f.): Mayor 101.

41. *Heis theos* ('God is one') is taken to be a formula for exorcising by, e.g., Mussner 139.

42. *Cf.*, e.g., D. E. Hiebert, 'The Unifying Theme of the Epistle of James', in *The Bib Sac Reader*, ed. J. F. Walvoord and R. B. Zuck (Chicago, 1983) 143–154 (148).

43. *Cf.* Ropes 215. According to Laws 128, v. 19b is intended by James 'to indicate the necessary outcome of faith, if it is a live faith, and the impossibility of its existing alone. For the demons, belief in the God who is one produces a response of fear . . .'. But in view of the clearly negative connotation of the verb 'shudder' as used here, the point of v. 19b is more likely to be the *uselessness* of the demons' kind of faith than its productivity. If there is reference to the latter, it is probably also ironical, as taken by Moo 106f. (following F. J. A. Hort).

44. Nicol, 'Faith and Works' (see n. 4 above), contends that in our pericope (2:14–26) faith is not intellectual acceptance only but 'true, saving faith' (14, *cf.* n. 7 above), that 'the whole pericope is concerned, not with differing kinds of faith, but to stress that faith must issue in works', and that James 'does not equate the demons' faith with the Christian faith-without-works in terms of content, but only in so far as they are of no help before a judging God' (15). Subsequently, however, he writes: 'James . . . addresses himself to a Church that is *dying or dead of orthodoxy*, whose members have faith and are proud of it, but who do not live it out. He tries to arouse them by emphasising that Christians who do not show their faith by deeds *cannot call themselves Christian*' (20, emphases added). This is tantamount to admitting that James is arguing against the *dead orthodoxy* of *nominal Christianity*, and it is difficult to see how the faith in question can still be described as 'true, saving faith'.

45. Some consider v. 20 to belong with vv. 18f. (e.g. P. H. Davids *The Epistle of James* [NIGTC; Grand Rapids and Leicester, 1985] 119), but it is more naturally taken as introducing the verses which follow, since the question 'do you want evidence . . .?' leads one to expect that the demonstration will follow (*cf.* Zmijewski, 'Christliche "Vollkommenheit" ', 62, who cites in support the fact that both v. 20 and v. 21 are in the form of a question). The use of *de* ('but', AV, RV) rather than *oun* ('therefore') in v. 20 also shows that the verse is meant to prepare for the following reference to Abraham (so Mussner 139f., though he nevertheless makes v. 21 the beginning of a new paragraph).

46. Some hold that the word *kenos* ('foolish') is the linguistic equivalent of *rhaka* ('Raca', Mt. 5:22; *cf.*, e.g., A. Oepke, *TDNT* 3.660); but others think that there is no connection between the two words (Oesterley [see n. 17 above] 447a) or that to compare *kenos* with *rhaka* is out of place (Mussner 140).

47. R. Bultmann, *TDNT* 1.708 takes *gnōnai* ('to know') to refer to 'specifically theological knowledge' which 'grows, e.g., out of the study of Scripture'. But the NIV rendering (similarly RSV, 'to be shown') adequately conveys the sense.

48. On the superiority of this reading to *nekra* ('dead', *cf.* vv. 17, 26), preferred by Hodges, 'Light on James Two', 341 n. 1, see Metzger, *Textual Commentary* 681.

49. In accordance with his view that vv. 18–21 is James's description of the one-sided 'works-only' position of the second *tis* ('someone'; see n. 22 above), Zmijewski, 'Christliche "Vollkommenheit" ', 62f. with n. 71 emphasises that v. 20 is differently formulated from v. 17, which describes James's own conception: James speaks of faith without works as 'dead' (*cf.* v. 26), not 'barren'; and he brings into relief the *'isolation'*

of faith (*kath' heautēn*, *cf.* the *monon* ['alone'] of v. 24). Considerable difficulties, however, are involved in Zmijewski's view: (i) It is highly unlikely that the example of Abraham (v. 21) is cited by the second *tis* whereas that of Rahab (v. 25) is cited by James; particularly in view of the same form in which the two examples are dressed (noted by Zmijewski, 66f.), it is much more probable that both are cited by *James* as examples of genuine faith, with the lessons drawn after each example has been given (vv. 21, 22–24; 25, 26; *cf.* J. A. Motyer, *The Tests of Faith* [London, 1972] 54). (ii) It follows that it is highly unnatural to put v. 21 in the mouth of the second objector and vv. 22f. in the mouth of James. Zmijewski's explanation of the abrupt beginning of James's response (63f.) is not convincing, and to understand the present tense *blepeis* ('you see') in v. 22 in a futuristic sense ('you will see from my exposition which follows', 64) is surely forced. (iii) Zmijewski has exaggerated the differences between what probably are basically synonymous expressions (vv. 17 and 20; see also 60 on vv. 18b [our 18d–e] and 22).

50. The Greek particle *ou* ('not') indicates that an affirmative answer is expected (*cf.* n. 9 above).

51. This title is most natural in the mouth of a Jew, but is not impossible for a Gentile Christian (1 Clem. 31:2): *cf.*, e.g., Dibelius–Greeven 161. Burchard, 'Zu Jakobus 2. 14–26', 40 takes 'our' not in the sense of 'of Jews and Christians' but 'mine [referring to James] and yours [referring to the objector]'. This interpretation is unlikely to be correct, in view of the stereotyped character of the term (Lk. 1:73; Jn. 8:53; Acts 7:2; Rom. 4:12; *cf.* Rom. 4:1).

52. Hiebert 192.

53. *Cf.*, e.g., P. H. Davids, 'Tradition and Citation in the Epistle of James', in *Scripture, Tradition, and Interpretation* (*Fs.* E. F. Harrison) ed. W. W. Gasque and W. S. Lasor (Grand Rapids, 1978), 113–126 (quotation from 115).

54. The plural occurs six more times in the epistle (2:22a, b, 24, 25, 26; 3:13). *Cf.* in particular, on the one hand, *ex ergōn* ('by works', vv. 21, 24, 25), *ek tōn ergōn* ('by works', v. 22b), *ek tōn ergōn mou* ('by my works', v. 18e), *tois ergois autou* ('with his works', v. 22a), and, on the other hand, *chōris tōn ergōn* ('apart from [your] works', vv. 18d, 20), *chōris ergōn* ('apart from works', v. 26). The use of the term in 3:13 (*ta erga autou*, 'his works') is similar to 2:18c and 22a. (All the English renderings above are from the RSV.) The singular *ergon* ('work') occurs in 1:4, 25.

55. Dibelius–Greeven 160.

56. Laws 135.

57. Walker, 'Allein aus Werken', 175f. fastens on the wording of v. 21 and insists that in Abraham's justification 'works have all the worth' with none for faith; he further (176f.) brings 2:10 into the discussion of 2:21, drawing the conclusion (which to him is the only possible one) that 'works are for James so highly meritorious that in their vicinity even sin against all the commandments melts into nothingness' (177). Such extreme views serve to underline the pivotal importance of determining the meaning of the verb 'justify' for the interpretation of this verse (*cf.* n. 68 below).

58. E.g. Ropes 217; Windisch 19 (on v. 25).

59. 'To save' is not listed by G. Schrenk, *TDNT* 2.211–219 (*TDNTA* 175f.) among the meanings of *dikaioō* ('justify') either in Scripture (including LXX) or in profane Greek; *cf.* BAGD 197f. (*s.v.*); J. H. Thayer, *A Greek–English Lexicon of the New Testament* (New York, n.d.) 150f. (*s.v.*).

60. So, respectively, Dibelius–Greeven 162f. and Balz–Schrage 32. Similarly, J. Jeremias, 'Paul and James', *ExpT* 66 (1954–55) 368–371 (370f.) speaks of James using the verb here (and in v. 25) in the *analytical* sense ('God recognises the fact of the existing righteousness', in contradistinction to Paul's use of it in the *synthetic* sense *('God adds something, He gives righteousness to the ungodly')*. *Cf.* also E. Grässer, 'Rechtfertigung im Hebräerbrief' ['Justification in the Epistle to the Hebrews'], in *Rechtfertigung* (see n. 2 above) 79–93 (84, on Jas. 2:21); M. L. Soards, 'The Early

Christian Interpetation of Abraham and the Place of James within that Context', *IBS* 9 (1987) 18–26 (18–20).
    61. Moo 109f. (emphasis added); *cf.* 47f.; Davids 132.
    62. Moo 109.
    63. *Chambers Twentieth Century Dictionary*, ed. A. M. Macdonald (Edinburgh and London, 1972), s.v.
    64. Those who take the verb in this demonstrative sense include, *inter alios*, J. A. Ziesler, *The Meaning of Righteousness in Paul. A Linguistic and Theological Inquiry* (SNTSMS 20; Cambridge, 1972) 128f.; O. P. Robertson, 'Genesis 15:6: New Covenant Expositions of an Old Covenant Text', *WTJ* 42 (1980) 259–289 (286f.). *Materially* the same is the view of those who take the verb here in the declarative sense of 'pronouncing/declaring righteous', but add in explanation that 'it concerns *evidence that can be seen* by men' (C. Brown, *NIDNTT* 3.370) or that 'it is a man's works which declare him righteous by *showing* that he is a man of faith' (O. Michel, *NIDNTT* 1.605) (emphasis in both quotations added).
    J. Buchanan, *The Doctrine of Justification* (London, 1961) 259 plausibly says of Abraham: 'He was ACTUALLY justified before [Gen. 15:6]; but there was here a divine DECLARATION of his acceptance, which expressly referred to his obedience, as the fruit and manifestation of his faith [Gen. 22:12,16,18]'. But the term *'declarative* justification' does not fit in the case of Rahab; for this reason also it seems better to take the verb in its *demonstrative* sense.
    65. Moo 109, 111, respectively.
    66. Robertson, 'Genesis 15:6', 287.
    67. This is the only place in vv. 21–23, which deals with Abraham, where the pronoun 'his' is used with 'works'. In contradistinction to the other instances of plural 'works' listed in n. 54 above, 'his works' here is most naturally understood of the good works which Abraham performed during the course of his life of faith. The view proposed by J. G. Lodge, 'James and Paul at Cross-Purposes? James 2,22', *Bib* 62 (1981) 195–213 (199 n. 10) — 'Since the works are in a context of offering upon an altar (Jas 2, 21) . . . the plural is used in the sense of the Levitical "service of the Lord" ' — is unconvincing.
    The mention of Abraham's faith here is not as sudden as it appears: according to our exegesis of v. 21, it is implicit in the assertion that Abraham was 'justified by works'. A hint of Abraham's faith has been detected in the confession of v. 19 that 'God is one', since in Jewish tradition Abraham was known as one who had turned from idols to serve the one God (Davids 128f.); but the suggestion appears doubtful to me, since the confession is there used negatively.
    68. E.g. Debelius–Greeven 163; Balz–Schrage 32. Walker, 'Allein aus Werken', 177–180 goes further and assigns *no* place to faith in Abraham's justification, since he subordinates the interpretation of v. 22 to his exegesis of v. 21 (*cf.* n. 57 above).
    69. *Cf.* R. Y. K. Fung, 'The Forensic Character of Justification', *Themelios* 3/1 (Sept. 1977) 16–21.
    70. When the verb (*synergeō*) is used of God as the subject, explicit (Mk. 16:20) or implied (Rom. 8:28, *cf.* RSV), such a derogatory sense is surely ruled out. 'The "iterative" imperfect *synērgei* . . . implies the coexistence of faith and works in Abraham over a period' (Lodge, 'James and Paul', 199f.) — from beginning (Gen. 15) to end (Gen. 22) (E. Lohse, ' "Glaube und Werke" — zur Theologie des Jakobusbriefes' [' "Faith and Works" — on the Theology of the Letter of James'], *ZNW* 48 [1957] 1–22 [5]). The weakly attested variant *synergei* (present tense) — favoured by, e.g., Schlatter 201 and taken by him as a dramatic present — is clearly secondary and may be explained as being due to a desire to emphasise the *general* significance of the statement (*cf.* Zmijewski, 'Christliche "Vollkommenheit"', 64 n. 80).
    71. Cranfield, 'Message of James', 169. *Cf.* Mussner 145f., who rightly observes

that the 'synergism' implied by the verb *synērgei* is not to be taken in an 'additive' sense.

72. As Mussner 142 remarks, 'perfection' (*Vollendung*) is more than and different from 'completion' (*Ergänzung*). The verb occurs only this once in the epistle. The cognate adjective (*teleios*) occurs five times (1:4a, b, 17, 25; 3:2), and each time the sense is 'perfect' (see NASB) rather than 'complete'.

73. *Cf.*, e.g., A. Ross, *The Epistles of James and John* (NICNT; Grand Rapids, 1967) 54; J. I. Packer, *IBD* 844c (whence the first quotation).

74. Reicke 34. On faith as prior to works *cf.*, e.g., E. E. Ellis, *Paul's Use of the Old Testament* (Grand Rapids, 1981) 87; G. Bertram, *TDNT* 7.876 (*TDNTA* 1117). Laws 134 states: 'The relation between Abraham's faith and his works is not properly one of consequence, demonstration or confirmation, all of which terms assume a measure of distinction between the two: for James they go together in a necessary unity.' But a measure of distinction (not synonymous with separation) is unavoidable (*cf.* v. 22), unless one simply equates faith and works, which surely one cannot do.

75. H. W. Heidland, *TDNT* 4.290 finds it 'not possible to say anything very definite about the precise meaning of *logizesthai* ['to be credited'] here'.

76. Schrenk, *TDNT* 2.201 with n. 44.

77. *Cf.* Dibelius–Greeven 163–166, 168–174 (quotations from 165, 172, 174). Similarly, Schneider 20 speaks of James as failing to grasp 'the decisive and fundamental significance' of Gen. 15:6.

78. *Cf.*, e.g., Laws 133; Davids 129f.

79. J. I. Packer, *IBD* 844c. *Cf.* A. E. Travis, 'James and Paul, A Comparative Study', *SWJT* 12 (1969) 57–79 (65).

80. Cranfield, 'Message of James' (see n. 5 above), 168. *Cf.* Buchanan, *Justification* 257f. On the other hand, Ziesler, *Righteousness* holds that 'the purpose of the quotation is not to explain the way of acceptance with God' (183) and that here 'there is . . . for James no element of imputation; . . . Gen. 15:6 is quoted, but with Gen. 22 in mind' (132).

81. R. N. Longenecker, *Biblical Exegesis in the Apostolic Period* (Grand Rapids, 1975) 199f.; *cf. idem*, 'The "Faith of Abraham" Theme in Paul, James and Hebrews: A Study in the Circumstantial Nature of New Testament Teaching', *JETS* 20 (1977) 203–212 (204f.).

82. *Cf.* Mussner 143; J. I. Packer, *IBD* 844c. Examples of other interpretations are: (1) Gen. 15:6 is taken by James as a prophecy which was fulfilled by Gen. 22:9, i.e. it 'expressed in advance the divine verdict, which was then confirmed by the offering up of Isaac' (G. Delling, *TDNT* 8.82; *cf.* Balz-Schrage 32). (2) In a way typical of the midrashic method, James takes Gen. 15:6 'as a prognostication of Abraham's faith in trial, referring specifically to the sacrifice of Isaac in chapter xxii' (I. Jacobs, 'The Midrashic Background for James II, 21–23', *NTS* 22 [1976] 457–464 [458], *cf.* 461f.; Davids 129). (3) In the sense that 'it *established* and *interpreted* Gen. 15:6', the event of Gen. 22 was a fulfilment, i.e. 'a divine suprahistorical (*überhistorisch*) verdict delivered on Abraham's entire life' (Adamson 131; *cf.* Dibelius–Greeven 164). (4) Gen. 15:6 found its ultimate significance and meaning in the sacrifice of Isaac, by which Abraham's faith was perfected (*cf.* Mayor 104; Moo 113). On various facets of the theme of Abraham's faith, *cf.* Longenecker, *art. cit.* (previous note).

83. *Cf.* Laws 136f. (quotation from 137).

84. *Cf.* L. C. Allen, 'The Old Testament in Romans i–viii', *VE* (1964) 6–41 (18): ' "Righteousness" in Gen. xv.6 is a covenantal concept, implying acceptance by God. Isaiah xli.8 sums it up in the word "friend" as James saw when he connected the two verses'; G. Stählin, *TDNT* 9.168: 'Due to the link with Gn. 15:6 the meaning of *philos theou* ["friend of God"] is very close to "he who is just through faith" '.

85. In other words, we take the *kai* ('and') of v. 23c as parallel, not with the *kai* of v. 23a (as in Moo 114) but with the *kai* of v. 23b (as in Dibelius–Greeven 164).

86. Hamann, 'Faith and Works' (see n. 34 above), 36 (*cf.* Mussner 148). Martin 33 rightly insists that v. 24 must be interpreted in the light of the context.

87. Via, 'Right Strawy Epistle' (see n. 7 above), 257. *Cf.* Longenecker, 'The "Faith of Abraham" Theme', 206.

88. *Cf.* J. A. Fitzmyer, in Reumann, *'Righteousness'* 221 (§414).

89. *Cf.* Cranfield, 'Message of James', 169f. and Laws 137, respectively. According to Schlatter 204, James said *monon* ('only', adverb), not *monēs* (adjective, agreeing with *pisteōs*, 'faith'), because he could not conceive of a believing that is isolated from acting.

90. *Cf.* Reumann, *'Righteousness'* 157 (§278), and Buchanan, *Justification* 371 (*cf.* 372), respectively. The words 'by logical inference' are intended to indicate that the thought of forensic justification is not contained in the verb 'justify' in vv. 21, 24, 25 (as though it meant 'show to be justified'), but that a man who is shown to be a genuine believer is necessarily someone who has, through faith, been justified in the forensic, declarative sense.

91. This force of *homoiōs* is further borne out by the fact that vv. 21 and 25 'run parallel verbally . . .: name plus qualification plus *ouk ex ergōn edikaiōthē* ['was he/ she not justified'] plus works described by a participle [or participles]' (Nicol, 'Faith and Works', 9).

92. Davids 132f.

93. The aorist participles *hypodexamenē* ['gave lodging to'] and *ekbalousa* ['sent . . . off'] may be construed as explicatory (RV, NEB) or temporal (AV, RSV, NIV, NASB), or even causal (MHT 1.230).

94. E.g., Laws 138. Others emphasise the hospitality motif as that which links the two OT characters both in Jewish tradition and in James (e.g., R. B. Ward, 'The Works of Abraham', *HTR* 61 [1968] 283–290 [287]); but James's failure to mention the Gen. 18 incident is rightly considered 'a serious problem with this theory' (Moo 117).

95. Ropes 225. This consideration supports the translation 'even' rather than 'also' (e.g., RSV) for the first *kai* in v. 25.

96. Dibelius–Greeven 167 n. 99; *cf.* Davids 133.

97. R. Jamieson, A. R. Faussett and D. Brown, *A Commentary, Critical and Explanatory, on the Old and New Testament* 2.489, cited in Hiebert 200f. *Cf.* Reicke 35.

98. Sidebottom 45f. *Cf.* Burchard, 'Zu Jakobus 2. 14–26', 31f.

99. *Cf.* Davids 133.

100. Martin 35f. *Cf.* Reumann, *'Righteousness'* 152 (§270).

101. P. B. R. Forbes, 'The Structure of the Epistle of James', *EQ* 44 (1972), 147–153 (152).

102. Hamann, 'Faith and Works' (see n. 34 above), 33.

103. Travis, 'James and Paul' (see n. 79 above), 58.

104. Via, 'Right Strawy Epistle' (see n. 7 above), 255, 257, 265, 266, respectively.

105. *Ibid.*, 255–257.

106. M. Evans, 'The Law in James', *VE* 13 (1983) 29–40 (38, 38f.). On the meaning of 'law' in James, *cf.* also Moo 48–50.

107. So, e.g., W. W. Wessel, *ISBER* 2.961f. R. N. Longenecker, 'On the Form, Function, and Authority of the New Testament Letters', in D. A. Carson and J. D. Woodbridge, eds., *Scripture and Truth* (Grand Rapids, 1983) 101–114, classifies James as a 'conventional tractate letter' (106) which, however, 'probably . . . was first a sermon representative of James's teaching' (105).

108. So, e.g., Ropes 10–16 and L. G. Perdue, 'Paraenesis and the Epistle of James', *ZNW* 72 (1981) 241–256, respectively.

109. Cranfield, 'Message of James', 156. *Cf.* E. Fry, 'The Testing of Faith. A Study of the Structure of the Book of James', *BibTrans* 29 (1978) 427–435; the title of Motyer's exposition on James, *The Tests of Faith* (see n. 49 above); Hiebert 43, 'Unifying Theme' (see n. 42 above), and the subtitle of his exposition (see n. 13

above). J. B. Souček, 'Zu den Problemen des Jakobusbriefes' ['On the Problems of the Letter of James'], *EvT* 18 (1958) 460–468 (463), correctly cites 'the problem of the verification of faith in life' as one of the recurring motifs of the epistle.

110. *Cf.* Fry, *art. cit.*, 431f. (*cf.* 435); G. R. Beasley–Murray, *The General Epistles* (Bible Guides 21; London and New York, 1965) 32.

111. Mayor cxxxi.

112. The declarative sense (as taken by, e.g., Moo: see at nn. 60, 61 above), does not fit so well.

113. A. S. Geyser, 'The Letter of James and the Social Condition of His Addressees', *Neot* 9 (1975) 25–33 (31, *cf.* 28). The latest proposal to read James as a polemic against Paul — 'in *indirect form* and without naming the opponent' — is that by M. Hengel, 'Der Jakobusbrief als antipaulinishe Polemik' ['The Letter of James as Anti-Pauline Polemic'], in G. F. Hawthorne with O. Betz, eds., *Tradition and Interpretation in New Testament* (*Fs.* E. E. Ellis; Grand Rapids and Tübingen, 1987) 248–278 (quotation from 253, emphasis original).

114. E. F. Harrison, *Introduction to the New Testament* (rev. ed.; Grand Rapids, 1974) 392. According to Hengel, however, James is arguing on the basis of oral knowledge of Pauline theology, 'which to him is on the whole *strange and doubtful*' ('Der Jakobusbrief', 255, emphasis supplied).

115. J. A. T. Robinson, *Redating the New Testament* (London, 1977) 127f.

116. Nicol, 'Faith and Works' (see n. 4 above), 20. Mussner 130 aptly points out that the pronoun *auton* ('him') at the end of v. 14, which refers back to the foregoing *tis* ('a man'), cannot possibly have the apostle Paul in view.

Apropos of the view under discussion and the majority view today (see next paragraph of text), it is not irrelevant to note the following observation by J. A. Brooks, 'The Place of James in the New Testament Canon', *SWJT* 12 (1969) 41–55 (51): 'There is no evidence . . . that the early church [i.e. the church of the first two centuries] saw in James a conflict with the theology of Paul and that for this or any other theological reason was slow to accept the book. Indeed, if the book was known at all [prior to the beginning of the third century], the mere fact it was ignored is an indication that it did not provoke controversy of any kind.'

117. R. Bultmann, *Theology of the New Testament*, 2 vols. (ET, New York, 1955) 2.131; Dibelius–Greeven 178–180; W. G. Kümmel, *Introduction to the New Testament* (ET, Nashville, 1975) 410 (*cf.* 413); W. Marxsen, *Introduction to the New Testament* (ET, Oxford, 1968) 227f., 229; J. A. Fitzmyer, in Reumann, '*Righteousness*' 220f. (§413).

118. E.g. J. D. G. Dunn, *Unity and Diversity in the New Testament* (London, 1977) 251f. For the suggestion that there is a possible historical setting for the controversy in James's self-defence, see R. P. Martin, 'The Life-Setting of the Epistle of James in the Light of Jewish History', in G. Tuttle, ed., *Biblical and Near Eastern Studies* (*Fs.* W. S. LaSor; Grand Rapids, 1978) 97–103 (102 n. 19).

119. D. Guthrie, *New Testament Introduction* (London, 1970) 765, and Plumptre 72, respectively.

120. *Cf.* Jeremias, 'Paul and James' (see n.60 above) 368–371.

121. According to Braumann, 'Der theologische Hintergrund des Jakobusbriefes' (see n. 11 above), 410 the thesis that 'faith saves' (*cf.* 2:14) is understandable apart from Paul, inasmuch as baptism presupposes faith and promises salvation to the candidate for baptism. But the author's attempt (406–408) to show that baptism appears as the background in various places of the epistle (especially 1:21; 2:14; 4:12; 5:15, 20) does not appear convincing to me.

122. *Cf.* e.g., Beasley–Murray 29; James and Paul 'are travelling on different lines and do not have as much as a sight of each other'; Ross, as at n. 130 below.

123. Hamann, 'Faith and Works', 33, 39–41 (quotation from 40). *Cf.*, e.g., Mayor lxxxix–xcviii (especially xcii–xciii).

124. J. G. Machen, *What Is Faith?* (Grand Rapids, 1969) 205, and Guthrie, *Introduction* 765, respectively.

125. Walker, 'Allein aus Werken', 192, 191.

126. E.g. J. A. Faulkner, J. Murray, G. W. Bromiley, *ISBER* 3.1171.

127. W. Barclay, *The Letters of James and Peter* (Philadelphia, 1976) 74.

128. E.g. J. Atkinson, 'Justification by Faith: A Truth for Our Times', in J. I. Packer *et al.*, *Here We Stand, Justification by Faith Today* (London, 1986) 57–83 (68).

129. These terms are from H. Küng, *Justification. The Doctrine of Karl Barth and a Catholic Response* (ET, London, 1964) 304, and Plumptre 72, respectively.

130. Ross 53; *cf.* Beasley–Murray, as in n. 122 above.

131. J. Murray, *The Epistle to the Romans* (NICNT; Grand Rapids, 1968) 1.351.

132. L. Morris, *The Cross in the New Testament* (Exeter, 1967) 314f. Our remark in n. 90 above should here be recalled.

133. Travis, 'James and Paul' (see n. 79 above), 61.

134. Davids 50f., and Moo 102, respectively. With Moo 101f., *cf.* Nicol, 'Faith and Works' (see n. 4 above), 20.

135. *Cf.* Moo 46; Küng, *Justification* 304.

136. L. Morris, *The Apostolic Preaching of the Cross* (London, 1960) 261.

137. E.g., D. Guthrie, *New Testament Theology* (Leicester, 1981) 599.

138. G. Schrenk, *TDNT* 2.201.

139. F. F. Bruce, 'Justification by Faith in the Non-Pauline Writings of the New Testament', *EQ* 24 (1952) 66–77 (75).

140. J. Calvin, *Institutes of the Christian Religion*, 2 vols. (ET, London, 1957) 2.114 (3:17:11). Calvin was convinced that the Spirit, who has spoken both by Paul and by James, 'cannot be at variance with himself'; his desire to 'make James consistent with the other Scriptures and with himself' led him to the conclusion that James 'is speaking of the manifestation, not of the imputation of righteousness, as if he had said, Those who are justified by true faith prove their justification by obedience and good works, not by a bare and imaginary semblance of faith': *ibid.* 2.113 (3:17:11), 115 (3:17:12). With regard to the expression 'prove their justification', our remark in n. 90 above may once again be recalled.

On scriptural harmony, *cf.* J. I. Packer, 'Infallible Scripture and the Role of Hermeneutic', in *Scripture and Truth* (see n. 107 above) 325–356 (350, point [2]).

141. It is a particular illustration of the fact that 'the diversity in the New Testament very often reflects diverse pastoral concerns, with no implications whatsoever of a different credal structure' (D. A. Carson, 'Unity and Diversity in the New Testament', in *Scripture and Truth* [see n. 107 above] 65–95 [86, with elaboration on 86–89]).

142. Brooks, 'Place of James' (see n. 116 above), 55. *Cf.* Mussner 150.

143. From a slightly different perspective, Jeremias is correct in saying that 'James has his full right to stand *after* Paul' in that 'his message can be understood only after Paul has been understood' ('Paul and James' [see n. 60 above], 371*b*, emphasis added).

144. Tasker 10. *Cf.* Nicol, 'Faith and Works', 23 (writing with apartheid in view?): 'The danger of which James warns us exists in our time and in our own country — the danger of a Christianity that is slow to act concretely. . . . His letter deserves special attention in this country.'

NOTES TO CHAPTER 9

1. *Instit.* III.11.1. cited in Paul Schrotenboer, ed., 'An Evangelical Perspective on Roman Catholicism II', *ERT* 11 (1987) 81.

2. *The Freedom of the Christian*, cited in Paul Schrotenboer, ed., *art. cit.* 81. *Cf.* Martin Luther, *Table Talk*, ed. T. G. Tappert (Philadelphia, 1967) 340.

3. G. C. Berkouwer, *Faith and Justification* (Grand Rapids, 1964) 18.

4. R. P. Shedd, *Man in Community* (Grand Rapids, 1964) 59–71.

5. H. G. Link, *NIDNT* 3.161. *Cf.* J. Cheeseman, P. Gardner, M. Sadgrove, T. Wright, *The Grace of God in the Gospel* (London, 1972) 46.

6. *All of Grace*, cited by D. Hunt, *Beyond Seduction* (Eugene, 1987) 86.

7. A. W. Tozer, 'The Waning Authority of Christ in the Churches', *Great Sermons of the 20th Century,* compiled by P. Gunther (Westchester, 1986) 9–15.

8. See B. L. Smith, 'The Bible and Morality', *Themelios* 6 (1969) 45f.

9. J. I. Packer, 'Put Holiness First', *Christian Life* (May, 1985) 47.

10. R. F. Lovelace, 'Evangelical Spirituality: a Church Historian's Perspective', *JETS* 31 (1988) 26.

11. M. Griffiths, *Take My Life* (Chicago, 1967) 14.

12. From the writer's recollection of a lecture given at New College, University of Edinburgh, in 1954.

13. *Cf.* R. Nicole, 'Universalism: Will Everyone Be Saved?' *CT* (Mar. 20, 1987) 32–39. Note P. Tillich's comment 'Simply accept the fact that you are accepted', in his *The Shaking of the Foundations* (New York, 1948) 162; cited by L. O. Hynson, *To Reform the Nation* (Grand Rapids, 1984) 99.

14. *Cf.* J. F. MacArthur Jr., *The Gospel According to Jesus* (Grand Rapids, 1988) R. C. Sproul (in the publisher's blurb) comments, 'This book provides a much-needed refutation of the false dichotomy between Saviour and Lord that threatens evangelical theology.' MacArthur exposes the current departure from the orthodox Christian view of justification.

15. R. Wager, 'This So-Called Lordship Salvation', *Signal Magazine,* cited in *Confident Living* (July/Aug. 1987) 55.

16. Many have pointed to the common misinterpretation of 1 Cor. 3 that sees in this chapter two distinct types of Christians. Such a view denies one of the central blessings of the new covenant (Heb. 8:6–10). It does not distinguish between saving and spurious faith (Jn. 2:22f.; 12:42f.; Lk. 8:13; Acts 8:12–22, etc.). It omits repentance (Acts 20:20f.), presents a false assurance (Heb. 6:8; 12:14; 1 Pet. 1:15ff.), and threatens a reversion to antinomianism requiring a second work of grace to pass from a 'carnal' to a 'spiritual' Christian. See further, J. F. MacArthur Jr., *The Gospel, op. cit. passim.* For a contrary viewpoint see, Z. C. Hodges, *The Gospel Under Siege* (Dallas 1981) 114f.

17. *Early Christians of the Twenty-first Century*, cited by H. G. Hendricks, *Taking a Stand* (Portland, 1979) 170.

18. P. Feine, *Theologie des Neuen Testaments* (2nd ed. 1911), cited in J. A. Faulkner, J. Murray and G. W. Bromiley, 'Justification', *ISBE* (revised) 2.1171.

19. C. C. Ryrie, *Biblical Theology of the New Testament* (Chicago, 1959) 116f., cited in D. Fuller, *Gospel and Law* (Grand Rapids, 1980) 150f. See L. S. Chafer, 'No Christian is under the law as a rule for life.' *He Who is Spiritual* (Chicago, 1940) 73.

20. L. Crabb, *Inside Out* (Colorado Springs, 1988) 62.

21. *A Serious Call to a Devout and Holy Life*, ed. J. Meister and others (Philadelphia, 1955) 105.

22. C. E. B. Cranfield, 'St. Paul and the Law', *SJT* 17 (1964) 49.

23. Matthew as a whole reflects the Jewish view of 'righteousness' as conduct expected of a disciple (5:20). In the last judgment works will be taken into account (Mt. 12:37). Nevertheless, entrance into the kingdom depends on following Jesus. *Cf.* D. Moo, *James* (Leicester, 1985) 111.

24. *Cf.* W. Bousset and H. Gressmann, *Die Religion des Judentums* (Tübingen, 1926) 375; cited E. Schweizer, *Lordship and Discipleship* (London, 1960) 24.

25. In John the call of Jesus is always addressed to the individual.

26. P. T. Forsyth, *Christian Perfection* (London, 1899) 56, 73, cited in R. F. Lovelace, *op. cit.* 28.

27. *Cf.* E. Schweizer, 'Discipleship and Belief in Jesus as Lord', trans, H. F. Peacock, *NTS* 2 (1956) 89.

28. E. Schweizer, *Lordship, op. cit.* 18.

29. J. R. W. Stott, *The Cross of Christ* (Leicester, 1986) 278f.

30. O. Cullmann, *Early Christian Worship*, trans. A. S. Todd and J. B. Torrance (London, 1953) 105–109.

31. R. F. Lovelace, *Renewal as a Way of Life* (Downers Grove, 1985) 18.

32. C. H. Dodd, *Gospel and Law* (Cambridge, 1957) 42, cited in W. J. Cameron, 'Pauline Ethics', *Themelios* 7 (1970) 44.

33. Luke does not discriminate between 'heal' and 'save' in his use of *sōzō*.

34. C. Spurgeon, *All of Grace* (repr. Chicago, 1984) 40.

35. L. Morris, 'Introduction to the *Benefit of Christ*', by J. Valdes and D. Benedetto, ed. J. M. Houston (Portland, 1984) xxvii.

36. For a convincing analysis of the controversy between K. Stendahl's understanding of the centrality of salvation history and E. Käsemann's view of justification by faith, see N.T. Wright, 'The Paul of History', *TynBull* 29 (1978) 62–64; also Juan Stam, 'Significado Teológico do Los Acontecimientos Históricos', *BolT* 29 (1988) 16.

37. H. Bavinck, 'Sanctification', in M. Erickson, ed., *New Life* (Grand Rapids, 1979) 169.

38. *Ibid.*

39. J. A. Faulkner, J. Murray, G. W. Bromiley, 'Justification', *ISBE* 2.1169. *Cf.* C. S. Storms, 'Jonathan Edwards on the Freedom of the Will', *TrinJ*, 3 (1982) 168f.

40. C. E. B. Cranfield, 'Gospel', 47.

41. W. Manson, 'Notes on the Argument of Romans 1–8', in *Studies in Memory of T. W. Manson* (Manchester, 1959) 161.

42. N. T. Wright, *art. cit.* 71.

43. W. Manson, 'Notes', 160f.

44. *Cf.* F. Davidson, R. P. Martin, 'Romans', in *NBCR* 1028.

45. B. L. Ramm, *Questions About the Spirit* (Waco, 1974) 71.

46. L. Goppelt, *Theology of the New Testament*, 2 vols. (Grand Rapids, 1981–82) 2.145.

47. B. Waltke, 'Evangelical Spirituality', *JETS* 31 (1988) 13.

48. *A Vision for Missions* (Edinburgh, 1985) 22f. J. Edwards said, 'I have often had sweet complacency in God, in views of His glorious perfections and the excellency of Jesus Christ. God has appeared to me a glorious and lovely Being, chiefly on the account of His holiness. The holiness of God has always appeared to me the most lovely of all His attributes' — cited by W. R. Newll, *Jonathan Edwards Contrasted with Modernist Preachers* (Chicago, n.d.) 1.

49. R. Y. K. Fung, 'Justification by Faith in 1 and 2 Corinthians', *ERT* 2 (1981) 177f.

50. *Ibid.* 179.

51. *Cf.* J. Cheeseman, *et. al., Grace* 47f., and L. Goppelt, *op. cit.* 2.145.

52. *Cf.* B. Reicke, 'Worship in the New Testament', *New Testament Essays*, ed. A. J. B. Higgins (London, 1959) 198f.

53. N. T. Wright *art. cit.* 70.

54. S. S. Smalley, 'The Christ–Christian Relationship in Paul and John', in *Pauline Studies*, eds. D. A. Hagner, M. J. Harris (Exeter, 1980) 97.

55. N. T. Wright, *art. cit.* 71.

56. 'The Christian Life a Life of Tension?', *Pauline Studies, op. cit.* 81. Always a sinner, always just, always penitent (engaged against sin, the flesh and the devil) was the trilogy Luther understood as describing the reality of justification. See H. Strohl, *O Pensamento da Reforma* (São Paulo, 1963) 95.

57. D. G. Barnhouse, *God's Heirs* (Grand Rapids, 1963) 145f., cited in J. M. Boice, *Foundations of Christian Faith* (Downers Grove, 1986) 137f.

58. J. Ellul, *The Subversion of Christianity* (trans. G. W. Bromiley; Grand Rapids, 1986) 5.

59. *Ibid.*

60. C. E. B. Cranfield, 'St. Paul and Law', 60. N. A. Dahl says that the 'new man' is not simply the converted individual but an eschatological entity, personal, corporate and pneumatic, nearly identical with Christ himself whom the baptised have put on and ever again are to put on (Gal. 3:27; Rom. 13:14): *cf.* his 'Christ, Creation and the Church', in *The Background of the New Testament and its Eschatology*', eds. W. D. Davies and D. Daube (Cambridge, 1964) 436.

61. D. A. Carson, 'Pauline Inconsistency', *Churchman* 100 (1986) 12.

62. Preface to a special collection of *Hymns and Sacred Poems*, 1739; *cf.* A. C. Outler, in L. O. Hynson, ed., *To Reform* 9.

63. *Ibid.* 10.

64. *Cf.* P. Althaus, *The Ethics of M. Luther* (Philadelphia: Fortress, 1972) 13; cited in L. O. Hynson, *ibid.* 93.

65. J. H. Westerhoff III, *Will Our Children Have Faith?* (New York, 1983) 98f.

66. J. H. Springer, 'Grace, Favour', *NBD* 443.

67. *Cf.* Brother Lawrence, 'I hope the affliction God has sent him will prove a wholesome remedy to him . . . it is an accident which should engage him to put all his trust in Him', *The Practice of the Presence of God*, ed. H. Martins (London, 1956) 29.

68. Carlos Alberto de Quadros Bezerra writes, 'We do not believe in the heresy of impeccability nor perfectionism, that defines itself in proud pharisaic terms such as, "I don't sin".' He prefers 'freed from' or 'living victoriously over sin's power'. Once reborn, the Christian is 'holy and free from accusation'. *Agape* (Nov. 1988) 1.

69. J. I. Packer, *Keep In Step with the Spirit* (Old Tappan, 1984) 145–163.

70. Pastor Glênio Paranaguá writes, 'The perfect God who created the perfect man in his humanity and is consequently free, can save perfectly fallen man so that he can live the perfect life of a child of God . . . for God nothing is impossible (Lk. 1:37) . . . This total salvation is a demand of God's perfect nature . . . [and] means a total freedom from sin' — in *Folha de Londrina* (Mar. 27, 1988) 11.

71. B. Waltke, 'Spirituality', 22.

72. Cited in J. Blanchard, ed., *Gathered Gold* (Welwyn, 1984) 214.

73. *Ibid.*

74. B. L. Ramm, 'The Glorification of the Soul', in *New Life* 201.

75. *Apostolic and Post-Apostolic Times* (ET, London, 1970) 31.

76. H. Berkhof, *Christian Faith* (Grand Rapids, 1979) 453.

77. Theodore Beza, cited in R. Alderson, *No Holiness, No Heaven* (Edinburgh, 1986) 2.

78. *Cf.* H. Berkhof, *op. cit.* 437.

79. R. Alderson, *op. cit.* 29.

NOTES TO CHAPTER 10

1. Of course, there is poverty in the North Atlantic too. For instance, there are thousands of homeless people in the U.S.A. But poverty in the Third World is more acute since it is an *epidemic* lack of opportunities for the vast majority. Can we close the gap between the North and South? Perhaps, but we must frankly contrast the misery of minorities with the radical poverty of majorities.

2. Even though for Augustine 'every thing' is from grace (grace is needed to keep God's commandments, to perform good acts and even faith is a gift of grace), there are also some comments in early writings that can be interpreted otherwise.

3. Gustavo Gutiérrez, *We Drink From our Own Wells* (ET New York, 1985) 108.

4. Gutiérrez, *ibid.* 91.

5. Gutiérrez, *ibid.*

6. Gustavo Gutiérrez, *A Theology of Liberation* (ET New York: Orbis, 1973) 7.

7. Gutiérrez, *ibid.*
8. Gutiérrez, *ibid* 200.
9. Juan Gutiérrez Gonzalez, *Teología de la Liberación Evaporación de la Teologia*, (México, 1975) 61.
10. Gutiérrez, *Liberation* 151.
11. Emilio Antonio Núñez, 'Heirs of the Reformation', *Occasional Essays* (Costa Rica) 7/1 (June, 1980) 13 (emphasis his). Núñez adds: 'To believe in Jesus Christ means, as well, to make a serious commitment to him, to his church, and to society. We do not accept Jesus Christ in order to avoid our moral responsibilities and to live as we please, once we have obtained an insurance policy for all eternity. There are serious ethical demands inherent in the gospel.'
12. Justo L. González, *A History of Christian Thought*, a vol. 2 (Nashville, 1971) 40.
13. González, *ibid.* 40–41.
14. Lausanne Committee for World Evangelization and World Evangelical Fellowship, *The Grand Rapids Report on Evangelism and Social Responsibility* (Wheaton, 1982) 16.
15. The problem with the word study of *tsdq* is ably presented in K. Koch, 'Ser fiel a la comunidad', *Diccionario Teológico del A. T.* vol. 2, ed. Ernest Jennie and Claus Westerman (Madrid, 1985) 639–668. For the relational concept *cf.* Gerhard von Rad, *Old Testament Theology*, 2 vols. (E.T. New York, 1962–65) 1.370–383.
16. Allen P. Ross, *Biblical Hebrew Handbook* (unpublished, Dallas 1981) 52 (emphasis his) 46. Some underline that the meaning of the word deals with the 'real relation between two parties' and the fact that behaviour was judged in accordance with 'concrete human relations', to the point that it is hard to see whether the God behind the covenant is ever considered. Léon Epstein, *Social Justice in the Ancient Near East and the People of the Bible* (London, 1986) 47–48.
17. Donald Guthrie, *New Testament Theology* (Downers Grove, 1981) 44.
18. Stephen Charles Mott, *Biblical Ethics and Social Change* (Oxford, 1982) 77.
19. E.g. Thomas Hanks, *God so Loved the Third World* (New York, 1983) 3–40. Hanks praises and to a certain extent depends on Jacques Pons, *L'Oppression dans L'Ancient Testament* (Paris, 1981) [see Hanks' comment, p. 128 n. 29]. The concern for the definitions of biblical social terms is here seen to be by no means confined to Latin American theologians.
20. See the book review by Thomas Hanks, *'L'Oppression dans L'Ancient Testament* by Jacques Pons', *Occasional Essays* (Costa Rica) 10/1 (June, 1983) 103–105; *cf.* José Miranda's translation, which views justice and righteousness as interchangeable terms.
21. *Cf.* Gottfried Quell and Gottlob Schrenk, *dikē* etc., *TDNT* 2. (1978) 174–225.
22. Plutarco Bonilla, 'The Content of the Evangelistic Message', *Occassional Essays* (Costa Rica) 9/2 (December, 1982) 36–37.
23. José P. Miranda, *Marx and the Bible: A Critique of the Philosophy of Oppression* (ET New York, 1974) 173.
24. Miranda, *ibid.* 178–179.
25. Hanks, 'L'Oppression', 103–105.
26. On the other hand, others have drawn attention to Hank's exegetical fallacies. The first part of his work is based upon word studies plagued with methodological errors. Failure to recognise the different meanings of a word in one historical period, reading the meaning of the word in one passage into all occurrences of that word, and basing theology upon word studies ruin some of Hanks's sound observations on the complexity of God's salvation. This basic criticism can also be levelled against Mirand's linguistic observations. Other criticisms of Hanks's work can be found in the review by Clayton Libolt, 'God So Loved the Third World: The Biblical Vocabulary of Oppression by Thomas Hanks', *Occasional Essays* (Costa Rica) 10/1 (June, 1983) 96–99.
27. John Finnis, *Natural Law and Natural Rights* (Oxford, 1984) 194. The basic

cultural milieu in which distributive justice flourished is described by Robert Goudzwaard, *Capitalism and Progress: A Diagnosis of Western Society* (Grand Rapids, 1979) 1–9; cf. pp. 1–32.

28. Gregory Vlastos, 'Justice and Equality', in Jeremy Waldron, ed., *Theories of Right* (Oxford, 1985) 44.

29. Vlastos 'Justice', 41.

30. Stephen Charles Mott, 'The contribution of the Bible to Economic Thought', *Transformation* 3–4 (1987): 25–23; see the responses by Milton W. Y. Wan, pp. 34–35 and Udo Middelmann, pp. 36–40.

31. For example, this concept is instrumental in determining justice in legal terms: 'Accordingly, in criminal justice (retributive or corrective), the norm is the formal equality of all before the law' (Mott, *Biblical Ethics* 71).

32. Wolfhart Pannenberg, *Christian Spirituality* (Philadelphia, 1983) 65.

33. Vlastos, 'Justice', 42–43.

34. Cf. Udo Middelmann, 'A Response to Stephen Mott', *Transformation* 3–4 (1987) 36.

35. Michael Novak, *The Spirit of Democratic Capitalism* (New York, 1982) 24–25.

36. Not only does Novak elaborate the division of powers concept in relationship to the idea of sin, he also claims that creation and the concept of community are important to an understanding of the basis of a liberal political economy. Michael Novak, *Will it Liberate?* (New York, 1986) 39–43.

37. The community concept is meant to affirm that wealth is for all and that capitalism does not necessarily foster 'rugged individualists'. *Cf.* the corporation concept; cf. Novak, *Will it Liberate?* 42–43.

38. Michael Novak, *Will it Liberate?* 75–95. See Chapters on 'Sin'; 'Providence and Practical Wisdom'; 'Community'; and 'The communitarian individual'. Novak, *The Spirit* 81–155.

39. Novak, *Will it Liberate?* 46, 85.

40. 'There is no argument against the fact that available social goods and services have to be increased if one is to enhance the possibility for social justice. A fair distribution under conditions of extreme scarcity can only lead to the universalisation of pauperism' (Ismael Garcia, *Justice in Latin American Theology of Liberation* (Atlanta, 1987) 144.

41. H. L. A. Hart, *The Concept of Law* (Oxford, 1961) 184. See here the criticism of natural law, pp. 181–189. For an evaluation of natural law, positive law, and natural right, cf. Garcia, *Justice* 111–138.

42. *Ibid.* 181–182.

43. Here we refer especially to Hart's interpretation as put forward in Hart, *The Concept* 165–167.

44. *Ibid.* From a legal perspective which retains closer links with morality, one may argue: 'Justice constitutes one segment of morality primarily concerned not with individual conduct but with the ways in which classes of individuals are treated'. (Hart, *The Concept* 163). When related to morality, the ground of legal justice seems to be more societal than individual, a conclusion that will surely be found much too narrow for theology.

45. *Ibid.* 165–167.

46. John Rawls' classic *A Theory of Rights* (Cambridge, MA 1971) has been widely pondered and criticised. It expounds basic principles that are strong and defensible, but according to Robert Paul Wolf, subsequent additions to the original idea of 'bargaining' are plagued with philosophical problems and make their application difficult, not to say impossible. See Robert Paul Wolf, *Understanding Rawls* (Princeton, NJ 1977). Here our concern is only with the social system idea, as it serves to embody social relations.

47. Pannenberg says: 'The problem is that the aspirations of social classes and of nations who think of themselves as oppressed are not necessarily justified. Whether

they are or whether their claims are excessive can be determined only by standards of justice . . . It is not by accident, of course, that Gutiérrez and other liberation theologians avoid head-on discussion of the concept of justice' (*Spirituality* 65–66).

48. This is the charge made by the Vatican's Congregation for the Doctrine of the Faith, 'Instruction on the Theology of Liberation' IV.6 (August 6, 1984).

49. For Pannenberg, 'Liberation Theology replaces ethics with social theory' (*Spirituality* 67). 'This is why in Liberation Theology, Marxism could replace an ethical theory of justice' (*Ibid.* 68).

50. The argument from the experience of oppression so ably used by Liberation theologians finds a powerful response, also from the realm of experience, in the following words: 'As a theology or philosophy of political economy, liberation theology is clearly at a pre-theoretical stage. It criticises. It exhorts. It stimulates. But is has not yet spelled out its future *institutional* form. Until it does so, it is not yet political but merely hortatory. Abuses of human rights are not curbed by exhortations but only by institutions functioning according to well-defined due process' (Novak, *Will it Liberate?* 34, emphasis his).

51. For a vibrant defence of Marxist ideology see Juan Luís Segundo, *Theology and the Church: A Response to Cardinal Ratzinger and a Warning to the Whole Church* (ET Minneapolis, 1985) 26–47.

52. Segundo, *Theology* 29.

53. Keith W. Whitelam, *The Just King: Monarchical and Judicial Authority in Ancient Israel* (Sheffield, 1979) 17–46. 'Given that in primitive societies the Law corresponded above all to customary right, *mishpat* often signifies custom or law, and it is only by later development that it comes to designate the corpus of laws, and therefore simple legislation. This term evolved above all among the prophets, where it shifted from its legal sense to an ethical and religious significance' (Epstein, *Social Justice* 47). For Mott, 'In assessing the level of justice in the society, the needs of the least advantaged member must be first identified; it is from that person's position that the social system is then evaluated' (*Ethics* 71).

54. Epstein, *Social Justice* 3–42.

55. C. René Padilla, 'New Testament Perspectives on Simple Lifestyle', in Ronald C. Sider, ed., *Lifestyle in the Eighties* (Exeter and Philadelphia, 1982) 55–56.

56. *Ibid.* 63.

57. *Ibid.* 64.

58. *The Grand Rapids Report* 50.

59. Erazim Kohák, *The Embers and the Stars: A Philosophical Inquiry into the Moral Sense of Nature* (Chicago, 1984) 168.

60. *Ibid.* 164.

61. Ismael García, *Justice* 97–98.

NOTES TO CHAPTER 11

1. *Cf.* H. George Anderson, T. Austin Murphy and Joseph A. Burgess, eds., *Justification by Faith. Lutherans and Catholics in Dialogue* VII (Minneapolis, 1985) 25. Somewhere Luther comes very close to the expression *articulus stantis et cadentis ecclesiae*, for he writes: 'If this article stands, the church stands; if it falls, the church falls.' *Op. cit.,* 320 n. 51.

2. *Inst.* III.11.1.

3. *Faith and Justification* (Grand Rapids, 1954) 17.

4. In fact, Trent and the Reformation polarised over six issues in the doctrine of justification: 1. the relationship between justification and sanctification; 2. the formal cause of justification: the imputation of Christ's righteousness or the impartation of God's own righteousness; 3. the nature of 'concupiscence'; 4. the nature of faith: is implicit faith enough or is the faith that justifies fiducial faith?; 5. the nature of the

eucharist and of the priesthood of the minister; 6. the Roman Catholic charge that the Reformers had no real place for subjective righteousness and holy living. *Cf.* C.O. Buchanan, E. L. Mascall, J. I. Packer and the Bishop of Willesden *Growing into Union. Proposals for forming a united Church in England* (London, 1970) 43ff.

5. G. C. Berkouwer, *op. cit.*, chap. 2.

6. *Cf.* R. A. Leaver, *The Doctrine of Justification in the Church of England* (Latimer Studies 3; Oxford 1979); and R. G. England, *Justification Today: The Roman Catholic and Anglican Debate* (Latimer Studies 4; Oxford 1979).

7. *Cf.* G. C. Berkouwer, *The Second Vatican Council and the New Catholicism* (Grand Rapids, 1965) 37.

8. *Cf.* Richard Stauffer, *Luther as seen by Catholics* (Ecumenical Studies in History; London: Lutterworth, 1967); Fred W. Meuser, 'The Changing Catholic View of Luther', in Fred W. Meuser and Stanley D. Schneider, eds., *Interpreting Luther's Legacy*, (Minneapolis, 1969) 40–54; P. Manns, *Martin Luther: Ketzer oder Vater im Glauben* (Hannover 1980); Gottfried Maron, *Das Katholische Lutherbild der Gegenwart* (Göttingen, 1982); Hans Scholl, *Calvinus Catholicus*, (Freiburg, 1974).

9. *Karakteristiek van het reformatorische Christendom* (Roermond, 1952) 348.

10. *Cf.* G. C. Berkouwer, *Second Vatican Council* 42.

11. Even as late as 1965 we still read in the introduction to the chapter on Grace in Karl Rahner, ed., *The Teaching of the Catholic Church* (ET Cork, 1967 [orig. 1965]) 367. (a condensed version of all the official decisions of the Church of Rome): 'It is not just that man is as though justified; he *is* justified. In this the Church's doctrine on justification is diametrically opposed to that of the Reformers who admitted only an external justification, a sort of attribution of Christ's righteousness to man while inwardly man remained a stranger to righteousness.'

12. H. Küng, *op. cit.* 11f.

13. *Recent Developments in Roman Catholic Thought* (Grand Rapids, 1958) 57ff.

14. *Rome: Opponent or Partner* (London, 1965) 101ff. *Cf.* also his statement on p. 198: 'Is Küng's interpretation of Barth wrong or of Trent? Since Barth himself testifies that Küng rendered his teaching accurately and interpreted it correctly, we come reluctantly to the conclusion that what Küng develops as the Roman teaching is not, or at least is not yet, officially the teaching of his Church.'

15. 'Justification: Barth, Trent, and Küng', *SJT* 34 (1981) 517–429.

16. Berkouwer, *Recent Developments* 63.

17. *Cf.* F. Barth, 'Römisch-katholische Stimmen zu dem buch von Hans Küng "Rechtfertigung" ', in *Materialdienst des Konfessionellen Instituts* 11 (1960) 81ff. It is interesting to note, however, that no one has suggested that what Küng claims to read in the intention of Trent is unorthodox: *cf.* G. C. Berkouwer, *Recent Developments* 44. Karl Rahner concluded that there is no doubt as to the 'orthodoxy of Küng's summary of the Catholic teaching on justification'.

18. *Theologie der Rechtfertingung bei Martin Luther and Thomas von Aquin* (Walberberger Studien: Theologische Reihe, Bd 4; Mainz, 1967).

19. G. C. Berkouwer, 'Convergentie in de rechtvaardigingsleer?', *GTT* 72 (1972) 129–157; Heiko A. Oberman, 'De rechtvaardingsleer bij Thomas en Luther', *Kerk en Theologie* 20 (1969) 186–191.

20. *Rechtfertingung bei Paulus. Studie zur Struktur und zum Bedeutungsgehalt des Paulinischen Rechtfertingungsbegriffs* (Münster, 1971) 286, 295–306.

21. *Wegwijzers naar de toekomst* (Hilversum, 1977) 73/4.

22. *Cf. Justification by Faith. Lutherans and Catholics in Dialogue VII* 62.

23. Quoted from Hywel Jones, 'ARCIC II Symposium', *Evangel* (Summer 1987) 19.

24. *Cf. Justification by Faith* 45f.

25. *CD.* IV.1, 530.

26. For the full text see *Worship* 46 (1972) 326–351, and *LW* 19 (1972) 259–273. Both the German and the English texts are also found in Harding Meyer, ed., *Evangelium — Welt — Kirche* (Frankfurt am Main, 1975).

27. For the full title, see note 1. This volume also contains the background papers of the dialogue. Furthermore, there is the companion volume: John Reumann, *Righteousness in the New Testament: 'Justification' in Lutheran–Catholic Dialogue* (Minneapolis, 1982). In the text of our paper we shall indicate the page number(s) of the document itself between brackets.

28. *Cf.* his *Iustitia Dei: A History of the Christian Doctrine of Justification*, 2 vols. (Cambridge, 1986).

29. ARCIC II *and Justification: an Evangelical Anglican Assessment of 'Salvation and the Church'* (Latimer Studies No. 26; Oxford: 1987) 31f.

30. *Cf.* B. J. Kidd, *The Counter-Reformation 1550–1600* (London, 1958) 64.

31. *Cf.* Alister E. McGrath, *Iustitia Dei* 2.63ff.

32. *Cf.* Alister E. McGrath, *op. cit.* 2.86ff.

33. *Cf.* also Canon 33: 'If any one shall say that the Catholic doctrine of justification as set forth by the Holy Council in this present decree derogates in some respect from the glory of God or the merits of our Lord Jesus Christ, and does not rather illustrate the truth of our family and no less the glory of God and of Christ Jesus — let him be anathema.'

34. *Cf.* G. C. Berkouwer, *The Conflict with Rome* (Philadelphia, 1958) 238: 'With Rome justification is based on sanctification, on sanctifying internal grace. The judgment of pardon through divine justification was in principle understood as an "analytical judgment", i.e., a statement of that which was already found in man now or will be found in him in his future perfection later on.'

35. My italics.

36. My italics.

37. My italics. The italicised words show how confusing such a statement is. Luther and the other Reformers never thought of justification as a 'legal fiction'. When God pronounces us righteous, we *are* righteous. But we are not righteous in ourselves, by inherent grace, but because we are clothed with the righteousness of Christ.

38. J. I. Packer and others, *Here We Stand. Justification by Faith Today* (London, 1986) 125.

39. *Op. cit.* 123.

40. G. C. Berkouwer, *The Second Vatican Council and the New Catholicism* 45.

41. *Acta Syn. Trid. cum Antidoto, Opera* VII, 477 — *Fides ergo sola est quae justificat, fides tamen quae justificat, non est sola. Cf.* also *Inst.* III.16.1: 'So it appears to be true that we are not justified without works, nevertheless not by the works.'

42. It was published in 1987 and is generally called ARCIC II. Again we shall mention the page number(s) in the text of the paper. A considerable number of articles and pamphlets on the document have been published. We mention the following: Alister McGrath, 'ARCIC II and Justification: Some Difficulties and Obscurities relating to Anglican and Roman Catholic Teaching on Justification', *Anvil* 1 (1984) 27–42 (this article, written long before the publication of the document, expressed some wishes on the part of the author); the entire issue of *Evangel* 5/2 (Summer 1987) 124, containing the text of the document and articles by Tim Bradshaw, Julian Charley, Roger Beckwith, Hywel Jones, and David F. Wright; McGrath, ARCIC II *and Justification*, see note 25; R. E. England, 'Salvation and the Church: A Review Article', *The Churchman* 101 (1987) 49–57; Paul Avis, 'Reflections on ARCIC II', *Theology* 90 (1987) 451–459; McGrath, 'Justification: the new ecumenical debate', *Themelios* 13 (1988) 43–48; *An Open Letter to the Anglican Episcopate*, Easter 1988, 1–12.

43. ARCIC II *and Justification* 44.

44. *Cf.* Wright, *art. cit.* 21ff.

45. *Open Letter* 10.

46. McGrath, *Themelios, art. cit.* 44f.

47. *Cf.* Jones, *art. cit.* 18; and McGrath, *Themelios, art. cit.*, 46.

48. *Cf.* McGrath, *Themelios, art. cit.*, 47.

49. *Cf.* Avis, *art. cit.* 55f.

50. *Cf. Justification by Faith* 42f. 'Christ associates the work of the church with himself and is present by his power in the sacraments, so that the liturgy is an exercise of Christ's own priesthood' (42).

51. *Art. cit.* 34–35.

52. *Art. cit.* 22.

53. Quoted by Robert Doyle in *The Australian Church Record* (April 27) 1987.

54. *Cf.* the chapter on Mary in G. C. Berkouwer, *The Conflict with Rome* 152–178. *Cf.* also his *The Second Vatican Council and the New Catholicism* 221–248.

55. Karl Barth, *CD*, IV.1, 514–528.

56. My italics.

57. *Cf.* Barth's sermon on the two criminals who were crucified with Christ, in his sermon collection *Deliverance to the Captives* (London, 1961) 75–84. Barth says here that these two criminals were 'the first certain Christian community' (77). He does not deny that there is a difference between the two men: the one acknowledged who Jesus was and what he did in his suffering and death for all men; the other shared in the general mockery. But then he continues: 'This is certainly an important and notable difference between the two criminals. But we shall not dwell on it today. For the difference is not important enough to invalidate the promise given so clearly, so urgently to both of them, indeed without distinction' (81). A little later he goes much further and says that both of them were covered by the word of Paul in Rom. 6:8. Therefore, 'these two criminals were the first two who, suffering and dying with Jesus, were gathered by this promise into the Christian fold' (82).

58. G. C. Berkouwer, *The Triumph of Grace in the Theology of Karl Barth* (Grand Rapids, 1956) 266ff.

59. Karl Barth, *CD* IV.1, 747.

60. G. C. Berkouwer, *Triumph of Grace* 274f.

61. For a thorough criticism of Barth at this very point, see also Alister E. McGrath, *Iustitia Dei* 2.170ff.

62. *Cf.* Wright, *art. cit.* 23.

NOTES TO CHAPTER 12

1. It also means right, justice, virtue, but Radhakrishnan agrees that it stands for 'the law of right living, the observance of which' secures both happiness and salvation (*moksha*). *Dharma*, evolved by the collective conscience of the people, has thus come to mean rule, custom, tradition, law, conduct.

2. S. Radhakrishan says that 'while it [Hinduism] gives absolute liberty in the world of thought, it enjoins a strict code of practice. The theist and the atheist, the skeptic and the agnostic, may all be Hindus if they accept the Hindu system of culture and life. What counts in Hinduism is conduct, not belief' — *The Hindu View of Life* (London, 1980) 34. As we shall later see, this 'culture and life' boil down to a sociological system of castes.

3. *Varna* means colour, but here it means the colour of skin or race. There are four *varnas* called 'castes' in English: *Brahmana* — the priest-caste; *Kshatriya* — the warrior caste; *vaishya* — the business/worker caste; and *shudra* — the serving caste (normally known as the casteless or the low caste, as its members were not allowed into temples to worship gods). There are four *ashramas*, or stages of life: *balashrama* — childhood; *brahmacharyashrama* — the chaste (youth); *grihasthashrama* — married life; and *vanaprasthashrama* — the forest state (when in the evening of life one is expected to renounce everything and spend one's last days in meditation). These stages of life apply, of course, only to men. To achieve *punya* or credit on the good side of one's *karma* (works), one is expected to meet the demands of *varna* and *ashrama*. Thus *varnashramadharma* means the tradition or duty or religion of four castes and four stages of life.

4. This is precisely parallel to Immanuel Kant's logic for life after death: since the results of our actions are not fully received in our lifetime he inferred life after death to be a theological necessity; but the Hindu thinkers went a step further, in suggesting that the recompense may well take more than one birth!

5. *Chandogya Up.*, Book V, Hymn 10, Verse 7 (in what follows all numerical references to Hindu scriptures are in this form: book, hymn, verse), in Robert Ernest Hume, *The Thirteen Principal Upanishads* (Oxford, 1983). All the quotations from *Upanishads* are from this work.

6. Loving devotion to a personal deity is found in many 'modern sects' of Hinduism, such as *Vaishnavism, Saivism, Krishnaism, Ramaism*. It is more or less established that this aspect of faith and devotion to a personal deity (nearest to the New Testament *pistis* ['faith, faithfulness']) and God's grace, *prasada* (nearest to the New Testament *charis* ['grace']) are developments in Hinduism influenced by the Christian gospel. For further study see Kulandran, *Grace: A Comparative Study of the Doctrine in Christianity and Hinduism* (London, 1964), and Fr. Zacharias, *An Outline of Hinduism* (Alwaye, 1956) 408–415.

7. It is hard to get a coherent picture of the teaching of the *Gita*. While the first commentary (earlier ones seem to have been lost) on *Gita*, by Sri Sankara, makes *Samkhya* and *Yoga* (both are philosophical traditions as well as values) its chief thrust, later commentaries have tried to find it in *Bhakti* ('loving devotion'), others to reconcile all Vedantic teaching in *Gita*, and so on. Sankara's commentary says: 'The aim of this *Gita-shasthra* [the Gita Scripture] is, briefly, the Supreme Bliss, a complete cessation from *samsara* [the earthly cycle of births and deaths] or transmigratory life and of [sic] its cause. This accrues from that Religion which consists in a steady devotion to knowledge of the Self, preceded by the renunciation of all works . . . Though the Religion of Works, which is enjoined on the several castes and religious orders, leads the devotee to the region of *Devas* [gods] . . . when practiced in a spirit of complete devotion to the Lord and without regard to the (immediate) results . . . forms also a means to the Supreme Bliss . . . *The Gita-Shasthra* expounds this two-fold religion' (*The Bhagvadgita* [Madras, 1985] 4–6.) Thus Gita highlights the *samkhya* (the way of knowledge) and *yoga* (the way of disciplined action). The *Gita* speaks also of *sankhyayoga, sannyasayoga, dhyanayoga, vijnanayoga, abhyasayoga*, etc.

8. Hindu sacred literature can be classified as follows:

1) *Vedasamhita* (about 1,000 B.C.), which consists of four *Vedas* — *Rigveda* (containing ritual prayers to various deities); *Samaveda* (a collection of liturgical songs sung at the time of sacrifices; *sama* means melody); *Yajurveda* (a collection of sacrificial formulae uttered at the time of sacrifices and their preparation); and *Atharvaveda* (a collection of domestic hymns and hymns for performing magic rites).

2) *Brahmanas* (1000 to 800 B.C.), priestly explanations concerning the sacrifices and rituals, along with allied magic formulae, myths and legends; *Kalpa-sutras*, or rules regarding sacrifices and other rites. Each *Veda* has its own set of *Brahmanas*, thus their number is very great. The chief ones are: *Aitreya, Kaushitaki, Tandya, Sadvinsa, Samavidhana, Taittreya* and *Sathapatha Brahmanas*. Though once *Brahmanas* were considered to belong to *sriti* (revelation), now they have been accepted only as *smriti*, (tradition).

3) *Upanishads* (800–600 B.C.): otherwise called *Vedanta*, or the end of the *Vedas*, for they come at the end of *Vedas*. While *Vedas* are prayerful hymns, *Upanishads* are philosophical abstractions. Here the simple Vedic insights have been divested of their religious garb and clothed anew with speculative discussion. So *Upanishads* are said to contain the cream of Vedic teaching, since such teaching is here distilled. The principal *Upanishads* are thirteen in number (*Brihadaranyaka, Chandogya, Taittreya, Aitreya, Kaushitaki, Kena, Katha, Isha, Prashna, Mundaka, Shwethasvatara, Maitri* and *Mandukya*). To this period belong also *Aranyakas*, monks' books of meditation and rules.

Other sacred Hindu literature, *puranas* (legends) and epics, are mostly myths of a religious and social character. The two great epics are *Mahabharatha* and *Ramayana*; *Bhagavadgita* (the song of God), which is next only to the sacred *Vedas* in authority as revelation, is part of the epic *Mahabharatha*. 'All Upanishads are the cows, the cowherd boy Krishna is the milker, Arjuna is the calf, the pure-minded are the consumers, and the ambrosial *Gita* is the delicious milk' (*Srimad Bhagvadgita* [Madras, 1984] 1).

9. One must bear in mind that terms like monotheism and polytheism do not have the same connotation for Hindus as for Christian readers, since the highest concept of the divine in Hinduism is impersonal.

10. *India, What Can It Teach Us?* 146.

11. I.164.46, which same thought is repeated as a refrain in III.55.

12. This statement is equivalent to *aham brahmasmi* ('I am Brahman'). These two root statements (*mulasuthras*) form the core of the Hindu advaitic (monistic) doctrine of deity.

13. This understanding of God has become quite popular among Christians, as it roughly corresponds to the trinitarian concept of God as the Father, Son and the Holy Spirit.

14. X.121.8.

15. See the author's article 'Hindu Prayer and Spirituality', in D. A. Carson, ed., *Teach Us to Pray: Prayer in the Bible and the World* (Exeter, 1990) 177–191, 338–343. For a detailed study of the Hindu concept of God, see further. Hendrik Kraemer, *The Christian Message in a non-Christian World* (repr. Grand Rapids, 1969 [orig. 1938]) 142–229; T. M. P. Mahadevan, *Hinduism* (Bombay, 1956); Fr. Zacharias, *op. cit.*; D. S. Sharma, *Hinduism Through the Ages* (Bombay, 1967).

16. Since such a search is a genuine thirsting after God, one could legitimately say that the religion of Hinduism (and indeed, by the same agreement, *any* religion) gets its resilience or appeal from this search.

17. *Rigveda* II.27.14.

18. *Brihadaranyaka Up.* I.4.15.

19. *Brihadaranyaka Up.* I.5.4.

20. *Taittreya Up.* VIII.2.1.

21. *Brihadaranyaka Up.* V.14.8.

22. *Rigveda* X.164.3.

23. *Rigveda* II.28.5.

24. *Rigveda* VIII.56.21.

25. *Rigveda* VIII.86.4–6.

26. *Chandogya Up.* V.10.9.

27. II.4.5 etc.; similarly, not for the love of sons, wealth, and the like are they dear, but for the love of the Soul are they dear.

28. *Srimad Bhagvadgita* 10–11.

29. *Rigveda* I.8.84; 124; II.23; IV.23; VII.86; X.92.

30. So S. Radhakrishnan, *The Heart of Hindustan* 28–29. In no Hindu scriptures do the terms *right* or *just* occur in any major way; instead the word *rita* occurs hundreds of times, thus confirming that the idea of right is fully covered by this term *rita*. Though the word *dharma* occurs in *Rigveda* once, it is there purely a proper name of a person.

31. Though the Christian doctrine of justification does not easily fit a shame culture, yet the objective guilt before God is always there. Further study is needed as to how this shame, this felt guilt, is properly related to the objective guilt. The lack of acknowledgment of this objective guilt can be easily explained: the eternal yearning of the Hindu heart for *shanti*, permanent peace, is an implicit indication of such an acknowledgment. Whenever some Hindu heart has been touched by the Holy Spirit through the gospel, there has always been an uncovering of a sense of guilt and a longing for God's gracious pardon.

32. *Chandogya Up.* V.24.1–2.

33. *Kathjopanishad* II.24.

34. *Taittreya Up.* II.9.
35. *Brihadaranyaka Up.* I.5.2.
36. As mentioned earlier, *Gita* does not major on the way of loving devotion or faith (*Bhaktimarga*) as the way of salvation, as many have tried to prove. Most researchers accept that *Gita* is an attempt to reconcile the various systems of thought, and so was developed over a period of time starting from about 1400 B.C. As the cult of Krishna worshippers gained strength, so Krishna was made the supreme God. But the idea of *Nishkamakarma*, acting without the expectation of rewards, is incontestably a new thought original with the *Gita*.
37. While 'fall' and 'nature' belong to the same perspective in Christian theology (as contrasted to the image of God), in Hindu thinking they are opposites. It is for this reason that in Hindu thought human freedom is equated with the 'fall' rather than the *imago dei*.
38. *Kathopanishad* V.11.
39. *Brihadaranyaka Up.* IV.4.5–7.
40. As is well known, there are several ways in which God and man are identified — or are separated: *Advaita* (monism — or non-dualism, as Hindus insist); *dvaita* (dualism); and *vishishtadvaita* (qualified monism).
41. *Maitri Up.* VI.20.
42. *Shwethasvatara Up.* I.7.
43. *Shwethasvatara Up.* I.11.
44. *Prashna Up.* I.10.
45. *Chandogya Up.* VII.2.1.
46. An even more explicit denial of the knowledge doctrine is found at *Kathopanishad* II.23: 'This Soul (*Atman*) is not to be obtained by instruction, nor by intellect, nor by much learning. He is to be obtained only by the one whom he chooses; to such a one that Soul (*Atman*) reveals his own person (*tanum svam*)'. Also in *Mundaka Up.* III.2.3. 'This Soul (*Atman*) is not to be obtained by one destitute of fortitude, nor through heedlessness, nor through a false notion of austerity (*tapas*). But he who strives by these means, provided he knows — into his *Brahma*-abode his Soul (*Atman*) enters'.
47. Thus the Hindu objection that justification by grace contradicts the holiness of God is baseless, since it is precisely because God is holy that justification of man before the holy God is necessary.
48. In *Rigveda*, an early hymn addresses sin as a deity (*Nirrti*), the deity of sin (I.86.10).
49. Friedrich Nietzsche's dictum, that to give is to kill, must be properly applied to *arbitrary* pardon, to the *arbitrary* condoning of sin, and not to the forgiveness of sin by paying its full cost.
50. Hindus are very familiar with the famous story of Yidhishtira on his way to heaven. Being the most righteous of men (his other name is *Dharmaraja* King of righteousness), he nevertheless had to trample over the bodies of his wife and brothers on his way to heaven; no one could accompany him to the heavenly bliss except his faithful dog! Until recently, there were hardly any philanthropic agencies among Hindus. Even those now active are all in one way or another copies of Christian ones.
51. Valmiki, the famous writer of the great epic *Ramayana*, was a hunter by caste, killing animals in order to feed his family. Once a deity appeared to him (so the story goes), and asked whether he was aware of the *karma* he was amassing by shedding the blood of living beings. Valmiki's reply was that he was not alone, but his wife and children also partook of the proceeds of the killing and so were equally guilty. The god asked him to go to get their consent as to whether they would participate in his punishment. To his astonishment, Valmiki found his family very willing to participate in the benefits of his sins, but not to take part in his punishment. Dejected, Valmiki renounced everything and thus became the enlightened writer of the great epic.

NOTES TO CHAPTER 13

1. *The Meaning of the Glorious Koran*, an explanatory translation by Mohammed Marmaduke Pickthall (New York, 1963) 48.

2. Syed Mahmudunnasir, *Islam, Its Concept and History* (New Delhi, 1984) 3.

3. T. Christy Wilson, *The Christian Message to Islam* (New York, 1950) 40.

4. Chris Marantika, '*Isa Almasih* in Indonesian Islamic Thought, A Study of the Message Relevant to Indonesian Muslims' (Unpublished Dissertation, Dallas Theological Seminary, 1978) 15–16.

5. David Penman, 'Islam', *Whenever Magazine* (Fall, 1977) 14.

6. Bong Rin Ro and Ruth Eshenaur, ed., *Toward an Evangelical Theology in Islamic Contexts* (Asia Theological Association, 1984) 381. Islam made an effort to prove that Christ's existence began at the time of his miraculous birth by means of the Virgin Mary. Arian discussion of the concept of *prōtotokos* in Colossians 1:15 as a proof of his humanity without eternal existence is often cited to back up this view. Proof of his eternal existence, therefore, is crucial to prepare the mind of Muslims to understand his incarnation.

7. Chris Marantika, a paper presented at the 'Project Firstborn Consultation' (on Islam) at Zeist, 1987, sponsored by LCWE.

8. *Cf.* Richard Stauffer, *Luther as seen by Catholics* (Ecumenical Studies in History; London: Lutterworth, 1967); Fred W. Meuser, 'The Changing Catholic View of (London, 1984) I.

10. George W. Peters, *Saturation Evangelism* (Grand Rapids, 1970) III.

11. 'Let the Earth Hear His Voice', ed. J. D. Douglas (Lausanne Conference Report, 1974).

12. *Surah* 1, the Opening (*Al-Fatihah*). The whole passage is considered among the most valuable and comprehensive revealed words of God.

13. Djohn Effendi, 'Men's Limitations, Freedom and Responsibilities', PRISMA, (No. 35, March, 1985) 110–119.

14. Muhammad Al-Nawaihi, '*The Religion of Islam: A Presentation to Christians*', *IRM* 55 (1976) 29.

15. *Cf.* Bong Rin Ro and Ruth Eshenaur, eds., *The Bible and Theology in Context* (Taiwan: ATA, 1984) 377.

16. Harun Hadiwiyono, *Iman Kristen* (Jakarta, 1973).

17. John Calvin, *Institutes of the Christian Religion I*, edited by John T. McNeill (Philadelphia, 1925) 38.

18. Bey Arifin, *Maria, Yesus Dan Muhamad* (Surabaya, 1974) 21.

19. Harbullah Bakry, *Nabi Isa Dalam Al Qur'an dan Nabi Muhamad*, dalam Byble (Solo, 1961) 24.

20. *Surah* 67:1, 2.

21. Donald Roland Richards, 'A Study of the Qur'anic References to "Isa" in the Light of Tafsir and Hadith', 54–59 (unpublished paper). His discussion concerning Christ's death and the meaning of *tawaffa* [= to cause to die] and *rafa'a* [= to raise up] is an excellent treatment of this subject.

22. *Surah* 4:157, 158.

23. Syed Mahmudunnasir, *op. cit.* 29.

24. Syed Mahmudunnasir, *ibid.*

25. *Surah* 4:17, 18.

26. Bey Arifin, *op. cit.* 59.

27. *Surah* 66:8.

28. Petrus Maryono, in a personal testimony, 1978. Mr. Maryono started a church in his house after his conversion in spite of the constant pressures from his Muslim relatives and friends.

29. Raden Abubakar S., in a personal testimony, Yogyakarta, 1988.

NOTES TO CHAPTER 14

1. Edward Conze defines the salvation of Buddhism as follows: 'Salvation . . . can be summed up in three negations — *Non-attainment, Non-assertion, Non-relying* — and one positive attribute — *Omniscience.' Buddhism: Its Essence and Development* (New York, 1959) 135.

2. Karl Barth, *CD* I.2.340.

3. *Ibid*. 341.

4. Seiichi Yagi, 'Paul and Shinran; Jesus and Zen: What Lies at the Ground of Human Existence?' in Paul O. Ingram and Frederick J. Streng, ed., *Buddhist–Christian Dialogue: Mutual Renewal and Transformation* (Honolulu, 1986) 204.

5. *Ibid*. 200. Yagi explains this correspondence more in detail in his *Paul and Shinran, Jesus and Zen* (Kyoto, 1986; in Japanese) 56, 57.

6. Barth, *Dogmatics*, I.2.343.

7. *Ibid*. 340.

8. *Tannisho* sec.2.

9. This is quoted from 'Shoshinge' in *Kyogyoshinsho* which is the celebrated poem or hymn composed by the great Shinran himself. This hymn is translated by Arthur Lloyds in his *Shinran and His Work* (Tokyo, 1910) 46, 47.

10. *Ibid*. 48, 49.

11. *Ibid*. 49.

12. *Ibid*. 51.

13. *Ibid*. 53.

14. This is quoted from the translation by D. T. Suzuki in 'The Sociology of Knowledge and Buddhist-Christian Forms of Faith, Practice, and Knowledge', cited by Morris J. Augustine in *Buddhist-Christian Dialogue* 43.

15. Lloyds, *Shinran* 52.

16. *Ibid*. 53.

17. *Ibid*.

18. *Ibid*. 49.

19. *Ibid*. 48.

20. *Ibid*. 49.

21. 'Introductory Essay' in James Buchanan, *The Doctrine of Justification* (London, repr. 1961) 5.

22. *Ibid*. 6.

23. *Ibid*. 7.

24. Shusaku Endo, *Silence* (trans. William Johnston; Vermont, 1969) 237. Endo lets the priest say: 'This country is a swamp. In time you will come to see that for yourself. This country is a more terrible swamp than you can imagine. Whenever you plant a sapling in this swamp the roots begin to rot; the leaves grow yellow and wither. And we have planted the sapling of Christianity in this swamp.'

25. Even Emil Brunner admits this difference clearly. He says: 'Frequently, indeed, it has been asserted that there is a parallel between the teaching of Luther and the religion of Amita Buddha; for one who trustfully calls on the name of Amita Buddha, whoever he may be, and whatever may be the character of his life, comes through this saviour (or deliverer) whom he trusts, to the goal, to nirvana, *sola gratia, sola fide*. But on closer examination the resemblance seems merely superficial. Amita Buddha is not God, the Creator and Lord, nor is he a historical revealer of God's will; he is a mythical figure, borrowing the name from the historical Buddha, but otherwise having nothing in common with him. He is not the Lord who mercifully deals with us on our own level, who reveals to us the mystery of His will; he is a religious hero, who, after he had already entered into nirvana, out of pity for men sacrificed his bliss in order to become a helper to man.' *Revelation and Reason* (trans. Olive Wyon; London 1946) 225–6

26. Buchanan, *Justification* 2.

27. *Ibid.* 5.

28. *Ibid.*

29. *Ibid.*

30. G. C. Berkouwer, *Faith and Justification* (Grand Rapids, 1954) 11.

31. Wolfhart Pannenberg, *Christian Spirituality and Sacramental Community* (London, 1984) 29.

32. *Ibid.* 94.

33. *Ibid.* 101.

34. *Ibid.* 94.

Index of Biblical Passages Discussed

Index of Names